REMAKING REALITY

Remaking Reality

U.S. Documentary Culture after 1945

EDITED BY

Sara Blair, Joseph B. Entin, and Franny Nudelman

The University of North Carolina Press | Chapel Hill

Manufactured in the United States of America
Designed by Rebecca Evans
Set in Minion by Tseng Information Systems, Inc.
The University of North Carolina Press has been a member
of the Green Press Initiative since 2003.

Cover photographs: (*top*) A screen capture from the 1946 film *Let There Be Light*; (*bottom*) *Yale March of Resilience, 2015*. Courtesy of the photographer, Alexander Zhang.

Library of Congress Cataloging-in-Publication Data
Names: Blair, Sara, editor. | Entin, Joseph B., editor. | Nudelman, Franny, editor. |
Kahana, Jonathan, 1966- contributor. | Tsika, Noah, 1983- contributor.
Title: Remaking reality : U.S. documentary culture after 1945 / edited by Sara Blair,
Joseph B. Entin, and Franny Nudelman.
Description: Chapel Hill : University of North Carolina Press, [2018] |
Includes bibliographical references and index.
Identifiers: LCCN 2017036472| ISBN 9781469638683 (cloth : alk. paper) |
ISBN 9781469638690 (pbk : alk. paper) | ISBN 9781469638706 (ebook)
Subjects: LCSH: Documentary mass media—United States—History—20th
century. | Documentary mass media—United States—History—21st century. |
Documentary mass media—Political aspects. | Arts—Experimental methods.
Classification: LCC P96.D622 U666 2018 | DDC 070.1/80973—dc23
LC record available at https://lccn.loc.gov/2017036472

A version of Rebecca M. Schreiber's essay in this book originally appeared as Chapter 6 in her book *Migrant Lives and the Promise of Documentation* (Minneapolis: University of Minnesota Press, 2018).

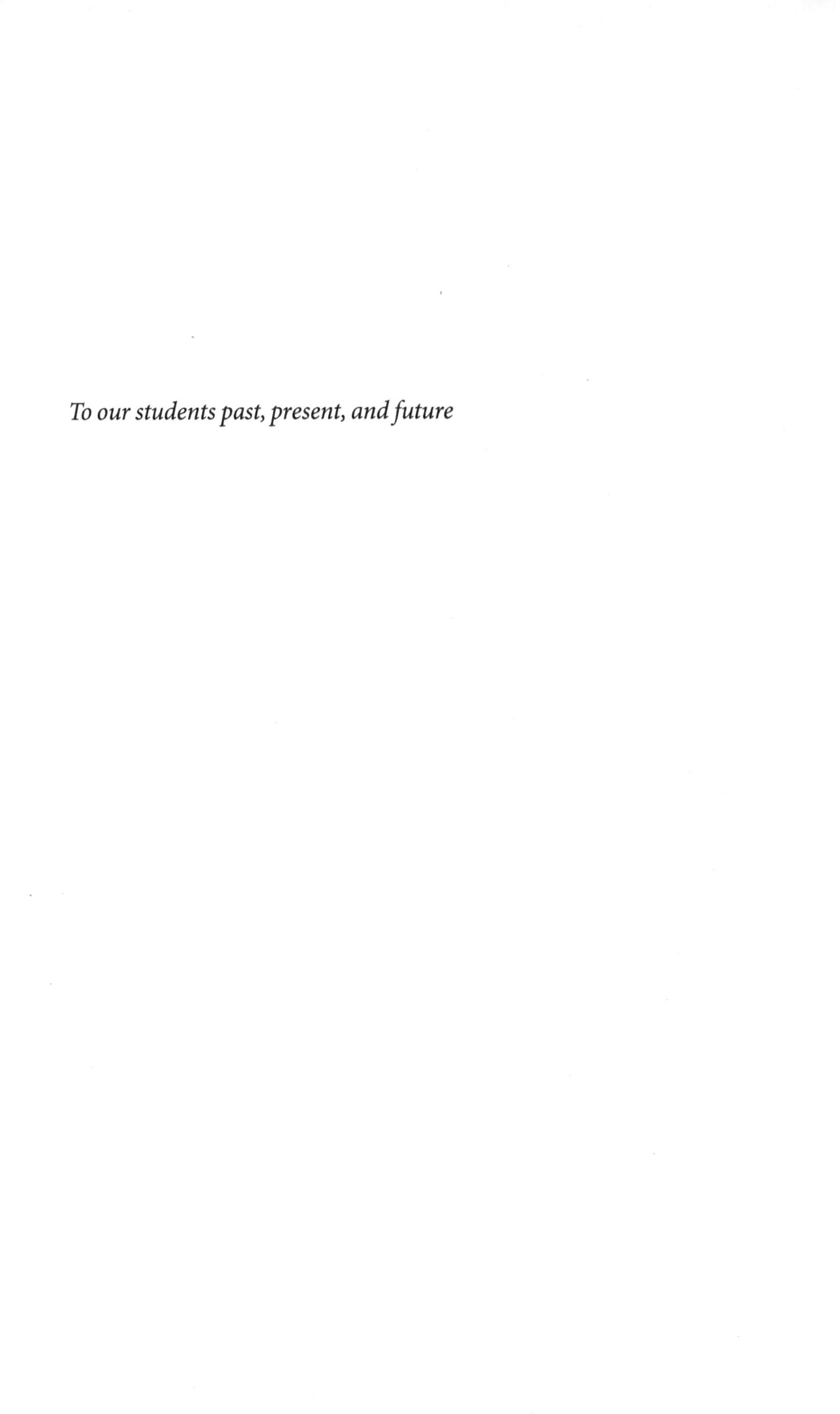

To our students past, present, and future

CONTENTS

Acknowledgments xi

Introduction 1
SARA BLAIR, JOSEPH B. ENTIN, AND FRANNY NUDELMAN

Let There Be Light and the Military Talking Picture 14
JONATHAN KAHANA AND NOAH TSIKA

Death in Life 35
Documenting Survival after Hiroshima
FRANNY NUDELMAN

I Saw It! 55
The Photographic Witness of Barefoot Gen
LAURA WEXLER

Speculative Ecology 83
Rachel Carson's Environmentalist Documentaries
DANIEL WORDEN

Participatory Documentary 99
Recording the Sound of Equality in the Southern Civil Rights Movement
GRACE ELIZABETH HALE

After the Fact 120
Postwar Dissent and the Art of Documentary
SARA BLAIR

Working Photography 151
Labor Documentary and Documentary Labor in the Neoliberal Age
JOSEPH B. ENTIN

Counterdocuments 172
Undocumented Youth Activists, Documentary Media, and the Politics of Visibility
REBECCA M. SCHREIBER

At Berkeley 192
Documenting the University in an Age of Austerity
MICHAEL MARK COHEN AND LEIGH RAIFORD

Afterword 210
MATTHEW FRYE JACOBSON

Bibliography 219
Contributors 235
Index 237

FIGURES

1.1 AND 1.2 Intake interviews with "psychoneurotic" soldiers at Mason General Hospital in *Let There Be Light* 19

1.3 Lieutenant James Stewart addressing his audience in *Winning Your Wings* 24

1.4 "Oh, God, listen!" from *Let There Be Light* 26

3.1 Mushroom cloud 68

3.2 Front cover of Keiji Nakazawa's *I Saw It* 68

3.3 Back cover of *I Saw It* 70

3.4 Page from *I Saw It* showing the bomb explosion 71

3.5 Page from Nakazawa's *Barefoot Gen: A Cartoon Story of Hiroshima* showing the bomb explosion 72

3.6 Double-page spread from Nakazawa's *Barefoot Gen: The Day After* showing the Aioi Bridge 73

3.7 Photo from *The Effects of the Atomic Bomb on Hiroshima, Japan*, showing the bomb's blast effects at the intersection of Bridge 23 and Bridge 24 74

5.1 Documentary album *Freedom in the Air: A Documentary on Albany, Georgia, 1961–1962* 110

5.2 Documentary album *Birmingham, Alabama, 1963: Mass Meeting* 114

6.1 Richard Avedon, *The Chicago Seven* 126

6.2 Richard Avedon, *Lt. Joe Hooper, The Most Decorated Soldier in Vietnam, Saigon, South Vietnam, April 15, 1971* 131

6.3 Richard Avedon, *Napalm Victim, Saigon, South Vietnam, April 29, 1971* 132

6.4 Richard Avedon, *The Mission Council, Saigon, Vietnam* 134

6.5 Martha Rosler, *Booby Trap* 140

6.6 Martha Rosler, *Cleaning the Drapes* 141

6.7 Detail from Martha Rosler, *The Bowery in two inadequate descriptive systems* 144

6.8 Detail from Martha Rosler, *The Bowery in two inadequate descriptive systems* 145

7.1 Milton Rogovin, *Untitled*, *Working People* series, 1976–1987 158

7.2 Milton Rogovin, *Untitled*, *Working People* series, 1976–1987 159

7.3 Allan Sekula, *Chief mate checking temperatures of refrigerated containers. Mid-Atlantic* 166

7.4 Allan Sekula, *Filling lifeboat with water equivalent to weight of crew to test the movement of the boat falls before departure. Port Elizabeth, New Jersey* 167

8.1 Screen shot from undocumented youth Angelica's video 180

8.2 Screen shot from "Undocumented Youth vs. Border Patrol Round 1—Mobile, Alabama" 185

9.1 Noor Jones-Bey, Tahirah Jones, and LaJuanda Asemota from "Thanks to Berkeley . . ." photo wall 196

9.2 "Occupy Everything" banner 198

9.3 Robert Lee, *Occupy Oakland May Day General Strike* 206

A.1 Alexander Zhang, *Yale March of Resilience, 2015* 211

FIGURES

1.1 AND 1.2 Intake interviews with "psychoneurotic" soldiers at Mason General Hospital in *Let There Be Light* 19

1.3 Lieutenant James Stewart addressing his audience in *Winning Your Wings* 24

1.4 "Oh, God, listen!" from *Let There Be Light* 26

3.1 Mushroom cloud 68

3.2 Front cover of Keiji Nakazawa's *I Saw It* 68

3.3 Back cover of *I Saw It* 70

3.4 Page from *I Saw It* showing the bomb explosion 71

3.5 Page from Nakazawa's *Barefoot Gen: A Cartoon Story of Hiroshima* showing the bomb explosion 72

3.6 Double-page spread from Nakazawa's *Barefoot Gen: The Day After* showing the Aioi Bridge 73

3.7 Photo from *The Effects of the Atomic Bomb on Hiroshima, Japan*, showing the bomb's blast effects at the intersection of Bridge 23 and Bridge 24 74

5.1 Documentary album *Freedom in the Air: A Documentary on Albany, Georgia, 1961–1962* 110

5.2 Documentary album *Birmingham, Alabama, 1963: Mass Meeting* 114

6.1 Richard Avedon, *The Chicago Seven* 126

6.2 Richard Avedon, *Lt. Joe Hooper, The Most Decorated Soldier in Vietnam, Saigon, South Vietnam, April 15, 1971* 131

6.3 Richard Avedon, *Napalm Victim, Saigon, South Vietnam, April 29, 1971* 132

6.4 Richard Avedon, *The Mission Council, Saigon, Vietnam* 134

6.5 Martha Rosler, *Booby Trap* 140
6.6 Martha Rosler, *Cleaning the Drapes* 141
6.7 Detail from Martha Rosler, *The Bowery in two inadequate descriptive systems* 144
6.8 Detail from Martha Rosler, *The Bowery in two inadequate descriptive systems* 145
7.1 Milton Rogovin, *Untitled*, *Working People* series, 1976–1987 158
7.2 Milton Rogovin, *Untitled*, *Working People* series, 1976–1987 159
7.3 Allan Sekula, *Chief mate checking temperatures of refrigerated containers. Mid-Atlantic* 166
7.4 Allan Sekula, *Filling lifeboat with water equivalent to weight of crew to test the movement of the boat falls before departure. Port Elizabeth, New Jersey* 167
8.1 Screen shot from undocumented youth Angelica's video 180
8.2 Screen shot from "Undocumented Youth vs. Border Patrol Round 1—Mobile, Alabama" 185
9.1 Noor Jones-Bey, Tahirah Jones, and LaJuanda Asemota from "Thanks to Berkeley . . ." photo wall 196
9.2 "Occupy Everything" banner 198
9.3 Robert Lee, *Occupy Oakland May Day General Strike* 206
A.1 Alexander Zhang, *Yale March of Resilience, 2015* 211

ACKNOWLEDGMENTS

We thank our contributors for bringing their expertise and creativity to this project and for sharing their vital commitments to the subject of documentary with such openness and flair. From the first, we conceived this book as a conversation—one that is ongoing—and we are grateful to our contributors for taking up the spirit of collaboration and improvisation and running with it. We have learned so much from the process of working with these essays, and the volume as a whole has been shaped and informed by each of them. We also want to thank our editor at the University of North Carolina Press, Mark Simpson-Vos, who has shepherded this book into being with great care, and the press staff for their exacting work and warm encouragement. Our families took an interest in the ins and outs of the project as it unfolded and diverted us when the time was right; our debt to them is a given as they make our work possible day to day. We dedicate this volume to our students as it is their tireless work, and inspired observations, that daily remind us why documentary matters.

Introduction

SARA BLAIR, JOSEPH B. ENTIN, AND FRANNY NUDELMAN

During the post–World War II period, a wide range of practitioners remade documentary expression in an effort to respond to a contemporary landscape that was, in the moment of its unfolding, both urgent and bewildering. Confronting in turn the atrocities of World War II, the social rebellions of the 1960s, and the inequalities of globalization, documentarians engaged in a rigorous rethinking of established practices and ideals. While they remained committed to portraying the world accurately and in realistic detail, they often did so in order to argue for its transformation and, by extension, to imagine alternatives to the conditions they recorded. They reconceived reality as the site of political conflict and collaboration, and documentation as instrumental to anti-institutional struggles for justice. At the same time, they understood that collective survival necessitated speculation—imaginings not tethered by observed detail—that might prefigure new forms of community and relatedness.

Our volume explores some of the signal developments in the field of documentary practice in the United States after 1945, with a particular emphasis on documentary activism and the formal innovation it engendered. We focus on documentary work that is committed to acting on the world it records and to activating audiences as participants in the making of that world. We argue for a broad conception of documentary that encompasses the varied, formally self-conscious experiments of postwar documentary: across a range of media and a sweep of some seventy years, we find practitioners—journalists and photographers, filmmakers and psychiatrists, professors and students—committed to documentary as a means of what Elaine Scarry calls "world-making." The documentarians represented in this volume build on and experiment with earlier modes and traditions as they explore the agency of documentary in unanticipated conditions and, in the process, create new and visionary forms of aesthetic, social, and cognitive practice. In response to Scarry's demand that "'making' itself become better understood," *Remaking Reality* explores the dynamic life of documentary in key postwar contexts, accounting for the work of documentarians as they innovate in response to the challenges of the present and, in the process, redefine both documentary and the reality it records.[1]

DOCUMENTARY MAKING

With our contributors, we develop a comprehensive portrait of documentary after 1945 that is at once formally inclusive and historically situated. Such consideration is timely. The last decade has witnessed a remarkable surge of critical interest in documentary practices and forms, produced by scholars in a variety of fields, as the urgency of questions about the social value of documentation has intensified.[2] Collectively, the essays gathered here allow us to revisit certain claims and assumptions often advanced by scholars of postwar documentary. Almost uniformly, this scholarship has focused on visual culture. While we explore developments in documentary film, photography, and video, we also consider the constraints that an exclusive emphasis on visuality places on our understanding of documentary practice. In his study of activist nonfiction, for example, Rob Nixon notes that visual media cannot easily capture the "delayed effects" of violence that "occurs gradually and out of sight."[3] The inclusion of documentary sound, drawing, and writing in this volume allows us to probe such delayed effects and, on this basis, to question the identification of documentary expression with the promise of immediacy and exactitude. Working across the media of sound recording, narrative journalism, drawing, photography, film, and video, we offer an expansive view of postwar documentary culture as it is characterized by diversity and intermediality. While this approach cannot produce an exhaustive account of that work within or across media, it makes visible the wide range of documentary practices, including interviews, collaborative documentation, and public testimony, that drives formal innovation in various expressive modes, and it demonstrates the relevance of new forms, like the graphic memoir and cell phone videos, in attempts to grapple with political and epistemological crises.

In addition to its multimedia scope and approach, our volume is also marked by a consistent yet flexible historicism. We are committed to accounting for the power of documentary expression in the specific historical contexts in which it unfolds, and the essays herein examine the relation between documentary practice and a range of crucial post-1945 moments, movements, and transformations, including the detonation of the atomic bomb, the civil rights movement, the Vietnam War, the emergence of the environmental movement, the financial collapse of 2008, and more. We consider the circumstances and events that shape documentary production as well as the ways in which documentary texts exceed these contexts, acquiring new meanings and establishing new lines of influence as they circulate and recirculate over time. Further, as we explain below, these texts often reach beyond the realist, indexical conventions of traditional documentary in order to confront historical conditions—such as nuclear war, ecological collapse, and globalization—that seem impossible to represent.

On the basis of this interdisciplinary, historicist approach, we find that many of the binaries that have traditionally organized discussions of documentary—between objectivity and subjectivity, realism and experimentalism, neutrality and participation, reformism and radicalism—prove to be fluid. Indeed, we argue that such binaries have obscured the dynamism of documentary making: many of the practitioners we examine cultivate and explore a dialectical relationship between documentarians, their subjects, and the conditions they observe. Documentary making is rarely solitary or univocal but rather "engaged" in the broadest sense as documentarians converse with their subjects, contend with events, critique their predecessors, and collaborate with other artists and activists. In our account, struggle and participation take center stage as documentarians reimagine their relationships to their subjects and audiences and create innovative, experimental forms of art that can reanimate our sense of what documentary is and what it can do in the world.

DOCUMENTARY ACTIVISM

Discussions of documentary have often assumed that documentary is essentially a pedagogical, even didactic, genre, marked by its capacity to shape policy and move audiences to action. This view of documentary practice reflects a focus in the U.S. context on New Deal–era documentary, specifically tied to state agencies charged with managing "relief" efforts through federally designed labor and "rehabilitation" programs. Indeed, New Deal documentary has provided an influential model of documentary practice in the United States that continues to shape the expectations of practitioners, scholars, and audiences.[4] As a result, discussions of documentary often take immediate social impact as their key evaluative criterion and implicitly reinforce an understanding of documentary as offering a transparent or objective rendering of social reality. We find that many postwar documentary makers did indeed see themselves, like their counterparts during the 1930s, as directly involved in shaping policy, building social movements, or advocating for individuals and institutions. The intensification of political life during the Cold War and the ominous specter of nuclear annihilation prompted a heightened urgency among many activists and artists for social transformation. In turn, the social movements of the 1960s sparked new attention to the role that culture can play in broad-based political change.[5] As a result, many postwar documentarians experimented with modes of advancing social and political struggle, recording the existing world not merely to improve reality but fundamentally to remake it.

In the aftermath of World War II, however, the reputation of objectivity was tainted by what Bill Nichols terms the "treacherous simplicities of unquestioned empiricism," now closely associated with genocide, total war, and the ominous power of large-scale institutions.[6] If the coevolution of documentary imaging and new weaponry prompted some to think critically about claims to transparency, others, inspired by anti-imperialist movements at home and abroad, took a closer look at the inequalities that structured the relationship between documentary makers and their subjects and tried to find ways to make visible and challenge this fundamental asymmetry.[7] Often, these critical reflections on the institutional history of documentary prompted practitioners to develop subjective approaches to their craft. From Michael Renov's exploration of the "autobiographical" mode in documentary film to recent studies of affect in photography, scholars have elaborated on the subjective turn in postwar documentary.[8]

Thus, even as they inherited a positivist model of the social agency of documentary texts, documentarians after 1945 were also—and often at the same time—skeptical about claims to transparency, accuracy, and objectivity, which they often associated with institutionalized violence and inequality. In step with these developments, documentary criticism from the 1970s through the 1990s, especially in photography, advanced a critique of the institutional ends of documentary observation by asserting that there is no "innocent" documentary. In this view, every act of documentary recording exercises power not only by shaping what can be seen and understood but also by extending the reach, authority, and disciplinary force of dominant institutions.[9] Yet even as these critics and practitioners warned against the capacity of documentary observation to extend the eye of the liberal, corporate state, they called not for the abandonment but rather for the reinvention of documentary as a critically self-reflexive, even radical practice that refuses both overinvestment in the subjectivity of the artistic and a naive faith in realism's presumed objectivity.

More recently, debates over the politics of documentary and its power to produce change have unfolded in a global context as documentarians work to identify the systems that structure the distribution of dwindling resources, producing extreme wealth and poverty in the age of global capital. In recent years, the agency of documentary has been mapped transnationally and the very idea that rousing compassion is a means to producing ameliorative action widely interrogated. Today, scholars weigh the power of documentary to make inequality visible and concrete against its tendency to naturalize or to sensationalize the suffering it depicts.[10] Debates over "compassion fatigue" and "sympathy porn" rage as scholars continue to attack, and to defend, what T. J. Demos refers to as the "ethnographic gaze and compassionate heart of conventional documentary."[11] Even as they make the case for social change, postwar documentarians engage in ethical deliberation on what it means to document and consume the pain of others and ask, as Susan Sontag puts it, whether the very privilege of witnessing may be "linked" to distant suffering in ways "we prefer not to imagine."[12]

In sum, analyses of documentary activism have been hindered by a contradictory characterization of post-1945 documentary—distinguished, on the one hand, for its embrace of subjectivity and, on the other, critiqued for its embrace of objectivity and, by extension, its complicity in imperialism, militarism, and neoliberalism. Our volume acknowledges both a history of experimentalism that explores extraordinary perceptual and affective states and a tradition of critique keyed to the opposition between objective and subjective modes, institutionality and resistance. We also work to complicate and move beyond these descriptions and debates in multiple ways, offering an account of documentary creation that is sensitive to uneven developments in the field and to the uncertainties surrounding the documentarian's own agency and intentions. We understand that documentarians not only are agents of power but also can themselves be subjected to power and are often made vulnerable by the documentary act. We recognize that documentarians can work both within and against dominant institutions, at the crossroads of multiple and conflicting channels of influence, inspiration, and intention. We understand that documentary's aspirations to spark direct action can coexist with long-term analysis and indirect effects. For these reasons, we read post-1945 documentary as engaged in, but not strictly confined to, complex, concrete, historically specific struggles, in which the terms and conditions of resistance are frequently quite fluid. Through such struggles, we maintain, the uneasy work of building counterpublics and social movements proceeds.

AFTER 1945 (OR, DOCUMENTARY TIME)

In histories of the twentieth century, "1945" signifies a violent rupture ushered in by the twin catastrophes of holocaust and atomic war. We perform a kind of balancing act by insisting that documentary practice after World War II was *not* radically discontinuous with its prewar traditions and at the same time adopting "after 1945," with all its rhetorical power, as our point of departure. We do so in order to foreground the sense of crisis that has been, paradoxically, a commonplace in contemporary culture and has proved immensely generative for documentary makers. Many postwar documentarians believed that the events of World War II had, as John Treat puts it, "split human history into halves," ushering in a present that was best defined by its extreme fragility and consequent unreality.[13] Indeed, the panic over collective survival triggered by the advent of nuclear weapons and, more recently, by the threat of climate change provides one explanation for the peculiar combination of pragmatic documentation, structural critique, and utopian speculation that characterizes documentary during this period. Since 1945, documentarians have innovated out of a sense of historical rupture, playing with the properties of recollection and the effects of trauma on representation as they rethink what documentary can accomplish in the face of possible extinction.

"1945" signifies the end of a war that made real the unthinkable of total war, systematic genocide, and planetary annihilation and occasioned the slow and ongoing work of documenting violence that is systemic and largely invisible. The documentarians represented in this volume simultaneously explore their own role as agents of social change and as creators of new and visionary forms of aesthetic, social, and cognitive practice. Their approaches extend the radicalism of earlier documentary in new and at times remarkable directions and, in doing so, generate our sense of documentary itself as a pliable, improvisatory form that has a special power—and responsibility—to respond to difficult and unexpected conditions. Together, the essays in this volume demonstrate a recognition among postwar documentarians that history moves in unpredictable ways and that cause and effect is a process riddled with gaps and uncertainties.

More specifically, our work expands on conceptions of time, and the temporality of action, that have shaped canonical understandings of documentary engagement and outcomes—and obscured the range of documentary experiments in the postwar era and beyond. In his widely influential account of documentary film, Bill Nichols contends that "the linkage between documentary and the historical world is the most distinctive feature" of the documentary tradition.[14] If anything has united the now vast body of critical work on documentary, it has been the presumption that this linkage is not only clear and instantly legible but instantaneous in effect—that documentary representation will produce immediate calls to action, real-time public campaigns for political or social reform, drives for swift and measurable amelioration or change. Frequently, the documentational act is instantaneous, and its temporal unity with the historical events it records conditions the expectation that it must produce immediate social change. But that structural tendency, we argue, obscures the rising interest among documentarians, across media and forms, in other temporal registers—slow time, variable time, experiential time—and the modes of knowledge, resistance, and transformation that they may enable. How then, in the wake of this legacy, to document—and ultimately create—change on a longer scale?

The inclusion of writing, drawing, and recorded sound in this volume helps us to probe and question the identification of documentary with the promise of immediacy, and exactitude, and to consider its largely unexamined role in producing a record of memory, reflection, and speculation that is by definition imprecise. Increasingly, documentary makers in the United States have explored the realities of trauma and threat, as well as the possibilities of resistance and recovery, that unfold beyond the scale of immediate capture and the framing of an ostensibly objective point of view. As Thomas Waugh notes, while some "committed" documentaries address their audiences through "gut-level calls to immediate, localized action," others represent "more cerebral essays in long-term global analysis."[15] Our documentarians not only intervene in concrete policy debates but also try to shape shared experience over time, exploring the power of foreknowledge, speculation, and retrospection in rendering the "slow violence" of inequality, cold war, and ecological disaster.[16]

This concern with temporality encompasses both the documentary response to urgent social needs and also the labor of documentary itself. In the face of the depredations of late and then global capitalism, the atomic bomb, the Holocaust, and intensified environmental damage, documentary makers have explored the possibility of alternative timelines for documentary expression. Postwar documentarians across media and forms, we stress, experiment not only with direct results—for example, direct action in cinema, or direct experience as the grounds of photographic practice—but also with new forms of what Martha Rosler has identified as "politically directed" affect, individual or collective but always "*directed toward change*."[17] For some documentary makers, that directedness involves close attention to the indirect, mediated nature of documentary expression and to the institutions of documentary art that critically refine *and* mobilize the will to change. Exploring documentary production across media, we open a wider view of documentary's evolving concerns with realities of social injury, and the possibilities of resistance and recovery, that unfold beyond the scale of immediate capture or even experiential time, in generational, planetary, or extra-human time.

CROSSCUTS AND THROUGH-LINES: WAYS OF READING

The organization of this volume reflects our commitment to a historicism that is at once local in its focus on individual cases and expansive as it thinks broadly and speculatively about the complex relationships between eras, influences, and texts. We identify important developments in documentary practice that belong to the period after 1945. At the same time, we resist a progressive or triumphalist logic in which postwar and contemporary projects supersede or move definitively "beyond" the assumptions of earlier practice. Accordingly, the essays in the volume follow a roughly chronological order that suggests, rather than makes structural, a thematic organization, as they move across varied terrain.

The volume begins with three essays that deal with the aftermath of World War II and explore the impact of military violence and state-sponsored documentary on the broader field of documentary expression. The three essays that follow broadly consider the anti-institutional stances of activist and revisionist documentarians of the 1960s and 1970s. The last three consider documentary projects that, in different ways, record the impact of neoliberal globalization on conditions of labor, learning, and citizenship. The range and richness of these case studies well serve the complex, ongoing evolution of documentary making from the immediate postwar moment to the present. But even as we remain committed to a historicist framework, we recognize that chronological ordering alone cannot do justice to the unexpected movements and unfamiliar synergies that the essays collected here produce and make legible. As photographer and theorist Allan Sekula has imagined late twentieth-century documentary practice, it takes unexpected "step[s] backward . . . and forward" as it revisits its aims; indeed, "to go forward," he suggests, its practitioners have had to "take several steps backward and recover abandoned paths."[18] In order to highlight the degree to which our cases reach backward, as well as forward and sideways, we offer the following through-lines, or crosscutting interests, that have shaped and emerged from the essays, extending and enriching the key concerns that generated the volume.

Participatory Documentary

In her essay, Grace Elizabeth Hale coins the term "participatory documentary," which helps us to conceptualize the role of documentary activism in combining the work of building social movements with the work of representing them. Several contributors to this volume examine activist documentaries in which populations, often positioned as objects of state-sponsored or liberal-reformist documentary, become agents, adopting innovative documentary forms to represent themselves and forge counterpublics united in common cause.

Hale's "Participatory Documentary: Recording the Sound of Equality in the Southern Civil Rights Movement" examines the work of noted New Left documentary makers Guy and Candie Carawan, who recorded documentary albums of mass meetings and protest actions during the southern civil rights movement. The production of these albums, Hale argues, which render the voices of African Americans denied official political representation in a segregated society, enacted a mode of participatory documentary, prefiguring the world to which its participants aspired. If Hale demonstrates the role of documentary sound in producing political participation, Rebecca M. Schreiber's "Counterdocuments: Undocumented Youth Activists, Documentary Media, and the Politics of Visibility" analyzes the role that digital videos play in building an oppositional community of undocumented youth in the contemporary moment. Specifically, Schreiber explores the circulation of digital videos—"counterdocuments"—by activists who recorded their personal stories and political actions through social media and other online platforms. In this way, young migrants challenged Obama administration policies that aimed to conceal or minimize publicity around the detention and deportation of undocumented immigrants and created an open, public space in which activists could share information and forge lines of mutual support and collective resistance. In "At Berkeley: Documenting the University in an Age of Austerity," Michael Mark Cohen and Leigh Raiford also address documentary's evolving capacity for political mobilization, focusing on the role of documentary photography and film in the struggle around austerity at the University of California, Berkeley. While the university administration used documentary's graphic appeal to enlist alumni in a fund-raising campaign that effectively naturalized the privatization of public higher education, students took up documentary forms to challenge the logic of neoliberalism. Working with Cohen and Raiford, who teach at UC Berkeley, student activists produced their own counterdocuments, repurposing documentary images that the university uses to sell education in an era of skyrocketing tuition fees, and rendering themselves as active participants in the struggle to reshape the university and the broader society. Read in conjunction, these essays suggest how a history of documentary making committed to participatory democracy continues to resonate in the key of the present and how that history continues to inform the project of documentary as it responds to and explores new medial and communicative forms.

Documentary Histories

A second strong thread or through-line for the volume is an interest in the way that documentary makers of the later twentieth century and the twenty-first have contended openly, deliberately, and generatively with the histories and limitations of the documentary project. Several essays make visible some of the ways in which documentary makers have departed from, and returned to, the legacies of documentary itself and argue that a key aspect of this self-consciousness about the labor of world making is a careful attention to documentary form. As they query and repurpose formal conventions, and the attendant assumptions, that precede them, these documentarians invite us to think about the history and the historiography of documentary in new ways.

Laura Wexler's "I Saw It! The Photographic Witness of *Barefoot Gen*" argues that Hiroshima survivor Keiji Nakazawa used the art of redrawing to challenge and rework aerial photographs taken by the U.S. Strategic Bombing Survey. In doing so, Nakazawa contested the documentary practices of the U.S. military and, more broadly, their power to produce and regulate knowledge. Claiming the perpetrator's perspective as his own, Nakazawa employed the formal flexibility of documentary manga to counter the military's mechanical objectivity, empower his own witnessing, and produce new forms of documentary truth. Sara Blair's essay on the redirection of photo-documentary practice by visual artists Richard Avedon and Martha Rosler also emphasizes the self-consciousness with which postwar figures represent and conduct their labor for a context of urgent social crisis and dissent. Both photographers experiment with the properties and forms of documentary imaging, wrested from its familiar contexts: Avedon in an evolving series of portraits of New Left leaders, activists, war prosecutors, and dissidents made in the United States and on the ground in Vietnam, Rosler in projects focusing on the role of photojournalism, documentary, and the media itself in perpetuating both a fog of war and a set of presumptions about documentary as a form of knowledge and power. Likewise, Joseph B. Entin's essay on Milton Rogovin and Allan Sekula emphasizes the self-consciousness with which these acclaimed photographers of labor generated new formal strategies to contend with the limitations of conventional documentary realism. Each, he shows, produced forms of labor photography attuned to the conditions of contemporary work and responsive to the widening social and economic forces shaping workers' experience—and each thereby reanimated, or reworked, the project of photo-documentary for a late industrial, emerging neoliberal context.

Documentary Imagining

A third through-line concerns documentarians who respond to trauma and social injury, attempting to represent events that will not conform to the techniques of documentary realism. Postwar documentarians ask how they can record the gradual effects of emotional distress, radiation poisoning, warming oceans; what formal, visual, narrative, or medial strategies would make this possible? Challenging the conventional twinning of documentary realism and real-world effects, several essays in the volume argue for the importance of what is rigorously imagined, exploring the role of filmic reenactment, immersive reporting, and speculative nonfiction in postwar documentary.

In their analysis of John Huston's *Let There Be Light*, Jonathan Kahana and Noah Tsika take the traumatized speech of returning World War II veterans, documented by the "military talking picture," as the foundation for a mode of documentary filmmaking that is characterized by its evocative elisions and gaps. The stammering, mumbling, and silence that characterize Huston's traumatized veterans establish both traumatic memory, evasive and partial, and reenactment, which builds narrative from these absences, as foundational to documentary filmmaking after World War II. Franny

Nudelman's essay, "Death in Life: Documenting Survival after Hiroshima," considers the influence of military psychiatry on documentary writing about Hiroshima survivors and, more broadly, on the "new" narrative journalism that flourished in the postwar decades. Examining the documentary writing of John Hersey and Robert Jay Lifton, who participated in the experimental treatment of traumatized soldiers and went on to interview and write about Hiroshima survivors, Nudelman constructs a genealogy of documentary nonfiction that grounds the immersive practices of new journalists, and their fascination with survivors, in the experimental techniques of military psychiatry. And in his essay, "Speculative Ecology: Rachel Carson's Environmentalist Documentaries," Daniel Worden argues that Rachel Carson's *Silent Spring* is not only a pathbreaking work of investigative journalism but also a daring act of imaginative projection. Rereading this seminal book in light of Carson's earlier writing about the ocean, which she portrays as vast and indecipherable, Worden reinterprets Carson's storied career and demonstrates her contribution to contemporary writing about climate change. Tasked with describing catastrophe that unfolds incrementally, Carson's speculative documentary defamiliarizes nature itself, performing the work of estrangement that survival may require.

As Matthew Frye Jacobson's concluding meditation on this volume reminds us, we live in a moment of flourishing documentary experiment that, like earlier moments, feels especially urgent. If the challenges we face seem frightening and strange, it is in part because we cannot fully comprehend them and are out of our depth as we try not only to reckon with uncertainty but also to write, teach, and agitate. All the more powerful, then, as Jacobson argues, is an understanding of documentary as "a way of knowing . . . an engagement *with* knowing." The essays in our volume do not provide a road map to projects of social transformation that lie ahead, or to the practices of documentation and world making that will inform them. But they do remind us that the struggle to record is an integral part of the struggle to produce knowledge and effect change and that new technologies, political configurations, and forms of violence and inequality will be met by innovative forms of expression. These essays aim to inspire critical thought across disciplinary boundaries and across time and, in doing so, allow us to recognize that the proliferation of vibrant documentary experiments we encounter today is deeply rooted in the struggles and innovations of the past. We offer them with the certainty that while documentation in itself will not resolve the challenges we face, it is an indispensable mode of engaging—and transforming—a world in need of repair.

NOTES

1. Scarry, *Body in Pain*, 19.

2. Among these projects, indicating the range of the broader interest in documentary practices and legacies, are Abbott, *Engaged Observers*; Azoulay, *Civil Contract of Photography*; Bogre, *Photography as Activism*; Hariman and Lucaites, *No Caption Needed*; Kahana, *Intelligence Work*; Mirzoeff, *Right to Look*; Stimson, *Pivot of the World*; and Zelizer and Tenenboim-Weinblatt, *Journalism and Memory*.

3. Nixon, *Slow Violence*, 2–3.

4. On 1930s documentary, see, among many other works, Stott, *Documentary Expression and Thirties America*; Trachtenberg, *Reading American Photographs*; Rabinowitz, *They Must be Represented*; and Allred, *American Modernism and Depression Documentary*.

5. Among other writings about the role of art and culture in the radical social change movements of the 1960s (and beyond), see Reed, *Art of Protest*; and Bryan-Wilson, *Art Workers*.

6. Nichols, "Voice of Documentary," in *Movies and Methods*, citation 261.

7. On the relationship between imaging and military technology, see Butler, *Frames of War*; Kozol, *Distant Wars Visible*; and Virilio, *War and Cinema*. On the impact of anti-imperialism on documentary film, see James, "Documenting the Vietnam War"; and Renov, "Imaging the Other."

8. See Renov, *Subject of Documentary*; Batchen, *Burning with Desire*; Brown and Thy Phu, *Feeling Photography*; E. Edwards, "Objects of Affect"; and Olin, *Touching Photographs*.

9. On the imbrication of documentary with liberal state and corporate power, see Tagg, *Burden of Representation*; Rosler, "In, around and Afterthoughts," in *Martha Rosler*; and Sekula, "Body and the Archive."

10. Some important texts that deal with the practice and ethics of documentary in a global context include Azoulay, *Civil Contract of Photography*; Dawes, *That the World May Know*; Demos, *Migrant Image*; Kennedy and Patrick, *Violence of the Image*; Kozol, *Distant Wars Visible*; Linfield, *Cruel Radiance*; Ritchin, *Bending the Frame*; and Sontag, *Regarding the Pain of Others*.

11. Demos, *Migrant Image*, xx.

12. Sontag, *Regarding the Pain of Others*, 103.

13. Treat, *Writing Ground Zero*, vii.

14. Nichols, *Representing Reality*, 9.

15. Waugh, *"Show Us Life,"* xiii.

16. Nixon, *Slow Violence*.

17. Rosler, "In, around and Afterthoughts," 191, in *Decoys and Disruptions*.

18. Sekula, "On 'Fish Story.'"

Let There Be Light and the Military Talking Picture

JONATHAN KAHANA AND NOAH TSIKA

THE EAR OF DOCUMENTARY

We expect a documentary interview, whether on film, television, or radio, to "coax people into revelations, showing unexpected intimacies, and particularly revealing moments where people are caught unawares," as John Ellis writes.[1] The interview and the confessional speech it fosters have become ubiquitous devices of ordinary social history and biography, so common in documentary and news media practice that we hardly recognize them as historiographic techniques, much less as practices with a history of their own. And at least as far back as the 1960s, when critics and producers began making arguments for the free-speech styles of *cinéma vérité*, against the more formal and scripted stagings of voice that had been conventional, it was possible to identify the interview as a method, one with predictable results. "When you interview someone," documentary cinematographer Richard Leacock remarked to Louis Marcorelles at the end of the 1960s, "they always tell you what they want you to know about them." Recounting this conversation in his book *Living Cinema*, Marcorelles agreed, calling the interview "the most banal kind of cinema there is."[2] But despite the fact that—or, indeed, precisely because—one could call the interview a "banal" and regular method of interrogation, it was also a historical practice: a practice with a history, as well as a practice *of* history. Regarded as such, it became impossible to reduce the documentary-specific use and meaning of interviews to words and their manifest content. This argument was embedded in Bill Nichols's definition, a decade and a half after Leacock and Marcorelles's conversation, of a "voice of documentary"—a technique never meant to be reduced to audible speech. The voice of documentary was, according to Nichols, a concept, a "moiré-like pattern formed by the . . . interaction of all of a film's codes."[3] This pattern could thus be understood to include the visual forms of narration, which carry the "point of view" of the film no less than its audible voices.[4] Extending Nichols and

Ellis, we could say that the paradigmatic cultural-critical faculty of American documentary after 1945—this medium's capacity for "showing" and "revealing... where people are caught unawares"—is paradoxically lodged in an *ear* of documentary, a faculty that can be alternately empathic, diagnostic, critical, and agonistic.

Unlike the voice or gaze of documentary, a metaphorical ear of documentary would take us some distance from the subjects and agents that have occupied the center of the frame of documentary practice and documentary history, off to the edge of a sharply registered image of documentary and into the range of cross-talk from its history: less a lens or optic on this history, one might say, than what Michel Foucault called a *dispositif*.[5] Against a progressive history of documentary, like that established by Erik Barnouw's epochal survey of the field, *Documentary: A History of Nonfiction Film*, written in the early 1970s, an ear of documentary can be less concerned with the constant updating, sharpening, and correcting of documentary's images and self-images and better attuned to the intermittence and discontinuity of documentary's discourse of realism, which, like an echo, moves both forward and backward and not necessarily along straight lines. This tendency has its origins in what we refer to here as the military talking picture, a particular discourse of American documentary dating to World War II and its cultural and disciplinary aftermath, including that of trauma and traumatic memory, conditions with their own history of revision and inconstancy.[6] In that period, it happens to intersect with an equally dotted line of documentary history, the trajectory of reenactment, which, like the documentary ear, has at times been so central to the discipline of documentary that it has gone unremarked for decades at a time, when it has not been simply dismissed or denigrated outright.[7] In the long final section of his 1946 collection of essays, *The Idea of History*, R. G. Collingwood proposes reenactment as a new critical method for historians, enabling them to understand history from both the "outside" and the "inside": unlike scientists, who may be content with a historical method that describes "sequences of mere events," philosophical historians put themselves in the position of historical actors and try to imagine what, in their context, their actions might have meant. But the historian "not only reenacts past thought, he re-enacts it in the context of his own knowledge and, therefore, in re-enacting it, criticizes it, forms his own judgment of its value, corrects whatever errors he can find in it."[8] If reenactment and the interview have seemed to run on separate tracks in the career of documentary since 1946, we aim, echoing Collingwood's formulation of a critical history of documentary's inner spaces of speech and consciousness, to restore their tangency here.

Prior to World War II, techniques of reenactment were simply one way among many for documentary filmmakers to "bridge the gap between past and present."[9] Over the course of the conflict, however, the dominant styles of narration used by filmmakers changed. The logic of this change is illustrated by the history of the military talking picture, a genre of American documentary prototypified by John Huston's Army Signal Corps documentary *Let There Be Light* (1946), a film that both reviews the effects of war and makes audio-visible forms of diagnostic retrospection then being developed by the U.S. military. Completed in 1946 and intended to be released to both military and civilian publics but kept out of commercial public circulation until 1980, *Let There Be Light* follows the progress of a group of returning soldiers suffering from what was then referred to as "battle fatigue." Becoming exemplary documentary subjects as they regain the power to move, speak, remember, and forget, the psychically wounded soldiers pass through a series of experimental treatments—all of them based, in some fashion, on speaking or reenacting their trauma—at Mason General, a military hospital in Long Island, New York. With a unique and prescient combination of testimonial interview, staged reenactment, and psychodrama—techniques that would remain dormant in the American documentary "tradition" until the 1960s, with the appearance of the so-called *cinéma vérité* documentary and a variety of later inflections and rejections of this style—Huston's film establishes a precedent for American social documentary film in the postwar era.

The military talking picture thus refers at once to a matter of theme and technique: a tropic tendency, in postwar investigations of soldiers and soldiering, to fetishize oration and audition as subjects and methods. The folds of this cinematic ear open onto many histories. In what follows, we propose a preliminary genealogy of this interdisciplinary faculty, focusing on one specific, perhaps anomalous, and certainly overdetermined particular case. Long withheld from commercial public release, Huston's *Let There Be Light* condenses a number of historical, scientific, and popular narrative approaches to the topic of combat trauma and its military treatment. It is a text that can be read as the buried precedent for postwar representations of soldiers' neuroses in American social documentary and popular cinema. As a document of medical science, Huston's film is not without its antecedents: among them, Army Signal Corps productions like *Psychiatric*

Procedures in the Combat Area (1944) and *Combat Exhaustion* (1945) and, even earlier, the British documentary film *War Neuroses* (Arthur Hurst, 1918), about the treatment of shell shock at a military hospital in Devon. But the profound impact of *Let There Be Light* and subsequent representational and discursive practices place it in a peculiarly generative position in American cultural history.[10]

In the early 1940s, the U.S. military, having studied the work of documentary filmmakers from Western Europe and North America—among them Pare Lorentz, John Grierson, and Humphrey Jennings—began to grasp the importance of oral communication as both a documentary device and an extracinematic objective, and often in explicit rebuke to the perceived authoritarianism of Nazi propaganda films. If Leni Riefenstahl's *Triumph of the Will* (1935) had functioned to manufacture consent in part by ceding its soundtrack to the public speeches of Nazi officials, then American military filmmakers, operating with a public relations mandate to resist Riefenstahl's illiberal approach, needed to find a way, at least some of the time, to enfold national and institutional imperatives into "democratic" vocal exchanges, striking a balance between pedagogy administered from above and questions posed from below. Hence the celebrated, if somewhat stilted, polyvocality of John Ford's *The Battle of Midway* (1942)—a film the *Washington Post* editorial board lauded, upon its release, as marking "the beginning of a new epoch in war pictures"[11]—which self-consciously combines a stentorian narrator and the folksy tonalities of the actors Henry Fonda and Jane Darwell, or the similar call-and-response soundtracks of documentaries about gender integration, such as the 1944 Army Signal Corps film *It's Your War, Too*, in which the reenactment of "typical" American misogyny leads to a litany of rebuttals (some more actorly than others). The authenticity of such diverse voices was hardly at issue in military contexts increasingly committed, both for budgetary reasons and by ideological design, to the practice of reenactment, a method whose usefulness the Signal Corps repeatedly touted in official memoranda and that was, despite the premium placed on authenticity by reviewers of Allied film propaganda within the military and without, regarded throughout the war as a legitimate documentary technique, one that might be freely mixed with an observational ethos to which it would soon seem inimical.[12] When the loss of actual combat footage, coupled with inter-Allied acrimony and looming deadlines, led the Signal Corps to commission a number of filmmakers, including John Huston, to stage reenactments for what would become *Tuni-*

sian Victory (1944), the military was well equipped to justify, at least internally, what to some observers might have seemed sheer, insupportable falsification.

In the case of *Tunisian Victory*, the practical necessity of reenactment only aided the film's objective, which was to furnish a model for close, *communicative* collaboration among Allied forces, interweaving equally prescriptive British and American voices. But while the vast majority of American military documentaries of the Second World War offered predetermined, carefully vetted, and skillfully directed voices designed to inspire spoken exchanges among members of the armed forces, some unexpected utterances and speech styles occasionally made their way into otherwise predictable documentaries, pointing toward the postwar emergence of the military talking picture as a forum not merely for unscripted, democratic chatter but also for accidents: confessional transgressions, polemical outbursts, and impediments to articulation that simultaneously reflected and set patterns for public debate. If knowledge of the imminence of combat makes it difficult for an officer to reenact one of his recent briefings in the 1944 Air Forces film *Target: Germany*, resulting in a painfully halting speech pattern at odds with the militaristic bombast of the language he employs, then similarly revealing vocal blunders are at the center of later films in which, appropriately enough, talking about war is hardly a simple or stabilizing task.

SPEECH IMAGES

Let There Be Light is one of the first documentary films of any kind in which the interview is used as a literally and figuratively symptomatic device. By no means is it the earliest use of the on-camera, synch-sound interview as a method for gathering and reporting empirical proof of social reality: Arthur Elton and Edgar Anstey's *Housing Problems*, made for the British Commercial Gas Association in 1935, or the recently rediscovered *Komsomol—Leader of Electrification*, Esfir Shub's 1932 Soviet propaganda film, or a number of Fox Movietone newsreels from the same era and earlier could all lay claim to that distinction. But it is certainly among the first documentary films in which speech serves as its own evidence—or, rather, in which the speech of ordinary individuals fails, through symptoms that Freud called "speech images," to speak for itself.[13] And, importantly, it is also one of the first documentaries produced under the aegis of the American military to eschew the scripted or reenacted interview, which prevailed among World War II training films, particularly those designed to dictate

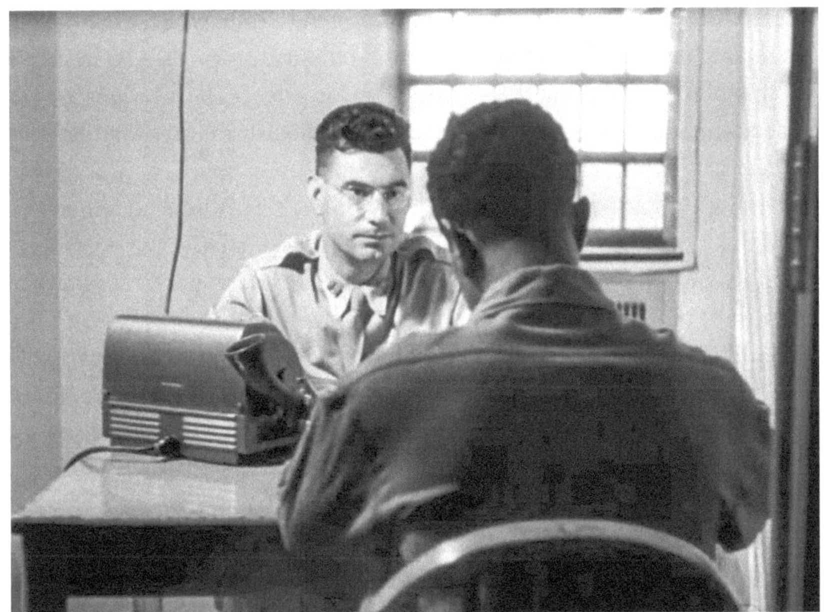

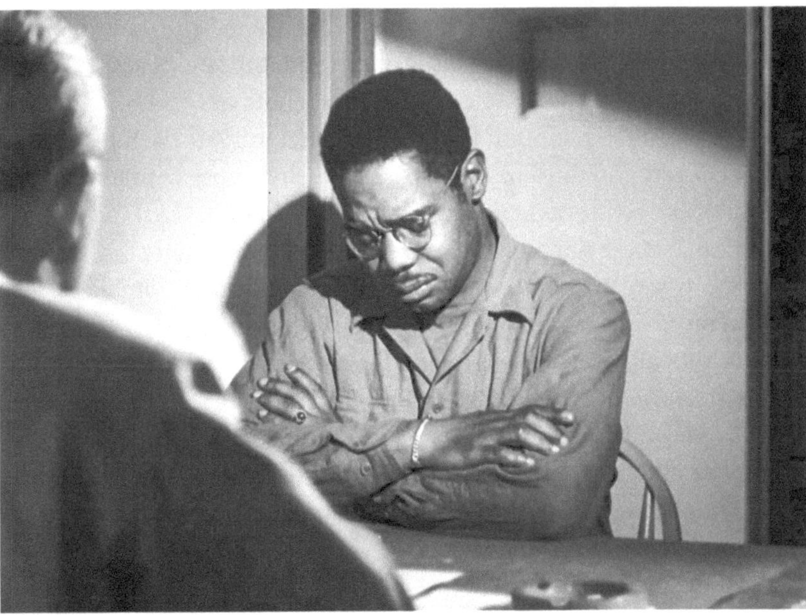

FIGURES 1.1 AND 1.2 Intake interviews with "psychoneurotic" soldiers at Mason General Hospital in *Let There Be Light*. Screen capture from digital video.

interactions between officers and infantrymen.[14] Rather than establishing a template for social behavior within the military, or for the serviceman's successful return to domestic settings, Huston's use of the interview serves to acquaint the viewer with the range of psychic disturbances that patients describe, in colloquial and often erratic terms, upon their arrival at Mason General Hospital in Long Island—a startling effect produced, cinematically, through the use of a "wipe," an editing device that here uncovers layer upon layer of trauma. Huston's montage of intake interviews serves the dual purpose of providing an entrée into the treatment methods at Mason General and underscoring the relatively high incidence of neurotic symptoms among returning soldiers, in keeping with the claims of the film's opening statement, which notes, somewhat conservatively, that "about 20% of all battle casualties in the American Army during World War II were of a neuropsychiatric nature."[15]

Intending what Huston privately called his "'psycho'" film[16] for wide release, as a means of quelling the anxieties of employers about the mental stability of returning veterans, the army reversed itself and restricted exhibition of the film, which had once been titled "The Returning Soldier—Psychoneurotics,"[17] to military installations and institutions and, upon request, to some educational settings. Relatively little was said by critics and scholars about the film until the ban was lifted in 1980, during a studio-driven effort to win the film a belated Oscar, when it began to be regarded by a number of critics as a prototypical work of *cinéma vérité*. Gary Edgerton rehearses these claims in one of the few scholarly treatments of the film, where he argues that Huston was "well ahead of his time" in his use of a "newer, more probing, and observational film style that was necessary to let these veterans, in a sense, speak for themselves." Edgerton calls Huston's approach *cinéma vérité*, in contrast to what he describes as the "authoritarian" style of the rest of the film, referring apparently to both the conditions of production and the use of dramatic reenactments and voice-over (by Huston's father, Walter) to illustrate the treatment and speedy recovery of the afflicted veterans, under the watchful eye of the experts at Mason General Hospital.[18]

Setting aside the progressivist notion of *cinéma vérité* as a historically necessary stage in the development of nonfiction filmmaking, one might indeed regard *Let There Be Light*, in its attention to accidental or pathological physical and vocal gestures and to the dynamic pressure of a filmed encounter between interviewer and interviewee, as an antecedent of the "direct" and "*vérité*" techniques developed in various North Atlantic countries in the late 1950s and early 1960s by documentary filmmakers inclined toward general-public audiences (as opposed to the institutional filmmakers, recording scientific or medical processes for the benefit of specialized, nonpublic audiences). Yet if the film fashioned a new discourse for American social documentary speech in the postwar era, this significance is better grasped by re-placing the film in its immediate cultural and institutional contexts rather than by returning it to its "proper" place in a biographical narrative of Hollywood auteurism or in a transhistorical ethos of documentary authenticity. That Huston's film is predated by such institutional productions as the 1944 Army Signal Corps film *Psychiatric Procedures in the Combat Area*, which sets several important precedents for Huston's approach—including by incorporating observational footage of interviews and various protracted treatment sessions—indicates the importance of peering beyond Huston's legend and taking a closer look at the legacy of military filmmaking, a mode of production within which, as was true of Hollywood in this period, the "genius of the system" might consist as much of technical refinements and thematic extensions as of original discoveries and works of expressive art.[19] *Let There Be Light* was produced during a transitional period in the military's long-standing engagement with mental illness as an object of institutional inquiry, as the shift to peacetime conditions occasioned new debates regarding recruitment and public relations and the role of documentary evidence therein. While historians have focused on the film's absence from public screens, remarkably little has been said about the place of the disorders and therapies we observe in *Let There Be Light* within discourses and practices of military psychiatry in the 1940s and 1950s, or about the institutional and popular cultures into which *Let There Be Light* and films dealing with similar material were released, including the audiences of the film at the command posts, military hospitals, and training facilities for which it was approved and the university, literary, journalistic, and mass-cultural spheres where psychology and psychopathology entered a sustained period of popular and critical fascination during and after World War II.

The concept of trauma did, of course, preexist the First World War, but it took its current form during and after the war, in the intersection of Freudian psychoanalysis and military psychiatry. Battle trauma had always been, and remains, a contentious topic among American military and political officials, in part because of its connection to psychoanalysis, and by 1980, when it was authorized by the American Psychological Association in the third edition of the *Diagnostic and Statistical Manual of Mental Disorders*, it had been largely stripped of its Freudian inflection. The American military's opposition to Freudian psychoanalysis is traceable to the First World War, when efforts were well underway among medical professionals to understand the psychosomatic consequences of combat. In a 1918 study for the *Journal of Nervous and Mental Disease*, Charles Rockwell Payne and Smith Ely Jelliffe pointedly cautioned against the pursuit of strictly somatic explanations for war trauma, suggesting that any effort to deny the threat of "emotional psychoneuroses" (and perhaps to resist the perceived encroachment of psychoanalysis on military medicine) would only harm the suffering soldier, as well as, by extension, the military itself.[20] Prior to the sustained psychiatric interventions of the late 1910s, the military had often embraced low blood pressure and various thyroid disturbances as medical explanations for soldiers' resistance to combat, and it was the groundbreaking work of British psychiatrists, including W. H. R. Rivers, that led to the expansive institutional reassessment of the emotional lives of combatants.

While the military could hardly be said to have heartily embraced psychoanalysis for its diagnostic and curative potential, World War II brought psychiatry to the battlefield, altering the military's official stance on various therapeutic practices, from narcohypnosis to group therapy. Throughout the 1940s, the military-sponsored psychiatric study of combat veterans would yield useful data on the various "anxiety states" affecting servicemen, data that often directly resulted from a range of speech therapies, including those depicted in *Let There Be Light*, in which the acts of speaking and listening serve a diagnostic and, ultimately, curative purpose for the victims of war trauma. These include a stuttering veteran suffering from what the narrator calls "battle tension": injected with a drug designed to "limber up [his] tongue," he suddenly exclaims, "Oh, God, listen, I can talk! Oh, there's nothing wrong!" In listening carefully to his own voice, and in exhorting a higher power to do the same, this man evokes the film's psychiatrically inflected thesis about the importance of mindful audition.

Even in the short history of the World War II factual film, however, *Let There Be Light* represents only one position in a wide field of investigation into the art and science of listening. In films like *Enemy Interrogation of Prisoners*, made in 1942 for the Royal Air Force, and *Resisting Enemy Interrogation*, a feature-length cautionary thriller made by the U.S. Army Air Force's First Motion Picture Unit in 1944, talkative British or American soldiers inadvertently reveal the location of military installations or the timing of bombing raids, having just enough time to regret their mortal error before a narrator explains the moral of the story: keep your mouth shut. The chatty, unreflective soldiers who appear in these docudramas are the loquacious mirror images of the reticent mumblers in Huston's film. And in fact, the U.S. Army was just as worried about soldiers who *did not* talk as about those who did. The official military historian for the Pacific and European theaters, S. L. A. Marshall, called the American forces in World War II "the mutest army we ever sent to war" and invented a method of postcombat group interview to address the problem of men who, he felt, had been "struck dumb" by the "magic" of communications technologies like radio, the telephone, the teletype, and television.[21]

We might say that the stammers, pauses, repeated words, transpositions, cries, and other forms of nonsense that make first-person interviews such compelling documentary evidence are, in their physicality, evidence of an "elsewhere" *within* speech, complementary to the "elsewhere" of classical documentary voice-over identified by Charles Wolfe as the dominant sonic structure—ideological and formal—of American documentary between roughly 1930 and 1960.[22] In *The Psychopathology of Everyday Life*, Freud, drawing on a contemporary term from linguistics, called these various kinds of interruptions of speech content by the sound of the voice "speech images," a term that is particularly useful for thinking about the documentary interview.[23] The nonfiction cinema of World War II is full of these speech images, both audible and audiovisual, and consciously or otherwise, *Let There Be Light* seems concerned, in its work with the subjects of traumatic speech, to trace and revise such contemporary scientific and historical talking pictures.

Take, for example, the Army Air Forces' 1942 recruiting short *Winning Your Wings*, released by the Office of War Information and Warner Bros. between 1942 and 1943 to more than thirteen thousand theaters (not to mention countless nontheatrical exhibition spaces nationwide). In *Winning Your Wings*, a familiar screen presence, Jimmy Stewart (now Lieutenant James Stewart), engages his audience in a pedagogical dialogue about what the Army Air Forces needs from ordinary "fellas." Bringing its star down to earth, the film constructs an audiovisual interaction—quite literally, an interview—between him and some curious young men. Even before the men pose their questions, Stewart's signature vocals syncopate his public address, at once managerial and folksy, with gestures of anxiety. After announcing, "I like to do some talkin'," Stewart repeats words unnecessarily, mutters incoherent syllables, and stops midline to substitute one term—"they"—or its opposite, "we." "It isn't as if it was a chore for me to

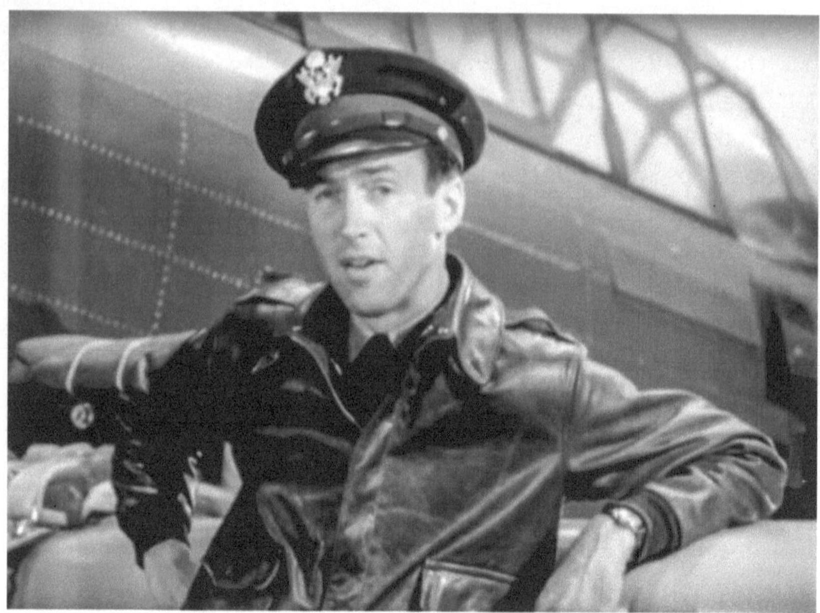

FIGURE 1.3 Lieutenant James Stewart addressing his audience in *Winning Your Wings*. Screen capture from digital video.

talk to you," Stewart assures his interlocutors, although it seems especially difficult for him to speak, as when he stutters through promises to skeptical men, declarations of the importance of teamwork, or observations about "a fellow who works at a filling station," whom Stewart initially misidentifies with a first-person pronoun before awkwardly shifting into a more appropriate third-person address. Since stuttering was one symptom that American military psychiatrists flagged during intake interviews of drafted and enlisted men, *Winning Your Wings* would seem, with the casting and performance of Stewart, to mobilize the repressive force of its institutional unconscious, a repression that resonates through the film's official dialects. Stewart admonishes his audience to "make no mistake" about the imminence of war, a point he addresses to the unconscious in that audience with the curious phrase "sooner than a lot of you realize," before making his own mistake over "we" and "they"—an especially interesting reversal in a time of war and a rather blunt manifestation of the dialectical character of the speech image as a form of self-expression.

But as one might also observe of the demotic vocal performances in the equally pandering Hollywood-army coproduction *The Battle of Midway*, where Henry Fonda and Jane Darwell, a pairing already known to moviegoers from John Ford's 1940 adaptation of *The Grapes of Wrath* as Tom and Ma Joad, speak the roles of ordinary folks, *Winning Your Wings* aims to strike a self-conscious balance between the professional expressivity of the Hollywood actor and the authenticity of documentary speech: Stewart's stuttering is first and foremost an expressive device, and his slips of the tongue in this performance are consistent with his style in other performance contexts. By contrast, the scenes of traumatic reenactment in *Let There Be Light*, in which nonprofessional actors demonstrate physical and psychological difficulty forming words, showcase a manifestly original trope: the symptom of a historic speech disorder.

Compare Stewart's shambling narration in *Winning Your Wings* with the justly famous scene from *Let There Be Light* in which a soldier suffering from a stutter is rescued in dramatic fashion from his own voice. In an interview with this patient, the doctor elicits the source of the patient's symptom: a memory of his own hearing, in the internal echoes of the sound of German shells. Before receiving an injection of sodium amytal, the preferred sedative-hypnotic drug at Mason General, the patient, identified as Hoffmeister, stutters uncontrollably as he struggles to communicate what troubles him. Told to lie down and wait for the sodium amytal to take effect, Hoffmeister eventually describes the experience of sedation as "just like seventh heaven" and soon extends the ecclesiastical similes to include God. "Oh, God, listen!" he screams, before calmly confessing that his former speech impediment "started with an *s*"—the letter that prevented him from completing words. When the doctor asks him to "go back to that 's'" and identify its significance, Hoffmeister struggles to do so, prompting the film's narrator, Walter Huston, to intercede for him, imposing an explanation that he claims Hoffmeister eventually provided (though we neither see nor hear any direct evidence of this in the film). Huston's narrator, in other words, talks over Hoffmeister, not only positing that the *s* reminded the soldier, onomatopoetically, of "the sound of death in combat" but also twice producing that sound. If it is uncanny that Hoffmeister's case so directly recalls the archaic concept of "shell shock," the explanation for war neuroses that psychoanalysis had worked to displace, during and after World War I, with a less mechanical and physical understanding of cause, what happens at the end of the patient's drugged self-analysis is equally strange: in his relief and excitement, he addresses himself to the ear of God, whom he commands to attend to his newly liberated speech—a speech liberated, that is, from the patient's own ear.

In a film both moving and deeply disturbing, these scenes of patients

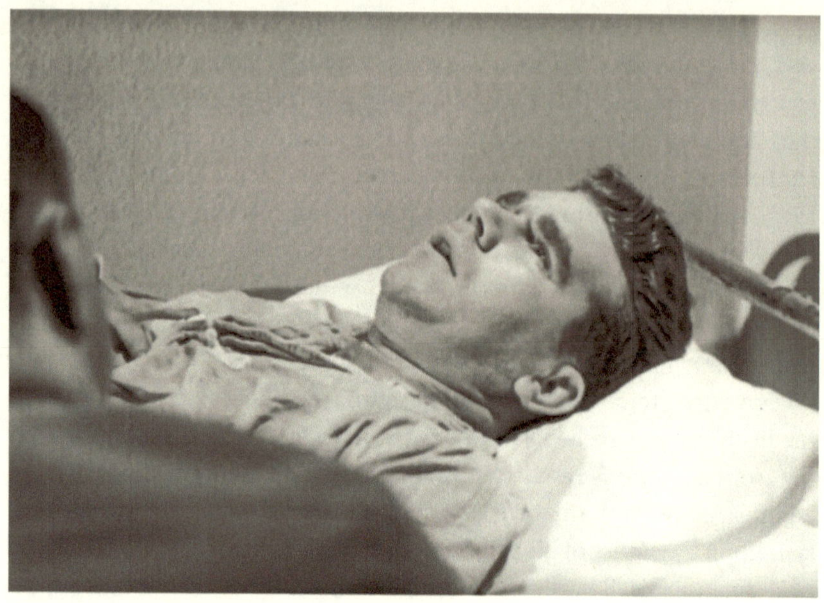

FIGURE 1.4 "Oh, God, listen!" from *Let There Be Light*. Screen capture from digital video.

undergoing drug-aided trips into their unconscious are perhaps the most unsettling, not least because it is difficult for the viewer of them to know for sure whether these performances are real or how much treatment time the editing condenses. Of course, the promise that the film makes in its opening title—that no scenes were staged—is immediately suspicious to modern viewers, especially given archival revelations about the frequency with which military-sponsored filmmakers like Huston, Frank Capra, and George Stevens staged combat scenes under the banner of actuality; indeed, Huston's own documentary *San Pietro*, promoted and received upon its release in 1945 as a filmed record of a key battle in the Italian Campaign, consists almost entirely of reenactments. The institutional utility of such reenactments would soon become so pronounced as to preclude the type of subterfuge in which Huston and other filmmakers engaged. When, in 1947, the army remade *Let There Be Light*, along with several other documentaries about military psychiatry, under the title *Shades of Gray*, it chose to open the film with a statement acknowledging both the moral virtue and the pedagogic effectiveness of reenactment. According to *Shades of Gray*, in order for "official case histories [to be] faithfully re-enacted," actors must impersonate the minutiae of mental illness. "Although actual patients are not shown," reads the film's opening statement, "their expressions, reactions, gestures, and speech have been carefully reproduced." What follow are scenes—some of them lifted almost verbatim from *Let There Be Light*—in which skilled actors uncannily recreate the transgressive behaviors of the patients in Huston's film, making it difficult to accept as necessarily authentic the awkward or disturbing mannerisms that those patients displayed for the cameras at Mason General. Perhaps further engendering suspicion about the authenticity of *Let There Be Light*, the film's opening disclaimer was in fact revised numerous times: archival files include hotel stationery on which someone—presumably John Huston himself—wrote and rewrote this disclaimer, with each new draft adding a denial designed to defuse criticism; a further, more official revision, approved by the Signal Corps for inclusion in the film's opening crawl, included the name of the hospital at which the film was shot, the claim that the film is "entirely authentive [*sic*]," and an assertion of the consent and close cooperation of the patients depicted therein.[24] All of these written statements, generated through a seemingly arduous process of internal adjudication and revision, are absent from the finished film, which favors a certain ambiguity, especially regarding the conditions of participation of each patient-subject. And although the official explanation for the ban on public screenings of *Let There Be Light* implied that these subjects had been exposed unawares, even though they had signed releases, nothing that we have seen in archival records of the film settles this question definitively at the level of production history.

The relatively familiar narrative of the film's initial suppression, so central to scholarly treatments of *Let There Be Light*, tends to conceal the history of its prominent display in a range of postwar settings. The lack of public, commercial availability of the film was, for over thirty years, simply the obverse of its broad institutional influence and its vivid contributions to the study of soldiering, documentary filmmaking, and especially psychoanalysis. Indeed, one might argue that the willingness of critics and scholars to embrace a "repressive hypothesis" about *Let There Be Light* and its abortive first life mirrors all too comfortably a consensus that emerged in the same period—the aftermath of the Vietnam War—about the human nature and scientific history of post-traumatic stress disorder. As Ruth Leys demonstrates in *Trauma: A Genealogy*, the study of trauma, particularly war-born trauma, itself suffers from a kind of traumatic memory over the century or so between its "discovery" and its enshrinement in the third edition of the *Diagnostic and Statistical Manual of Mental Disorders* as PTSD, subject to flare-ups of interest from physicians, scientists, and public health authorities during major wars and then to sporadic forgetting and revision. During World War II, Leys shows, a particularly intense debate erupted over the causes, meanings, and treatment of battle trauma, one that partly turned on the question of whether traumatic repetitions were "veridical depictions of the origin": that is, whether the signs and symptoms of trauma should serve, and should be treated, as a historical source or discourse.[25] While the most extreme position of scientific and cultural theorists of trauma has been to assert a direct relation between trauma and history, on the premise that trauma is otherwise an unrepresentable state, a condition in fact tantamount to a historical period, in its widespread effects on the culture containing it, Leys argues that a more accurate understanding of trauma in both scientific and cultural terms treats it less as a contagion or pandemic and more *as* discourse, subject to uneven development and local variation, replete with ambivalence and contradiction. Such was also the condition of *Let There Be Light*, as it began to generate and circulate through its initial publics.

As early as November 1946, a mere seven months after military police prevented the exhibition of the film at the Museum of Modern Art in New York, the War Department authorized the striking of new 35 mm prints of *Let There Be Light* for military use, including in the Army Pictorial Service film library, where it would be available upon request by military personnel.[26] Orders for new prints were frequent in the late 1940s, as numerous military hospitals continued to use Huston's film as a teaching tool; indeed, in electing to limit the exhibition of *Let There Be Light*, the War Department had emphasized the film's usefulness "to military professional personnel participating in the treatment of neuropsychiatric cases." Pursuant to the restriction of the film to military and psychiatric venues, the War Department had ordered the Signal Corps to furnish prints to the navy, the Army Medical Museum, the Neuropsychiatry Consultants Division of the Surgeon General's Office, "civilian professional groups as determined by the Surgeon General," and "all overseas theaters for showing to military personnel"; it also instructed the Signal Corps to loan the film's negative to the Veterans Administration for the striking of as many prints as necessary for use in its hospitals, outpatient clinics, and community outreach facilities.[27] Following the dramatic expansion of the film's military presence, the Association for the Advancement of Psychotherapy obtained a print of *Let There Be Light* in 1948, screening it at one of its well-attended monthly meetings at the Academy of Medicine; in a thank-you letter to the Signal Corps Photographic Center, association secretary Dr. Emil Gutheil noted that "the film was followed with the keenest interest by the doctors present," which only confirmed, for Gutheil, its lasting extramilitary value.[28]

Complicating the notion that the nonspecialist public was deprived of knowledge of *Let There Be Light* during the documentary's decades-long suppression, two popular magazines—*Life* and *Harper's Bazaar*—featured stills of the film along with information about its production and purpose.[29] In a 1946 letter to Army Public Relations, Dorothy Wheelock, the associate editor of *Harper's Bazaar*, noted the film's positive reception among the magazine's staff members, writing, "We think the film is one of the most important documentaries we have ever seen."[30] Later, in a letter to the Signal Corps, Wheelock attempted to distinguish her magazine's proposed coverage of the film from that of *Life*, reemphasizing the high esteem in which the film was held at *Harper's* and promising to promote its documentary legitimacy: "We do feel that the film is so terribly important and our treatment is simply on the film itself—how it happened to be made, and its great importance as an educational documentary."[31] Listening to Huston's traumatized combat veterans describe the sources of their neurotic symptoms, sometimes in ways that ran counter to the military's official claims, the *Harper's* audience, which consisted of the magazine's editorial board and art director, was one of several civilian groups to have engaged with *Let There Be Light* at the time of its official suppression, a fact that challenges retrospective critical assumptions about the distribution of knowledge of Huston's subject and methods during the immediate postwar period.

In addressing the ban—often in direct response to the various organizations and individuals who requested that it be lifted between 1946 and 1980—military officials occasionally cited the film's obsolescence as a tool intended to help win the war, despite the fact that it had never been earmarked for this purpose and was instead commissioned to aid postwar processes of reconstruction. As late as 1971, in response to an archivist's request to include *Let There Be Light* in a retrospective of Huston's films, an army official reiterated the specious claim that the documentary's subjects had signed consent forms strictly "in furtherance of the war effort," omitting the more persuasive arguments of those who, with increasing frequency following the suppression of Frederick Wiseman's *Titicut Follies* by the Supreme Judicial Court of Massachusetts in 1969, critiqued attempts to obtain consent from the mentally ill.[32] Contradicting its official position on the postwar irrelevance and inadmissibility of the identities of Huston's onscreen subjects, the military often pursued, with an eye toward institutional publicity, the very information that it sought to protect. In 1947, a Signal

Corps production executive wrote to Dr. Benjamin Simon, a psychiatrist at the Connecticut State Hospital who had served as a technical adviser to Huston, in order to obtain the name of one of the patients who appeared in *Let There Be Light*—"a patient in a paralytic stage who could neither walk nor talk" but who, after treatment, "talked freely, mentioning specifically that he had family troubles." Simon had requested a print of *Let There Be Light* for his clinical research; in return for providing one, the Signal Corps requested the identity of this former patient, apparently on the assumption that the man, who in Huston's film complains "that his parents were forever bickering and quarreling," could lend his story to the corps for the production of a film series on postwar social problems.[33] The military thus appeared to both endorse and dismiss the authority of Huston's interview footage—to alternately identify and repudiate its lasting relevance, leading to a complex and contradictory fabric of official justifications for the film's suppression.

War trauma had the force of a structure of feeling in postwar American culture, a structure that can be glimpsed not only in the narrative and characterological dimensions of particular documentary and realist films but also out into the broader orbits of cinema, where the massive wartime production of nontheatrical, nonfiction film continued to exert its effects on viewership. Although echoes of *Let There Be Light*'s characterology can be found in both American films and film criticism for at least a decade after the film's failed initial public release, well into the period of the Korean War, it was not until the codification of battle trauma as PTSD in the late 1970s—due largely to an activist group of progressive psychiatrists within the American Psychological Association, a result of their work with Vietnam war veterans, leading to the inscription of PTSD as a medically recognized and recognizable condition in the third edition of the *Diagnostic and Statistical Manual of Mental Disorders* in 1980—that the symptomatology of trauma could be explicitly registered in commercial documentary film as an individual and collective artifact of veterans' war experiences or could be fully incorporated into what Nichols called, around this time, the documentary "voice." The visibility and audibility of PTSD was raised in this period by films like *Interviews with My Lai Veterans* (Joseph Strick, 1970), which won an Oscar for best documentary short, and *Winter Soldier* (Winterfilm Collective, 1972). Both films gathered together American veterans of the war in Vietnam, in individual or collective portraits, and gave them the opportunity to admit to the torture, rape, and murder of prisoners and civilians, a series of horrifying performances whose aim was twofold: to provide vivid, firsthand support for the moral case against the war, and to corroborate arguments made by veterans' groups that veterans were suffering from the effects of what they had seen and done even after returning home. These filmed confessions, in other words, simultaneously announce in the first person acts of inhumanity committed by the speakers and, by serializing and collecting their testimony, attribute ultimate blame to the institutions that authorized both the atrocities confessed to and the rule of silence that made these public confessions necessary. Moreover, the cinematic performances of the veterans helped advance the claim that the veterans were themselves victims, troubled by their experiences and their memories to the point of melancholy or disassociation, a point made best on the curiously impassive or distracted faces of the men in *Interviews with My Lai Veterans*. For decades, when soldiers' reluctance to fight took the psychosomatic forms of fear, anger, sadness, and fatigue referred to as "shell shock" and "war neuroses," their symptoms, confessed to in therapeutic interviews, were treated as excuses, signs of deviance from the patriotic mean that psychiatry would correct.

After Vietnam, the innovation by veterans and psychiatrists of PTSD made trauma not only a kind of social norm, an ordinary and expected response to violence and terror, but a form of political collectivity, and such films as *Interviews with My Lai Veterans* and *Winter Soldier*, one might say, helped to turn the excuse of war trauma into an assertive, rather than a defensive, position. Traumatic memory becomes a standard device of critical documentary approaches to history in the Vietnam era, and its prevaricating, self-indicting, and confessional subjects can be found in many of the era's most significant cinematic studies of war experience: not only the experience of Vietnam but—as in Marcel Ophüls and Claude Lanzmann's interview-based studies of the buried histories of World War II, *The Sorrow and the Pity* (1969) and *Shoah* (1985)—of other conflicts, as well. Indeed, as Thomas Waugh notes in an influential article from 1975, the agonistic "new documentary" style of interview practiced by filmmakers like Ophüls and Emile de Antonio—a style that could be considered "new" only insofar as it was radically unlike the *cinémas vérité* whose methods and beliefs it challenged, in part by simply reviving a dormant mechanism of documentary speech—became a common denominator in antiwar and political documentary cinemas of the period and after, a tradition that continues to this day.[34] The wide variety of recent documentary, docudramatic, avant-garde, and narrative fiction film and video work about American military engagements, in which moving-image artists and their subjects take stock of the causes and consequences of the ongoing conflicts in Afghanistan, Iraq, and other sites of the "War on Terror," often use the documentary interview and its confessional subject to assert the psychic and social reality of trauma as an American historical event. The effusive yet hesitant confessants of the acknowledged and unofficial veterans of these most recent wars, from the self-incriminating amateur documentarians recounting their exploits at Abu Ghraib in Errol Morris's *Standard Operating Procedure* (2008), to Edward Snowden, the nervy NSA saboteur at the center of Laura Poitras's confessional portrait film *Citizenfour* (2014), can trace their origins to Huston's cine-medical laboratory. Well before *vérité*, *Let There Be Light* modeled a style of documentary historiography in which the subject's testimony is its own, only guarantee of truth, a radically disturbing proposition for the viewer of documentary when it supplements the authority of the camera to witness and to testify. Incorporating history into the subject of the interview, in whom the "elsewhere" of spoken truth in the documentary interview becomes a kind of inner ear, Huston's interpretation of the talking cure still illuminates the aural recesses of our military past.

NOTES

1. Ellis, "Dancing to Different Tunes," 57.
2. Leacock, quoted in Marcorelles, *Living Cinema*, 55.
3. Nichols, "Voice of Documentary," *Film Quarterly*, 18.
4. Ibid.
5. See Foucault's 1975 interview with *Le Monde*, in which Foucault first uses the term *dispositif* in a discussion of his book *Discipline and Punish*: Jambet, "Une interrogation sur les prisons." See also Foucault, *The History of Sexuality* and *Power/Knowledge*.
6. In her sweeping study *Trauma: A Genealogy*, Ruth Leys revises the received histories of trauma as a problem for medicine, neuroscience, and psychoanalysis, especially the post–Vietnam War era accounts of trauma that, Leys argues, reduce its paradoxes—paradoxes that also make it, she argues, difficult to write about in a linear, progressive, or evolutionary manner—and universalize its causes and effects.
7. For an economical account of the critical problem posed by reenactment, through the career of one of its most innovative practitioners, see Brian Winston's short essay "'Honest, Straightforward Re-enactment,'" where Winston goes so far as to suggest that the entire history of documentary might be rethought in terms of a taxonomy of reenactment. Elsewhere, in his account of Humphrey Jennings's wartime documentary *Fires Were Started* (1943), Winston writes, "Filming re-enactments was central to the 'creative treatment of actuality,' as Grierson's famous definition of the documentary has it. It was

not only permitted: it was in fact the cardinal mark of what made documentary different from other forms of non-fictional filmmaking, such as newsreels." Winston, *Fires Were Started*, 58.

8. Collingwood, *Idea of History*, 215.

9. Rosen, *Change Mummified*, 199.

10. For more on *War Neuroses*, see Cowie, *Recording Reality*.

11. "Midway Movie." The *Post* editors make this historic claim for the film because of, not despite, the "confused idea of the actual development of the battle" viewers would gain from its cinematography and its structure, "since great naval engagements are not thoroughly rehearsed like Hollywood spectacles." The film's soundtrack, which displays "the restraint and taste exhibited by Ford in his commercial pictures," is held to a different standard of authenticity.

12. See, for example, James Agee's review of *Memphis Belle*, where he comments that the film's "vigorous and pitiful sense of the presence, danger, skill, and hope of several human beings" is "so unobstreperously clear in the faces of all of them that I could not guess which shots were reenacted and which were straight records"—a confusion that troubles Agee not at all. Agee, "Films."

13. Freud, *Psychopathology of Everyday Life*, 79.

14. An example of this predetermined, prescriptive approach is 1943's *Introduction to the Army*, which dramatizes a "typical" intake interview designed to determine whether an enlistee is sexually "deviant"; the interview ends with a scripted declaration of the enlistee's avid heterosexuality—a model, in the film's terms, for heteronormative social interactions within the American armed forces. By contrast, the wartime military documentaries that presage Huston's approach in *Let There Be Light* offer far fewer behavioral blueprints. Since exhibitions of 1944's *Psychiatric Procedures in the Combat Area*, like exhibitions of 1945's similarly themed *Field Psychiatry for the General Medical Officer*, were initially restricted to officers and medical personnel, the film was free to incorporate observational footage both of actual intake interviews and of actual treatment sessions. For more on these and related films, see Tsika, *Traumatic Imprints*.

15. *Psychiatric Procedures in the Combat Area*, for instance, puts the figure at 25 percent.

16. Letter to Walter Karri-Davies, Universal International Films, Inc., 21 March 1946.

17. It was also known, at various stages of its development, as "The Returning Soldier—Nervously Wounded," "The Returning Psychoneurotic," and "What Is a Psychoneurotic?" See Record Group 111: Records of the Office of the Chief Signal Officer, 1860–1985, 111-M-1241, box 11 (hereafter RG 111).

18. Edgerton, "Revisiting the Recordings of Wars Past," 50, 46.

19. Unlike the conception of *Let There Be Light* that gradually emerged among its supporters as a kind of crossover product, screenings of *Psychiatric Procedures in the Combat Area* were reserved for officers and enlisted medical personnel.

20. Payne and Jelliffe, "War Neuroses and Psychoneuroses," 387. Denouncing various dismissals of psychoanalysis, the authors passionately argue that "shell shock" is "not a concussion but an emotion" (386). At the same time, however, they stress the aberrance of "war neuroses," referring to the afflicted soldier's "constitutional peculiarity" (387) and "special sensibilities" (388).

21. Marshall, *Men against Fire*, 136.

22. Wolfe, "Historicizing the 'Voice of God.'"

23. Freud, *The Psychopathology of Everyday Life*, 57–58.

24. "'Let There Be Light': Revised Narration," 7 December 1945, RG 111.

25. Leys, *Trauma*, 203.

26. "Daily Information Bulletin No. 50," Office of the Chief Signal Officer, 27 November 1946, RG 111.

27. Harry P. Warner, "Clearances on 'Let There Be Light,'" 11 March 1946, RG 111.

28. Emil A. Gutheil to Lt. Col. James B. Buchanan, 28 February 1948, RG 111.

29. Hersey, "Short Talk with Erlanger"; McFadden, "Let There Be Light."

30. Dorothy Wheelock to Chief, Army Public Relations, 27 January 1946, RG 111.

31. Ibid.

32. Jerry W. Friedheim to James B. Rhoades, 9 September 1971, RG 111.

33. James B. Buchanan to Benjamin Simon, 15 October 1947, RG 111.

34. Waugh, "Beyond *Vérité*."

Death in Life

Documenting Survival after Hiroshima

FRANNY NUDELMAN

Exaggerations and distortions are themselves products of the bomb.
—ROBERT JAY LIFTON, *Death in Life*

Writing in *politics* in 1946, Dwight Macdonald and Mary McCarthy delivered a scathing critique of John Hersey's recently published *Hiroshima*—a one-two punch, with Macdonald taking Hersey to task for what he did and McCarthy calling him out for what he failed to do. Together they set the terms for the often heated debate over Hersey's book and, implicitly, over the properties and purposes of documentary writing after 1945. Macdonald found the book so "dull" that he "stopped reading halfway through." He explained that the "dead-pan, keyed-down approach," which he terms a kind of "naturalism," is "so detached from the persons that Hersey was writing about that they become objects of clinical description." It is this clinical approach, which treats Hiroshima survivors as "white mice," that Macdonald objects to on both aesthetic and moral grounds.[1] If Macdonald critiques Hersey's bland style, McCarthy blames the conventionality of his reporting, which fails to capture what is earth-shattering about the destruction of Hiroshima. Specifically, she criticizes his dependence on interviews, the "classic technique for reporting such events," which render Hersey's characters banal and, moreover, substitute the irrelevant details of their daily lives for the reality of mass destruction. "The interview with survivors," she writes, "is a falsification of the truth of atomic warfare." She continues, "To have done the atom bomb justice, Mr. Hersey would have had to interview the dead."[2]

Both Macdonald and McCarthy were exacting in their characterization of Hersey's style, but without the benefit of retrospection they could not understand the complex relationship between clinical observation and narrative journalism or the role of the interview in redefining the relationship between life and death in the decades following World War II. Narrative journalism evolved and flourished in the postwar period as journalists experimented with the techniques of immersion, involving themselves more intimately with their subjects and frequently documenting the impact of reporting on their own emotions and outlook. Their writing often provided a record of the interaction between reporter and subject—an interaction they conceived as intense and potentially transformative. In this regard, narrative journalists were profoundly influenced by war-related developments in psychiatry that gave primacy to the clinical interview as a site of experimentation and healing in the aftermath of the war. In both psychiatric and journalistic contexts, the interview process allowed practitioners to rethink a model of documentary knowledge that assumes the neutrality of the observer and to develop an alternative model that emphasizes the expert's involvement in the documentary exchange.

This essay explores the influence of experiments in military psychiatry on two landmark books about Hiroshima survivors—Hersey's *Hiroshima* (1946) and Robert Jay Lifton's *Death in Life* (1968). Both Hersey and Lifton observed psychiatric experiments on traumatized American veterans before writing their accounts of survival in Hiroshima. Documenting the experiences of Hiroshima survivors, both authors grappled, if in different ways, with the ethical complexities they had encountered in treatment settings—Hersey in his work as a journalist and Lifton as a psychiatrist. Shortly before traveling to Japan in 1946, Hersey observed the experimental treatment of "psychoneurotic" veterans and wrote about it in a short story that probes the relationship between interviews and storytelling in a clinical setting and elaborates on the role of artifice and coercion in producing traumatic recollection. These were problems that he chose to sideline, however, when he arrived in Japan and stepped into the role of interviewer. Hersey's turn to the techniques of fiction in *Hiroshima*, which paved the way for the "nonfiction novels" of later new journalists like Norman Mailer and Truman Capote, functioned to obscure his complex relationship to his interview subjects. Although Hersey did not fully immerse himself in the emotions and inner lives of his subjects, as later writers would do, he understood that atomic warfare called for new forms of writing and took a small if hesitant step toward refashioning documentary prose for the nuclear age.[3]

More than two decades after the publication of *Hiroshima*, Lifton, who was a great admirer of Hersey's book, developed a different approach to writing about Hiroshima survivors. In his role as an army psychiatrist during the Korean War, Lifton had a chance to interview soldiers who had been subjected to the techniques of thought reform in Korean prisons. This experience alerted him to the complexities of the interview scenario and provoked his lifelong commitment to "bringing . . . the clinical interview, into historical perspective."[4] In *Death in Life*, Lifton reproduces interview testimony verbatim and, unlike Hersey, places his own emotional reactions to this testimony at the heart of his account. Documenting the marked detachment of Hiroshima survivors, he charges the observer, or "witness," with the burden of pained feeling. In the process, Lifton defines the state of being that he calls "death in life"—stunned and without feeling, alive and yet not fully so—that came to characterize victims of violence in the contemporary period.

Like Jonathan Kahana and Noah Tsika's essay in this volume, my essay explores the interview as "a historical practice: a practice with a history, as well as a practice *of* history," and argues for its impact on the career of documentary prose as well as documentary film. Observing the importance of survivor testimony to postwar documentary, we must ask after the institutional settings where such testimony was produced.[5] If documentary filmmakers and writers culled narratives of trauma and survival from reams of interview footage and transcribed testimony, that documentation was generated by a set of practices that are rarely analyzed. What Bill Nichols calls the "voice of documentary" belonged not only to traumatized subjects but also to the professionals who elicited and structured their recollections.[6] In their writing about traumatized veterans, Hersey and Lifton demonstrate that military psychiatrists, far from being objective, used interviews to prod veterans to remember scenes that they often preferred to forget and, at an extreme, to recollect events that had never occurred. Indeed, at times military experts engaged in experiments that bordered on the occult. In this essay, I contend that a fascination with the nuances of extreme experience that courses through the field of documentary writing after 1945 was significantly influenced by the institutional production of subjectivity in experimental settings where documentarians and their subjects collaborated—however coercive or unequal the nature of that collaboration—to produce survivor testimony.

John Huston and his crew were not the only documentarians at Mason General Hospital as the war came to a close: John Hersey also observed and documented the experimental treatment of traumatized veterans in his short story "A Short Talk with Erlanger." Although military censors suppressed Huston's documentary about the hospital, *Let There Be Light*, until 1980, Hersey's story appeared in *Life* magazine in October 1945, accompanied by stills from Huston's film and photographs by *Life* photographer David Scherman. "A Short Talk With Erlanger" is a close study of the narcoanalytic interview, during which traumatized veterans were drugged and questioned by psychiatrists, and the story examines the dynamics of military experimentation in careful detail.

As Macdonald's comment on *Hiroshima* demonstrates, from the time of its publication, debate over Hersey's *Hiroshima* has focused on the relationship between military and literary experimentation and, implicitly, on the ethics of documentary representation. World War II produced staggering developments in weaponry and techniques of genocidal destruction; once the war was over, practitioners in various fields—writers and military strategists, psychiatrists and physicists—began the process of recording and analyzing the effects of these new forms of violence and, in the process, producing knowledge out of destruction. Survivors, who had experienced war at its most extreme, were of special interest: in the psychiatric clinic, where traumatized veterans were treated and studied, and in the destroyed city of Hiroshima, practitioners in the interlocking fields of military science, psychiatry, and journalism used interviews to collect information about the effects of war on personality and belief.

In their influential *Men under Stress* (1945), psychiatrists Roy Grinker and John Spiegel described World War II as "a crucial experiment." Although it had proved "cruel, destructive and wasteful," they observed that the war offered "exceedingly valuable lessons."[7] Indeed, professional psychology came into its own during World War II, as psychiatrists and psychologists were called upon to test the mental health of soldiers entering the military and to treat the epidemic of soldiers who suffered from debilitating traumatic symptoms during the war. In particular, the decision to screen soldiers before they enlisted made the interview central to the conduct of the war and necessitated the training of professionals in interview techniques. The screening process was overseen by psychiatrist Henry Stack Sullivan, who was hired as military consultant to the draft in November 1940. In the decades preceding the war, Sullivan had reconceptualized the aims and methods of talk therapy: advocating for a view of psychiatry as primarily focused on relationships rather than on individual pathology, he took the dynamic interaction between psychiatrist and patient as a microcosm for social relatedness more broadly. Summarizing this approach in *The Psychiatric Interview* (1954), Sullivan wrote, "There are no purely objective data . . . and there are no valid subjective data." Instead, the psychiatrist is a "participant observer," and the "data which can be subjected to scientific study" lies "in the situation which is created between the observer and his subject."[8]

As soldiers and veterans flooded a relatively untried system, therapists applied a range of treatment techniques that included deep sleep therapy, hearty food, and recreation. Chief among these were forms of conversation—the intake interview, hypnosis, psychotherapy, group therapy—and, at an extreme, the process of narcoanalysis. Narcoanalysis (sometimes called narcosynthesis) was developed in the 1920s and 30s and popularized in the psychiatric community during World War II by Grinker and Spiegel.[9] In a narcoanalytic session, the patient receives a barbiturate injection (sodium amytal or sodium pentothal) that produces a state of twilight consciousness and primes the process of talk therapy. Throughout the session, as Grinker and Spiegel describe it, the "needle should be kept in the vein" and more of the drug injected if needed to maintain "the proper responsiveness."[10] During the narcoanalytic interview, the therapist—in classic analytic fashion—peels away layers of personality in order to access buried content with the aim of producing an "abreaction," in which the patient relives the foundational trauma. If the session goes well, the patient revisits the scene of trauma and is, in theory, cured through the process of recollection. Once the patient regains consciousness, the therapist reviews with him the recollections he experienced while drugged so that he will remember them, and in this way they together construct a narrative about the patient's traumatic wartime experiences. Narcoanalysis takes Sullivan's theorization of relationality to a bizarre extreme, amplifying and exaggerating the interactive properties of the clinical interview.

Huston's film documents two scenes of narcoanalysis in which one paralyzed veteran and one mute veteran are drugged, undergo a brief session of talk therapy, and are swiftly cured. Hersey's story "A Short Talk with Erlanger" focuses narrowly on this same technique, recounting a single narcoanalytic session in detail. In this story, Hersey represents clinical dialogue in which the authoritative, at times coercive speech of a military psychiatrist simultaneously excavates and produces traumatic memory. Although it is a composite portrait, with fictive elements, Hersey's story is rigorously precise in its rendering of narcoanalysis. In the name of accuracy, "A Short Talk with Erlanger" was vetted by at least three doctors who made extensive comments on it, including Grinker, who wrote, "You have done an amazing job and one that will stand professional scrutiny."[11] In addition, the story was reviewed by the "Surgeon General's Office and Review Branch," which made relatively minor alterations to the text that it stipulated were "corrections from the point of view of accuracy rather than the suppression of information."[12]

According to Hersey, "A Short Talk with Erlanger" was based on many sessions of narcoanalysis that he witnessed at Mason General Hospital,[13] and his archives contain sound recordings of these sessions. Psychiatrists were eager to document treatment, and yet there was no recording method that did not potentially interfere with the relationship between expert and patient. Sullivan worried that taking notes distracted the therapist from the subtleties of the patient's speech and body language and that recording devices had an "inhibiting effect" on clinician and patient.[14] At the same time, clinicians valued a transcript of the psychiatric interview that could be studied and used in teaching and consultation; even better was a sound recording that would capture not only the nuances of tone and inflection but also the stray yawn or sigh. As recorded on these SoundScriber discs, now barely audible, the narcoanalytic session is unpredictable and disorderly, conveying the exploratory nature of the process. Listening to these interviews, the vulnerability of the drugged patient comes across, but so does his recalcitrance, rudeness, and unpredictability. By extension, the authority of the therapist seems less firm as he tries various approaches and is at times thrown off his game. True to Sullivan's model of the psychiatric interview, these sound recordings convey the shifting and uncertain nature of the therapeutic relationship.

"A Short Talk with Erlanger" describes a narcoanalytic session conducted by an army psychiatrist with a traumatized veteran, inexplicably paralyzed from the waist down. During this session, Erlanger recalls many past difficulties—most significantly he remembers the death of his best friend in combat, for which he feels responsible, as well as the fact that his abusive father feigned a bum leg to get out of work. These recollections, prompted by the forceful suggestions of the psychiatrist, mark the beginning of Erlanger's recovery. Hersey's story, which consists primarily of dialogue between Erlanger and the unnamed "Army doctor," is a close study of the psychiatric interview that alerts us to the role of artifice and imagination in the clinical exchange. At every point, Hersey describes the way that the administration of sodium amytal guides and structures the interview process: "The nurse snapped the tourniquet tube loose and the doctor slowly pushed one cubic centimeter of 10% sodium amytal solution into the vein,

[and] left the needle point embedded."[15] The needle is left in Erlanger's arm so they can continue to dose him as the "talk" unfolds; the story is punctuated by the injection of more of the drug. In response to the combined probing of needles and questions, a sudden and "electrifying" change comes over Erlanger, and he begins to speak in the present tense. Dramatizing the process known as "abreaction," Hersey claims that the treatment process "cracked Erlanger's sense of time and threw him back again into the actual situation."[16]

If narcoanalysis was conceived as a crude version of psychoanalysis, tailored to the conditions of war in which many soldiers had to be treated very quickly, it also brought some of the more coercive aspects of the analytic relationship to the fore, as it made the drugged patient entirely vulnerable to the therapist's suggestions. During the narcoanalytic session, patients were uninhibited, so it was easier for them to recall painful experiences. By the same token, they were also more open to suggestion. British psychiatrist William Sargant recalled that in some instances of narcoanalysis, drugged patients were not encouraged to relive their earlier experiences but rather to imagine new ones that were similar to the traumatic event. In acute cases, he writes, "quite imaginary situations . . . could be suggested to a patient under drugs; though as a rule these were in some way related to the experiences which he had undergone. Much better results could often, indeed, be obtained by stirring up emotions about such imaginary happenings."[17] Throughout "A Short Talk with Erlanger," the coercive interrogatory bleeds into the disciplinary command that never pretends to neutrality but rather tells the drugged and suggestible Erlanger what he should remember.

In their description of the review process that follows the narcoanalytic session, Grinker and Spiegel write, "After the pentothal has worn off, the patient is pressed to recapitulate, while conscious, the material which he abreacted or remembered while under narcosis. He frequently states that he cannot remember what he has said but with pressure most of the associations can be recalled."[18] As Erlanger falls asleep the lieutenant colonel explains to him, "After you wake up, I'm going to have another talk with you, and I want you to remember everything that you've told me, *and some other things, too*."[19] Hersey's story describes the process of recollecting traumatic experience as an effect of military discipline, capturing the complexities of the narcoanalytic interview as it works alternately to recover and to instill the narrated particulars of trauma. When he traveled to Hiroshima seven months after publishing "A Short Talk with Erlanger," it was these very complexities that he did his best to expunge from his written account in hope that the journalistic interview, unlike its clinical counterpart, might record trauma in a manner unmarred by coercion.

When John Hersey arrived at the Reverend Kiyoshi Tanimoto's house in Hiroshima to conduct their scheduled interview, he was wearing an army uniform. Tanimoto, who would become one of *Hiroshima*'s six protagonists, later recalled his first impression of the American reporter: "He, being a war correspondent, put on an army uniform but, unlike a soldier, had about him the refinement of a literary man."[20] As a war correspondent, writing for *Time* and *Life* magazines during World War II, Hersey worked in collaboration with the military. He traveled to Japan with permission from General Headquarters of the U.S. Army Forces and, as the publication history of "A Short Talk with Erlanger" suggests, at times consulted with military personnel who vetted his writing. If Hersey's relationship with the U.S. military was close, it was not uncritical. Tanimoto recalled that at the beginning of their interview Hersey remarked, "'Various scientific investigations of damage inflicted by the atomic bomb have been carried out, but, I, different from them, want to investigate the damage from the viewpoint of humanism.'"[21] A literary man in military dress, Hersey sought to distinguish his project from a vast, militarized documentary enterprise.

Hersey traveled to Hiroshima in May 1946, on assignment for the *New Yorker*, to conduct interviews with atomic bomb survivors. He was one of the many experts who flocked to Hiroshima, among them the "engineers, architects, fire experts, economists, doctors, photographers, draftsmen," who contributed their findings to the *U.S. Strategic Bombing Survey*.[22] Hersey's interviews, and the resulting text, were part of a much larger effort to survey and record the effects of atomic weapons. And yet, Hersey and his editors at the *New Yorker* saw themselves as dissenters, trying to fill a gap in media coverage of the atomic bomb that had emphasized its magnitude and novelty while ignoring its effect on Japanese victims. Hersey's editors charged him with reconstructing the experience of Hiroshima survivors from their own perspective. To this end, he interviewed forty survivors and from this group chose six to focus on. Hersey relied heavily on the interview testimony of these characters, recounting the particulars they observed on the day of the bombing and in the days that followed. Harold Ross, the *New Yorker*'s editor in chief, was especially insistent, urging Hersey to exclude any detail that could not be securely attached to the perspective of one of these six people.[23] Ideally, this narrow focus would allow readers to identify more closely with Hiroshima survivors. As Hersey put it years later in a letter to a reader, "I didn't set out to 'prove' anything. I wanted to bring readers a sense of what it must have been like to be there."[24]

From the first, *Hiroshima* was praised, and promoted, for its ability to produce this sense of immediacy. One reader, featured in an ad for the Book of the Month Club edition of *Hiroshima*, put it this way: "This indeed is how it must have been—this is how it would have seemed to me, had I been there."[25] Readers who had an intense emotional response to the book—and they were legion—testified to its power to simulate presence. This was true not only for American readers, who were not there, but also for some Japanese readers, who were. As the writer and survivor Yōko Ōta put it in her review of the book, reading it was like "peering into a mirror."[26]

In order to give his readers a sense of "being there," Hersey absented himself from the scene of documentation. Years later he explained that in writing *Hiroshima*, "My choice was to be deliberately quiet . . . because I thought that if the horror could be presented as directly as possible, it would allow the reader to identify with the characters in a direct way. . . . This was one of the reasons why I had experimented with the devices of fiction in doing journalism, in the hopes that my mediation would, ideally, disappear."[27] Hersey assumed that the mediating presence of the journalist could only detract from the impression of experiential verisimilitude he wanted to create. By omitting quotation marks and keeping editorializing to a minimum, Hersey did his best to scrub the text clean of any traces of his involvement in the dialogic process that produced his documentation.

At the same time that Hersey wanted to convey the experiences of his informants, he also wanted to critique the "scientific investigations" conducted by the U.S. military. If Macdonald disliked Hersey's approach for too nearly resembling clinical science, Hersey admonished the U.S. military on similar grounds; throughout *Hiroshima*, Hersey portrays his subjects as victims of military science. His most scathing indictment comes in a chapter titled "Details Are Being Investigated" that culminates with President Truman's radio address describing America's new weapon as "the largest bomb ever yet used in the history of warfare."[28] In this passage, Hersey allows himself a sardonic aside, remarking that victims of this weapon—those who survived—would probably not have heard Truman's remarks and, if they did, were probably "too busy or too weary or too badly hurt to care that they were the objects of the first great experiment in the use of atomic power." As Dan Gerstle notes, "In emphasizing the experimental nature of the bomb, Hersey quietly carved out his moral position."[29]

The techniques of fiction provided a resource for Hersey as he tried to sublimate the interview process that, as his short story about Mason General Hospital indicates, is rife with coercion, conflict, and inaccuracy. Unlike later new journalists who explored and elaborated on the properties of voice as well as the interview dynamic, Hersey stripped the idiosyncrasies of the spoken word—his subject's and his own—from the text. What makes the book "dull," to borrow Macdonald's language, is not only the preponderance of undifferentiated narrative detail but also the fact that all six central characters share a single (and singularly uninflected) narrative voice. In *Hiroshima*, Hersey reproduced words without sound, suppressing not only his own voice—as it prods, queries, and guides—but also those of his interviewees.

Hersey wanted to devise a literary alternative to scientific investigation; instead, he wrote a book that confounds the distinction between empiricism and humanism. Hesitant to fully embrace the particularity and thus the limitations of his subjects' point of view, Hersey was also loath to relinquish the type of knowledge that military science affords. Hersey consulted the *U.S. Strategic Bombing Survey* while writing *Hiroshima* and incorporated details from it into his text. Indeed, despite Harold Ross's advice, the book is full of factual information—statistics, measurements, explanations—that Hersey, somewhat sheepishly, tucks into parentheses. Offering readers information that his interview subjects have no access to, Hersey stages his own unwillingness, or inability, to forgo scientific expertise. In this light, it is not entirely surprising that in 1947 the War Department requested permission to use *Hiroshima* for "instructional purposes" and to reprint it in the *Civil Affairs Digest*. Nor is it surprising that Hersey refused to grant his permission until General Douglas MacArthur lifted the ban on *Hiroshima*'s publication in Japan.[30]

While Hersey did not explain his purposes in writing *Hiroshima* until many years after it was published, the Reverend Tanimoto left a detailed account of his one and only meeting with Hersey. Tanimoto kept a careful record of his experiences in the days and months following the U.S. attack on Hiroshima that, it is worth noting, employs the same flat, descriptive prose that characterizes Hersey's narrative. The postscript to this unpublished diary focuses on his encounter with Hersey and his response to *Hiroshima*. Before meeting Hersey in person, Tanimoto sent him ten pages of his diary through Father Wilhelm Kleinsorge, a German priest who introduced the two men and was another of the six survivors featured in Hersey's book. When Tanimoto and Hersey met for their scheduled interview, Tanimoto's first question for Hersey was "how he considered about my manuscript."[31] "Quite moving," Hersey replied. During their interview, Tanimoto followed "in detail along the line of the manuscript" that he had already given Hersey, while Hersey "took memorandum of the gist in his note-book."[32] *Hiroshima* includes particulars from Tanimoto's written as well as spoken recollections. Months later, when Tanimoto had the chance to read *Hiroshima*, he was pleased with the extent to which Hersey's account resembled his own; indeed, he recalls that he was "surprised at the truthfulness and correctness of its description. He does not add his own story but lets us tell it freely."[33]

Hersey blamed military experimentalism for the obliteration of Hiroshima, even as he drew on official documents to transfigure testimony into narrative and, in the process, absent himself from the process of creating knowledge. Likewise, he used fictional technique to displace his interaction with his subjects—which in this case involved the exchange of manuscript pages—that might detract from the impression of verisimilitude. Tanimoto's diary offers a corrective of sorts, giving us a glimpse of the documentary exchange between Hersey and one of his subjects, an exchange that had a profound impact on *Hiroshima*. Tanimoto's account reminds us of the inherently unequal and potentially exploitative relationship between the interviewer who asks, transcribes, and interprets and the interviewee who approaches the interview process with his or her own designs. In this instance, Tanimoto's and Hersey's objectives were very much in step. Tanimoto appreciated Hersey's faithful transcription of his text and words, and he adopted Hersey's own language when he praised the work. "What echoes through the whole," Tanimoto wrote, "is his warm passion for humanity."[34] All the same, contemporary readers may be disconcerted by Hersey's failure to account more fully for his relationship to his sources. Even as Hersey critiqued military experiment in his effort to formulate a "humanistic" rendering of atomic destruction, he innovated in a way that obscured the voices of his subjects and their role in the creation of his narrative. Ultimately, *Hiroshima* was not detached, as Macdonald would have it, but rather perfectly ambivalent—to the point of ethical paralysis—on the subject of experimental knowledge.

Reviewing *Death in Life* for the *New York Review of Books*, Paul Goodman criticized Lifton's method of "psychiatric research" for producing "a new kind of Stoicism."[35] Rebutting this charge, Lifton recalled the similar charges that Macdonald had leveled against Hersey's *Hiroshima* more than twenty years earlier. Lifton writes, "Years ago Dwight Macdonald questioned the adequacy of a naturalistic approach for understanding what happened in Hiroshima. Psychological empiricism is a first cousin to literary naturalism. In conducting and researching about my study, I found myself pressing an empirical approach to its limits, and then moving beyond those limits."[36] For Lifton, "moving beyond" psychological empiricism entailed a speculative approach that at once extrapolated a model of traumatic experience from the testimony of Hiroshima survivors and laid bare the fact that the analyst was also a storyteller whose interpretations were partial and fallible.[37] His sustained inquiry into the relationship between the numbness of the trauma victim and the powerful emotions of the observer, who feels what the survivor cannot, has gone some distance toward shaping contemporary discussions of "witnessing" in therapeutic, journalistic, and activist circles.

Although Lifton admired Hersey's "stunning rendering of the bomb," he took a very different approach to narrating the experiences of Hiroshima survivors; eschewing the techniques of fiction—indeed, narrative of any kind—Lifton presented survivor testimony as a mass of densely contextualized detail that was difficult to order or assimilate.[38] Hersey's slim volume, written within months of the U.S. bombing of Hiroshima and Nagasaki, sought to counter spectacular images of mushroom clouds with a narrow focus on the daily lives of six individuals—and in this way to make real those experiences that had to date been represented to an American audience in impersonal terms. By contrast, Lifton used his training as a psychiatrist to write an oral history that would "relate the atomic survivor to general human experience."[39] In *Death in Life*, he constructed a panoramic context for the words of survivors and, at the same time, observed the way that survivor testimony affected him. At the outset of his book, Lifton rejects the notion that the researcher-writer "undertakes his study as a tabula rasa or uncontaminated 'instrument,'" describing himself as "shocked and emotionally spent" after each interview.[40]

Lifton's lifelong preoccupation with the role of the interview in healing, analyzing, and inflicting mental pain took hold in the late summer of 1953 when, in his capacity as a psychiatrist for the U.S. Air Force, he traveled from Inchon to San Francisco with 442 soldiers recently released from Korean prisons. Onboard the USS *General Pope*, Lifton had the opportunity to study the effects of "a large-scale, carefully organized, and coercive program of political indoctrination" on survivors.[41] In 1954 he published an article, "Home by Ship," in the *American Journal of Psychiatry* that was based on individual interviews and group therapy sessions that he conducted at sea. In this article, he observes the marked apathy of survivors and the psychiatrist's inevitable complicity in their mental suffering—ideas that he went on to explore more extensively in later work.

If the mass mobilization of World War II and the resulting influx of "psychoneurotic" veterans into institutions like Mason General facilitated the study of troubled veterans, the conditions of the Cold War made such study vital to military strategy. In the context of psychological warfare, the military tried to reproduce—or weaponize—the disorienting and destabilizing effects of war trauma so that they might be turned against the enemy. As psychiatrist William Sargant, who treated soldiers during World War II and went on to study the techniques of mind control, explained, "The recent war showed . . . that continual active combat experience with noise, excitement, fear and loss of weight and sleep, eventually produced breakdown in all temperamental types. . . . Therefore, if these underlying physiological principles are once understood, it should be possible to get at the same person, converting and maintaining him in his new belief by a whole variety of imposed stresses."[42] Clinicians used traumatized veterans to develop a better understanding of the influence of environment on personality; their findings, which could be applied to the task of healing, or destroying, consciousness, laid the groundwork for Cold War experiments in brainwashing and thought control.

When the first group of prisoners returned to the United States in April 1953, as part of the "Little Switch," the military was alarmed by their detachment and decided that later returnees should travel by boat rather than by plane so that they could have a two-week transition to begin the adjustment process in the company of other repatriates and under the guidance of psychiatrists. Lifton accompanied returning prisoners of war back to the United States as part of the "Big Switch." He described the "average repatriate," who seemed "dazed, lacked spontaneity, [and] spoke in a dull, monotonous tone with markedly diminished affectivity."[43] This lack of affect cast the ambiguity of his own position into relief; Lifton noted that returning prisoners of war regarded him with suspicion, and he understood that his interviewees might hesitate to confide in him when his reports could be used for "disciplinary purposes."[44]

As a result of his work with repatriating POWs, Lifton became interested in the relationship between coercion and belief and, specifically, between the psychiatric interview and the process of interrogation central to programs of indoctrination and torture. He moved to Hong Kong in January 1954 and spent the next year and a half interviewing people who had been subjected to indoctrination in Chinese prisons. His experience with both American repatriates and victims of thought reform set the stage for his later writing, which returned to the problem of trauma as it pertained to both survivors and perpetrators of war atrocity. In his books on thought reform, Hiroshima survivors, Nazi doctors, and Vietnam veterans, Lifton continued to theorize the detachment he observed in returning prisoners of war and to cultivate a mode of observation—partisan and self-aware—that might compensate for the lack of purpose and affect that characterized survivor testimony.

In May 1962 Lifton traveled to Hiroshima, where he spent six months conducting interviews with more than seventy survivors. At a time when nuclear annihilation had become a global threat, Lifton felt it was necessary to connect the particular experience of Hiroshima survivors to the broader problem of planetary survival. He described victims of the atomic bomb as "representative of a new dimension of death immersion" and surveyed their symptoms in order to produce a comprehensive model of survivorship.[45] Although *Death in Life* includes lengthy passages drawn verbatim from interviews, Lifton's subjects do not emerge as characters with life histories and stories that unfold. They are not identified by name but rather by occupation ("day laborer," "cremator") or by social role ("abandoned mother," "moralist"), and the reader will find it nearly impossible to keep track of them. Lifton's purpose is not to individuate his subjects but to use their experiences as the basis for a psychological profile of the special, if exemplary, condition of the atomic survivor. To accomplish this, Lifton used a "mosaic" structure that placed "the words of survivors . . . at the center of the work" and surrounded them with a wide range of contextual information on Japanese history, culture, and politics. As Lifton put it, somewhat wistfully, "The book grew into a long one, centered on the interviews but extending to every form of response to the weapon. I have sometimes thought that a more concise and simplified volume could have been much more widely read. . . . In contrast, I have frequently thought of John Hersey's *Hiroshima*, which I greatly admire, a short book written for a popular audience."[46] If the techniques of fiction helped Hersey to manage knowledge and affect in war's immediate aftermath, Lifton used the interview to expand on, aggregate, and structure a comprehensive account of traumatic experience.

Lifton found that Hiroshima survivors, like American returnees, often displayed a marked apathy. On this basis, he theorized the condition that he called "psychic numbing." Drawing on the language of his interviewees, Lifton recounts the way that survivors describe trauma by using the term "*kyodatsu-jōtai*, which means a state of despondency, abstraction, or emptiness, and may be translated as 'state of collapse' or 'vacuum state.'"[47] Lifton continues, "Also relevant is a related state which Miss Ōta described as so widespread . . . as to constitute a medical symptom—that of *muyoku-ganbo*, a listlessness, withdrawn countenance, 'expression of wanting nothing more,' or what has been called in other contexts 'the thousand-mile stare.' Conditions like the 'vacuum state' or 'thousand-mile stare' may be thought of as apathy, but are profound expressions of despair: a form of severe and prolonged psychic numbing in which the survivor's responses to his environment are reduced to a minimum."[48] Characteristic of Lifton's dialogic approach, this passage translates Japanese phrases and expounds on interview testimony at the same time that it brings Lifton's own clinical expertise to bear on the Hiroshima example by recollecting his experience treating veterans of the Korean War. In a footnote to this passage, Lifton cites his essay "Home by Ship" and explains that "the term 'thousand-mile stare' was informally used to characterize the facial expressions of American prisoners of war repatriated from camps in North Korea in 1953."[49] Lifton's investigation of "psychic numbing" links his own clinical observations of U.S. veterans, subjected to brainwashing, with the self-described experiences of atomic bomb survivors.

In *Death in Life*, Lifton theorized detachment as the mark not of objectivity but of trauma and insisted that the observer (clinician, ethnographer, historian) must reject detachment as an investigative stance. As he put it, "One cannot be neutral to the subject of the atom bomb."[50] Instead, the observer must cultivate a deeply empathic relation to the survivor and feel what the survivor cannot. In *Death in Life*, Lifton examines his responses to interview testimony as he swings between extremes of shock and detachment and, in the process, becomes what he calls elsewhere a "survivor by proxy."[51] Unlike Hersey, who was determined to correct American ignorance through a careful rendering of experiential detail, Lifton's book stages the complexity of immersive research but does not manage to bring survivor experience to life. In his reply to Paul Goodman, Lifton admits that "anyone who writes about the subject must in important ways fail."[52] It was up to other writers to turn an immersive approach to reporting—marked by the author's own vulnerability—into a literary method capable of conveying the survivor's perspective and, at its outer reaches, speaking for the dead.

In an essay written in 1980, well after the "new journalism" had come of age, Hersey forcefully condemned it. In "The Legend on the License," he blamed new journalists Truman Capote, Tom Wolfe, and Norman Mailer for effectively destroying journalism with their experiments in hybrid form. He charges each writer with attempting to pass off invention as truth and objects as well to their use of an intrusive voice that makes the person of the journalist more important than the facts reported on. In an interview, he explained that in new journalism "the element of the subjective that appears under the surface of fiction came to the surface . . . so that in the end, the figure of the journalist became more important than the events being written about."[53] Hersey feared that the idiosyncrasies of voice, especially the voice of the journalist, would turn reportage into fiction. In the face of these developments, he asserted that the "time has come to redraw the line between journalism and fiction" by following two simple rules: "The writer of fiction must invent. The journalist must not invent."[54]

It is not hard to turn the tables on Hersey and find the same flaws in his reporting from Hiroshima. One might observe that before arriving in Japan he had already decided to model his narrative on Thornton Wilder's novel *The Bridge of San Luis Rey* (1927), using multiple perspectives on a single disaster to simplify the "very complex story of Hiroshima."[55] He decided to focus, as Wilder had, on a small group of people whose "paths crossed each other and came to this moment of shared disaster," and upon arrival in Hiroshima he began "right away looking for the kinds of people who would fit into that pattern."[56] Such observations simply underscore a truism—that narration (like other forms of representation) will bear the imprint of the writer's experience, assumptions, and imagination. There is no way around it. But then again, one might observe that one of the most graphic and sensational images in *Hiroshima*—a woman's hand comes off when the Reverend Tanimoto tries to drag her to safety—can be found in Tanimoto's memoir as well as in "A Short Talk with Erlanger," written months before Hersey left for Japan. Even as the writer's own perspective is limited by inclination and experience, he is on occasion subject to impressions, or even knowledge, that originate outside his ken.

I think it is fair to construct a loose genealogy of narrative nonfiction for the postwar period in which the interview method is increasingly embedded in the process of storytelling and writers come to conceptualize the documentary endeavor as, like the interview itself, an unstable mix of observation, intuition, and projection. In this context, the difference between Hersey's writing and the writing of later new journalists is not, as Hersey would have it, that they invented and he did not, but that they saw invention and observation as co-constituents of reality, otherwise known as fact, and tried to find ways to cultivate accurate and reliable forms of invention, frequently by immersing themselves in conversation with their subjects over extended periods of time. As Tom Wolfe put it, new journalists "developed the habit of staying with the people they were writing about for days at a time, weeks in some cases. They had to gather all the material the conventional journalist was after—and then keep going."[57] As the interview process becomes more involved, it bleeds into the telling, suffusing the character and texture of the narrative and transforming the writer, who turns himself over to his sources and finds the voices of his subjects speaking through him.

In some instances, this immersive approach allowed writers to document the experiences of the dead, as Mary McCarthy had once demanded. Truman Capote's *In Cold Blood* (1965) uses the experience of murderers facing execution to explore the condition of "death in life" and to test and expand the properties of the interview to include the voices of dead victims. With his "nonfiction novel," Capote hoped to "explore whole new dimensions in writing that would have a double effect fiction does not have—the very fact of its being true, every word of it true, would add a double contribution of strength and impact."[58] Capote based his narrative on extensive interviews over the course of many years, not only with friends and acquaintances of the murdered Clutter family, but also with the murderers themselves, who were, as Capote observes, the last people to see the Clutters alive. On this basis, Capote spoke not only for his interview subjects but also for the victims he had never met. Capote's attempt to describe their experience of being murdered, and to insist on this description as "true," is a profound accomplishment that places speculation, impeccably grounded in extensive research, at the heart of a new narrative journalism. These developments reach a high-water mark with Norman Mailer's *Executioner's Song* (1979). Mailer never met his protagonist, Gary Gilmore, who was dead by the time Mailer began work on the project. And yet, inheriting eleven thousand pages of interview transcripts, Mailer was able to plumb Gilmore's experience—conditioned by an array of social contexts and yet unaccountable—in a comprehensive way. It is significant, in this light, that he took "voices" as a central conceit for his project—titling the first half of the book "Western Voices" and the second half "Eastern Voices"—and explored Gilmore's interest in life after death in some depth.

Early on, Macdonald offered a powerful account of Hersey's style but was too quick to align Hersey's detached, descriptive prose with the neutral gaze of the disinterested spectator. By contrast, Lifton's account of "psychic numbing" allows us to interpret Hersey's "dead-pan, keyed-down approach" as an expression of his sensitivity to the survivor's sense of detachment. Indeed, Hersey's flat style very much resembles what John Treat has described as the "distilled, terse prose" produced by Japanese survivors in the years following the war, and it can be regarded as one point of origin for what Treat calls the "evolving language" of atomic atrocity.[59] In this light, Hersey's *Hiroshima*, however cautious, represents an early experiment in immersive journalism, a process that proved so hot to the touch that Hersey retreated from the most radical implications of his own endeavor. Although his stay in Hiroshima was brief and he refused to immerse himself in the experiences or perspective of his interviewees, his subjects did manage—at least in Tanimoto's opinion—to speak through the text. In this way, Hersey set the stage for later writers who would "move beyond" literary empiricism and document the influence of voices, muted by suffering, that could be only faintly heard.

NOTES

I am grateful to the contributors to this volume who have in various ways helped me to develop and refine this essay—in particular to Jonathan Kahana for his invaluable feedback and to Sara Blair and Joseph Entin for their editorial guidance and unfailing generosity.

1. Macdonald, "Hersey's 'Hiroshima,'" 308.
2. McCarthy, "Hiroshima *New Yorker*," 367.
3. On the impact of nuclear weapons on literature, see Cordle, *States of Suspense*; Grausam, *On Endings*; Nadel, *Containment Culture*; Norris, *Writing War in the Twentieth Century*; and Saint-Amour "Bombing and the Symptom."
4. Lifton, *Thought Reform and the Psychology of Totalism*, vii.
5. For two important books that take up the production of testimony in its institutional setting, see Felman and Laub, *Testimony*; and Dawes, *That the World May Know*.
6. Nichols, "Voice of Documentary," *Film Quarterly*.
7. Grinker and Spiegel, *Men under Stress*, vii.
8. Sullivan, *Psychiatric Interview*, 3.
9. For an account of Grinker and Spiegel's contribution to World War II military psychiatry and, especially, the development of narcoanalysis, see Shephard, *War of Nerves*, 212–15, and Leys, *Trauma*, 190–228. While Grinker and Spiegel coined the term "narcosynthesis," I have opted for the more widely used "narcoanalysis" throughout.
10. Grinker and Spiegel, *Men under Stress*, 390.

11. Grinker's handwritten comments on a draft of "Short Talk with Erlanger," Hersey Papers, box 12.

12. "Re Neuro Psychiatrics by Hersey," October 16, 1945, Hersey Papers, box 12.

13. Hersey, *Here to Stay*, 138.

14. Sullivan, *Psychiatric Interview*, 51.

15. Hersey, "Short Talk with Erlanger," 109.

16. Ibid., 114.

17. Sargant, *Battle for the Mind*, 17–18. On the role of fantasy in narcoanalysis, see Shephard, *War of Nerves*, 209–10.

18. Grinker and Spiegel, *Men under Stress*, 392.

19. Hersey, "Short Talk with Erlanger," 122, emphasis mine.

20. Kiyoshi Tanimoto, "John Hersey's Visit to Hiroshima," Hersey Papers, box 37.

21. Ibid.

22. This list comes from a summary of the *USSBS* that Hersey used in his research. "Atomic Bomb: First Official Report on Damage to Japan; Full Text of U.S. Strategic Bomb Survey's Findings," *United States News*, July 5, 1946, 64, Hersey Papers, box 37.

23. Yagoda, *About Town*, 189.

24. Letter to Jeffrey Bauman, November 17, 1955, Hersey Papers, box 37.

25. "An Extra Book in November," Hersey Papers, box 37.

26. Yōko Ōta, "Not Reminiscence, but a Symbol of Today's History," *Japan Readers' News*, April 27, 1949, Hersey Papers, box 37.

27. Dee, "Art of Fiction XCII: John Hersey," citation 228. It is also worth noting that Hersey's "quietness" extended beyond the text, as he refused to give interviews until the mid-1980s when he spoke, at length, in this interview.

28. Hersey, *Hiroshima*, 49.

29. Gerstle, "John Hersey and *Hiroshima*," 94.

30. Unsigned letter to Colonel Vickers, Hersey Papers, box 37.

31. Tanimoto, "John Hersey's Visit," n.p.

32. Ibid.

33. Ibid.

34. Ibid.

35. Goodman, "Stoicism and the Holocaust," citation 18.

36. Lifton, "Victims of Hiroshima."

37. I draw my emphasis on "speculation" from Daniel Worden's essay "Speculative Ecology: Rachel Carson's Environmental Documentaries," published in this volume, and am indebted throughout to his theorization of the role that speculation plays in postwar documentary.

38. Lifton, *Witness to an Extreme Century*, 92.

39. Lifton, *Death in Life*, 3.

40. Ibid., 5, 10.

41. Lifton, "Home by Ship," citation 732.

42. Sargant, *Battle for the Mind*, 205.

43. Lifton, "Home by Ship," 735.

44. Lifton, *Witness to an Extreme Century*, 12.

45. Lifton, *Death in Life*, 540.

46. Lifton, *Witness to an Extreme Century*, 143.

47. Lifton, *Death in Life*, 86.

48. Ibid., 86–87.

49. Ibid., 86.

50. Lifton, "Experiments in Advocacy Research," 3.

51. Ibid.

52. Lifton, "Victims of Hiroshima."

53. Dee, "Art of Fiction XCII," 245.

54. Hersey, "Legend on the License," 25, citation 3.

55. Dee, "Art of Fiction XCII," 226.

56. Ibid., 226–27.

57. Wolfe and Johnson, *New Journalism*, 21.

58. Interview with Roy Newquist (1964), in Capote, *Truman Capote: Conversations*, citation 40.

59. Treat, *Writing Ground Zero*, 34, 20.

I Saw It!

The Photographic Witness of Barefoot Gen

LAURA WEXLER

The drawing, instead of marking the site of a departure, began to mark the site of an arrival.

—JOHN BERGER, "Drawn to That Moment"

INTRODUCTION

If trauma, by definition, is repressed experience and therefore constitutive but difficult to document, by how much does the difficulty of documentation increase when government censorship ferociously bars access to that experience? If the infamous gap between living and knowing that marks the site of any subject's own traumatic narrative is also legally enforced, how much wider does that fissure grow? And if the experience itself is literally without comparison, how can it be possible to represent it meaningfully within a documentary form?

Few have faced more obstacles to recognizing and expressing their own accounts of trauma than the survivors of Hiroshima and Nagasaki, the *hibakusha*,[1] whose direct experience of the horror of nuclear bombing remains unique in the history of the world. Censorship, denial, and incomprehension have all characterized their existence and remain potent into the second and third generations of survivors in the Japanese population in general. Any traumatic narrative must deal with blank spots and the missing pieces of memory where what was undergone could not be processed. And yet, the struggle of the *hibakusha* to survive, to witness, and to warn has shaped new expressive forms in film, photography, and the literary arts.[2]

This essay concerns one of those new forms, what critics have called the "atom bomb manga" that came into being in postwar Japan in 1966 with the publication of *Kuroi Ame ni Utarete* (*Pelted by Black Rain*, 1968), about a group of young Japanese adults involved in the black market after the war. The author of these books, Keiji Nakazawa (1939–2012), a successful Tokyo-based cartoonist, was a child survivor of the 1945 atomic bombing in Hiroshima. Nakazawa did not begin his career by addressing this event.

But by the end of his career the preponderance of his fifty-nine published works would consider either wholly or partially the causes and effects of the atomic bombing. Chief among them are a short autobiographical manga, *Ore wa Mita* (1972), which was published in English as *I Saw It: The Atomic Bombing of Hiroshima: A Survivor's True Story* by EduComics in 1982, and a magisterial ten-volume series, *Hadashi no Gen*, or *Barefoot Gen*, published in Japanese between 1972 and 1985 and translated into English between 1978 and 2009. Because of his focus on the self-described effects of the atom bomb on survivors as evidence, Nakazawa is widely considered an innovator in documentary comics, which historian Hillary Chute explicates as follows: "The essential form of comics—its collection of frames—is relevant to its inclination to document. *Documentary* (as an adjective and a noun) is about the presentation of evidence. In its succession of replete frames, comics calls attention to itself, specifically, as evidence. Comics makes a reader access the unfolding of evidence in the movement of its basic grammar, by aggregating and accumulating frames of information."[3]

In what follows, I will argue that the authority of Nakazawa's atom bomb manga rests not only on his use of personal experience as evidence, as he often claimed, but also on his destabilizing of the disciplinary regime that regulates the mechanical eyewitness image, that is to say, his upending of the truth claims of documentary photography itself. I have called this tactic "transmedial revision." The term does not simply mean to redraw photographs but something more fundamental: to recombine media forms in a way that exposes the photograph's claim to witness as too narrowly self-reflexive. By incorporating drawings of military photographs into his first-person survivor accounts, Nakazawa sets his own experience against the photographic record. He deploys his own eyewitness in confrontation with post-bomb photography and thereby challenges the adequacy of the accepted documentary representation of the depicted events.

This essay focuses on a small selection of Nakazawa's transmedial drawings of the explosion and of the Aioi Bridge in *I Saw It* and *Barefoot Gen*, comparing his drawings with the photographic record. Comparisons that warrant further study throughout his work on the atom bomb include but are not limited to Nakazawa's drawings of the scenes at first aid shelters photographed in the days immediately following the blasts "by Japanese investigators or news agencies" such as Professor Nishima, a famous physicist, and by the Bunka-sha Agency of medical activities at Hiroshima prior to the arrival of the Atomic Bomb Casualty Commission, among others; his reconceptions of the bodies of victims, who also figure in medical researcher Averill Liebow's photographs of the wounded taken between Liebow's arrival in the city with the Joint Commission for the Investigation of the Effects of the Atomic Bomb in Japan on 13 October 1945 and departure on 23 November; and his wholesale revisions of images of public transportation or schools or huts uniformly pictured as nearly uninhabited by the United States Strategic Bomb Survey (USSBS). Primary evidence of Nakazawa's long-standing interest in the aerial view is found in the form of these drawings themselves and perhaps also in the large aerial photographic view pinned to the wall of his studio and visible in the film *Barefoot Gen's Hiroshima*. Additional archives of "A-bomb–related materials used in creating his works" are contained in the Hiroshima Peace Memorial Museum.[4]

Nakazawa's artistic excursions into these materials helped to establish photographic exposure as a new platform for the graphic display of buried knowing. By this I mean not exposure *in* the photograph but exposure *of* the photograph. Nakazawa's brilliant re-rendering of the aerial documentary photography file of the USSBS and on-the-ground documentation in other official photographic records expanded the register of *hibakusha* testimony. In Nakazawa's hands, the state control that spun and censored knowledge also created the opening for a dialectical image that both highlights and deconstructs official viewpoints. That comics could work with photographs in this way gave the *hibakusha* story a new power of resistance against its long-enforced prior silencing. Nakazawa showed how countercurrents and buried precedents can be made available for a post–World War II documentary history alongside of or in opposition to the mantle of mechanical instrumentalism such photography had assumed within mid-twentieth-century military goals. The written history of post-1945 documentary photography, by and large an archive of victors, awaits further development in this vein.

ATOM BOMB MANGA

Nakazawa's work in *Ore wa Mita* has been very important to the creation of documentary comics as a genre, if not always recognized by robust sales to the general public. Chute argues, in *Disaster Drawn: Visual Witness, Comics, and Documentary Form*, that through his work "we can understand the return to *drawing to tell*, the reemergence and creative expansion in our contemporary world of the power of the hand-drawn image, against the backdrop of [the] . . . saturation of mechanical objectivity and the discourses of technological power that shaped the atomic age."[5] In "Globalizing Comic

Books from Below: How Manga Came to America," comics artist Leonard Rifas assigns the importance of Nakazawa's work to the use of his own lived experience, as well as that of others, to "help increase understanding about issues, but [to] do it in such a way that preserves the drama of real life so that you can see how these facts get generated." Rifas believes such "public interest comics" can be "a tool for raising social awareness."[6] Rifas was the only American publisher of Nakazawa's *I Saw It* in four-color comic book format, and in 1976 Rifas published two volumes of *The Barefoot Gen* series as *Gen of Hiroshima* as well. Though the series was cancelled after those two volumes, Rifas's efforts received strong endorsements from a long list of socially conscious cartoonists, including R. Crumb, Harvey Kurtzman, Will Eisner, Trina Robbins, Sharon Rudahl, Art Spiegelman, Larry Gonick, Spain Rodriguez, Justin Green, Guy Colwell, Joyce Farmer, Melinda Gebbie, and Kim Deitch. Nakazawa, in Japan, worked in isolation from this group, but the underground comix movement lent support, through Rifas's connections, for his work to be published in the United States. Rifas writes, "Thanks to the underground comix movement, I had a way of distributing Nakazawa's violent manga without worrying about the Code."[7] The Comics Code was instituted in the United States in 1954 and in one form or another continued into the early 2000s. It required mainstream distributors to display a seal that, among other things, guaranteed that the publication did not contain "scenes of excessive violence" or "lurid, unsavory, gruesome illustrations."[8] Underground comix successfully evaded such controls. Rifas also published *I Saw It* in the United States after the point when the self-censorship of violence demanded by the Comics Code was breaking down, extending its reach.

Virtually simultaneously, a small group of volunteers called "Project Gen" began to publish volumes of the longer *Hadashi no Gen* in English book format. *Maus* author Spiegelman helped support their English edition of *Barefoot Gen* by writing an introduction in which he described Nakazawa's powerful effect upon his own work. "*Gen* haunts me. . . . The first time I read it was in the late 1970s, shortly after I'd begun working on *Maus*, my own extended comic-book chronicle of the twentieth century's other central cataclysm. . . . *Gen* deals with the trauma of the atom bomb without flinching. There are no irradiated Godzillas or super-mutants, only tragic realities."[9]

Initially, some expressed (and still do express) doubts that the comics genre, be it in a printed book or classic comics format, could be robust enough for material of this weight and complexity. Others were open to the possibility. In 1983, when Rifas wrote to ask him for an endorsement, Noam Chomsky politely declined but replied that "maybe that is the way to reach people. I don't know. Your general point, in your letter, I very much agree with. It is necessary, somehow, to find ways to reach an audience that isn't attuned to elaborate analysis and documentation. . . . I am glad to see that you are working on it." Frederic Wertham, author of the controversial *Seduction of the Innocent* (1954), was not convinced. "I think of course that anything that goes against atomic war deserves attention. But I have doubts whether the comic-book brutality in the first part of the book is effective as an antiviolence message," he responded to an inquiry by Rifas.[10] But by now it is clear that an entire generation of artists, empowered by the successful interventions of the underground comix movement and influenced both directly and indirectly by Nakazawa's example, has doubled down on the project of researching and representing humankind's disasters in comics form. These artists not only see no contradiction between painstaking research and its presentation in comics but also consider comics an advantage for their documentary work. Particularly respected among those who have followed this practice is Joe Sacco, who drew comics to record daily life in the wake of genocidal violence in Goražde and Palestine. Spiegelman, another tireless researcher, believes that comics are especially powerful testimonial documents because "the small scale of the images and the directness of the medium that has something in common with handwriting allow comics a kind of intimacy that also makes them surprisingly well suited to autobiography."[11] He concludes that "the vividness of *Barefoot Gen* emanates from something intrinsic to the comics medium itself and from the events Nakazawa lived through and depicted."[12] As Chute has argued in *Disaster Drawn*, autobiographical historical comics are now broadly accepted "as nonfiction—as a form of documentary—as a form of witnessing."[13]

Such comics have also come to occupy a prestigious place in the production of critique. Histories of manga, including *Manga* by Paul Gravett, *Comics, Comix and Graphic Novels* by Roger Sabin, and *Manga, Manga* by Frederik Schodt, give Nakazawa's intimate images a prominent role in countering the grand narratives of the twentieth century.[14] Through his multiple depictions of *hibakusha* trauma, Nakazawa demonstrated that graphic storytelling, rather than diminishing and distorting reality, could approach the lived experience of the survivors of Hiroshima more closely from a popular, working-class point of view than did official documentary photographs, which usually did not arise from such a social position.

In *Documentary Graphic Novels and Social Realism*, Jeff Adams considers documentary comics like Nakazawa's to be a radical form of popular resistance to aesthetic regimes such as documentary. They are "intelligible to the broad masses, adopting and enriching their forms of expression, assuming their standpoint, confirming and correcting it."[15] Adams argues that such comics are actually a form of critical social realism. "They deal textually and visually with disruptive social or political events, and their various critical devices may be said to reveal something of the underlying social configurations."[16] Above all, they demystify the lies and half-truths told by those in power by presenting the lived experiences of ordinary people that conflict with official stories. The particular achievement of *I Saw It* and *Barefoot Gen* is that in one way or another Nakazawa's work was able to intervene, against the limits of the history of the bomb that had been conveyed in the period of overt government censorship during the occupation of Japan.

TRANSMEDIAL REVISION

Transmedial revision—Nakazawa's strategy I am examining here—sets documentary's instrumental knowledge against itself. Neither Japanese militarism nor the brute fact of the U.S. bombing escapes his condemnation. His redrawing of official images makes possible a clearer view of their dehumanization of "the other" through a closer-to-hand, more humane depiction. It amplifies his ability to represent the disastrous consequences of the use of the atomic bomb.

As I will later show, Nakazawa consulted photographic images from the USSBS, among other sources. By 1966, when Nakazawa began to draw his first atom bomb manga, *Pelted by Black Rain*, the public record of such images was rich. Some of the USSBS images had been made immediately available in public outlets such as *Life* magazine to inform the public of the extent of American victory and Japanese defeat. Other images were released gradually, as censorship ended after the occupation, in the public press and in touring exhibitions. *Pelted by Black Rain*, which appeared in May 1968, is a fictional account considered the inaugural "'atomic bomb manga,'" writes Chute.[17] But documentary photographs were available.

His deployment of official photography in comics was both a formal and a functional innovation. In *The Origins of Comics: From William Hogarth to Winsor McCay*, Thierry Smolderen traces the fascination that cartoonist A. B. Frost developed for photography beginning in the 1880s, which ranged from mimicry to irony in his own constructions of sequential narrative. Word balloons and label texts had been featured in English cartoons since George Cruikshank. According to art historian Steef Davidson in *The Penguin Book of Political Comics*, the French Situationists were the first to join the two forms. They pasted "thought balloons" from comic strips cut from the popular press onto photographs, and the resultant collages, like earlier ones that John Heartfield used to pillory the German fascist press, conveyed a range of subversive meanings they called *détournement* (diversion).[18] Nakazawa applied the technique to American military documentary photographs, redrawing them and then adding his own editorial points. Photographs customarily leave traces all over manga because artists use them as preparatory sketches for landscape and background as well as for inspiration. But to understand that the photograph itself is the discursive trace—the sign to seek—was Nakazawa's special insight.

Functionally, it was also a breakthrough. Nakazawa's revisions convey his experience of the bombing of Hiroshima with exceptional force. Drawing is of course fundamental to the manga form, natively a hybrid of hand-drawn sequential images and text. Unless it is to be computer generated, an atomic bomb manga must be drawn. On the other hand, photography is fundamental to the period of modernity, whose negative epiphany is the bomb. In atom bomb manga, the ancient act of drawing meets an expressive threshold in the atomic bomb; like the Holocaust, the bombing of Hiroshima was (and remains) a crisis of representation. In combining the two dialectically, Nakazawa was able to use drawings of photographs to critique the photographs themselves, sharpening the contradictions.

What were these contradictions? First, the USSBS could and did persuasively record the scale of the destruction of Hiroshima. The aerial view is suited to the sweep of the destruction. Nevertheless, the panoramic perspective was also insufficient. Disaster on the ground played out in thousands of unique, individual, personal lives that could be rendered only in particularity, as distinct from the camera's wide-angle or distanced objectification. Conversely, drawing is intimate, the mark of a human hand, as Spiegelman points out, and it was therefore better suited for that task. But the intimate private world of *hibakusha* knowledge rarely figured in official discourse. As a consequence of the Allied victory, photographic images of the devastation were largely, though not entirely, made by the American forces. These images overwhelmingly display the victors' point of view. Some were meant to underline the fact that the Japanese were military aggressors, and the USSBS survey shows extensive damage done to individual barracks, bunkers, factories, and railroads, attesting to the continuing military functionality of the city, despite the fact that in its recent history, as Liebow reported, "the military importance of this center had waned and it was serving largely the function of a quartermaster depot."[19] Hence, a number of the images seek to justify taking Hiroshima as a military target. At the same time, many others show the vast destruction of businesses, hospitals, places of worship, homes, schools, banks, and light rail and civil infrastructure generally, which were part of the war effort but had previously escaped bombing in the war. Because these last, as domestic images, also could fuel impressions of the Japanese as victims themselves, they could "humanize" an enemy said to be less than human. Nakazawa's double-facing practice puts the difficulty of controlling all these factors into view. For him, to resee and then redraw the military photographs of Hiroshima was to incorporate them into a form of storytelling that complicated the ethical and political claims of both sides.

Nakazawa's invention intervened in the mechanical objectivity of the camera, which represents the most deadly common aspiration of the atomic age. By "objectivity" I mean not only that such photographs could be mechanically produced but also that interpretation was managed as well.[20] Transmediating the photographs from the USSBS literally expanded upon, or "drew out," subaltern perspectives. In circulating their own photographs, the Allies claimed the moral victory of ending the war. But Nakazawa's manga competed with the official tale about the history of ruin. His perspectives highlighted the ambiguous historical relationships responsible for the invention and use of the bomb and castigated subsequent denials of the full range of responsibility.

Nakazawa's recourse to drawing was not the same as the mark-making of the military or the civil authorities in sketches, maps, and charts. Nor was it akin to a therapist's use of victims' drawings to heal individuals through direct expression of remembered trauma. It differs by many degrees of art and intentionality from the famous survivor drawings published in *Unforgettable Fire*, in 1977, which are searing but artistically crude accounts.[21] Rather, this drawing practice in sequential narrative sought to reverse the power relations of the extant documentary record. It aimed to speak back and, further, to wound the viewer by registering his distance from what, to paraphrase art historian W. J. T. Mitchell, the photographs officially "want."[22]

In the following discussion I will first describe what Nakazawa tells of his experience as a survivor of the bombing of Hiroshima. Then I will present a portfolio of close readings of some representative examples of his remedial interventions in *I Saw It* and *Barefoot Gen*, chiefly his drawings of official documentary photographs of the aerial reconnaissance images of the bomb. This portfolio is meant to be suggestive rather than comprehensive. Finally, I will consider what it is that drawing, in particular, offers to the photographic record and why this particular kind of transmediation plays such a powerful role in Nakazawa's work. By way of conclusion, I will briefly suggest some further avenues for rethinking documentary photography, and post-1945 documentary in general, along these lines.

SURVIVING THE BOMB

Nakazawa was a single individual among many thousands of survivors of the bombing of the city, and he strove to tell both his own and others' stories. On 6 August 1945, at 8:15 a.m., the six-year-old Keiji stood in the shadow of the gate of the Kanzaki Elementary School in Hiroshima, hesitating a bit near the foot-thick concrete wall before entering his first-grade class and talking with the mother of a classmate, when he "happened to look up": "The *Enola Gay* cut its engines, penetrated quietly to the heart of Hiroshima, and dropped the atomic bomb, raising the curtain on hell. Even today, if I close my eyes, the colors of the atomic bomb the moment it exploded come floating right up. A pale light like the flash of a flashbulb camera, white at the center, engulfed me, a great ball of light with yellow and red mixed at its outer edges. Once that violent flash burned itself onto my retinas all memory stopped."[23] Small, stricken, and stunned, young Nakazawa himself could have seen relatively little of the immense, immediate destruction accomplished by the bomb. Yet *Ore wa Mita—I Saw It*—was the title given to his first autobiographical account. In the recent film *Barefoot Gen's Hiroshima: The Story of Nakazawa Keiji*, he describes how, emerging from shock, he found his vision had become literally photographic, explicitly linking the picture-making machine to his own body: "It was a procession of ghosts. I walked among them, like this. My eyes were like the lens of a camera, snapping pictures of everything I saw. Images of how the scene looked were etched on my memory."[24] He embodied this seeing in many scenes of his autobiography, among them the trauma of learning about the death of his father, sister, and brother under their collapsed house in the firestorm that followed the bombing; the frightful sight of the walking dead with peeling skin trailing from their hands and feet, their eyes and guts spilling out; the corpse-clogged rivers and body-strewn trees; the cruelty of others who refused asylum and hoarded food; the omnipresent hunger;

the illness of his mother and the death of his newborn baby sister; and the heart-hardening necessity to put the past aside and move on. This was his own experience.

In the subsequent series *Hadashi no Gen*, the individual autobiographical "I" of his initial narrator, Keiji himself, became the voice of a composite fictionalized eyewitness named Gen. Like the real Keiji, Gen starts out as a six-year-old, but as he grows up, Gen ranges over much more territory and recounts profound encounters with many more persons than did the autobiographical small boy in *I Saw It*. Yet the authorial claim is still based on lived experience. "Gen is my alter ego, and his family is just like my own," Nakazawa asserts. "The episodes in *Barefoot Gen* are all based on what really happened to me or to other people in Hiroshima."[25] "What really happened" has a double meaning; it asserts a personal documentary authority, and it also implies that other accounts might not be so faithful. Here is also where further research into the experience of the views of "other people in Hiroshima" had to have begun.

Nakazawa did not set out to embody this history. Originally apprenticed to a sign painter, he left Hiroshima for Tokyo in 1961 at the age of twenty-two to become a manga creator, or cartoonist, and soon became successful. But Tokyo life was also a negative epiphany. In Hiroshima, the existence of survivors was at least acknowledged. Nakazawa was "shocked" by the discrimination he encountered against *hibakusha* in Tokyo: "When talk of home arose and I mentioned to acquaintances that I'd experienced the atomic bombing in Hiroshima, the glances sent my way were indescribably chilly and strange, and I was bewildered—I couldn't recall ever having experienced such hateful looks."[26] His initial reaction was to disavow his own experience. "I resolved never to speak the words 'atomic bomb' again. When I went to bookstores and there were books about the atomic bomb on the shelves, I averted my eyes and moved on. When the characters 'atomic bomb' leapt out of a newspaper article, I didn't read a word of that article. I truly came to hate the word and the characters 'atomic bomb.'"[27]

Indeed, the *hibakusha*'s tale was commonly a story that went for a long time untold. Certainly it was nowhere in the public record. Censorship in Japan before 15 August 1945 and subsequent military occupation by the American victors prohibited for years any organized public recognition of what had occurred. As political scientist Richard Tanter states, a silence was "constructed": "There were three strands to official American policy towards information about Hiroshima and Nagasaki. First, access to Hiroshima was denied to Allied journalists. Second, public discussion of the topic was banned in Japan. Finally, through the censorship and official disinformation program as a whole, Western perceptions were channeled in such a way as to minimize understanding of the human, as opposed to the physical, destructiveness of the weapon."[28] Tanter remarks that "the first step in the attempt to suppress the truth about Hiroshima was to attack claims of radiation illness, and to deny authority to Japanese-sourced accounts of Hiroshima and Nagasaki."[29] It took six years—precisely the length of the American military occupation—for the first Japanese newspapers to show photographs of keloid scars on the bodies of the victims of the nuclear bombing.

Whereas more information might not have saved the survivors from bodily suffering, their separation and isolation increased the gap between living and knowing, which is the enabling condition of trauma. The most destructive result of this censorship regime was that the lack of public discussion and the suppression of medical reports impeded medical research and information about treatment of *pika*, or radiation illness, about which little was actually known. This denial of information was itself a secondary attack, extending the sense of abandonment felt by the wounded population, which was another deep consequence of the use of the bomb. Deprived of knowledge about what was happening to them, victims of radiation sickness died by the thousands immediately and at a more measured pace throughout subsequent days, weeks, months, and years. Fearing contagion, a majority of Japanese avoided contact with known *hibakusha*, who were also subsequently deemed unmarriageable due to anticipation of genetic damage once radiation was identified as the cause of illness. The actual effects, according to the Atomic Bomb Casualty Commission, included cancer, leukemia, shortened life span, loss of vigor, growth and developmental disorders, sterility, genetic alteration, abnormal pigmentation, hair loss, and epidemiological changes.[30]

The Japanese government did not begin to pass laws for substantial relief for the *hibakusha* until the mid-1950s. The loss of the chance to know—and to be known for—the personal experience that characterized each survivor individually also damaged society as a whole. The toxic suppression of information extended the bitter harvest of the war. Long after "humanization of the enemy" could lead to any conceivable softening of American resolve to fight, both the Americans and the Japanese averted their gaze from the complex and continuing suffering of so many survivors, or conversely, as in the singular instance of the "Hiroshima Maidens," turned their medical care into a gendered spectacle.[31] And all the while, as Tanter observes, "the occupation authorities were meticulously collecting scientific information on the bomb and its health effects for American scientific consumption."[32]

In 1966, Nakazawa's mother died in the Hiroshima Atomic-bomb Hospital in Hiroshima after a long, debilitating illness. He was outraged that the American-run hospital immediately requested permission from the family to do an autopsy. "I couldn't forgive the ABCC [the hospital]," he wrote in 1995 in his non-manga autobiography, *Hiroshima: The Autobiography of Barefoot Gen*. "It didn't offer bomb victims a single bit of help. It treated them as specimens, guinea pigs. Always hot on the trail of bomb victims for the purposes of their own country's nuclear war, it took the data it collected back to the United States."[33] After his mother's cremation, Nakazawa found that only small slivers of her bones remained in the ashes, unlike in normal circumstances where a lot of bone remained. At that point, he realized that "radioactive cesium from the bomb had eaten away at her bones to the point that they had disintegrated. The bomb had even deprived me of my mother's bones."[34] Subsequently, something shifted inside him and he was, as he put it, "overcome with rage. I vowed that I would never forgive the Japanese militarists who started the war, or the Americans who had so casually dropped the bomb on us."[35] In the crucible of this grief he "came to want to avenge our Nakazawa family. I resolved to fight a one-man battle: 'Say who—the Japanese government? The U.S. government?—was responsible for the war and the atomic bomb! Speak! Speak! Speak! Never forgive!"[36]

In 1972, *Boys Jump Monthly* published *Ore wa Mita*, a forty-five-page manga autobiography, and in 1973 the autobiographical character Gen Nakaoka was born. Nakazawa's editor suggested that he continue working on the story, and Nakazawa agreed. *Barefoot Gen* was serialized at the rate of sixteen pages a month, eventually totaling its full ten volumes. By that time, newspaper images of the first photographs of post-bomb Hiroshima were widely available, as were hospital records and journalistic accounts. Nakazawa, working furiously, was actively seeking more knowledge, as were the twenty thousand people who came to see the *Unforgettable Fire* exhibition of drawings at the Hiroshima Peace Memorial Museum between 1 and 6 August 1974.[37] Drawing upon such information to deal with his own personal crisis guided Nakazawa's attention to the quality and individual texture of *hibakusha* knowledge being held under erasure.[38] He thought there was a great power in every person's counternarrative. He wrote, "If each single Japanese person who was dealt a grave blow by the war and the atomic bomb musters all his bitterness to wage an angry struggle, he can smash those guys who rejoice at war and the atomic bomb. It's not something a group of people can do."[39] And he set out to wage this struggle. Notably, this was not simply a campaign for remembering and against forgetting; it was an affective campaign, mobilizing the emotion of anger and maneuvering against disdain. In Nakazawa's hands, each individual *hibakusha*'s memory rebukes the American grand narrative. The difference between them is sharply rendered. In the next section, I will examine a sample of Nakazawa's drawings as examples of the insurgent potential of suppressed *hibakusha* witness.

PICTURING THE BOMB

Among those who could be said to have "rejoiced at the atomic bomb" were the American victors, who while acknowledging its horrible destruction nevertheless credited it with ending the current war and, they hoped, deterring the next. For many Americans, what came to be the iconic photographs of the bomb were proof of American might. The earliest photographs of the atomic bombing allowed to reach a wide audience were aerial photographs of the towering cloud formed by the Hiroshima explosion and the more tightly configured mushroom of Nagasaki, both taken by the retreating planes. The circulation of American photographs of Hiroshima and Nagasaki commonly compared not the effects of each nuclear attack on Japan but the strength of each kind of bomb relative to the other, for the sake of intimidating Russian eyes. They were meant to signify America's peerless nuclear prowess. These images, published in *Life* magazine in 1945, displayed the awesome capacity of the American military, chiefly for the sake of the Soviets, whom the Americans then understood to be mounting their own threat to the West (fig. 3.1).

But Nakazawa's depictions of the iconic mushroom cloud convey another perspective. In the main, they diminish American claims. In *I Saw It: The Atomic Bombing of Hiroshima: A Survivor's True Story*, a postage stamp–sized drawing of the Hiroshima bomb cloud appears near the upper-right corner on the cover of the comic, but it is by no means compelling and only somewhat bigger than the imprint of the price ($2) at the lower left, whose form it mirrors.[40] On the other hand, a giant image of a sweating and screaming Keiji, atomic fire reflected in his huge and horrified eyes, commands attention. The viewer is situated so as to have the choice of looking at or looking with Keiji, undermining certainty about what the picture "wants" (fig. 3.2).

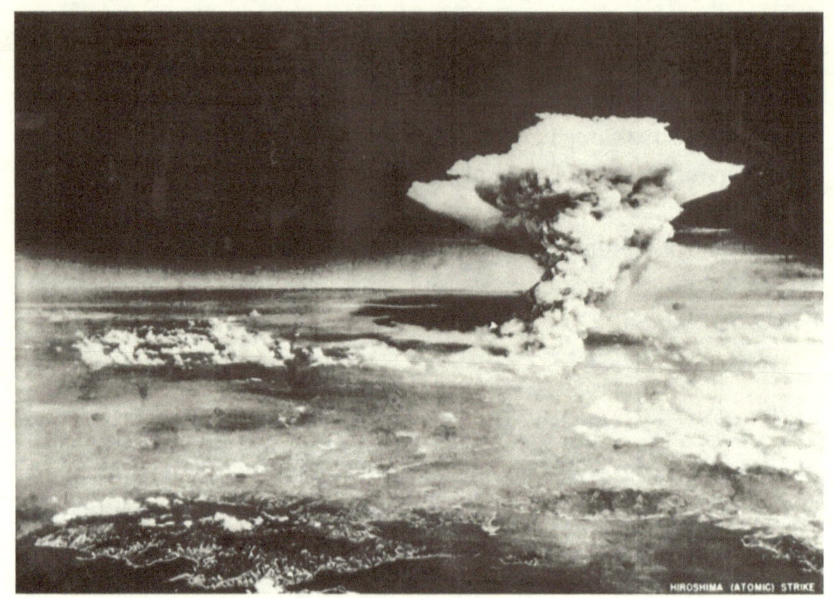

FIGURE 3.1 Mushroom cloud, HG273, U.S. Army. Reprinted by permission of the Hiroshima Peace Memorial Museum.

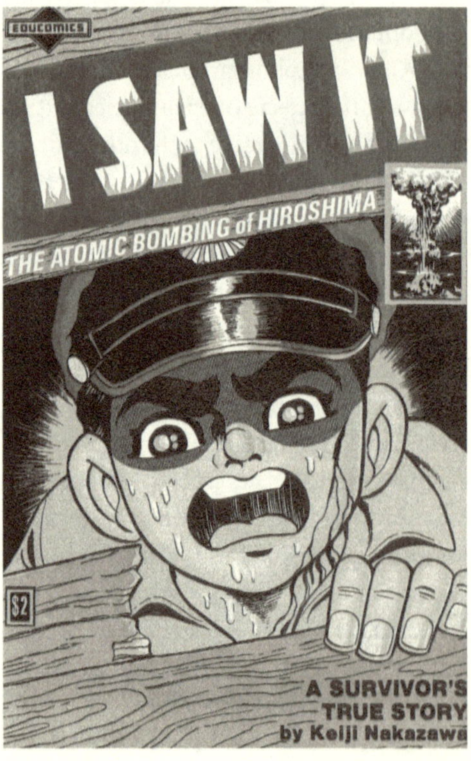

FIGURE 3.2 Front cover of Keiji Nakazawa's *I Saw It*, English-language edition, 1982. Used by permission of Misayo Nakazawa, arranged with Japan UNI Agency, Inc.

A giant Keiji appears on the back cover too, along with a different depiction of the cloud. This time the cloud is enormous, arising from the devastated city. It does not take the iconic form but rather fits eyewitness descriptions of what it looked like from the ground: "an enormous mass of clouds . . . [which] spread and climbed rapidly . . . into the sky. Then its summit broke open and hung over horizontally. It took on the shape of a monstrous mushroom with the lower part as its stem—it would be more accurate to call it the tail of a tornado. Beneath it more and more boiling clouds erupted and unfolded sideways . . . the shape . . . the color . . . the light . . . were continuously shifting and changing."[41] Like Walter Benjamin's angel, Keiji is running forward but blown backward by the force of the blast. He clearly wishes to draw what he sees, but his brushes are scattered. The cloud is more imposing than the city, but Keiji is larger still. He looks back accusingly toward the viewer, with whom this time his eyes securely lock. The eyes, more furious than frightened, show outrage. Closest of all, a titanic diagonal black banner proclaims "I Saw It" in white block letters suggestive of a newspaper headline. The words are at once a simple statement and an accusation. Despite the ruined city, the lethal cloud, and the counter-winds of history, the banner is a declaration that this boy will depict the atrocity, *as he sees it*, and not the USSBS (fig. 3.3).

The bomb cloud is particularly revealing. By the time that Nakazawa drew *I Saw It*, a small number of Japanese views had been published, including a found photographic image of the mushroom cloud taken from the ground. Its round shape is quite different from the aerial view of the American bombers. In *I Saw It* the bomb repeatedly takes the Japanese form: concentric circles of a "flash" of light seen from the ground. In the story itself, the image of the cloud is easily contained in a narrow panel that is only half a page tall. Unlike the stories in the American press, the narrative does not fetishize the awesome power of the bomb but moves swiftly on to the damage it has done to buildings, plants, and people. The mirroring half-page panel shows a living tree being bent and snapped by the atomic wind that is also blowing a hurricane of roof tiles across the churning air. Tree, tiles, and wind are curved, like the explosion. These two panels frame a third that is vertically bisected. This panel contains the faces of a boy (Keiji) and a woman (the mother of a schoolmate) being hit by the blast. The people are much larger, because they are closer, than either the nuclear explosion or the tree. Nakazawa refuses to show the atomic cloud as a separate transcendental symbol, putting his drawings at odds with photographic rep-

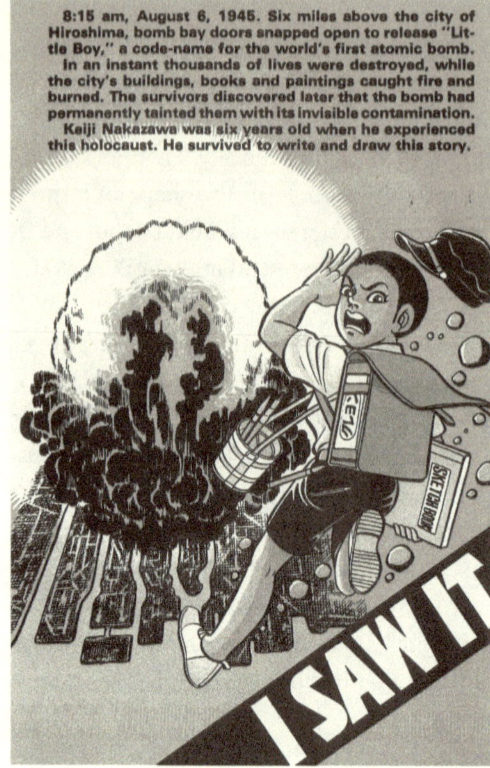

FIGURE 3.3 Back cover of *I Saw It*. Used by permission of Misayo Nakazawa, arranged with Japan UNI Agency, Inc.

resentations (fig. 3.4). Even when he draws the cloud at full height from a distance, it is immediately counterbalanced by the close-up view (fig. 3.5).

But in another sense the witnessing that Nakazawa invented was not only to use manga as a genre that could address the atomic bomb. Rather, he simultaneously found a new way to contextualize it. He peeled ideological content away from the scientific and political visualization of the time and examined the desire of the photographic image from a different point of view. This process of contesting what photographic documentary wants was painful but necessary, like debridement of a wound.

The most vivid example is found in the second volume of the *Barefoot Gen* series, *The Day After*, where a full double-page spread vehemently confronts the reader. Its size is unique in the whole ten volumes. The drawing is a reproduction of a USSBS aerial view. A vast flattened plane extends to the mountains ringing the city in the distance, while black clouds glower and swaths of heavy black ashes in the rivers simulate reflections of buildings and trees on their banks that no longer exist. There is nothing alive to be seen on the ground. Architectural landmarks still standing loom up out

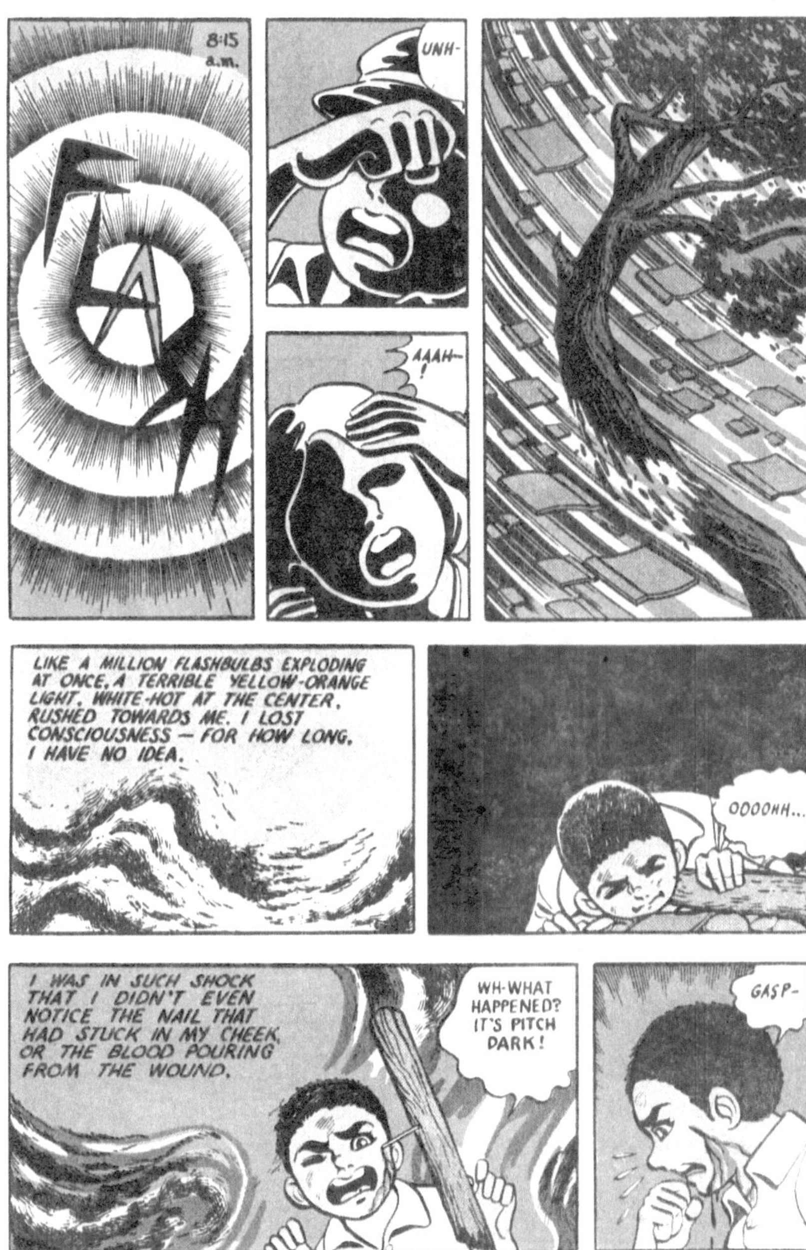

FIGURE 3.4 Page from *I Saw It* showing the bomb explosion. Used by permission of Misayo Nakazawa, arranged with Japan UNI Agency, Inc.

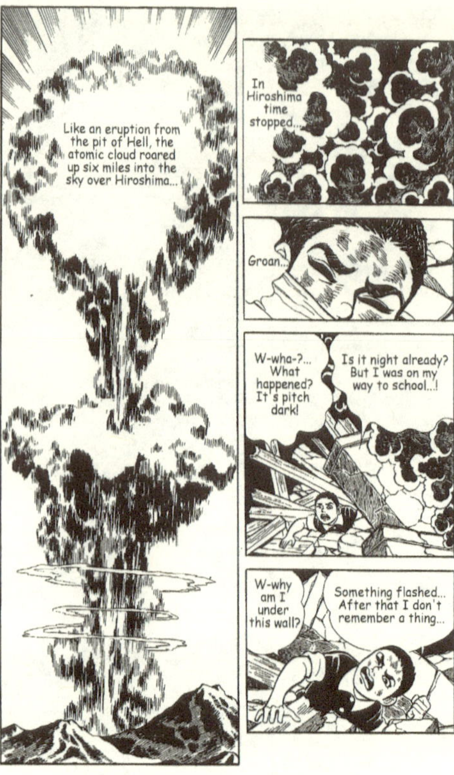

FIGURE 3.5 Page from Nakazawa's *Barefoot Gen: A Cartoon Story of Hiroshima* showing the bomb explosion. © Keiji Nakazawa. All rights reserved. Reprinted by permission of Last Gasp.

of the debris to grab the viewer's attention as on a strategic map. The point of view hovers hundreds of feet in the air. Over it all an enormous figure of Gen rears up. A colossus in judgment, its angry eyebrows are knitted over large, accusing manga eyes disgusted by the Americans, the Japanese, and everybody else (fig. 3.6).

But what is he seeing? Unlike the back and front covers of *I Saw It*, Gen is looking neither at the fire nor at the viewer. Rather, his focus is internal. He is registering how the victors are seeing his city. The photograph was one of the most famous documentary images taken by the USSBS, titled *BRIDGES 23 and 24, 4H/ GZ860–1000. October 14–November 26, 1945. USSBS 3:93, Photo 70-XII* (fig. 3.7). Taken just a few days after the bombing, it recorded the extent of the destruction for the benefit of American civil engineers, who now had to redesign the civil defense architecture of the United States in anticipation of a nuclear attack. The caption reads, "Intersections of Bridge 23 (left) and Bridge 24 (right). All damage from blast effects. Bridge 23 (860 feet to GZ, 2,170 feet to AZ). Bridge 24 (1,000 feet to GZ, 2,230 feet to AZ)."[42]

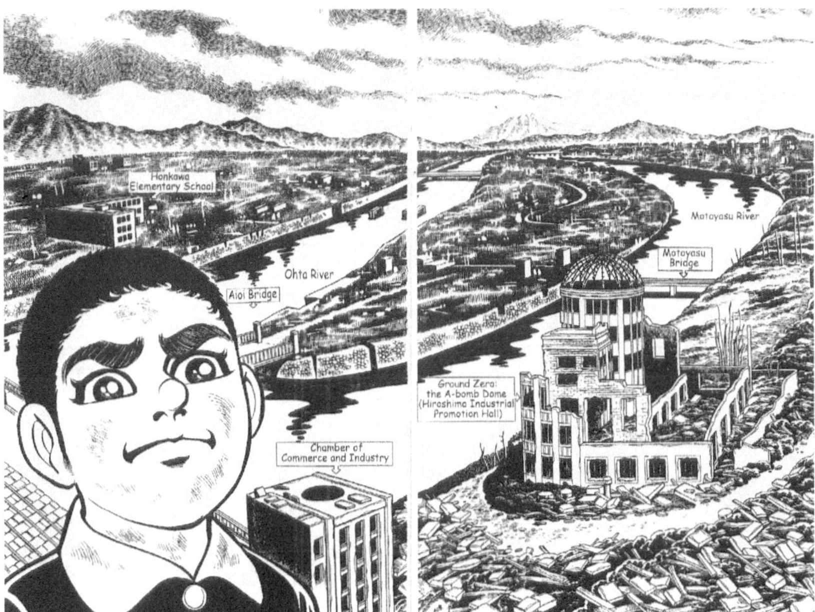

FIGURE 3.6 Double-page spread from Nakazawa's *Barefoot Gen: The Day After* showing the Aioi Bridge.

Usually there are no people in the USSBS images. But poignantly, this photo of the bridges shows little people walking, riding bicycles, even apparently boarding a trolley car. They too would have had stories to tell, although the USSBS photographer did not seek them out. But Nakazawa rejects any fantasy that might have been on offer about conversing with such *hibakusha*. In his drawing there are no people. No one loved remains. There is nothing in the drawing that Gen desires to see. Neither are the bodies in the rivers, the burned corpses in the streets, and the blinded, still-walking zombies—with their flayed skin trailing from their wrists and ankles—to be found. The city is a vast field of rubble seen from a distance, and the photograph, distinct from the drawing, wants us to accept this as a victory.

Emergent in the drawing is also Gen's consciousness that the photograph is a revelation of how the *hibakusha* are being looked at by the victors. The Aioi Bridge was the original ground zero targeted by the bombers, who missed only by a short distance. The photograph thus shows how close the American military came to technocratic perfection. Gen's eyes reflect this moment of realization about the photograph. If the documentary tradition expects the viewer to accept its vantage point, Gen refuses. Instead, he

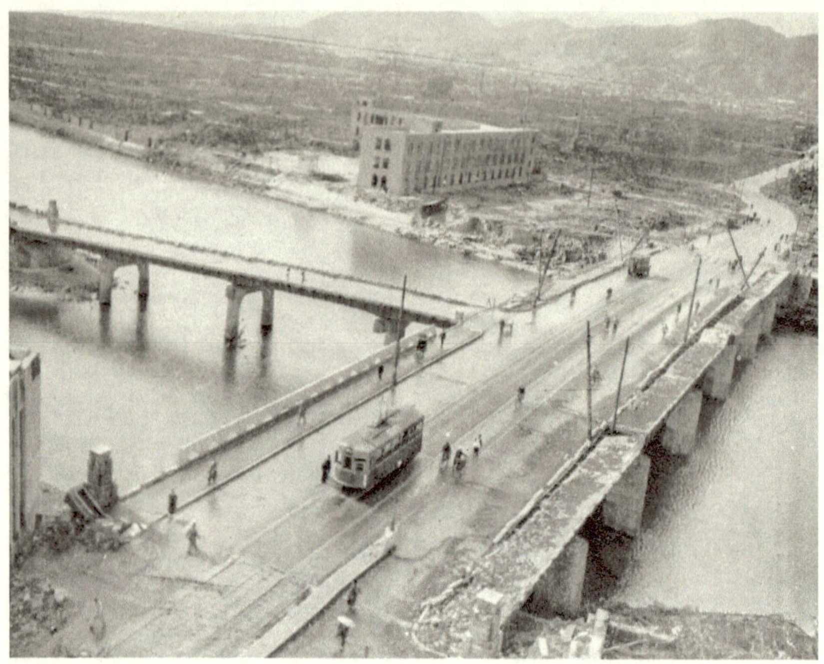

FIGURE 3.7 Photo from *The Effects of the Atomic Bomb on Hiroshima, Japan, Volume III*, showing the effects of the bomb's blast at the intersection of Bridge 23 and Bridge 24. International Center of Photography, Museum Purchase, Robert Capa and Cornell Capa Acquisitions Fund, 2011.

imports it into his own story and shows why it is unacceptable. The photograph, redrawn, is an indictment of all those whose acts made it possible. Even the big cloud is small in comparison with Gen's avenging face. It is an image of what Walter Benjamin called "dialectics at a standstill." As the philosopher and cultural critic observed in *The Arcades Project*, "It is not that what is past casts its light on what is present, or what is present its light on the past; rather, the dialectical image is that wherein what has been comes together in a flash with the now to form a constellation."[43]

Nakazawa loved drawing manga. Although he had not originally wanted to make manga from his experience, when he did, the sequential form of graphic narrative, constructed frame by frame from memory, may also have been helpful for recapturing an analytically consequential understanding of cause and effect in the world. Chute and others have described such a fit between manga and traumatic memory generally.[44] But Nakazawa's remediated *photographs* also registered what otherwise could not be shown or remembered. This was not the seemingly objective truth of the photographed scene itself, or its lived experience, but the emergence of its social meaning. The potential for a new kind of documentary realism to emerge from the gap between the photograph and the drawing is a very important contribution to the art of manga and the history of postwar documentary. Transmedial revision allows this buried vantage point to emerge.

But why specifically the medium of drawing, and why specifically photography? In the following discussion I will examine those questions further by turning to John Berger's writings on drawing. In Berger we have a brilliant theoretician of what "another way of seeing" allows.

DRAWING CONCLUSIONS

Nakazawa described what he saw at ground zero in his autobiography, *Hiroshima: The Autobiography of Barefoot Gen*. There are no photographic referents for the brutal scene:

> The Trolley street from Funairi Naka-cho as far as Saiwai-cho was a human exhibition, inhuman forms utterly transformed. Naked bodies moving sluggishly, burned by rays and trailing blackened bits of clothing like seaweed. Moving forward, glass splinters from the explosion sticking into all parts of their bodies, spurting blood. People whose eyeballs hung down their cheeks and trembled; they'd been blown out by the sudden pressure of the blast. People whose bellies had been ripped open, trailing a yard of intestines, crawling on all fours. Shrikes impale fish and frogs on dead tree branches, storing them to eat later; people too had been sent flying and hung from tree branches, impaled. I ran among these horrific humans, threading my way, crying out, searching for family.[45]

Nakazawa also drew these awful images. In his autobiography he makes a connection between the smoke and fire caused by explosion and the tools of his trade: India ink, water, and paper. The implication is that drawing is a kind of knowledge uniquely suited to this task: "Drop India ink into water, and it thins and spreads. Smoke just like pale ink covered the sky and wafted all about. The sky was like an ink painting: boards and sheets of metal danced helter-skelter into the sky, quite like birds. Every now and then, out of the collapsed row of houses a dragon's tongue of bright red flames crawled, disappeared, moved. Aghast, I burned that scene onto my retinas."[46]

In *I Saw It* and *Barefoot Gen*, the smoke and gore of the atomic wasteland make one long passage, but they do not reappear. Unlike current constructions of post-traumatic stress disorder that consider flashbacks as a key indicator, in each book the trauma of the bomb stays in place in time. Instead, what Nakazawa repeats is his struggle to make the drawing in the first place. "I drew what happened on the day the bomb fell. Even my editor responded negatively to the harsh scenes that unfolded in the burned-out ruins of atomic wasteland: he said, 'It's horrible.' But I continued to struggle, unable to re-create the truth that was still burned onto my retinas."[47] The obsessive exhaustiveness of the 2,500-page *Barefoot Gen* opus gives some impression of the intensity of this struggle. "Rereading my own work made my flesh crawl. It was really tough. . . . Even though I was ruining my health, I finally completed it. From the start of the serialization, it had taken fourteen years."[48]

Unlike a photographic image, each drawn mark on paper describes something one observes. What one is able to observe depends, in turn, on one's access to one's own memory. Some of Nakazawa's own sketches may indicate that is was difficult for him to forge this access. Rifas observes, "I was shocked at the crudity of Nakazawa's pencils in the autobiography [Richard] Minear translated. . . . I was even more shocked by some of his sketches at the Peace Museum. His work could succeed because his wife, Misayo, inked it so sweetly. The stories were his and about him, making her role secondary . . . but her contribution was so vital!"[49] It would be interesting to compare these particular sketches with others in his archive at the Hiroshima Peace Memorial Museum. In drawing, one traces not only the physical appearance of the object but also one's connection or disconnection to one's own experience. "It is the actual act of drawing that forces the artist to look at the object in front of him, to dissect it in his mind's eye and put it together again," John Berger observes, "or if he is drawing from memory, that forces him to dredge his own mind to discover the content of his own store of past observations."[50] Over time, this process results in self-discovery for the maker. "A drawing of a tree shows, not a tree, but a tree being-looked-at," writes Berger.[51] The tree being-looked-at reflects one's own self, looking. Apparently, disturbances remained in Nakazawa's visual field.

Yet how can drawing represent impressions or memories when, as in this instance, the events and hence the memory of the first atomic bombing are completely unprecedented? Other events of violence in other kinds of war may look quite similar, but the underlying narrative diverges. Such a drawing cannot show the being-looked-at of anything, because a knowing seer does not exist. Drawing is visceral; one draws in relation to the entire physical being. But the embodiment of a traumatized person vis-à-vis the traumatic event is partial and interrupted. The organized self has been destroyed. If to draw an object, according to Berger, one must see it, internalize it, and then reconstruct it, the trauma of Hiroshima makes this repertoire impossible. This trauma is not the missing of experience but the impact of experience that does not get portrayed. In crucial ways, the traumatized observer is fragmented or even missing. In parallel, a narrative of surviving an atomic bombing had yet to exist.

Such a barrier to seeing does not exist with photography. As Roland Barthes puts it in *Camera Lucida*, "Not only is the Photograph never, in essence, a memory," but it "*fills the sight by force*, and . . . nothing in it can be refused or transformed." The camera makes a picture that seems in itself to be complete.[52] A photograph commonly records things that are not yet fully observed and even makes an impression of things that have never yet been seen, filling in the holes and securing the opportunity for future discovery. Trauma can affect the act of taking a picture, inhibiting the choice of a moment or restricting access to the threshold of a scene, but it will not generally preclude the camera from making an image. Once subjected to the automatized process, however difficult it may be to make the exposure in the first place, the scene will be recorded whether or not meaning is conveyed.[53] But this is not true of drawing. With a drawing, you must see where you are going. "Another way of putting it," writes Berger, "would be to say that each mark you make on the paper is a stepping-stone from which you proceed to the next, until you have crossed your subject as though it were a river, and have put it behind you."[54] Nakazawa's drawing of the photographic record shows Hiroshima being-looked-at by a self that is crossing over by looking at the photograph.

Nakazawa clearly looked at many photographs of what it was so hard for him to draw. Comparing USSBS photographs taken in the days after the bombing with his drawings, one can easily discern some source material for what ultimately became a strong, sinewy black line inked by Masayo in the twisted beams and poles and timbers and wires of the USSBS prints. He draws the ruined schools, the collapsed houses, and the torqued trolley lines as the photographs show them.[55] But Nakazawa's drawings of the dead move him beyond what the photographs show. Robert Jay Lifton notes that the Allies were taught that the Japanese would die with a salute to the emperor on their lips. In reality, those who spoke before they died chiefly called out for their mothers, "an effort to reassert the ultimate human relationship in the face of death's severance," as Lifton puts it.[56] By adding their cry to his drawings of the photograph, Nakazawa is looking at himself looking and reclaiming what is human from the victors' armed gaze. In another horrific example, Nakazawa draws Gen, wordless, looking into a pail that contains the bones and skulls of his brother, sister, and father. The skulls are precisely rendered. Gen's mother, also looking, eventually tells him, "All . . . all our hopes are gone now, Gen. . . . We know . . . they're really dead,"[57] and they begin slowly to comprehend that they must carry on without them. In the story's diegesis, they try to "go far from these bad memories."[58] But in drawing the bones in the bucket, Nakazawa observes his own unsustainable flight from remembrance and now knows that it is unsustainable. As Berger discovered when he too drew a body—that of his own deceased father—in watching this seeing, instead of being "the site of a departure," his drawing has become "the site of an arrival."[59]

AFTERIMAGE

Nakazawa's antiwar manga have traveled widely. The volunteer organization "Project Gen" has translated the many volumes of *Barefoot Gen* into English and other languages and devoted itself to teaching about the bomb's devastation; it has developed school curricula as well. There have been three live-action films of *Barefoot Gen*, an opera, and two animated films released internationally. Although he is not universally praised in Japan, Nakazawa's admirers also include other comics artists who seek to convey the experience of a wide spectrum of kinds of survivors. Spiegelman stated that he took inspiration from *Barefoot Gen* while in the process of creating *Maus* when "*Gen* burned its way into my heated brain with all the intensity of a fever dream. . . . I've just reread the books recently and I'm glad to discover that the vividness of *Barefoot Gen* emanates from the work itself and not simply from my fever."[60] Nakazawa once said that he wished to travel "together with Gen . . . to various places and collect material—Chernobyl, Semipalatinsk, the Urals in the old Soviet Union; Nevada and Three Mile Island in the United States; the islands of the South Pacific (Bikini, Muroroa); Auschwitz; Nanjing in China."[61] His admirers have gone forward in that spirit to tell other kinds of stories, as he wished to do himself.

But I believe that another important part of Nakazawa's legacy is specifically his way of seeing photographic seeing. There is today a growing group of astute practitioners, among them Art Spiegelman, Joe Sacco, Alison Bechdel, and Marjane Satrapi, and scholars such as Leonard Rifas, Hilary

Chute, Mihaela Precup, Marianne Hirsch, Robin Bernstein, Nina Mickwitz, and Jeff Adams, among many more, who recognize that the transmedial revision of documentary photography offers opportunities especially suited to witness both historical violence and the social trauma of its erasure. Sacco's remarkable achievements in wartime comics—*Palestine*, *Safe Area Goražde*, and *Footnotes in Gaza*—are one example. Shigeru Mizuki's *Showa* and Emmanuel Gilbert's *The Photographer: Into War-Torn Afghanistan with Doctors without Borders* and *Alan's War: The Memories of G.I. Alan Cope* are others. Sacco works in the interstitial space between the news photograph and its hand-drawn copy. He has said that he draws because it is virtually impossible to get a shot of the perfect instant. "When you draw, you can always capture that moment. You can't always have that exact, precise moment when someone's got the club raised, when someone's going down. I realize now there's a lot of power in that. It's a bit scary in a way, because you're capturing moments like that constantly from panel to panel."[62] In redrawing documentary photographs, Sacco can curate his story to show the perfect instant that emerges from the interplay of suppression and discovery. Capturing "dialectics at a standstill" is his way of rethinking documentary's trail. Gilbert, on the other hand, redraws photographs so that they can be recognized as photographs, and the shock of his repossession of them in that manner, in sequence with his drawings, estranges the technocratic narrative, at once so central and so far from the U.S. war in Afghanistan. Through these and other transmediations, it is quite possible to discern that Gen is traveling still.

NOTES

I would like to thank Toby Appel, Courtney Baker, Robin Bernstein, Daniel Botsman, Hillary Chute, John Dower, Jessica Hernandez, Taylor Jardno, Caren Kaplan, Mihaela Precup, Leonard Rifas, Ono Seiko, John Whittier Treat, and Linda Truilo for helpful comments and practical support in the writing of this essay; audiences at Stanford, Yale, and the "Picturing Photography in Graphic Memoirs" session at the 2013 MLA for their generous responses to my presentations of this work; and Colin Turner of Last Gasp Press, Misaya Nakzawa and Ayumu Kiryu of Japan UNI Agency, and the International Center of Photography for permission to reproduce images.

This essay is dedicated to my father, Bernard I. Kaplan (1916–85), second lieutenant, U.S. Army Signal Corps, Pacific theater, Occupying Forces, Osaka, Japan, 1945, who loved to read the funnies and hated the war.

1. *Hibakusha* is the Japanese term for atom bomb survivor. It literally means "bomb-affected-people."
2. Early achievements in film, photography, and the fine arts include *Summer Flowers*

by Hara Tamiki; *City of Corpses* by Ota Yoko; *Poems of the Atomic Bomb* by Toge Sankichi; *Hiroshima Mon Amour* by Alain Resnais; the sculptures of Kita Kazuaki; the *Hiroshima Murals* of Maruki Iri and Maruki Toshi; and the photographs of Ken Domon and Shomei Tomatsu. In the United States, the iconoclastic force of the Underground Comix movement in the 1960s and 1970s also permitted the production and circulation of antiwar art, but widespread truth telling in the general population about the effects on the civilian population of the atomic bombing of Hiroshima remained difficult.

3. Chute, *Disaster Drawn*, 2.

4. Nishima and other Japanese photographs were published in Liebow, "Hiroshima Medical Diary." The USSBS photographs are published in Barnett and Mariani, *Hiroshima*. Nakazawa's own collection of atom bomb materials is at the Hiroshima Peace Memorial Museum.

5. Chute, *Disaster Drawn*, 112. See also Mickwitz, *Documentary Comics*; and Bernstein, "'I'm Very Happy to Be in the Reality-Based Community.'"

6. Rifas, "Globalizing Comic Books from Below," 141.

7. Leonard Rifas, personal communication with the author, 20 December 2016. Nakazawa's sense of distance in Japan is recorded in his interview with Alan Gleason. Gleason, "Keiji Nakazawa Interview."

8. See Amy Kiste Nyberg, *Seal of Approval: The Origins and History of the Comics Code* (Jackson: University Press of Mississippi, 1998); and Charles Hatfield, *Alternative Comics: An Emerging Literature* (Jackson: University Press of Mississippi, 2005).

9. Spiegelman, "*Barefoot Gen*," n.p.

10. Quoted in Rifas, "Globalizing Comic Books from Below," 166.

11. Spiegelman, "*Barefoot Gen*," n.p.

12. Ibid.

13. Chute, *Disaster Drawn, 1.*

14. As cited in Adams, *Documentary Graphic Novels and Social Realism*, 89.

15. Ibid., 39.

16. Ibid., 9.

17. Chute, *Disaster Drawn*, 116.

18. Thierry Smolderen, *The Origins of Comics: From William Hogarth to Winsor*, trans. Bart Beatty and Nick Nguyen (Jackson: University Press of Mississippi, 2014); *McCay*, Davidson, *Penguin Book of Political Comics*, 62, quoted in Adams, *Documentary Graphic Novels and Social Realism*, 70.

19. Liebow, "Hiroshima Medical Diary," 67.

20. See, for instance, Daston and Gallison, *Objectivity*; Sekula, "Instrumental Image"; Deriu, "Picturing Ruinscapes"; Kaplan, "Dead Reckoning"; Wexler, "Heightened Histories"; J. Scott, "Evidence of Experience"; Nichols, *Introduction to Documentary*; Stott, *Documentary Expression and Thirties America*; and Jacobs, *Documentary Tradition*.

21. Japanese Broadcasting Corporation (NHK), *Unforgettable Fire*. These pictures were displayed at the Hiroshima Peace Memorial Museum on 1–6 August 1974. Among them is a survivor's view of the Aioi Bridge. See also J. Berger, "Hiroshima."

22. Mitchell, *What Do Pictures Want*, xv. "The question to ask of pictures from the standpoint of a poetics," writes Mitchell, "is not just what they mean or do but what they

want—what claim they make upon us, and how we are to respond. Obviously, this question also requires us to ask what it is that we want from pictures."

23. Nakazawa, *Hiroshima*, 34–35.

24. *Barefoot Gen's Hiroshima*.

25. Nakazawa, "A Note from the Author," in *Barefoot Gen: A Cartoon Story of Hiroshima*, n.p.

26. Nakazawa, *Hiroshima*, 146.

27. Ibid., 147.

28. Tanter, "Voice and Silence in the First Nuclear War," n.p.

29. Ibid.

30. Tsuzuki, "Report on the Medical Studies of the Effects of the Atomic Bomb."

31. See https://en.wikipedia.org/wiki/Hiroshima_Maidens.

32. Tanter, "Voice and Silence in the First Nuclear War," n.p.

33. Nakazawa, *Hiroshima*, 150.

34. Nakazawa, "Note from the Author," n.p.

35. Ibid.

36. Nakazawa, *Hiroshima*, 152.

37. For example, Leonard Rifas relates that Nakazawa "redrew a panel in *Barefoot Gen* when I pointed out that Albert Einstein had not worked on the atomic bomb, and that in volume nine, he gave an unreliable account of the American response to North Korea shooting down a spy place. I do not trust Nakazawa as a *historian*, but he's very important as a *witness*." Personal communication with the author, 20 December 2016. Nakazawa's own rich archive is available in the Hiroshima Peace Memorial Museum.

38. Martin Heidegger's term *sous rature* is precise in this context.

39. Nakazawa, *Hiroshima*, 152.

40. Rifas states, "As I remember it, I was the one who instructed the colorist to insert that Nakazawa-drawn mushroom cloud into Nakazawa's splash page drawing for *Ore wa Mita* which became the cover of *I Saw It*, to further tip off American (and other English-speaking) readers about what Nakazawa had seen." Personal communication with the author, 20 December 2016.

41. Quoted in Lifton, *Death in Life*, 19.

42. Barnett and Mariani, *Hiroshima*, 17.

43. Benjamin, *Arcades Project*, 463. Originally published in German in 1983 as *Das Passagen-Werk*, *The Arcades Project* comprises Benjamin's notes on nineteenth-century Parisian bourgeois life written between 1927 and 1940.

44. Chute, *Disaster Drawn*.

45. Nakazawa, *Hiroshima*, 38–39.

46. Ibid., 35–36.

47. Ibid., 164–65.

48. Ibid., 166, 168.

49. Rifas, personal communication with the author, 20 December 2016.

50. J. Berger, *Berger on Drawing*, 3.

51. Ibid., 71.

52. Barthes, *Camera Lucida*, 91.

53. One Japanese eyewitness at Hiroshima, Yoshito Marsushige, started to photograph as soon as forty minutes after the blast but managed to make only five images and spoke of how repugnant it was to him even to use his camera at that juncture. Nonetheless, despite his ambivalence, the photographs he did take do exist.

54. J. Berger, *Berger on Drawing*, 3.

55. Compare, for instance, the many USSBS photographs of schools found in Barnett and Mariani's *Hiroshima*—the Yamanaka Girls High School, Fukuromachi Grammar School, Sanyo Middle School, Takeya Grammar School, Sotoku Middle School, Misasa Grammar School, Koko Private Grammar School, Funairi Grammar School, Honkawa Grammar School Auditorium, Honkawa Grammar School, Temma Grammar School, Hiroshima Daini Junior High School, Hijiyama Grammar School, and Koyin Grammar School Auditorium—with his drawings of the gate and wall of his own Kanzaki Primary School before the blast and the schools attended by himself and other child survivors in Hiroshima afterward.

56. Lifton, *Death in Life*, 22. "Trained to go to their deaths with the phrase 'Long live the Emperor' on their lips, they instead called out 'Mother!'"

57. Nakazawa, *Barefoot Gen: A Cartoon Story of Hiroshima*, 191.

58. Ibid., 194.

59. J. Berger, *Berger on Drawing*, 72

60. Spiegelman, "*Barefoot Gen*," n.p.

61. Nakazawa, *Hiroshima*, 172.

62. Joe Sacco with Hillary Chute, "Can you draw what you don't understand?," in Chute, "Joe Sacco."

Speculative Ecology

Rachel Carson's Environmentalist Documentaries

DANIEL WORDEN

But the long trend is toward a warmer earth;
the pendulum is swinging.
—RACHEL CARSON, *The Sea around Us*

Rachel Carson's work of literary nonfiction *Silent Spring* (1962) is often celebrated for its legislative effect. Carson's book documenting the harmful effects of DDT and other pesticides, it is noted frequently, was central to the creation of the Environmental Protection Agency, by executive order of Richard Nixon in 1970, and the nationwide ban on the use of DDT in 1972. The immediate reception of *Silent Spring* as a pressing work of activist documentary has just as much to do with the work's speculative imaginings as it does with its more traditional journalistic content. Though primarily lauded as the origin point of modern environmental legislation, Carson's *Silent Spring* is part of a larger trajectory in her documentary writings about nature, one that is concerned not just with regulating chemicals like DDT but also with a broader reorientation of our relation to the environment in a way that can make visible, and therefore allow us to begin to think of alternatives to, the structural conditions of environmental harm that have led to the crisis of climate change. Carson's prose blends nature writing, science writing, investigative reporting, and lyrical imagining into a mode that I will describe in this essay as "speculative documentary." This mode blends traditional reportage with visions of (usually apocalyptic) futures both to emphasize the "slow violence" of pollution and climate change and to ground that violence and its long-term effects in our everyday lives.[1]

What Carson's *Silent Spring* consolidates, I argue in this essay, are New Deal–era documentary forms aimed at a broad public and a more speculative documentary form emergent in Carson's earlier writings, one that used lyrical speculation about the future to represent both the vast network of marine ecology, from the shorelines to the deepest reaches of the sea floor, and the effects of seemingly mundane chemicals like DDT. In her writings about the ocean, ecological networks, and human-made toxins, Carson articulated and popularized a mode of speculative documentary suited to grappling with environmental problems, and especially with climate change, by making available a conception of the world in which ecological systems are estranged from and even unrecognizable by the humans who inhabit them. By undoing the familiarity of "nature" as a stable other to culture, Carson produces a documentary account capable of projecting the future from present-day actions, thus advocating for changes to behaviors that otherwise slowly, and perhaps invisibly, lead to catastrophe. This method has become central to environmentalist documentary. For example, Al Gore's award-winning account of climate change, *An Inconvenient Truth*, opens with speculation, inviting readers "to use our moral imaginations and to project ourselves across the expanse of time, 17 years into the future, and share a brief conversation with our children and grandchildren as they are living their lives in the year 2023."[2] This kind of speculative imagining is necessary to making climate change and other environmental problems visible. Carson's synthesis of nature writing, science writing, investigative journalism, and imaginations of the future into "speculative documentary" helped to make available a mode of documentary writing and filmmaking that is capable of and has become a prominent way of representing climate change, environmental harm, and the necessity of environmental activism in the late twentieth and early twenty-first centuries. Only through speculation about the future can environmentalist documentaries present climate change and other forms of environmental crisis as immediate problems.

SPECULATIVE DOCUMENTARY

Rachel Carson's *Silent Spring* is about the proliferation of pesticide-spraying programs after World War II. Documenting DDT and other pesticides' effects on water, soil, plants, fish, birds, and mammals (including humans), *Silent Spring* is written in a lyrical yet journalistic style, intertwining scientific data, industry history, and information about spraying programs with reflections about nature's importance, anecdotes about victims of pesticide toxicity, and apocalyptic imaginings of a world forever poisoned. As Gary Kroll has documented, *Silent Spring* is not a singular text but a "polysemous" one, appearing in multiple forms, from its initial magazine publication to its publication as a book and distribution through the Book of the Month Club and even its treatment on TV.[3] Moreover, Carson's reportage on pesticides followed and relied upon earlier reports doubting DDT's safety. Employed by the U.S. Fish and Wildlife Service, Carson herself had written press releases warning fish processing plants about DDT's toxicity in 1945 and 1946.[4] *Silent Spring*'s publication as a book, then, was part of a longer progression of reportage and dissemination, less a singular text than a process that could then be consolidated around a concrete object. Following the book's publication, Carson's account of pesticides would be disseminated even further through television and government documents, including, in 1963, an episode of the news program *CBS Reports* and a report on pesticides from President Kennedy's Science Advisory Committee.

As was evident even before *Silent Spring* was published by Houghton Mifflin, Carson's writing was defining and propelling the environmentalist movement forward in the 1960s. As Rob Nixon, the Rachel Carson Professor at the University of Wisconsin, Madison, noted in a recent editorial, Carson's *Silent Spring* and its reception have a sobering effect, a double-sided sense of both the possibilities for environmental change and its limits: "We can seldom expect outright environmental victories, just indispensable, heroic holding actions, in which writers of conscience—as interpreters and witnesses—have a vital role to play. Sure, Carson didn't live to see the Clean Water Act of 1972 and the Safe Drinking Water Act of 1974 that her writings helped inspire. But she also didn't live to see U.S. Vice President Dick Cheney, a former Halliburton chief executive, chair the energy task force that resulted in the 2005 bill exempting high-risk hydraulic fracturing (fracking) from the requirements of those same two acts."[5] As Nixon points out, celebrations of *Silent Spring*'s legislative impact can occlude the persistent and worsening problems of environmental pollution and escalating climate change, let alone legislative mandates that have undone or bypassed the regulations the book helped to put in place. Thinking of *Silent Spring* as speculative documentary, though, allows one to find in the book both an activist argument about government legislation and a vision of the environment that demands a recognition of environmental exploitation and its long-term effects—a recognition of the slow accumulation of damage and toxicity that activities like fracking produce—that cannot be fully repaired by regulatory triumphs.

Involvement in governmental reports was not new for Carson, who had worked for almost ten years in the U.S. Fish and Wildlife Service, where she "wrote pamphlets and press releases, and edited scientific papers generated by other Fish and Wildlife staff."[6] Owing to Carson's own experience and the role her writings played in legislation, her work clearly partakes in and is an important late part of the tradition of government-sponsored documentary forms associated largely with the New Deal, documentary forms that, like Pare Lorentz's film *The River* (1938), tend to celebrate technology, government, and humanity's ability to reshape the environment for the better. What makes Carson's work distinct from those government-sponsored, often sentimentally humanist forms, though, is her twinned focus on legislative action and the vast temporal sweep of ecology that displaces human society as central to the world. This ecological framework is evident in *Silent Spring*, but it was crafted and refined in Carson's earlier books about ocean ecology. These earlier ocean books—*Under the Sea-Wind* (1941), *The Sea around Us* (1951), and *The Edge of the Sea* (1955)—engage in a hybrid documentary form much like *Silent Spring*, though they are descriptive rather than activist in their ultimate intent.[7] While rooted in federal patronage of oceanography and her own experiences working for the U.S. Fish and Wildlife Service, Carson's ocean writings importantly speculate as much as they report and disseminate scientific information.[8] As Philip Cafaro claims about Carson's first book, *Under the Sea-Wind*, she combines "an imaginative, phenomenological exploration of other consciousnesses with the latest researches in scientific natural history."[9] It is this imagining of other consciousnesses, such as *Under the Sea-Wind*'s character Scomber the Mackerel, coupled with her lyrical passages about deep time that produce a speculative documentary form, one that remains key to environmentalist documentary writing and film today.

Through her blend of science and nature writing with speculative imagining about the futures of increasingly over-fished and toxic ocean life, Carson's books often produce a sense of a doomed future. Indeed, in the 1952 documentary film adaption of Carson's *The Sea around Us*, written and directed by Irwin Allen, who would later make the successful disaster films *The Poseidon Adventure* (1972) and *The Towering Inferno* (1974), a series of Technicolor scenes of glaciers shedding ice into the ocean concludes the film on an ominous note about temperatures rising across the globe and the concomitant rise of ocean levels. The film closes with the phrase "The End?," presaging both Allen's future career in disaster films and Carson's sublime approach to nature.[10] Gary Kroll notes that Carson was disappointed with Allen's adaptation of her book, citing a letter in which Carson wishes that the film version of *The Sea around Us* had been made with the "beauty, the dignity, and the impressiveness of the Pare Lorentz script for *The River*."[11] Lorentz's New Deal documentary *The River* concludes with an account of how the Tennessee Valley Authority and the Farm Security Administration are controlling rivers, to improve farmland and restore rivers, optimistically stating, "We had the power to take the valley apart—we have the power to put it together again."[12] Though she was unhappy with it as a film adaptation, Allen's *The Sea around Us* nonetheless captures, in its ominous warning of environmental catastrophe, the way in which Carson presents a longer view than Lorentz's documentary, one that emphasizes not the rehabilitation of society but its ultimate and inevitable collapse. Rather than engaging in a sentimental humanist account of social flourishing and the renewed control of nature, as we see in *The River*, Carson offers, through speculation, a more realistic view of the environment over time.

Gesturing not to a hopeful future occasioned by liberalism but instead to a disastrous future facilitated by human interference with ecological systems, Carson's approach to the environment speculates about our apocalyptic future and in so doing challenges the public to imagine alternatives to seemingly mundane activities. Indeed, Irwin Allen's 1961 science fiction film *Voyage to the Bottom of the Sea* would hinge on a giant fire in the sky that threatens to extinguish all life on Earth by raising the planet's temperature. Featuring crumbling glaciers and nuclear warheads, *Voyage to the Bottom of the Sea* dramatizes, in the guise of an adventure story, the kinds of apocalyptic visions lyrically and presciently documented in Carson's writings about the warming oceans and our toxic environments.[13] Thus while Carson's prose trades in a kind of sensational imagining similar to Allen's, it is only through that speculation that she is able to begin to describe the larger consequences of climate change.

As Michael Schudson states in his influential *Discovering the News*, literary journalism of the 1960s often takes on a subjective, challenging tone in order to make visible what might otherwise be obscured by the "standard of objectivity" in print journalism.[14] Carson's contribution to this subversive, critical tradition in literary nonfiction is the synthesis of nature writing, lyrical reflection, and speculative representations of the future. Moving from ecosystems to pesticide production, Carson documents nature as a function of economic, oceanic, and biological processes rather than as a static end in itself to be conserved and celebrated. *Silent Spring* takes part in both traditions ascribed to critical journalism of the 1960s by Schudson—"a literary tradition and a muckraking tradition."[15] At once investigative and speculative, Carson's prose blends a distinctively imaginative style with investigative strategies, including endnotes to support *Silent Spring*'s claims. This synthesis of the investigative and the speculative can be traced through Carson's own career, and it has led to a wide swath of speculative documentaries that seek to make visible environmental damage, the climate change crisis, and the need for large-scale environmentalist reform.

In an influential essay that helped to define the shift from ecocriticism to what is commonly referred to now as the environmental humanities, Lawrence Buell claims that "contemporary toxic discourse effectively starts with *Silent Spring*."[16] Moving beyond romantic notions of nature as separate from human activity, toxic discourse, in Buell's argument, "insists on the interdependence of ecocentric and anthropocentric values. It underscores the point that environmentalism must make concerns for human and social health more central and salient than it traditionally has if it is to thrive, perhaps even to survive."[17] However, in her *Sense of Place and Sense of Planet*, Ursula K. Heise notes that the discourse of toxicity often replicates what it purportedly disavows, "the fundamentally pastoral vision of ecology . . . a vision that understands ecological systems as harmonious and balanced networks and that sees nature as self-regenerating if left on its own."[18] Moving beyond this pastoral vision has proven difficult, and Heise argues, in a later essay, that science fiction is one site where ecology has been thought of as thoroughly enmeshed within human culture, as a part of global networks that cannot be nostalgically bracketed off from late capitalism. As Heise asserts, modern environmentalism must imagine "a human society that will live its future life in Martian ecologies, no matter the planet."[19]

What Carson offers, even in her early writings on the ocean, is a blend of what Buell describes as "toxic discourse" and what Heise describes as imaginative representations of ecology as part of a global network. Carson is not nostalgic for pristine nature but instead a thinker who imagines ecology as in a constant, yet slow, state of change and flow. In *The Sea around Us*, Carson describes the sea as both one entity and not an entity at all, but movement: "There is, then, no water that is wholly of the Pacific, or wholly of the Atlantic, or of the Indian or the Antarctic. The surf that we find exhilarating at Virginia Beach or at La Jolla today may have lapped at the base of antarctic icebergs or sparkled in the Mediterranean sun, years ago, before it moved through dark and unseen waterways to the place we find it now. It is by the deep, hidden currents that the oceans are made one."[20] Carson's network thinking—her emphasis on the fluidity of the ocean over our geographical boundaries—casts the ocean as fluid and porous, as something that undoes the names that describe it once one looks at water itself. That is, the ocean, and ecology more broadly, presents the nonfiction writer with a representational dilemma. Traditional nomenclature fails to capture the reality of the ocean, and Carson's speculative documentary prose aims to represent the "deep, hidden currents" otherwise obscured.

In *Under the Sea-Wind*, Carson described writing about the ocean precisely as such:

> In planning this book I was confronted at the very outset with the problem of a central character. It soon became evident that there was no single animal—bird, fish, mammal, or any of the sea's lesser creatures—that could live in all the various parts of the sea I proposed to describe. That problem was instantly solved, however, when I realized that the sea itself must be the central character whether I wished it or not; for the sense of the sea, holding the power of life and death over every one of its creatures from the smallest to the largest, would inevitably pervade every page.[21]

Carson's central character, then, is a vast ecological network, one that makes human society seem temporary, yet also one that requires representation through a human framework, characterization. What Carson's prose stages, then, and what allows her to engage in the various tropes and imaginings of *Silent Spring*, is a dialectic representation of nature, as both other to human society and as the network on which human society is based. Toxicity and equilibrium, ultimately, are synthesized in Carson's view, as ecological systems were never stable entities in the first place but in balance only in a very short temporal view. This understanding of ecology exceeds the temporal limits of traditional journalism and documentary by attempting to represent what cannot be directly observed or documented.

THE NATURE OF *SILENT SPRING*

As noted above, Carson's *Silent Spring*, like many of her earlier works about marine life and ocean ecology, was initially published in the *New Yorker* magazine, a venue best known for its "smart" commentary on urban life. On the surface, Carson's writings seem at odds with the *New Yorker*'s editorial focus, yet as Jamin Creed Rowan has argued, Carson's ecological texts mirrored the magazine's understanding of the city as a network. Comparing Carson's prose to Jane Jacobs's writing about the city, Rowan demonstrates how "like the community of sea creatures Carson describes at sea's edge, the pedestrians on Hudson Street compose a deeply interconnected yet anonymous social web."[22] While her earlier works might, on first glance, fit within the tradition of nature writing continuous from nineteenth-century nonfiction such as Henry David Thoreau's *Walden* (1854)—works that find in the natural world an escape and difference from culture—Carson's writing also makes it clear how nature writing is, and always was, just as much about nature's intertwinement with culture as it was about drawing a stark dichotomy between the cultural and the natural. Carson's ecological networks mirror the urban flows of the postwar city, entailing, in the worst-case scenario, the naturalization of exploitative structures and, in the best-case scenario, the decentering of normalized hierarchies. In *Silent Spring*, especially, this enlarged vision of nature as culture is necessary, for only through that lens can one begin to understand the permanent, long-term, large-scale effects of pesticide toxicity.

From *Silent Spring*'s title and its opening chapter, "A Fable for Tomorrow," Carson begins her record of increased organic pesticide use in the United States and its harmful effects on plants, animals, water supplies, and soil with a vision of future apocalypse. Like many works of environmentalist nonfiction to follow it, *Silent Spring* begins not with facts or experience but with speculation, a narrative about a before ("There was once a town in the heart of America where all life seemed to live in harmony with its surroundings") and an after ("Then a strange blight crept over the area and everything began to change. . . . On the mornings that had once throbbed with the dawn chorus of robins, catbirds, doves, jays, wrens, and scores of other bird voices there was now no sound; only silence lay over the fields and woods and marsh").[23] Borrowing a familiar trope from *The Communist Manifesto*, Carson then concludes the first chapter of *Silent Spring* with a claim about what her documentary prose will make available as knowledge: "A grim specter has crept upon us almost unnoticed, and this imagined tragedy may easily become a stark reality we all shall know."[24]

Carson figures this possible "stark reality" in two temporal registers—the slow time of pollution, which results in small changes to the ecosystem that, compounded, become disastrous, and the immediate, catastrophic event. As she writes, "The full maturing of whatever seeds of malignancy have been sown by these chemicals is yet to come."[25] While in this view, toxicity is hidden until catastrophic ("an irreversible malignancy will slumber long and undetected until finally—its cause long forgotten and even unsuspected—it flares into the open as recognizable cancer"),[26] Carson also documents more sudden, noticeable effects of toxicity. The central reference point for this is the death of songbirds, which is invoked in the book's fictionalized first chapter only to be returned to, as fact and not as fiction, in chapter 8: "Over increasingly large areas of the United States, spring now comes unheralded by the return of the birds, and the early mornings are strangely silent where once they were filled with the beauty of bird song. This sudden silencing of the song of birds, this obliteration of the color and beauty and interest they lend to our world have come about swiftly, insidiously, and unnoticed by those whose communities are as yet unaffected."[27] This alliterative "sudden silencing of the song of birds" echoes *Silent Spring*'s title, shushing through prose the silencing occasioned by DDT.

Another major work of documentary prose, also serialized in the *New Yorker* two years after *Silent Spring*, ends with a similarly alliterative phrase, as the detective Alvin Dewey walks away from the tombstones of the Clutter family, a family murdered at the beginning of Truman Capote's "nonfiction novel" *In Cold Blood*: "Then, starting home, he walked toward the trees, and under them, leaving behind him the big sky, the whisper of wind voices in the wind-bent wheat."[28] Capote's alliteration produces the effect of the word "why," reinforcing the book's critique of capital punishment—a critique made not overtly but through Capote's sympathetic representation of convicted murderer Perry Smith as a product of abuse and misdirected artistic ambitions. Carson's "shush" functions similarly, as an alliterative flourish that, in its repetition, emphasizes the open-endedness of this kind of documentary prose's provocation, as the text's lyrical design can potentially echo and repeat beyond the boundaries of the print book in the reader's mind.[29]

While Carson figures natural cycles and equilibrium as persistent and as inevitably returning after a disruption such as the use of DDT, *Silent Spring* also chronicles the irreversibility of some pollution and toxicity—the ways in which "the living world was shattered."[30] In the book's concluding chapter, "The Other Road," Carson argues that in forests, "with a minimum of help and a maximum of noninterference from man, Nature can have her way, setting up all that wonderful and intricate system of checks and balances that protects the forest from undue damage by insects."[31] In this contradiction—between nature as irreversibly damaged and nature as always striving to an equilibrium—lies Carson's conception of nature. At once redemptive and beyond human interference and also completely determined by human activity, nature in *Silent Spring* is a marker of an other to human culture and a figure for human culture's growing reliance on the manipulation and production of the natural world as a source of revenue. Carson's images of apocalypse and deep time, of the inevitable washing away of human society, coupled with her representation of the irreversible changes human society has contributed to the environment, stage this dialectical approach to ecology, one in which humans are both temporary and permanent agents among other organic and inorganic entities in the environment, never certain about their place in a fluid system.

The permanent harm done by humans is rendered clear when Carson casts an everyday object as saturated with foreign toxins: "The common salad bowl may easily present a combination of organic phosphate insecticides. Residues well within the legally permissible limits may interact."[32] Carson then projects, through the toxic salad bowl, an apocalyptic vision of the environment: "The world of systemic insecticides is a weird world, surpassing the imaginings of the brothers Grimm—perhaps most closely akin to the cartoon world of Charles Addams. It is a world where the enchanted forest of the fairy tales has become the poisonous forest in which an insect that chews a leaf or sucks the sap of a plant is doomed. It is a world where a flea bites a dog, and dies because the dog's blood has been made poisonous, where an insect may die from vapors emanating from a plant it has never touched, where a bee may carry poisonous nectar back to its hive and presently produce poisonous honey."[33] Carson's representation of the "slow violence" of environmental degradation and displacement is punctuated by these moments of everyday toxicity, of sudden death and contamination.[34]

In his reading of the 1963 *CBS Reports* episode "The Silent Spring of Rachel Carson," which gave Carson's warnings about pesticides an even broader audience, Finis Dunaway argues that the media spectacle produced around *Silent Spring*, similar to other media coverage of environmental problems such as nuclear testing, pollution, and climate change, "narrowed the scope of *Silent Spring* to single out DDT as the nation's sole pesticide danger. The repeated emphasis on DDT, while lending legitimacy to the ban, also worked to marginalize systemic critiques of industrial agriculture and the increasing reliance on pesticides."[35] The reduction of Carson's critique to DDT bypasses her larger ecological framework, one in which DDT is merely one example of human society's slow violence, and also one in which human society is temporary, destined to be washed away. This perspective lends itself less to environmental policy than to science fiction, and this is perhaps why *Silent Spring*'s speculative vision of apocalypse is followed up with chapters and endnotes about the present, not the future. Carson's careful documentation and citation practices in *Silent Spring* are evidence of a pragmatic concern—that speculative documentary will be received as "merely" speculative rather than seen as founded on scientific evidences and principles. As Mark McGurl has noted, deep time lends itself to genre fiction, and especially science fiction and horror, for unlike literary realism, works of genre fiction are "willing to risk artistic ludicrousness in their representation of the inhumanly large and long."[36] This is, in part, evident in *Silent Spring* and countered in the text by endnotes and citations. What makes *Silent Spring* unique, in this instance, is its dialectical staging of what McGurl refers to as the "posthuman comedy" of deep time, in which human society is rendered absurd in the grand sweep of time, and of the stasis and silence of postwar America. Carson's speculative documentary prose imagines an important shift from everyday life in the present to the future that our economic and social systems are making, thus grounding the time travel of speculative documentary in empirical data about everyday life in the present.

Silent Spring argues for a more mindful use of science in pest control while also emphasizing how ecology is a vast system that exceeds human society. In *Silent Spring*, Carson traces how her ecosystem thinking, emergent alongside urban planning ideologies that would be appropriated into fantasies of organic synthesis between work and life, can produce not a sense of organic equilibrium but a recognition of dynamism, change, and political responsibility.[37] Following Timothy Morton, Carson's *Silent Spring* denies nature's status as ontologically distinct from culture and politics.[38] Even more than this, though, Carson's mode of speculative documentary positions the speculative documentation of the future as central to environmental activism.

This imperative to document the future is taken up by later environmentalist documentaries, from the counterhistory in the film *Who Killed the Electric Car?* (2006) to the environmental damage described in Bill McKibben's *Eaarth: Making Life on a Tough New Planet* (2010). To focus briefly on one example: Werner Herzog's 1992 film *Lessons of Darkness* engages in the kind of estrangement from place and time that allows one to view our world as transient, as polluted and unsustainable, bound to give way. The film is composed of documentary footage shot in Kuwait after the first Gulf War. Centering on scenes of the Kuwaiti oil fires and the oil workers trying to contain them, Herzog narrates the film as an alien observer, introducing the footage in the film as being of "a planet in our solar system" and going on to say about an oil worker standing in front of a wall of flames, gesturing and stomping on the ground, "The first creature we encountered tried to communicate something to us."[39] The communication is, of course, unintelligible. Perhaps the worker is showing us that the wall of flame is coming from below the ground, that the fire is crude oil aflame, but Herzog neither interviews the figure nor speculates about the meaning of his gestures. Instead, the viewer is left not with a sense of aestheticized violence (something that the film was initially accused of upon its first festival screenings) but with a sense of how environmental catastrophe estranges one from the environment, displacing the familiar and the everyday so completely as to render human communication and human agency moot. In *Lessons of Darkness*, this rendering moot is also part of its temporal and spatial reach—one of the film's chapters is titled "A Dinosaur's Feast," featuring shots of large machinery moving around Kuwaiti oil fields. The chapter title's reference to the organic beings, the dinosaurs, who decomposed into petroleum, is ironic—it is not the dinosaurs who feast on their crude remains, but these large machines. The dinosaurs here are not reptiles but fossil-fuel-burning engines, facing extinction on a burning planet. This kind of imaginary can capture the temporal span necessary for thinking of our everyday actions and structures of environmental exploitation as slowly leading to catastrophe.

REPRESENTING CAPITALISM AND CLIMATE CHANGE

Central to Carson's *Silent Spring*, but not named as such, is the engine driving the exploitative use of pesticides: late capitalism. Indeed, Carson's *Silent Spring* made available not only the environmentalism of the late twentieth century but also contemporary environmentalist politics that focus on capitalism and economics. As Nixon notes in his editorial on Carson, the ways in which legislation has been manipulated to conform to corporate interests have actively impeded the legislative triumphs occasioned by *Silent Spring*: "Even the prescient Carson could not have imagined this: an America where corporations are now legally people, replete with human rights, thereby endangering the rights of us noncorporate humans—ordinary, mortal citizens whose right to an unpoisoned future Carson rose up to defend."[40] The problems facing us today require something more than the advocacy of legislation and regulation, and this was anticipated even in Carson's earlier books about the ocean. For Carson, ecological time necessitates a shift in perspective, a recognition of and sense of obligation toward the dark patches of unknown life that precede and will follow the human species.

In a chapter about eels in *Under the Sea-Wind*, for example, Carson imagines a distant future: "As the waiting of the eels off the mouth of the bay was only an interlude in a long life filled with constant change, so the relation of sea and coast and mountain ranges was that of a moment in geologic time. For once more the mountains would be worn away by the endless erosion of water and carried in silt to the sea, and once more all the coast would be water again, and the places of its cities and towns would belong to the sea."[41] This moment of speculative documentary poses a subtle counterpoint to the logic of conservation, as the environment is valuable not as a resource for human life but because it will exist after humans have vanished.

Carson's *Silent Spring* and the environmentalist documentary tradition that follows from it—works such as Edward Abbey's *Desert Solitaire* (1968) and John McPhee's *Control of Nature* (1989), and more recently Elizabeth Kolbert's *The Sixth Extinction* (2014) and Naomi Klein's *This Changes Everything* (2014)—strive to represent the mutual imbrication of nature and culture through imaginings of the future that reach beyond the limits of conventional journalism. Carson's sublime imagery often offsets capitalism as temporary, as in this passage from *The Sea around Us*:

> In the artificial world of his cities and towns, he often forgets the true nature of his planet and the long vistas of its history, in which the existence of the race of men has occupied a mere moment of time. The sense of all these things comes to him most clearly in the course of a long ocean voyage, when he watches day after day the receding rim of the horizon, ridged and furrowed by waves; when at night he becomes aware of the earth's rotation as the stars pass overhead; or when, alone in this world of water and sky, he feels the loneliness of his earth in space. And then, as never on land, he knows the truth that his world is a water world, a planet dominated by its covering mantle of ocean, in which the continents are but transient intrusions of land above the surface of the all-encircling sea.[42]

Our place in this world is transient, Carson reminds us, even if our effects on this world will be permanent.

Contrary to Carson's faith in the decentering force of the sea, and as Allan Sekula documented in his work of photography and prose *Fish Story* (1995), late capitalism nonetheless transformed our relation to the sea at the time *Silent Spring* was being written, published, and read through the "containerization of cargo movement: an innovation pioneered initially by United States shipping companies in the latter half of the 1950s, evolving into the world standard for general cargo by the end of the 1960s. . . . Factories become mobile, ship-like, as ships become increasingly indistinguishable from trucks and trains, and seaways lose their difference with highways. . . . This historical change reverses the 'classical' relationship between the fixity of the land and the fluidity of the sea."[43] Carson's ocean loses its difference from the land, yet this entails not the sea's taming by late capitalism but late capitalism's own instability, its own entrance into the speculative imaginaries that Carson associated with the sea. As Joseph B. Entin argues in this volume, Sekula's *Fish Story* details how documentary representations of labor must always be provisional, and this provisionality is, in the work of Carson and other environmentalist documentarians, where speculation can chart possible pasts and futures.

Since *Silent Spring*, environmental documentary has come to engage in both activism, often aimed at specific legislative action or consumer awareness, and speculation about what comes after our current economic and energy regime. Climate change has made this twofold mode of representation even more necessary, as it demands recognition of the role industrialization has played in reshaping the environment. This poses a representational problem, as Dipesh Chakrabarty has noted, because "one never experiences being a concept."[44] It is here that Carson's writings continue to be useful, for they do allow one to experience exactly this—the conceptual nature of deep time and the twin pulls of hopelessness and individual activism that can accompany a recognition of one's place within a system. The author of the science fiction *Southern Reach* trilogy, a dazzling representation of an othered environment not understood by the humans who live alongside it, recently tweeted that his trilogy was "all based on the video game of Rachel Carson's *Silent Spring*."[45] It is this kind of speculative imagining—a never-created video game of a work of documentary prose, leading to a science fiction trilogy about an environment unrecognizable by humans who formerly inhabited it—that *Silent Spring* has made possible and this kind of thought that may continue to allow us to grapple with the reality of climate change.

NOTES

1. The concept of "slow violence" comes from Nixon, *Slow Violence*.

2. Gore, *Inconvenient Truth*, 11.

3. Kroll, "'Silent Springs' of Rachel Carson," 404.

4. See Souder, *On a Farther Shore*, 113–14.

5. Nixon, "Rachel Carson's Prescience."

6. Souder, *On a Farther Shore*, 23.

7. As Gary Kroll has noted about *The Sea around Us*, the best seller that allowed Carson to leave the U.S. Fish and Wildlife Service to work as a full-time writer, the book is "part nature writing" and "an equal participant in the literature of science writing. As

an established form of journalism, science writing emerged in the 1920s as an effort to inform the lay public of the many scientific advances of the day." Kroll, "Rachel Carson's *The Sea around Us*," 120.

8. As Kroll argues, Carson's ocean books participated in and documented the scientific discoveries gained from the "federal patronage lavished [on] the oceanographic sciences in return for important data on a large range of ocean statistics that were crucial for the military's execution of the war effort—a new partnership that lasted well into the Cold War." Ibid.

9. Cafaro, "Rachel Carson's Environmental Ethics," 68.

10. *The Sea around Us*, directed by Irwin Allen.

11. Carson quoted in Kroll, "Rachel Carson's *The Sea around Us*," 128.

12. Script of *The River*, directed by Pare Lorentz, 1938, http://xroads.virginia.edu/~1930s/film/lorentz/riverscript1.html.

13. For more on science fiction and environmentalism, see Canavan and Robinson, *Green Planets*.

14. Schudson, *Discovering the News*, 160–94.

15. Ibid., 187.

16. Buell, "Toxic Discourse," 645.

17. Ibid., 639–40.

18. Heise, *Sense of Place*, 140.

19. Heise, "Martian Ecologies," 469.

20. R. Carson, *Sea around Us*, 147.

21. R. Carson, *Under the Sea-Wind*, 3.

22. Rowan, "New York School of Urban Ecology," 603.

23. R. Carson, *Silent Spring*, 1–2.

24. Ibid., 3.

25. Ibid., 226.

26. Ibid., 233.

27. Ibid., 105.

28. Capote, *In Cold Blood*, 343.

29. See Franny Nudelman's essay in this volume for a more robust account of how postwar documentary represents these kinds of ghostly voices.

30. R. Carson, *Silent Spring*, 68.

31. Ibid., 293.

32. Ibid., 32.

33. Ibid., 32–33.

34. See Nixon, *Slow Violence*.

35. Dunaway, *Seeing Green*, 31.

36. McGurl, "Posthuman Comedy," 538.

37. For a reading of how Carson's ecology mirrors Jane Jacobs's urban planning vision and how both reinforce social hierarchies within late capitalism, see Kinkela, "Ecological Landscapes of Jane Jacobs and Rachel Carson."

38. See T. Morton, *Ecology without Nature*.

39. *Lessons of Darkness*, directed by Werner Herzog.

40. Nixon, "Rachel Carson's Prescience."

41. R. Carson, *Under the Sea-Wind*, 162.

42. R. Carson, *Sea around Us*, 15.

43. Sekula, *Fish Story*, 49. See Joseph Entin's essay in this volume for an analysis of how *Fish Story* represents changes to labor, another important facet of Sekula's work.

44. Chakrabarty, "Climate of History," 220.

45. Jeff VanderMeer, Twitter post, October 23, 2014, 11:46 a.m., https://twitter.com/jeffvandermeer/status/525357671839326208.

Participatory Documentary

Recording the Sound of Equality in the Southern Civil Rights Movement

GRACE ELIZABETH HALE

In a mass meeting in Albany, Georgia, in 1962, the sounds of a church packed with people fill in around the edges of the voice of the minister. Point by point, the Reverend Ben Gay lists and boldly rejects the issues raised in the Albany City Commission's report. Anger strains at his voice as he starts out loud and builds in volume. Audience members breathe and shuffle in their seats and increasingly sound their assent. Their "Amens" and "Yeses" and "That's rights" punctuate his phrases, fill in his pauses, and weave around his words. Layers of call-and-response structure the exchange—the commission and Gay, Gay and the people at the mass meeting, Albany movement participants and people who are not present but later listen to this recording.[1]

The commission charges that blacks do not pay much tax, Gay announces; he then offers his reply: "Since they own the large end of the income, they have a right to carry the tax burden." The audience claps and shouts in approval. "I wish someone would remind them that one of the reasons we are protesting now is that we want to get into the bracket where we can pay more taxes!" Gay pauses, and the clapping and shouting build. People talk to each other. Then Gay resumes his indictment. The commission charges that African Americans have too high a crime rate. Carrying "the psychological maladjustments that segregation imposes on us play[s] a big part in the crime we commit. And if the cause is stopped, the effect will certainly cease." A man yells out "That's right" somewhere close to the mic. Destroy Jim Crow, and "the Negro won't have to get him some liquor on Saturday to forget about how he was treated on the job." Yeses, shouting, laughing, and clapping fill the church.

His voice shaking with outrage, Gay next challenges the "sneak attack on our morals" in the commission's comments about African Americans' "high rate of illegitimacy." "I think it is a shame and a disgrace to be attacked about something for which the attacker is responsible." He pauses, and the crowd shouts assent. "Maybe these city commissioners were not told by their fathers and their grandfathers and their contemporaries"—laughter and "huhs" ring out—"that for three hundred years" (more voices join in support in the background) "they did everything that was humanly possible to destroy all family ties that would have existed among the negro through the system of slavery." Gay stops, and "Amens" and other shouts fill the gap. "The negro man and woman were mated as stock according to what they thought would produce the best specimen for the auction block of slavery." The shouting and clapping explodes. "Mothers and fathers, children from their mothers, they were sold asunder from the auction block." The audience shouts louder. "And here less than four generations after their grandfathers did this to us he comes and blames us"—Gay drags out the word "blame"—"for not having better family ties." The rising voices of assent create a wall of sound.

Members of this Albany audience weave their voices around the speaker and each other, creating parts that do not blend together but instead fit next to each other to fill the soundscape. In their musical manner of "bearing up" the individual speaker, as well as in the long-meter hymn singing that opens this meeting, they model an active, participatory form of engagement. They transform Gay's speech and indeed the entire mass meeting into a collective performance. After Gay finishes speaking and the meeting ends, many of these audience members will take their participation, their enactment of their collective agency, out of the church and into the streets and jails.[2]

The Albany movement was one of many city-centered movements that emerged across the South in the first half of the 1960s. During these heady days of mass activism—a burst of organizing I call the short civil rights movement—nonviolent mass protests and local actions replaced lawsuits as the center of the struggle. Led by the National Association for the Advancement of Colored People Legal Defense Fund, African Americans had already won in the federal courts, which had declared voter discrimination and racial segregation unconstitutional. Still, in many parts of the region, these legal rights did not mean much in practice. Activists mounted a series of nonviolent protests and concentrated regional and local organizing in response: the lunch counter sit-ins in 1960 and 1961, the 1961 Freedom Rides, the city-centered movements from 1962 through 1965, the Mississippi Freedom Summer in 1964, and the Selma march in 1965. Participation—people in the streets and in the jails and at the courthouses—helped turn legal rights into rights that southern blacks could live. In Albany, for example, Student Nonviolent Coordinating Committee (SNCC) organizers Charles Sherrod and Cordell Reagon arrived in October 1961 and began working with students at Albany State College, including Bernice Johnson. Mass protests erupted in December 1961 as these students and older Albany residents tried to make the city comply with an Interstate Commerce Commission's ban on segregation in interstate bus terminals.[3]

During this period, activists across the South made nonviolent direct action into a kind of political performance art. As M. S. Page, a leader of the Albany movement, said in 1962, "These people know what to do when you fight back. They don't know so well when you don't." Faced with the unexpected, southern whites often responded with anger and brute force. The nonviolence of the protesters, activists knew, highlighted the violence of the segregationists. In this context, organizers increasingly thought about how to conduct demonstrations in order to produce effective stories and images. Journalists, photographers, and camera operators working for regional and national newspapers and local and national television networks, activists understood, could extend the impact of their actions. Supportive media coverage functioned as a kind of documentary evidence. Participants then and scholars more recently have described this growing self-consciousness about how to shape activism to generate strategic representations as a key characteristic of the southern civil rights movement and the New Left it inspired. In nonviolent direct action, activists worked to "stage" the live event, creating the image they wanted journalists to capture and circulate.[4]

Rather than depend upon outsiders, some organizers in the early 1960s began collaborating directly with other organizers to create a low-budget and innovative set of countermedia practices. They employed faster film speeds and 35 mm cameras, 8 and 16 mm movie cameras, self-built darkrooms, WATS telephone lines, Ampex and Nagra audio-recording equipment, mimeograph machines, community radio stations, and independent record companies with ties to the folk music revival to transform documentary work into a form of activism. The recording of the Albany mass meeting in which Gay speaks is part of one example of this work, the documentary album *Freedom in the Air: A Documentary on Albany, Georgia, 1961–1962* recorded by Guy and Candie Carawan and sold by SNCC. Other examples of activist media practices include documentary record albums recorded and produced by the Carawans for Folkways Records; Berkeley community radio station KPFA's audio documentary *Freedom Now!*; the audio recordings of Alan Ribback; the documentary pamphlets produced by Students for a Democratic Society, SNCC, and the Congress of Racial Equality; the documentary photographs produced by SNCC staffers Danny Lyon, Clifford Vaughs, and others; the Southern Documentary Project founded in 1964 by Matt Herron; Harold Becker's 1964 film *Ivanhoe* about SNCC activist Ivanhoe Donaldson; and Edward Pincus's 1964 film about community organizing in Mississippi, *Black Natchez*. Activist countermedia functioned as a mechanism of what scholar Wini Breines has called "prefigurative politics," a process in which organizers tried to live as if the world they were fighting for already existed. The documentary materials produced in this way united form and function. They represented participants' experiences and agency in their content, and material existence served as evidence of that very experience and agency.[5]

The documentaries produced by civil rights–era countermedia practices are not liberal documentaries, in the scholar Martha Rosler's apt definition, works that ask the members of their audiences to write their congressmen. They are instead what I want to call participatory documentaries. Rather than simply address audiences imagined as having the agency to think and act in the modern world, these documentaries present people as possessing the agency to think and act themselves, as what Rosler has called "experiencing subjects." Their mode of affect does not, like liberal documentary, hinge on sympathy or even empathy but on participation, arousal, and engagement.[6]

Participatory documentary drew on important precedents like the depression-era collaboration between Frontier Films, the Highlander Folk School, and local people in producing the 1937 documentary film *People of the Cumberlands*. Guy Carawan, in fact, was working for Highlander when he first met southern civil rights activists. In the 1960s, however, activists and documentary makers grew increasingly self-conscious about their representational strategies. They began to understand the boundary between the subjective and the objective—the world outside the still, film, or television camera or tape recorder and the world as imagined by the activist or documentary maker—as brittle and porous. Many factors contributed to this shift. The postwar folk music revival's emphasis on participation intersected in important ways with the short civil rights movement's focus on mass activism. Participation—on a continuum from singing along at a live performance to sitting in at a lunch counter or on a bus—demonstrated commitment and produced community solidarity, but it also enabled people to express and share their feelings and act out the social transformation they were trying to create. It placed the experiencing subject at the center. The Newport Folk Festival in 1963, a world in which blacks and whites, working-class and middle-class Americans, rural residents and city dwellers came together, was not just a fantasy. It was a reality, something people attending collectively experienced. Similarly, some young civil rights activists in the South created the integrated world—blacks and whites eating and working and living together—that many of them were also working to achieve.[7]

In this context, the production of audio recordings, still photographs, printed pamphlets and books, and films became a tool for remaking and not just representing the world. Activists' focus on the right of people to represent themselves increasingly meant both the right to vote as well as the right to collaborate in creating the documentary record. Instead of simply external, "objective" accounts of events, participatory documentary presented internal, subjective accounts of participants' experiences. It foregrounded, rather than denied, the relationship between documentary subjects and documentary viewers. It positioned representational work as activism rather than as preceding, supplementing, or transcending activism.[8]

In making the subjectivity of southern African Americans their subject, activist documentary makers did not just document the short civil rights movement. They also helped produce a new reality, a participatory democracy in which African Americans were citizens. Blurring the boundaries between cultural and political representation, participatory documentary literally represented the voice in the form of an audio recording. It also figured the voice as a metaphor for the vote. In this way, cultural representation both demonstrated the need for and functioned as a substitute for political representation.[9]

THE SOUND OF EQUALITY

When Guy and a then-pregnant Candie Carawan arrived in Albany in February, the people were already singing. The Carawans knew SNCC field secretary Cordell Reagon, a Nashville native, Freedom Rider, and skilled song leader and activist. The other field secretary, Charles Sherrod, was also a talented singer. In southwest Georgia, Sherrod and Reagon found many gifted singers practicing a variety of group singing styles. Guy heard some of the Albany students singing at a voter registration meeting in Georgia in January. "If the young people could sing so powerfully," he wondered, after he heard them, "what about their parents and grandparents?"[10]

Soon after the Carawans' trip to Albany, Candie wrote a letter to her parents: "They have such a live-wire movement going there with everyone participating—across class and age lines. We had a lot of contact with students, some who have been kicked out of Albany State College for participating in the demonstrations." She also described their documentary work there: "We recorded some wonderful singing by the students—modern and traditional—and some archaic lined-out hymns by the older people at the mass meeting. We also taped a soul stirring traditional sermon, 'The Eagle Stirreth Her Nest,' with a new interpretation for the current situation. We recorded people of all ages telling what they hope for." Sometime that spring, Guy took the tapes to New York City, where Alan Lomax helped him edit the materials into an audio documentary. Vanguard pressed the record, and SNCC sold *Freedom in the Air: A Documentary on Albany, Georgia, 1961–1962* to raise funds.[11]

Documentary record albums like *Freedom in the Air* are a now mostly forgotten type of a little-studied documentary form, the audio documentary. Audio documentaries were central to the emergence of participatory documentary in the civil rights movement. In part, technological changes, including the production of first wire and then tape recorders, made audio recording easier, and these formats, which did not have to be developed, were low in cost in comparison to film. Audio documentaries also emerged for historical reasons. Most important, they fused two major mid-twentieth-century forms of audio documentary work—current events reporting on the radio and salvage-inspired music collecting. Field recordings of rural southern musicians made by John Lomax and Alan Lomax in the 1930s, for example, encouraged a broader interest outside the region in southern music and culture.[12]

By the late 1940s and early 1950s, folk musicians and music collectors had access to recording equipment and the expertise to use it. They knew people like Moses Asch, founder and owner of Folkways Records, who produced a diverse roster of records including anthologies of old commercially recorded songs then out of print, field recordings made around the world, collections of songs by both rural musicians and contemporary urban folksingers, animal sounds, and sound effects. Asch did not pay much—sometimes he did not pay at all—but he seemed to make his decisions about what to put out based on his desire to document the global soundscape rather than on commercial potential. The album format provided a solution to the distribution problem as commercial radio stations increasingly turned away from variety formats and broadcast mostly music after the spread of television. Documentary albums circulated in the same distribution systems as other albums. Folkways, for example, sold civil rights documentaries to some of the same people who bought folk music albums.[13]

Despite the red-baiting of the early 1950s, an older fusion of music and left political organizing had survived the decade in places like the Highlander Folk School's citizenship training workshops and the performances of left musicians like Pete Seeger. Lomax and Seeger, young members of the Old Left, met younger activists and musicians like Guy Carawan who would help build the New Left through their shared love for folk music. In this way, the Old Left managed to salvage and pass on some of its organizing tradition through the folk music revival. Networks of Old Leftists, folk music clubs, college student folk enthusiasts, and, later, friends of SNCC chapters and other civil rights support groups provided a small market for civil rights audio documentaries, which were often played and listened to collectively at meetings.[14]

Sometime in the early 1950s, after Guy Carawan graduated from Occidental College in Los Angeles and studied for a master's degree in sociology at UCLA, he traveled across the South. Along with his folk musician friends Jack Elliot, a future Woody Guthrie disciple, and Frank Hamilton, who would help found Chicago's Old Town School of Folk Music, Carawan learned new songs and new skills, like how to busk for funds and bum places to stay. In part, Carawan went to meet his father's relatives in North Carolina and see the southern countryside where both of his parents grew up. In 1953, he visited the Highlander Folk School and met Zilphia Horton, its first musical director. Between 1953 and 1959, Guy spent some time in New York participating in the growing folk music revival there. He stayed two months with Alan Lomax, who had moved to England to escape McCarthyism, and took advantage of his mentor's contacts as he traveled around Europe and, in 1957, to China and the Soviet Union. When he returned to the United States, he immersed himself in Lomax's Library of Congress recordings and continued traveling and performing. By the summer of 1959, with Pete Seeger's recommendation, he returned to Highlander to work as a volunteer.[15]

At a workshop on community development in August, Guy met activist song leaders and ministers who had participated in the Montgomery bus boycott. For the first time, he recalled later, he "felt" a palpable connection between the music and the politics. He was hooked. The next April, Lomax wrote him at Highlander: "While I was squirreling around in the past, you were busy in the present, and how I envy you. It must be wonderful to be with those kids who are so courageously changing the South forever."[16]

Audio documentaries fit the needs of civil rights organizers for formal and material reasons as well. Sound was an important movement tool. White southerners never succeeded in segregating the soundscape. Noise, voices, and music did not stay within racially labeled spaces. As historian Robin Kelley has argued, making noise—whether yelling, speaking, clapping, stomping, or singing—functioned as a form of opposition to segregation. Music, in particular, has a complicated relationship to racial categories. Beginning in the early nineteenth century, as scholar Eric Lott has argued, minstrelsy mixed and circulated a variety of musical traditions, moves, fantasies, and desires, even as it also expressed white supremacist ideas. In the early twentieth century, both the commercial music business and the practices of folklore scholars and fans worked in competing ways to racially categorize music, a history documented by Karl Hagstrom Miller. At the same time, some musicians and fans performed and listened to music across these sonic color lines. Music worked both to make and unmake racial identities and raced spaces. In no other place in the United States was this more fraught than in the South, where proximity enabled white and black musicians to share rhythms, tones, melodies, licks, and keys even as segregation insisted on a rigid separation. The spread of recorded music, in turn, created new possibilities and problems as it enabled more intimate styles of address, like the rediscovered blues of Robert Johnson, the subtle crooning of Nat King Cole, and the sexy soul of Sam Cooke to move across racial boundaries. Civil rights audio documentaries used the space-making power of recorded sound to challenge the spatial order of the segregated South.[17]

Guy and Candie Carawan met when the Nashville movement emerged as part of the student sit-in movement sweeping through the South in 1960. A Los Angeles native and a student at Pomona College, Candie Anderson moved to Nashville in the spring semester to attend Fiske University as an exchange student. In early April, Highlander hosted a workshop to connect student organizers across the region. Candie attended the Highlander workshop along with a group of students from Fiske. Guy, by then in charge of music programming at Highlander, had a talent for tweaking melodies and lyrics to make songs easier to sing and to connect them to current protests. That weekend, he taught participants songs he had collected from activists attending Highlander events and on his travels and songs that had been collected in the previous decade by Zilphia Horton.

Two weeks later, some of the participants in the Highlander workshop attended the youth leadership conference that Ella Baker organized at Shaw University in Raleigh. There, they taught these songs, including "We Shall Overcome," to the other student leaders at what became the founding conference of SNCC.

Late that spring, Guy traveled the 180 miles from Knoxville to Nashville to reconnect with the activists there. As Carawan wrote in the liner notes for his first documentary album, *The Nashville Sit-In Story*, "After spending two months in Nashville going through some of the history making events and being in daily contact with the students I decided to try and record some of the spirited singing and new songs that had grown up around the movement. Then the idea hit me that the songs would mean more to people if they were put in the contexts from which they came. Slowly a skeletal outline formed in my mind which wove together the songs, narration and scenes to be recreated." He convinced a local recording company, Willard Electronics, to record the singing, reenacted scenes, and interviews. Mel Kaiser, owner of Cue Recording Studios in New York, helped him edit the piece. Candie assisted in writing the jail scene, and she and other young activists including Diane Nash, James Bevel, and John Lewis participated in the reenactments and the singing. This collaboration produced a format that Guy and Candie would perfect two years later on the Albany record by replacing the reenactments with recordings of mass meetings.

In August, Guy and Highlander activist and educator Septima Clark held the first workshop on music in the movement to systematically collect, teach, and distribute what were increasingly called "freedom songs," continuing the work begun in April. At the end of the workshop, Carawan and Clark gave participants a mimeographed songbook. Guy then traveled to the Southern Christian Leadership Conference (SCLC) and SNCC's fall conferences and gave away copies of the songbook and the Nashville record. Flying in from Pomona, where she had returned to finish college, Candie too attended the SNCC conference in Atlanta, and Guy and Candie began dating seriously.

Working for Highlander and connected to SNCC, Guy received invitations that fall and spring to visit and sing with local movements. Everywhere he went, he met local singers, learned new tunes, and adapted and shared old ones, creating and spreading a growing repertoire of freedom songs. According to unpublished accounts of these years that Candie and Guy wrote later, he was acutely aware of the problem he posed as a white man teaching African Americans songs with roots in their history. For Guy, the songs "seemed very right for the situation and it was more like reminding people about them than teaching something totally new," a way of "tapping the wellspring of a resource already in the community." "Through trial and error working with groups at Highlander," the Carawans later wrote, "Guy had learned to play the songs in a style on the guitar and banjo that invited the congregation to join in, and as soon as that happened, as he put it, 'people could sing circles around me.'"[18]

In February 1961, Guy organized a Highlander-sponsored concert at Carnegie Hall in New York City to celebrate the one-year anniversary of the start of the sit-in movement. Students from Nashville and Montgomery sang freedom songs, and Pete Seeger performed. Birmingham's Reverend Fred Shuttlesworth described the growing movement down south. The Carnegie Hall concert took the form of an audio documentary performed live. The next day, Guy took the singers to the Folkways studio and recorded a second civil rights documentary record, *We Shall Overcome: Songs from the Montgomery and Nashville Freedom Movements*. In March, he and Candie married in California.[19]

By the fall, meetings in Jackson with Freedom Riders released from jail made it clear to Guy that his role in the movement needed to change. Writing about this period in 1965, Carawan described hearing many "good, experienced singers." They "knew how to get freedom singing going and could do it much better than I. I also found my guitar and banjo were even getting in the way sometimes of the unaccompanied group singing style, with its free-swinging body movement, hand-clapping, and foot-rhythms[,] that is part of Negro church background." With a modesty he would display for the rest of his life, Carawan searched for another role: "I decided to spend my time and energy trying to document the freedom struggle through books and records and to confine my own song leading to areas where they didn't know the songs."[20]

Candie and Guy Carawan spent the next few years lugging their not particularly portable Ampex tape recording machine and microphone to places like Albany, Birmingham, and Greenwood, where they recorded local activists speaking and singing in mass meetings and describing their lives and movement work. Because of their previous work as participants, their contacts with both student activists and older activists, and their documentary work, including *The Nashville Sit-In Story* and the Highlander songbook, the Carawans got access. They set up their equipment in places where still and movie cameras were banned for fear visual images would fall into the hands of police or of members of the Citizens' Councils or the Sovereignty Commission or the Klan. They became the most prolific and important audio documentary makers working in the civil rights movement. Their audio recordings represented the movement from the perspective of participants, what it sounded like to be inside the world activists made for themselves. On their albums, "the voice of the people" served as a synecdoche for political participation—one kind of recorded voice standing in for another, the ballots their subjects were not allowed to cast. As Guy Carawan wrote to James Forman, executive secretary of SNCC, "I am convinced now after playing the Albany documentary for a number of good-sized audiences of people who are not in the South and are uninformed about what goes on there that I can really move and exhilarate them."[21]

FREEDOM IN THE AIR

When the old lined-out, long-meter hymn begins, opening side A of the documentary record album *Freedom in the Air*, the emphasis is on sound, not words. In what the Carawans describe as "a very slow surge style," the singers draw out each syllable into multiple rising and falling notes that weave together into a shimmering wave of sound. This is not standard, Protestant church hymn singing but something entirely different, haunting and deep, a sound that marks a break from everyday life. As this singing fades out, a strong southern male voice speaks the name of the place, with the accent on the second syllable, as locals pronounce it: "All-BEN-ny. "All-BEN-ny, Georgia"—Reverend Gay pauses here to let the tension build before continuing—"is on the brink of ruin. It's TIME that Albany have some DEMOCRACY here! It's time that we move out of the old ruts of life and begin to contend for the things that ALL Americans OUGHT to have!" His voice crackles and strains with passion. He is not just speaking. He is testifying. He is commanding. "All of Albany is now REELING under the impact of this great request we're making, just to be first class citizens, just to be as ANYBODY else, just to walk the streets with dignity and reside with honor." They have heard, he stresses, "the voice of democracy," calling them to pray and protest and persist until they achieve victory. As he finishes speaking, the sound of the old long-meter hymn surges up again in the sound mix. This is not normal life, the sounds recorded here suggest. This is something heightened, something backed by the spirit. This is something sacred (fig. 5.1).[22]

The next brilliant edit simultaneously marks and contradicts this point. As the long-line singers stretch out a syllable that sounds like "heeeee," the

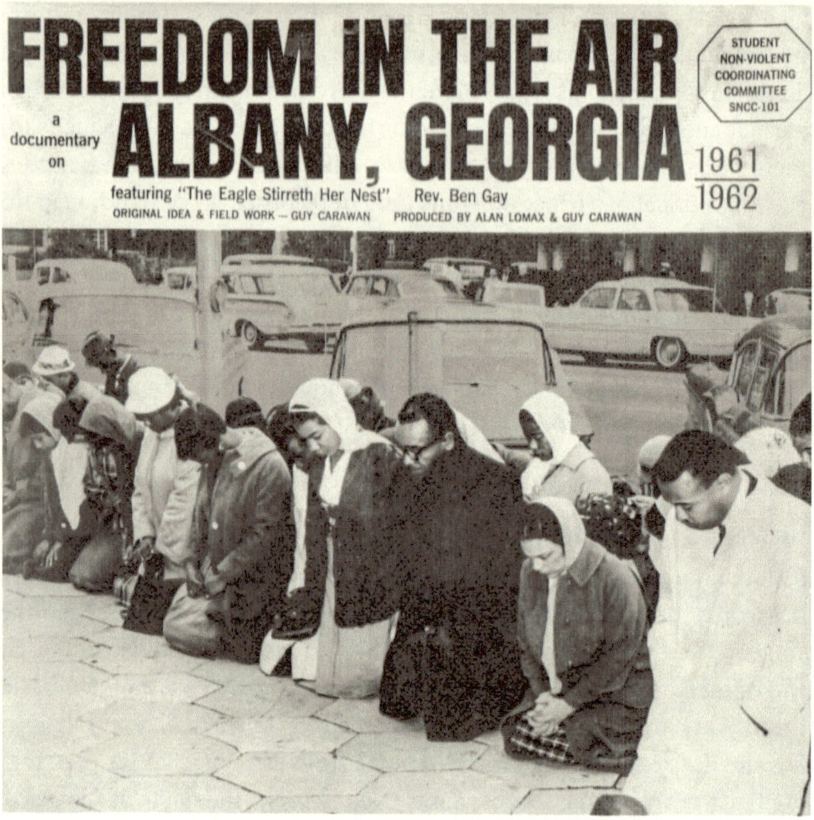

FIGURE 5.1 Documentary album *Freedom in the Air: A Documentary on Albany, Georgia, 1961–1962*, recorded by Guy and Candie Carawan, released by SNCC Records, and sold by the Student Nonviolent Coordinating Committee. Author photo.

sound of young voices singing "hallelujah" rises in the mix. The song is "Woke Up This Morning with My Mind Stayed on Freedom," described in the Carawans' notes as "a new version of an old gospel song . . . sung by college students at a jam session." The piece is performed mid-twentieth-century black gospel quartet style, with multipart harmonies and no accompaniment. After the "hallelujahs," the singers hit the verse and repeat it three times: "Walking and talking with my mind set on freedom." Five "hallelujahs," the last particularly drawn out, form the chorus. The segment ends with a jazzy turn as the young singers clap and rhythmically scat "walk, walk," pause, "walk, walk," pause, "walk, walk, with your mind on freedom." As they repeat this phrase, the sound fades down and a man who introduces himself as M. S. Page, executive secretary of the Albany movement, begins to talk in a calm and easy speaking—not preaching—

voice. Performed in a contemporary gospel style, popular even outside of church, "Woke Up This Morning with My Mind Stayed on Freedom," along with the grain of Page's voice, moves the sound and with it the movement back into contemporary and secular life. *Freedom in the Air* suggests that all of these spaces and all of these people, like all of these sounds, make the movement.[23]

On the rest of side A, speaking and singing voices alternate, coming together to convey both the story and the feel of the Albany movement. After Page describes how the movement has drawn everyone in Albany together, the voice of Bernice Johnson (later, after her marriage to Cordell, Bernice Johnson Reagon) moves up in the mix. She is singing the opening line of a new version of an old religious song, "Over My Head," and she uses melisma to draw out this last word before continuing, "I see freedom in the air." After just one line, the documentary pushes her singing into the background while Charles Sherrod describes how people were scared even to talk to them when he and fellow SNCC organizer Cordell Reagon first came to town. Bernice's strong singing of "Over My Head" takes over again, and the phrase here describes the way the singing takes over from Sherrod's voice as well as civil rights organizers' ability to imagine victory. Sound and words together conjure both divine intervention and the power that comes from being able to see as well as hear and feel an alternative reality. Then the documentary cuts back to Sherrod as he describes how he and Reagon went to nightclubs and churches and Sunday schools, anywhere black people gathered: "It took a long time to unenslave their minds. This was the first task." The voices of Sherrod, Albany student activist and later SNCC field secretary Charles Jones, and Page alternate with more singing, this time a small group of students performing "You Better Leave Segregation Alone."

This song in particular embodied the connections between the Caravans and other activists across local movements. Students in Nashville had first adapted Little Willie John's 1959 and 1961 R and B hit "Leave My Kitten Alone" during the sit-in movement there, changing the words and adopting a harmonizing, a cappella style. The song traveled to Jackson when Nashville activists joined the Freedom Rides. From there, former Freedom Riders—including Cordell Reagon—brought it to Albany. Here, the documentary includes the lines "You better leave"—and the students stretch out the last word across multiple beats—"segregation alone. / Because they love segregation like a hound dog loves a bone." As the documentary shifts to Jones speaking, the last line fades out as an echo, "a bone, a bone, a bone."

Jones and Page continue describing the development of the Albany movement in late 1961 as Albany State students are expelled from school and peaceful protesters try to integrate the segregated facilities at the bus station and elsewhere. The documentary incorporates excerpts of students singing "No segregation / no segregation / no segregation over me. / Before I'll be a slave / I'll be buried in my grave." Then Page, in his measured, smooth voice, describes the city as a police state: "They have dogs, big ones too, they have thugs, big ones of those too. And the whole system is predicated on one thing, keep the black man down." Then the old long-meter hymn comes back in and continues as Sherrod explains how the movement is so large now that participants hang onto the balconies and out of the windows, overflowing the two big churches used for mass meetings.

The rest of side A is the sermon version of a freedom song. Here, the Reverend Gay adapts the traditional African American sermon "The Eagle Stirreth Her Nest" to a new message. Eagles, as this story goes, build their nests out of thorns, woven with straw. When it is time for the young eagles to leave home, the mother eagle pulls the thorns into the inside of the nest and makes it uncomfortable for them to stay. "Somebody came and turned thorns up in this mess of segregation in which we've been living," Gay shouts, "stirring up the Negroes of Albany." Like those baby eagles, Albany blacks need to leave the nest, leave segregation and whatever small comforts they might have known in this world behind, and move into the world of freedom. After Gay finishes this story, he returns directly to the movement. "God," he insists in his loud and straining voice, "is using the Negro to save this nation." The United States cannot lead the world filled with people of color, and "the people of the world are asking, 'What about the Negroes of Albany? If you can't give them their rights, you cannot speak to us.'" Gay's segment ends with his urging listeners to continue boycotting downtown merchants. Side A ends with students singing more of "Woke Up This Morning with My Mind Set on Freedom," this time with foot stomping as the "walk, walk" part repeats and fades out.

In *Freedom in the Air*, the different styles of music serve as a metaphor for the different generations and classes of African Americans in the Albany movement. Older, more rural, and often more working-class participants in the mass meetings perform the old long-meter hymns. Many participants of all ages sing hymns and spirituals adapted for the movement in a more contemporary, black church style. Young people incorporate gospel, R and B, and jazz influences into their revisions of older songs and recent hits. *Freedom in the Air* edits all these different singing styles into one story. In interview segments included in *Freedom in the Air*, the older activist Page and the younger activists Sherrod and Charles Jones describe how participation in the movement works in the same way, creating unity across generational and class lines. "Doctors and lawyers and teachers and domestics walked together to jail and got to know each other in the cells as they sat with each other and felt, breathed, and slept . . . their own desires to be free," Jones says. "But more than that, they got to know each other as people, not as classes. . . . And in the cells that housed some seven hundred of Albany citizens grew a bond of togetherness that has characterized Albany more than anything else." The audio documentary describes, as the liner notes say, the way SNCC workers "use their previous experience, energy, and enthusiasm to help Negro communities give form and expression to their discontent." It also is a form of that work. It is an artifact that produces that form and expression.

As Fiske University sociologist Lewis W. Jones writes in a section of the liner notes titled "About This Record and Its Documentors," "No place else can so finely focused insight into the cultural basis of the movement to desegregate the South be found. Anyone who listens to this recording will have the tones and quality of feeling in his ears when he reads a news story or studies one of the volumes written about the struggle." Structure, sound, and content all work together. *Freedom in the Air* enacts through its form what people in Albany enact through their singing, praying, and protesting. Even the title of the documentary—also the title of a freedom song—works on multiple levels. Freedom in the air is God; it is the world the protesters are trying to achieve, and it is the music.[24]

BIRMINGHAM

A little more than a year after their trip to Albany, the Reverend Charles Billips invited Guy and Candie Carawan to Birmingham, Alabama, to sing with the congregation at his New Pilgrim Baptist Church and record the mass meetings there. Representatives of the SCLC were in Birmingham to bolster the local organization, the Alabama Christian movement, led by Fred Shuttlesworth, in its ongoing protest campaign. Part of a group of reinforcements, the Carawans arrived on 5 May 1963 with SNCC executive secretary James Forman, SNCC mentor Ella Baker, the comedian and civil rights supporter Dick Gregory, and the singer Joan Baez. Two days earlier, Bull Connor had used police dogs and high-pressure water cannons on demonstrators. As the Carawans wrote in the liner notes, when they tried to enter Billips's church, Sheriff Connor arrested them. Billips led his congre-

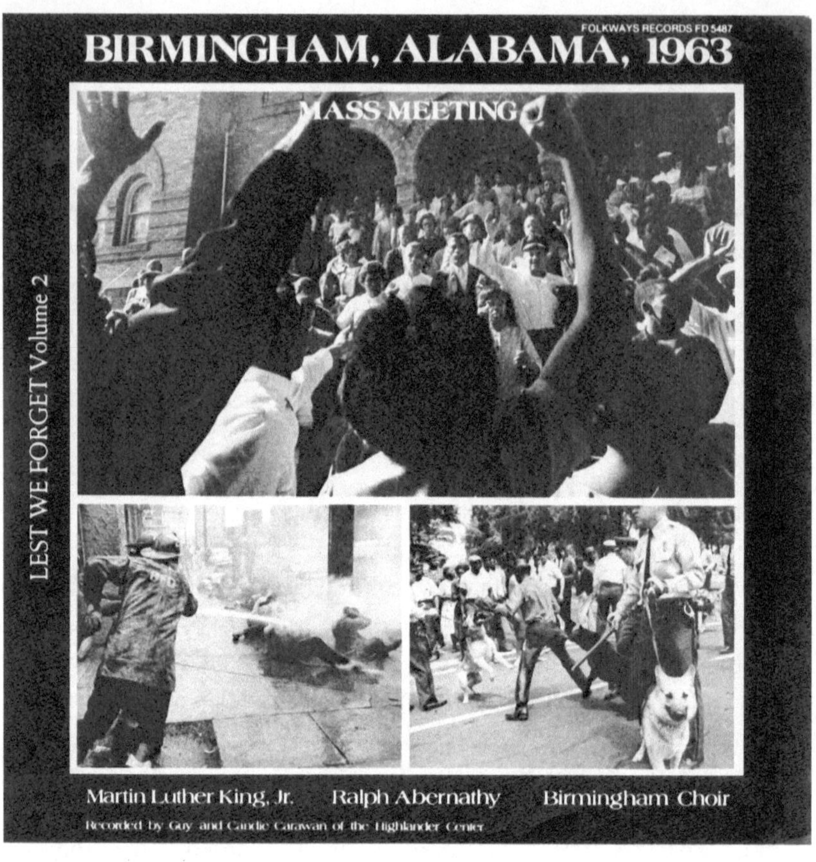

FIGURE 5.2 Documentary album *Birmingham, Alabama, 1963: Mass Meeting*, recorded by Guy and Candy Carawan, released by Folkways Records in 1980 as volume 2 of *Lest We Forget*. Author photo. By permission of Smithsonian Folkways Records, Smithsonian Institution.

gation out in spontaneous protest. Prevented from proceeding a few blocks to the jail, the by-then crowd of about two thousand people kneeled in the street in prayer while Billips shouted at Connor, "Turn on your water! Turn loose your dogs! We'll stand here 'til we die!" Despite Connor's orders, the firemen hesitated, refusing to turn the hoses on people praying. The police and firemen instead let the marchers walk to a nearby park to pray.[25]

Released from jail the next day, the Carawans grabbed their Ampex and their only microphone, checked on their one-year-old son, and rushed to the church just in time to record that evening's civil rights meeting. *Birmingham, Alabama, 1963: Mass Meeting* documented the Birmingham movement in the midst of the confrontation (fig. 5.2). It records the choir singing and at times the congregation joining in. It documents SCLC leaders Martin Luther King Jr. and Ralph Abernathy speaking. It also captures the feel of the room, the mood in the air there in the sanctuary, and the use of humor and of song to break the tension and the fear.[26]

Ralph Abernathy, for example, is alternately serious and funny, lyrical and blunt. He starts by reminding the crowd that "we stand today on the threshold of freedom" and that "if the Negro is to be free, he must free himself." Then he describes recent events, including the success of the march on 5 May. "They have those same dogs. They still have the water hoses and the water but they didn't use it. We have already won a victory here in Birmingham. And all we have to do is keep marching." The recording conveys the sound of the crowd clapping and shouting, the response growing every time Abernathy pauses in his description of how they have filled the jail and the jail yard. He continues, "And on the morrow when they look up and see that number coming, I don't know what they are going to do!" Members of the congregation break into laughter and shouting. Together, they feel their victory and their strength.

Birmingham, Alabama, 1963: Mass Meeting also records the singing. After a traditional performance of "Swing Low, Sweet Chariot," for example, song leader Cleo Kennedy leads the church choir straight into a variation that builds in force and volume and transforms the spiritual into a powerful gospel song about activism. "Why don't you swing down, sweet chariot, stop and let me ride," the singers sing and repeat and circle back. Sometimes several voices just chant "swing, swing." The lyrics ring out with action phrases—"you may ride" and "you may fly"—that reverberate through the sanctuary. God is on their side in this place and is going to let them ride. As the song continues, congregation members join in on the repeated lines, and the chorus of "let me ride" echoes loudly. The sound of singing, even more than Abernathy's words, makes the collective strength of the participants, together in this place built of sound and in this church, palpable and present. Like *Freedom in the Air*, the *Birmingham, Alabama, 1963* recording documents this collective embodiment, the intensity and the solidarity and the courage, the emotions that make the movement run. It conveys the experiences of participants, what it feels like to be inside of the movement. A rare intimacy is on offer here. Listeners can share the crackle of anger that African Americans risked their lives to express in other venues. They can feel the humor and bravado participants express to hide their barely checked fears. They can hear the way the rising volume of group singing provides sonic evidence of the way courage can grow in a community. *Birmingham, Alabama, 1963* is documentary as activism—a representation of people actually talking to their political representatives rather than asking the documentary audience to write for them. This, it suggests, is what political and social equality sounds like. Unlike *Freedom in the Air*, however, *Birmingham, Alabama, 1963* could not also participate in the larger movement for civil rights at the time because it was not released as an album until 1980.[27]

Guy and Candie Carawan helped create new documentary practices that spread throughout the New Left and beyond in the late 1960s and 1970s—a participatory praxis that worked to embody as well as to present a new reality. Participatory documentary thrived in the 1970s and early 1980s, as federal agencies like the NEA and NEH, state humanities councils and nonprofits, universities, and foundations funded documentary practices. Documentary makers, working in collaboration with communities from Mississippi delta and Appalachian settlements to Alaskan Native villages and Lower East Side Puerto Rican neighborhoods, produced hundreds of now mostly forgotten documentaries as part of an explosion of community-based media making. Unlike during the New Deal period, an earlier era of widespread, public documentary making, no central repository in the 1970s collected and archived this work. The particular stories documented and the way new collaborative forms shaped how the people who made or saw or heard these documentaries thought about history have mostly been lost. At stake is any historically grounded understanding of today's participatory media.

A practice based on the tension between the subjective and objective, uninterested in neutrality, and intent on trying to convey its subjects' experience was inherently political and, from a contemporary perspective, often radical. Participatory documentary offered a different emotional model from the one built into earlier documentary forms. While liberal documentary worked to produce an emotional experience in the viewer, participatory documentary tried to communicate the experience of the documentary subjects, the participants. Participation—in protests, in any other aspect of a movement, in making a documentary, and in the act of listening to or watching a documentary—linked individuals and their experiences into a collective subjective. In the Carawans' civil rights audio documentaries, finding a voice became the key act in the collective work of building the new world in which everyone could be a citizen.[28]

NOTES

1. *Freedom in the Air: A Documentary on Albany, Georgia, 1961–1962* (Student Non-Violent Coordinating Committee, SNCC-101), produced by Guy Carawan and Alan Lomax, manufactured by Vanguard Records. This is also the source of quotes in the next two paragraphs. I bought my copy on eBay, but the documentary is archived as FT 9649 and FT 9650, Carawan Collection. For information about this recording, see Freedom Singers file, folder 10, box 130, Student Nonviolent Coordinating Committee Papers (hereafter SNCC Papers); and box 10, folder 814; box 12, folder 134; and box 8, folder 85, in the Guy and Candie Carawan Collection #20008 (hereafter Carawan Collection). On call-and-response, see Floyd, *Power of Black Music*.

2. Guy Carawan, "Albany Voices: Old and New," notes for unreleased Folkways album, box 12, folder 134, Carawan Collection. On the Albany Movement, see C. Carson, *In Struggle*; Formwalt, *Looking Back, Moving Forward*; "Documents from the Albany & Southwest Georgia Movements"; "Albany Movement"; and Formwalt, "Albany Movement."

3. Branch, *Parting the Waters*; *Pillar of Fire*; C. Carson, *In Struggle*; Hogan, *Many Minds, One Heart*; Arsenault, *Freedom Riders*; Payne, *I've Got the Light of Freedom*; Hall, "Long Civil Rights Movement and the Political Uses of the Past"; and Cha-Jua and Lang, "'Long Movement' as Vampire."

4. On journalists and the civil rights movement in the South, see *Reporting Civil Rights: Part One* and *Reporting Civil Rights: Part Two*; M. Berger, *Seeing through Race*; Bodroghkozy, *Equal Time*; and Torres, *Black, White, and in Color*. On staging the "live" event, see Cook, *National Guard Confronting Demonstrators*, a photograph of protests in Cambridge that shows SNCC photographer Danny Lyon taking a photograph in Cambridge, Md.; and Lyon, *Memories of the Southern Civil Rights Movement*, 139.

5. Breines, *Community and Organization in the New Left*.

6. Rosler, "In, around and Afterthoughts," reprinted in *Decoys and Disruptions*.

7. On documentary work during the 1930s and 1940s, see Stott, *Documentary Expression and Thirties America*; Pells, *Radical Visions and American Dreams*; and Kahana, *Intelligence Work*. On the folk music revival, see Robert Cantwell, *When We Were Good*; and Hale, *Nation of Outsiders*.

8. Rosler, "In, around and Afterthoughts," reprinted in *Decoys and Disruptions*.

9. The documentary materials produced within the movement have all too often been used by scholars as transparent illustrations "of what actually happened" rather than as consciously created tools of political struggle. The essential exception is Raiford's *"Imprisoned in a Luminous Glare."* On African Americans as subjects/citizens, see Rankine, *Citizen*. Scholars have also barely studied the use of documentary practices by the segregationist opposition and government officials at the local, state, and federal levels. For one statewide documentary effort, see the Mississippi Sovereignty Commission papers, http://mdah.state.ms.us/arrec/digital_archives/sovcom/, accessed 15 October 2015.

10. "Go Tell It on the Mountain: Recording the Movement," unpublished writings, box 8, folder 85, Carawan Collection.

11. Candie Carawan's letter to her parents is quoted in ibid. *Freedom in the Air: A Documentary on Albany, Georgia, 1961–1962* is hard to find because unlike most civil rights documentary albums, it was not released by Folkways Records. Folkways is now

Smithsonian Folkways, and most of the catalog can be purchased and downloaded online, including the liner notes.

12. On John Lomax and Alan Lomax's collecting work, see the Lomax Family Collections at the American Folklife Center, Library of Congress.

13. Goldsmith, *Making People's Music*; Olmstead, *Folkways Records*.

14. Evans, "Black Folk Music," reviews both *Freedom in the Air* and *The Story of Greenwood, Mississippi*. Guy Carawan, La Jolla, Calif., to Jim Forman, Atlanta, 15 May 1962; and Jim Forman, [Atlanta], to Carawan, La Jolla, in Carawan, [November 1962], box 70, folder 4, SNCC Papers. See also sales figures in Vanguard Records File, reel 10, Student Nonviolent Coordinating Committee Microform Edition, Ann Arbor, UM-I, 1994.

15. Unpublished writings, "Chapter 2: The Civil Rights Years," no page numbers, includes a copy of a letter from Myles Horton, Highlander School, [Monteagle,] Tenn., to "Friends of Highlander" introducing Carawan, August 1959, and a copy of a letter from Guy Carawan to "Friends of Highlander," box 10, folder 103, Carawan Collection.

16. "Excerpt of a Letter from Alan Lomax to Guy Carawan in April of 1960," published in the liner notes for *Freedom in the Air: A Documentary on Albany, Georgia, 1961–1962*.

17. Kelley, *Race Rebels*; Miller, *Segregating Sound*; Deleuze and Guattari, *Thousand Plateaus*; Kun, *Audiotopia*; Shank, *Political Force of Musical Beauty*; and Johnson, *Spaces of Conflict*. On the reception of Nat King Cole in the South, see Thompson, "Nat 'King' Cole's Civil War."

18. *The Nashville Sit-In Story* (Folkways FH 5590, 1960), conceived, coordinated, and directed by Guy Carawan; Guy and Candie Carawan, "Chapter 2: The Civil Rights Years," part of unpublished manuscript, box 10, folder 103; Guy Carawan and Candie Carawan, "'This Little Light of Mine, I'm Gonna Let It Shine': The First Sing For Freedom," unpublished writing, box 8, folder 85; and Candie Carawan, résumé, box 10, folder 102, all in Carawan Collection. James Bevel's interview for the *Eyes on the Prize* documentary series is available at http://digital.wustl.edu/cgi/t/text/text-idx?c=eop;cc=eop;rgn=main;view=text;idno=bev0015.0491.010; Diane Nash's interview for *Eyes on the Prize* is available at http://digital.wustl.edu/cgi/t/text/text-idx?c=eop;cc=eop;rgn=main;view=text;idno=nas0015.0267.075.

19. *We Shall Overcome*. I found their marriage license in "California Marriage Index, 1960–1985," at FamilySearch, https://familysearch.org/ark:/61903/1:1:V6NB-MKM, accessed 28 August 2015. Guy H. Carawan and Carolann M. Anderson were married on 17 March 1961. See unpublished autobiographical writings and other materials in box 8, folder 85, and box 10, folder 103, Carawan Collection.

20. Guy Carawan and Candie Carawan, "Chapter 2: The Civil Rights Years," box 10, folder 103, Carawan Collection.

21. Carawan to Jim Forman, 15 May 1962, quote. See also Forman's reply, Forman to Carawan, [November 1962], in Carawan, box 70, folder 4, SNCC Papers. SNCC membership is a fluid term across this period. Field secretaries earned little and were frequently not paid. Local volunteers were also considered in many cases staff. Attendance at SNCC conferences also swelled after Freedom Summer. See Forman, *Making of Black Revolutionaries*.

22. *Freedom in the Air: A Documentary on Albany, Georgia, 1961–1962* (see also quotes in the next few paragraphs); Carawan notes labeled "Voices—Old and Young—Albany,

Georgia," box 12, folder 134, Carawan Collection. On lined-out, long-meter hymn singing as practiced by African Americans, see "Dr. Watts Singers," Mississippi Folklife Folk Artist Directory, http://www.arts.state.ms.us/folklife/artist.php?dirname=watts_doctor, accessed 15 October 2015.

23. Carawan notes labeled "Voices—Old and Young—Albany, Georgia," box 12, folder 134, Carawan Collection.

24. Jones, "About This Record and Its Documentors."

25. For interviews of participants in the Birmingham movement and historical documents, see http://www.crmvet.org/tim/timhis63.htm#1963bham, accessed 15 August 2015.

26. *Birmingham, Alabama, 1963: Mass Meeting*, released on Folkways Records, FD 5487 (see also the quotes in the next few paragraphs).

27. On the circulation of these recordings, see the clipping of a review in the *Reporter* (7 December 1963) and SNCC News Release, box 130, folder 10, SNCC Papers. See also Vanguard Records file, reel 10, Student Nonviolent Coordinating Committee Microform Edition, Ann Arbor, UM-I, 1994.

28. Today, what we might call neoliberal documentaries emphasize the emotional experience of the documentary maker.

After the Fact

Postwar Dissent and the Art of Documentary

SARA BLAIR

Accounting for the career of postwar photography, received histories have emphasized a decisive turn against documentary image-making. In the two decades following World War II, they agree, photo practitioners made a critical break with documentary practice, leaving behind what came to be seen as its "often naïve—or at least oversimplified—belief in the medium as an instrument for social change."[1] Skeptical about explicit claims or presumptions of transparency, authenticity, and objectivity that buttressed earlier documentary interventions, practitioners are said to have turned inward, redirecting documentary aesthetics and techniques toward more subjective aims.[2]

This canonical view has descriptive power, but it has occluded the social conditions that transformed possibilities for documentary's postwar social engagements.[3] Beginning in 1947, with the publication of the first Attorney General's List of Subversive Organizations—naming, among such leftist stalwarts as the Communist Party and the Abraham Lincoln Brigade, the New York Photo League, then the most robust center for documentary photo production in the United States—documentary makers confronted radically new conditions for their work.[4] In the context of emerging Cold War politics, the defining concerns of New Deal–era documentary practice—poverty, workers' rights, housing conditions, the experience of socially marginal Americans, and social inequality—became categorical grounds for state suspicion. Targeted for real or imagined connection of their ongoing commitments to institutions held suspect by the attorney general, Cold Warriors, and the House Un-American Activities Committee (HUAC), documentarians of the late 1940s and 1950s had strong motivation to adopt "increasingly personal and . . . progressively private" modes of practice.[5] Subjected to red-baiting, loyalty tests, and blacklisting, they found themselves confronting the foreclosure of opportunities for work and publication.[6] As one historian of the era notes, "the documentary gaze" itself "had come to be suspected of being un-American," and "its repression was relentless."[7]

Redirection of documentary practice toward the expression of "personal alienation"—a mode that more readily conformed to the approved Cold War ideology of liberal individualism—helped provide cover for image makers.[8] Over time, it also enabled a triumphalist reading of the longer postwar evolution of photographic practice. With the landmark exhibition *New Documents* at New York's Museum of Modern Art in 1967, curator John Szarkowski set the terms for the critical framing of postwar photography's decisive break with documentary practice. A new, postwar generation of photographers, he argued, "has directed the documentary approach toward more personal ends. Their aim has been not to reform life, but to know it, not to persuade but to understand."[9] What characterizes this "new document" in Szarkowski's view is "the belief that the world is worth looking at" just as it stands—and the photographer's "courage to look at it without theorizing" (in other words, without thinking in collectivist, systemic, or overtly social terms).[10] Under the sign of the snapshot, with its cool, arch, and wayward vibe, form and formalism trump social engagement; authenticity and photographic agency alike are conditioned on the achievement of unconventional, even illegible, aesthetic effects. Widely hailed as a landmark for twentieth-century photography, *New Documents* revalued photography as fine art by suppressing the formal experimentation of socially conscious documentary work and by insisting on a self-conscious, irreversible break with its transformational aims.[11] R.I.P. documentary; long live the politically distanced, aesthetically challenging New Document.

This framing of a postwar subjective turn has been highly influential—and, in an important way, misleading. Far from vanishing, documentary histories and commitments had a powerful afterlife in postwar photographic practice, particularly in the era of rising protest and dissent against the failures of the postwar corporatized, military-industrial state. By the late 1960s, at the moment of Szarkowski's throw-down, photographers working within the very art institutions whose influence his practice extended were returning with new interest to models of socially conscious practice. After the fact, we might say, critical aesthetic experiments with the documentary legacy constituted an important effort to reanimate an ethos of social engagement on new and more self-conscious terms—not least by revisiting the agency of documentary itself. Focusing on projects by Richard Avedon and Martha Rosler, I argue after Jonathan Kahana and Noah Tsika in this volume for a history of buried antecedents in documentary image-making, whose importance both to postwar U.S. histories of photography and to a tradition of critical thinking about the aesthetics of social transformation has been obscured. Read in tandem, Avedon's and Rosler's work exemplifies a postwar trajectory of politically engaged photography that grounds its agency not in state-dominated or instrumental action but in critical reflection. It also makes clear that the turn to interiority said to characterize postwar photography is party to a complex negotiation of the legacies of documentation, one that continues to be informed by earlier practice as it seeks not to move beyond social engagement but to reanimate it on new grounds.

Richard Avedon (1923–2004), storied fashion photographer and portraitist, is hardly an obvious exemplar of the career of post-1945 documentary. At a critical moment in postwar culture and in his own practice, however, Avedon's work explored generative questions about the work of documenting contemporary social reality, about the cultural uses of objectivity, and about the distinctive power of the photograph as a technique for making visible the most stubbornly evasive aspect of historical experience (and, in the postwar context, of documentary engagement itself): power and its exercise. Departing sharply from his more familiar achievements, his work from 1969 to 1971 focused closely and rigorously on political dissent, New Left activism, and antiwar protest. Indebted as it was in prosecution to Avedon's institutional affiliations and celebrity—he himself noted that his commercial practice "made it possible for me to be my own Ford Foundation, my own Guggenheim"—this body of work was also a pointed testing and redirection of the legacies of documentary imaging.[12] Attention to its methods clarifies the reach of documentary's postwar afterlives and antecedents in the context of urgent dissent and widening social injury.

From the outset, Avedon's practice took shape in response to shifting postwar documentary and photojournalistic modes. He began his career during World War II in the U.S. Merchant Marine, as a service photographer assigned to make ID photos, and went on to produce dynamic fashion work that was inseparable from his interest in reportage and street imaging. Notably, one of Avedon's first forays into exhibition was his contribution to the 1948 show *This Is the Photo League*, mounted by that group in an (unsuccessful) effort to combat blacklisting and charges of subversion.[13] Photographs documenting the street life of a postwar Rome recovering from fascism became literally central to Avedon's first photo-text, the landmark volume *Observations* (1959).[14] Likewise, his harrowing documentation of the lives of mentally ill patients in a state institution in Jackson, Louisiana, anchored the civil rights–focused volume he produced with writer-activist James Baldwin, *Nothing Personal* (1964). Much earlier, in 1949, Avedon's street-inflected fashion work had led *Life* magazine to offer him an opportunity to create an entire issue of the journal documenting "Avedon's New York."[15] Although he ultimately aborted the assignment, the images he shot for the project in such familiar sites of socially conscious encounter as Harlem and the Lower East Side suggest an urge to rethink the historical premises of documentary imaging—in particular, its disciplinary interest in what Avedon called "the man on the street"—to redirect the possibilities for camera work as a mode of social engagement.[16] Along these lines, Avedon gave the photo-text accompanying the Whitney Museum of American Art's 1994 retrospective of his half-century-long career the suggestive title *Evidence*.

But if the mode of documentary and a strain of self-reflexivity about its histories remain "constant" in Avedon's work from the inception of the postwar era, both take on new life at the critical juncture of 1969.[17] By his own account, vitriolic response to the social commentary of *Nothing Personal*, with its confrontational images of white supremacists and civil rights activists alike, had left him "blank," unable to make "meaningful" portrait work—an index to Avedon's foundational interest in the portrait as a mode of transformative social knowledge.[18] In the summer of 1969, however, Avedon began working on a new portrait project, titled "Hard Times," to engage with key figures of antiwar, Black Power, feminist, and other radical dissent from America's policies at home and abroad, and within the New Left itself.[19] In collaboration with writer Doon Arbus (the daughter of photographer Diane Arbus), Avedon planned a photo-text book that would "respond to the demands of the time" and make visible "how people survive and what they consider important . . . right now."[20] In this context, Avedon's method took new shape. Putting aside his signature camera—the handheld Rolleiflex, with its distinctive square format—he found new use for a very different one. Taking up his 8-by-10-inch large-format Deardorff, the archetype of earlier site-based documentation, he transformed it as an instrument for enhancing interaction between photographer and subject. Committing to what he called "that ancient camera," he elided its links with the project of Walker Evans, who made his iconic images of Depression-era dispossession, including his photographs of Alabama tenant farm families, with a Deardorff loaned by the Farm Security Administration.[21] Instead, Avedon foregrounded a lineage that historically began with Mathew Brady, whose documentation of the ravages of Civil War battlefields informs the social aims of "Hard Times" just as Brady's landmark studio portraiture did its formalism.

Critics have noted that the pursuit of "Hard Times" generated Avedon's signature style: off-center framing; cropping and fragmentation of subjects' bodies; an unrelieved white background with which all traces of context and extenuating detail are erased. These signal aesthetic choices shaped and were shaped by Avedon's aim of finding a way to confront the defining reality of the era: the individual and collective struggle for social transformation. One of his first "Hard Times" subjects, civil rights attorney and activist Florynce Kennedy, whose image he made on 1 August 1969, gave Arbus an interview to accompany her portrait that reflects on the power of Avedon's camera and the uses to which he now sought to put it. Kennedy notes: "I use the law as a hustle and then I confront society in the way that it dreads most, which is to expose its phony hypocrisy. . . . Those of us who are unimaginative, unskilled, untutored must do such routine things as putting our lives on the line."[22]

Beyond his singular use of a dynamics of confrontation via the portrait form, Avedon would echo Kennedy's language nearly word for word in describing the subjects of the most ambitious early session of "Hard Times," the Chicago Conspirators. That notorious group—including Youth International Party (Yippie) cofounders Abbie Hoffman and Jerry Rubin, Students for a Democratic Society leader and author of the Port Huron Statement Tom Hayden, and Black Panther Party cofounder Bobby Seale—had been charged with conspiring to cross state lines to incite riots at the 1968 Democratic National Convention. In late September 1969, Avedon and Arbus attended the opening week of the trial, using a room at the Chicago Hilton (latterly the convention hotel) as a makeshift studio for portrait sessions with the defendants, their attorneys, and other movement figures. In a radio interview of July 1970 describing the critical importance of these sessions to his broader interest in documentation of the moment, Avedon asserted, "I consider the seven defendants to be heroic men in that they're doing for all of us what we should be doing. Or should have done a long time ago. . . . These men are putting their lives on the line."[23]

Avedon's much-remarked innovations in group portraiture, coalescing with his work around the trial, turned in a specific sense on visualizing this claim.[24] He and Arbus were present in the courtroom in Chicago on 5 November 1969 when presiding judge Julius Hoffman—who had earlier ordered that Seale be gagged and manacled to his chair for his appearances in court—severed Seale's trial from that of his codefendants, henceforth known as the Chicago Seven.[25] That day, Avedon and Arbus invited them to a group portrait session that resulted in a landmark document. Arranging his subjects linearly against the distinctive white background, compressing them tightly within the pictorial space—note the gap on the far right, intended to mark the absence of Seale—Avedon shot three carefully sequenced images for a triptych portrait that self-consciously invoked the genre of the police lineup (fig. 6.1). (Reflecting what Allan Sekula has identified as the "double system" of photographic portraiture, which simultaneously produces both power and deviance, Avedon would tell a reporter in 1970 that he "used to go down to the post office and look at the 'Wanted' pictures because that's where it's at.")[26] Putting the defendants on this line, literally framing them as fractured, riven, disjointed, Avedon turns the question of complicity back on the trial itself—and more broadly on the very constructions of law and order, democratic process and the failures of democracy, that the photograph's viewers were actively making in their everyday lives. To the extent that the seven had been, as Paul Roth argues, transformed by the charges against them into heroic agitators, exemplars of "an insurrectionary conspiracy," they became "symbolic" of the emerging "relationship between the Vietnam-era state and its citizens."[27] Alone together in the image, pressing against one another and the boundaries of the frame, they also press on the viewer the question of what it means, as Avedon put it, to "wor[k] toward a common goal . . . to make the country America."[28]

The Chicago Seven image is exemplary of the achievement of "Hard Times" as curator Jane Livingston describes it: invention of "the group portrait as photo-reportage," a mode unprecedented in the history of photography.[29] However unlikely the formal genre of portraiture as a means of engaging social urgencies, Avedon was particularly interested in using it to reactivate a self-reflexive strain of earlier twentieth-century documentary practice. In conception, execution, and dissemination, the work of "Hard Times" was deliberately photo-textual—"a way," Arbus put it, "of representing the people, and their passions, and their causes, with words and pictures."[30] She conducted her interviews with portrait subjects in Avedon's studio, typically during the shooting sessions themselves, thereby pressing the question of an appropriate relationship between voice and embodiment, words and image. Some critics have speculated that key photo-texts of the New Deal era—for example, Dorothea Lange and Paul Taylor's *An American Exodus*, which published interview excerpts alongside photos—

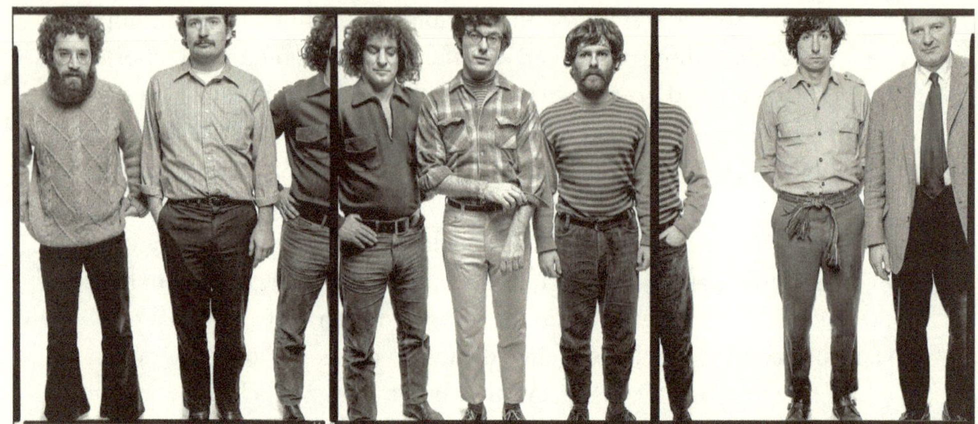

FIGURE 6.1 Richard Avedon, *The Chicago Seven*: Lee Weiner, academic radical; John Froines, academic radical; Abbie Hoffman, Yippie; Rennie Davis, revolutionary; Jerry Rubin, Yippie; Tom Hayden, revolutionary; Dave Dellinger, pacifist, Chicago, 5 November 1969.

may have influenced the approach of "Hard Times." If anything, however, its dialogical thrust suggests how strenuously Avedon and Arbus worked to revalue photo-text synergy and friction to address the context of New Left dialogue and dissent. For Avedon, the resulting document in the form of a photo-text book was revelatory in this way. Producing and encountering it was, he noted, "like discovering a new form."[31]

Moreover, "Hard Times" was predicated from the outset on exploiting the tension between a still-lingering presumption of the evidentiary value of the photograph (particularly the photographic portrait) and the awkwardness and uncertainty of experiential narrative. Arbus wrote up the interviews as first-person stream-of-consciousness rife with ellipses and complex associative logic. Abbie Hoffman's text, paired with a solo portrait in which Hoffman holds a rifle and gives viewers the finger, "FUCK" emblazoned on his forehead, opens this way: "Living in America I expect to get killed. I mean, . . . I've been active for a long time. I've seen Mississippi and I've seen the rest of the country turn into Mississippi. So going to jail or dying or any of those things . . . I don't know . . . what's the difference? Both times you're like—you're removed from, uh . . . the streets. From what you feel you have to do. . . . Dying is . . . I don't know. It makes a better movie but . . . what's the difference? [ellipses original]."[32]

Some thirty years later, a *New York Times* reviewer opined that the project's interviews were "hilariously disjointed."[33] In the moment of their production, that disjunction was both found and purposive, documented and formalized. It communicates not only painful intensity but also an epic struggle to order the ongoing experience of social injury, personal and collective. Throughout, the intensely subjectivist cast of the interviews makes the project not less but more convincingly documentary—that is, more sharply reflective of the real impact of inequality, failed social promises, and the disturbing powers of the state. Set against and alongside one another, Avedon's images and Arbus's interviews stake a claim for the necessity of a more subjective, self-reflexive mode of documentation appropriate to the moment of "Hard Times."

At the same time, however, the project continues to mobilize the effects of conventional documentary objectivity. The latter is activated by Avedon's signature use of the visible marks of the Deardorff's plate-holder; in his portrait images, it appears as a hard black edge—dramatic and Brechtian in effect, "proof" against darkroom manipulation. Likewise, in the eventual publication of much of the photo-reportage of "Hard Times" in the volume

The Sixties (1999), Arbus and Avedon chose to mimic the material form of her interview archive, replicating in the text the Courier font of Arbus's typewritten interview drafts. Commissioned by IBM in 1955, quickly setting an industry standard, Courier had powerful associations with documentational practice, including journalism and governmental communications. (Among other things, it remained the default typeface of the U.S. State Department until 2004.)[34] Linking the work of "Hard Times" with the practices of to-the-moment reportage, Avedon and Arbus offer it, in and after the fact, as a series of dispatches from the front lines of the movement.

That framing after the fact reflected the actual conduct of the project's climactic work, a series of portraits Avedon shot in Vietnam during April 1971 near the shifting front lines of the unraveling U.S. military engagement. It was by any measure a fraught moment with respect to the prosecution of the war. Major troop drawdowns were under way. Antiwar activism by citizen groups, including the highly visible Vietnam Veterans against the War, had been intensifying; public support was ebbing. In March, U.S. forces sustained punishing defeat in major engagements near the border of Laos, and President Nixon's policy of "Vietnamization" increasingly appeared to be magical thinking. Stateside, the Capitol building in Washington, D.C., had been damaged the previous month by a bomb for which the radical Weather Underground claimed credit. At the close of the month, Lieutenant William Calley was convicted for the murder of twenty-two civilians during the 1968 My Lai massacre and sentenced to life imprisonment. This was the immediate context in which Avedon sought to extend the project of "Hard Times," working in Saigon and on in-country trips to the Mekong Delta and to various firebases, airbases, and military camps around Phu Bai and Hue, near the DMZ.[35] On the ground in Vietnam, he pressed the uses of portraiture as photo-reportage so as to bring Americans at home face to face with fellow citizens "mak[ing] the country America" through the exercise of power, military service, and dissent alike.

Avedon's method for creating the Vietnam images is worth noting. Arbus stayed behind to manage the New York studio; his two senior assistants, who were guest nationals with U.K. citizenship, were ineligible for State Department travel clearance. In their place Avedon took his technical assistant Larry Hales, a self-described "naïve 23-year-old Midwestern lad" who had just received conscientious objector status from the Selective Service.[36] Avedon's preliminary outreach to intended portrait subjects in-country insisted on his own identity as a political noncombatant. Formal letters of request for sittings declared that "Mr. Avedon . . . has no political views to promote in his work; he is a very special kind of photographer"; "He is an *artist*" (emphasis original).[37] Hales's trials of pacifism and the kind of distance it necessitated are painfully evident in his numerous letters home from Saigon, which express the deep wish "to remove myself far away from this war, the USA, the whole machine," coupled with "a strange responsibility" for observing firsthand; the difficulty of imagining "how I'll go back home" but also "how I'll go forward"; the devastating "blur" of "life and death"; the anguish of not "carry[ing] demons" for the soldiers they encountered.[38] Hales's private writings clarify what a stance of conscientious detachment under such conditions exacted—and what constituted a shooting war, then and there, as a mode of documentary practice.

Whether or not Hales's struggle to achieve a distance shaped by his conscientious objector commitments entered into the project, Avedon's shifting invocations of his own status as artist and of the institutional cover of journalism suggest how deftly he anatomized codes of documentary objectivity. Officially on assignment for *Vogue* to "produce a series of photographs documenting . . . the American Woman Nurse in the hospitals, in the field," and also for *Look* to produce portraits of diplomatic and military leaders, Avedon secured access and considerations from agents for the secretary of defense, the Pentagon, and the State Department.[39] (Among other things, he and Hales received Military Assistance Command press passes awarding them the simulated rank of major, which allowed them to "fly free anywhere in country" in military vehicles "and bump off those with less rank.")[40] In an informal shooting script Avedon wrote for review by the assistant secretary of defense, he noted that his key aim was "to give a sense of the vast number of people involved and to convey the cooperative nature of the effort in which they are engaged."[41] Precise yet anodyne, that description itself provides cover for the work of making visible the full range of actors—military, civilian, bureaucratic, American, Vietnamese, and more—producing war and potential war crimes, disinformation and body counts, a charged network of war powers and of resistance to them.

Avedon's Vietnam venture lasted just over a month. Among his portrait subjects were members of the South Vietnamese underground antiwar movement and their American collaborators, soldiers returning to base "strung out" after patrol in the bush, others posing with Vietnamese sex workers, and victims of the notorious Tiger Cages at Con Son Island prison, in which, in an evolving tradition of outsourced black ops, political prisoners were tortured by South Vietnamese police trained and funded by the United States.[42] In none of these instances was Avedon documenting or exposing conduct unbecoming, atrocities, or casualties in a conventional way. But his commitment to a rigorous, unvarying mode of portrait presentation—suppressing context, evading trauma so as to allow participants to embody it—afforded all his subjects equal agency as figures attesting to those realities.[43] In his growing archive of portraits and in the exhibitions and publications designed to disseminate them, Avedon and his collaborators created contexts and environments in which individuals variously and tragically damaged by the war, including those in uniform, would come "eye to eye" with viewers stateside and with one another.[44] (In this respect, he may have been building on the success of the summer 1970 midcareer survey of his work at the Minneapolis Institute of Arts, which included Avedon's triptych of the Chicago Seven. The show featured "room after room of massive photographs" of movement figures and state actors "who may never have met in life" hung so that they could "look into one another's eyes.")[45] In numerous instances, visual resonances between unlikely pairs of subjects make shockingly visible the state of moral emergency.

A case in point is Avedon's chilling portrait of Lieutenant Joe Hooper—the most decorated American soldier in Vietnam, winner of a Medal of Honor and thirty-six additional commendations for his service during two tours of duty (fig. 6.2).[46] Leaning forward in the frame, his neck and chest weighted with military bling, Hooper flashes a rictus grin, exposing nearly all of his crooked, unusually large teeth. The disturbing effect is intensified by the resonance of Hooper's portrait with another of a select few that Avedon shot, not against his signature white rolls of paper, lugged to Saigon and remote military outposts all the way from New York, but against a gray background, whose "Victorian romanticism" he invoked to heighten affective tension (fig. 6.3).[47] Here, that tension runs unsettlingly high: the unnamed subject is the survivor of a napalm attack. Her rotted teeth, gutted eye, and unadorned black garment offer a chilling afterimage or counterimage to the heroic veteran's military history and self-presentation. Encountered in the sequences Avedon created, one reviewer noted grimly, "The napalm victim's face stops us dead."[48]

The current of exchange Avedon creates between his subjects has its most dramatic effects in the key shoot of his tour in Vietnam, the object of much of his prenegotiation with military officials and journalistic sponsors, and the "principal motivation for his coming": a group portrait of the U.S.

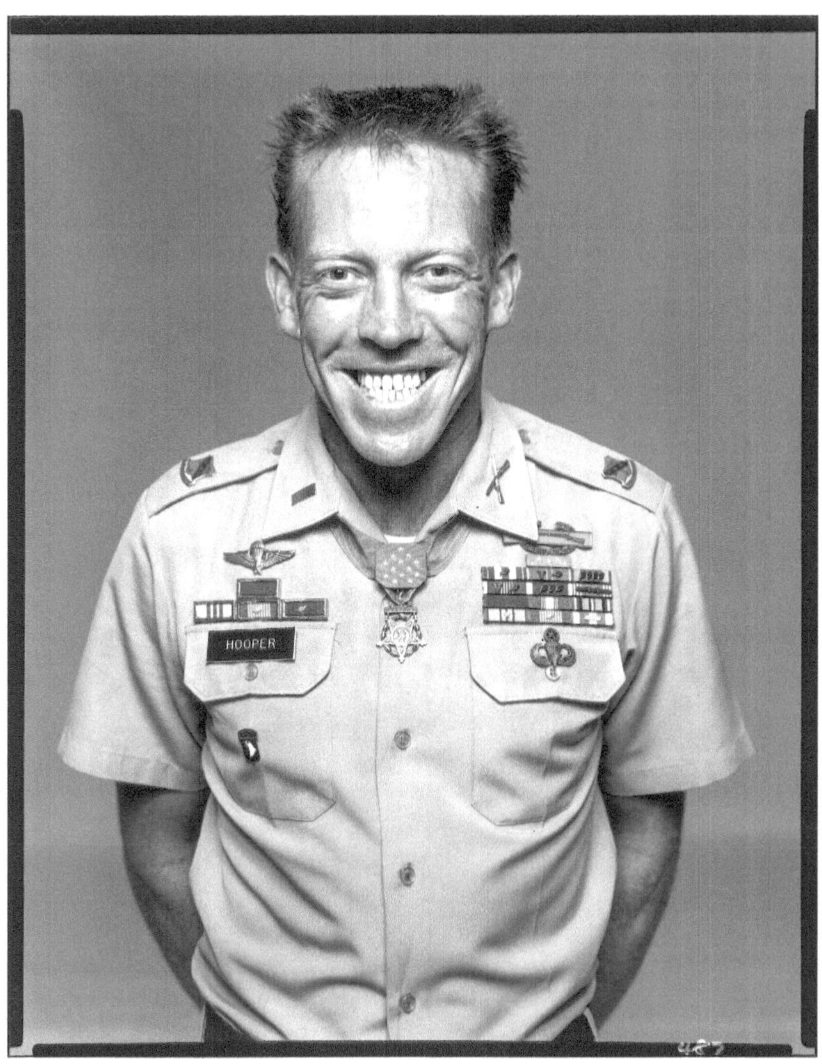

FIGURE 6.2 Richard Avedon, *Lt. Joe Hooper, The Most Decorated Soldier in Vietnam, Saigon, South Vietnam, April 15, 1971*. © The Richard Avedon Foundation.

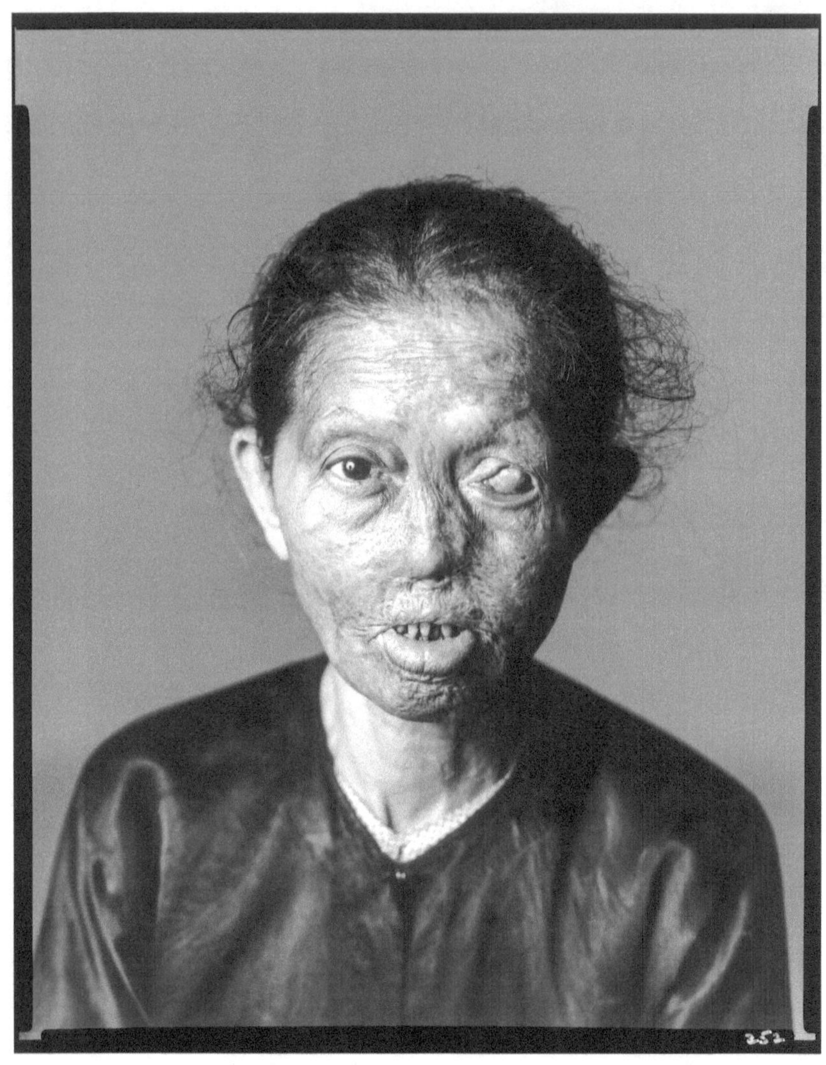

FIGURE 6.3 Richard Avedon, *Napalm Victim, Saigon, South Vietnam, April 29, 1971.* © The Richard Avedon Foundation.

Mission Council (fig. 6.4).[49] A policy advisory led by the U.S. ambassador, the Mission Council included senior civilian and military officials coordinating strategies and relations with the South Vietnamese. The list of their titles reads like a brief for a critique of liberal-managerial state power. In his final portrait session of the trip, Avedon managed to assemble the entire council with the exception of CIA station chief Theodore Shackley (known as the "Blond Ghost," he was notorious both for his skill at covert ops and for his avoidance of cameras) in a secure room in the American embassy in Saigon; General Creighton Abrams arrived by chopper on the roof.[50]

Posing the group in a police lineup as he had the Chicago Seven, Avedon shot a five-part portrait of the men in suits and uniform who were making cold, chemical, and covert warfare in the name of American democracy. Of this remarkable act of photographic capture, Hales wrote (in palpable disbelief), "The war machine's shadow souls are ours (almost)."[51] Facing off within the archive and on display against soldiers under command, victims of U.S.-supported napalm bombings, committed antiwar activists, and survivors of secret interrogations, the members of the Mission Council lining up for their portrait by Avedon make fully visible—as even the most incendiary documentation of damage and atrocity could not—what one observer called "something more insidious than war": the "terrifying picture of business as usual."[52]

New York Times correspondent Gloria Emerson, who accompanied Avedon and Hales on their in-country tours and enabled access to sources throughout the trip, went even further. She noted that the aim of his imaging in "Hard Times" was "to take the romance and the lying out of pictures" altogether.[53] Deploying the portrait form, Avedon turns the lens not just on the face of state power and the victims of its exercise but on the labor and agency of documentation itself. Among his group portraits in-country are a significant number featuring journalists, photojournalists, and bureau chiefs and correspondents—including Emerson herself—associated with outlets ranging from the *Times*, *Newsweek*, *Time*, and the *Washington Post* to *Chin Luan* and the *Village Voice*. Collectively, these portraits read as a who's who of the remarkable on-the-ground reporting from Vietnam.[54] Even as Avedon relied on his fellow observers' experience, contacts, and support—"we will help you *terribly*," Emerson promised in a letter encouraging him to come to Vietnam—he made these agents of an unprecedented shooting war continuous with the public and private subjects of their activity, equally available for examination as producers of "Vietnam" and of a

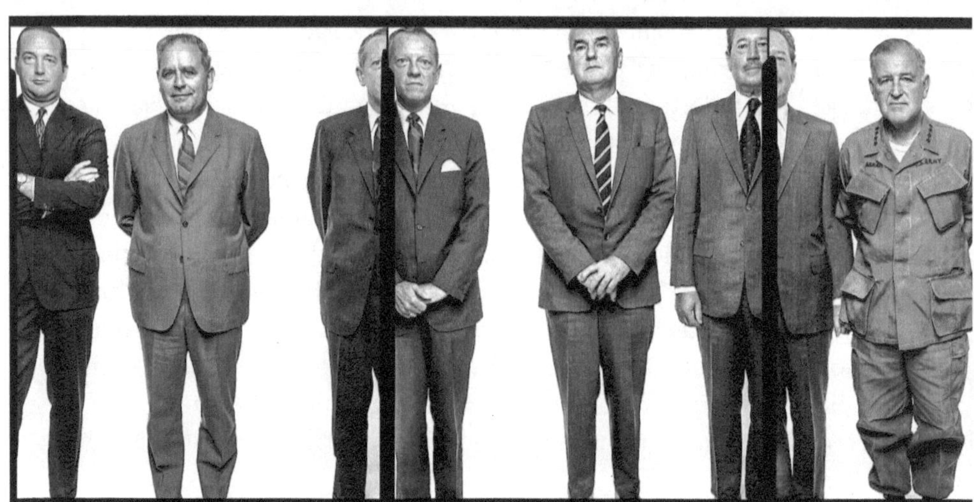

FIGURE 6.4 Richard Avedon, *The Mission Council, Saigon, South Vietnam*: Hawthorne Q. Mills, Mission Coordinator; Ernest J. Colantonio, Counselor of Embassy for Administrative Affairs; Edward J. Nickel, Minister Counselor for Public Affairs; John E. McGowan, Minister Counselor for Press Affairs; George D. Jacobson, Assistant Chief of Staff, Civil Operations and Rural Development Support; General Creighton W. Abrams Jr., Commander, United States Military Assistance Command,

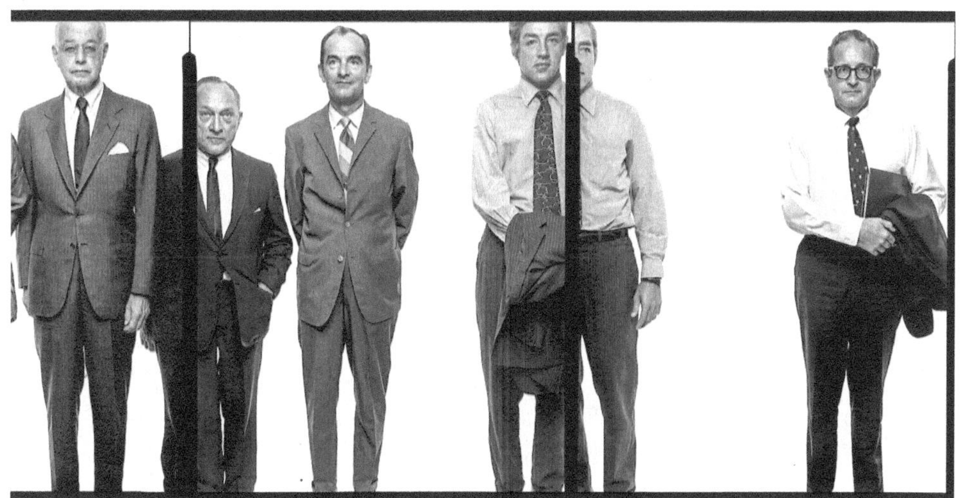

Vietnam; Ambassador Ellsworth Bunker; Deputy Ambassador Samuel D. Berger; John R. Mossler, Minister and Director, United States Agency for International Development; Charles A. Cooper, Minister Counselor for Economic Affairs; and Laurin B. Askew, Counselor of Embassy for Political Affairs, Saigon, South Vietnam, 28 April 1971. © The Richard Avedon Foundation.

will to change state policy, ideological dispositions, and the public mind.[55] For these portraits, Avedon eschewed the police lineup format in favor of more informal, expressionist groupings. The resulting images convey collective activity in which the work of documenting the war in words and pictures is not made heroic but available for understanding as a critical form of practice.

Along these lines, we might consider Emerson's interview, produced in the context of a group portrait of journalists Avedon made in Vietnam for "Hard Times":

> Once I got so desperate—the Americans had started bombing Hanoi—I ran to the National Press Center where they give the briefings . . . a forty-year-old woman running through the streets in the middle of the night . . . and I wrote on the wall in Magic Marker, Father, forgive. They know not what they do. And I don't even believe in God. Who is Father? Father, forgive, they know not what they do. But there were no other words in the whole English language.
>
> If they found out it was me they would have sent me home. New York Times correspondents must not go running around at two o'clock in the morning writing, Father, forgive, they know not what they do. But afterward I thought how there's no way . . . no one, no one to whom you can say we're sorry.[56]

If Emerson's narrative intersects with what we recognize as new journalism—subjective, turned back on the conditions of its own production and of eye-witnessing—it has been invited, or even commanded, by Avedon's portrait work. Enabling her enactment, in word and image, of the lived experience of documenting the war, Avedon succeeds in making visible the networks of complicity and despair, the moral exigencies of documentation, in a profoundly new way. That his practice has been seen as discontinuous with these exigencies—explicated by the institutional logic of the museum and celebrity or the approved role of the artist working from an aesthetic distance—misses the moment of "Hard Times." Avedon's pursuit of dissent as a subject matter and a relation to power, culminating in Vietnam, constitutes a notable experiment in the redirection of documentary and reportage. His project's reanimation of their conventions, and interest in the work and experience of negotiating them, belongs to a more expansive account of the career of documentary practices being revalued in postwar contexts. Avedon's practice also provides a useful vantage point from which to consider more explicit revaluations of documentary and its legacies. To one such producer, whose work has been a landmark in the history of postwar documentary, I now turn.

In the years before the emergence of "Hard Times," as Avedon struggled to reimagine meaningful social uses of the portrait form for a context of radical dissent from imperial war abroad and unequal citizenship at home, artist Martha Rosler had already begun an extended examination of the suppressed links connecting them. Unlike Avedon, Rosler had informal and significant formal training in visual art production—first, in her native Brooklyn, at Brooklyn Museum Art School and Brooklyn College, where she attended the abstract painter Ad Reinhardt's course on East Asian art, and later in the maverick MFA program at the University of California, San Diego, whose distinctive emphasis on the philosophical underpinnings of contemporary art attracted artists like David and Eleanor Antin, John Baldessari, and Allan Sekula and put her in the orbit of theorists Fredric Jameson, Jean-François Lyotard, and Herbert Marcuse and filmmaker Jean-Luc Godard. But another durable influence on Rosler's practice, she has suggested, was a social justice and protest tradition, a sensitivity to "the public and the political" that was activated in her early yeshiva training and experience in the culture of left and Jewish-left New York.[57] That social context, closely linked with the historical project of socially conscious imaging, continued to inform Rosler's interest in aesthetic practice and theory as well as her awareness of the limits of documentational practices, which she entered into in connection with her antiwar and feminist activism. Shortly after graduating from Brooklyn College in 1965, Rosler began working in the medium of photomontage. She was drawn to its possibilities as a technique for confronting the power of contemporary image culture—in particular, photojournalism and its documentation of the war. Rosler's first major series, titled *House Beautiful: Bringing the War Home* (1967–72), reflected this engagement.[58] It would shape not only her commitment to an activist aesthetic practice but also a profoundly influential critique of documentary and its social uses.

When she began *Bringing the War Home*, Rosler may have been aware of the history of photomontage as a tool of anti-fascist, anti-imperial activism in Weimar Germany and interwar Europe. (Of the radical photomontagist John Heartfield, for example, she later noted, "I think it's not possible to know nothing of him.")[59] But her uses of photographic materials were independent of that precedent; they grew organically out of her experience of the distinctive conditions of American photo-documentation and reportage in Vietnam. To begin with, Rosler set out to literalize the realities of encounter that would come to be encapsulated in Michael J. Arlen's notion of Vietnam as the first "living room" war, whose unprecedented film coverage of military campaigns and casualties produced what he acerbically described as a "keyhole view" of America's engagement.[60] Rosler was less concerned with medium-specific misdirection—the effect produced by millions of Americans watching "a picture of men three inches tall shooting at other men three inches tall . . . tamed by the enveloping cozy alarums of the household," as Arlen put it—than with the effects of bringing documentary footage of the war into the heart of middle-class American life, only to naturalize a false segregation of the postwar consumer paradise of home from the military-industrial logic and the matériel deployed in the killing fields.[61] Rosler's "frustration" with this effect encompassed not just "the images we saw in television and print media," she later noted, but even "anti-war flyers and posters" that defined the visual culture of protest. There, too, "the images we saw were always very far away, in a place we couldn't imagine."[62]

To attack that disjunction, Rosler began working with photographs and photo-text page spreads spliced from the pages of *Life* magazine, carefully assembling and rephotographing them. Critics have noted the importance to her choice of *Life*'s historical role in institutionalizing print medial segregation of editorial and advertising modes, documentary war coverage and domestic feature writing.[63] (There is also, of course, the irony of the title and brand power: during World War II, the journal was so iconic that Joseph Goebbels's propaganda machine produced a parody of its iconic cover titled *Death*, featuring a skull in a GI's field helmet, for distribution to Allied soldiers.) But Rosler's initial use of *Life* resonates in other ways, in particular with histories of photo-documentary production. Launched in 1936 by media mogul Henry R. Luce, *Life* was premised on the narrative and cultural value of "pictures" and their power to enable readers "see life; to see the world; to eyewitness great events"; the journal's development of the photo-text form has been recognized as its singular, critical achievement.[64] Early contributors included Farm Security Administration–employed photographers Dorothea Lange, Carl Mydans, John Vachon, and Gordon Parks, as well as famed documentary image-makers W. Eugene Smith and Robert Capa (who died in 1954, the victim of a landmine, while he was documenting anti-French resistance activity in Vietnam). Widely celebrated for its war coverage, historical and contemporary, *Life* had won the prestigious National Magazine Award in March 1967 for photographer

Henri Huet's disturbing series documenting the experience of a U.S. medic, Private First Class Thomas Cole, wounded in action in An Thi.

Reflecting the course of the U.S. engagement, *Life*'s photographic coverage had grown increasingly grim. But even as it gave space to documentation of the intensifying brutality of the conduct of the war, its pages reflected a calculated bid to win back a readership eroded by the explosion of televisual experience. Those pages were dense with color features focusing on such absorbing matter as the careers of celebrities and the space program, juxtaposed, in the journal's busy visual style, with postwar lifestyle advertising. As *Bringing the War Home* unfolded, Rosler included images from *House Beautiful* and other glossy popular home and design magazines in the project. The use of *Life* as a key source for both registers of her photomontage work—war and home, anesthetized domesticity and traumatic worldliness—was, however, critical. It helped Rosler take aim not only at the ideological effect of separate spheres and the central role of mass media in perpetrating it but equally at the debasement of documentary practice and its transformative potential.

Among its varied images, *Bringing the War Home* includes *Beauty Rest*, in which an all-American couple with a young child, the father holding aloft a detailed toy aircraft, lounges on a deluxe, cheerfully patterned mattress; the family bed is incongruously set in a home that has been ravaged by flood. *Booby Trap* moves out of doors, where a gleaming late-model Cadillac Eldorado convertible, empty of riders, is parked on a rutted road that trails off in the distance into unkempt foliage (fig. 6.5). The car's sleekly designed bumper abuts a crude assemblage of hoop, spikes, and bolts—a bicycle destroyed beyond repair. Here, Rosler, suggests, the false seduction of America's emblematic commodity is at once the real booby trap and the source of the geopolitical aggression that is its material expression. Yet another image in the series, *First Lady (Pat Nixon)*, repurposes a glowing celebrity portrait of its subject in elegant White House quarters. In Rosler's image, however, a picture visible behind the First Lady, in an ornately gilded frame that rhymes with the color of her gown, features a woman in extreme distress, her body riddled by bullet wounds. On closer inspection this image-within-the-image turns out to be a still photo of Faye Dunaway in the landmark finale of the 1967 Arthur Penn film *Bonnie and Clyde*, whose unprecedented, shockingly graphic violence offered viewers a powerful metonym for "the senseless violence that American youth [were] walking into with the Vietnam War."[65]

In each of these photomontages, the tension between ideological regis-

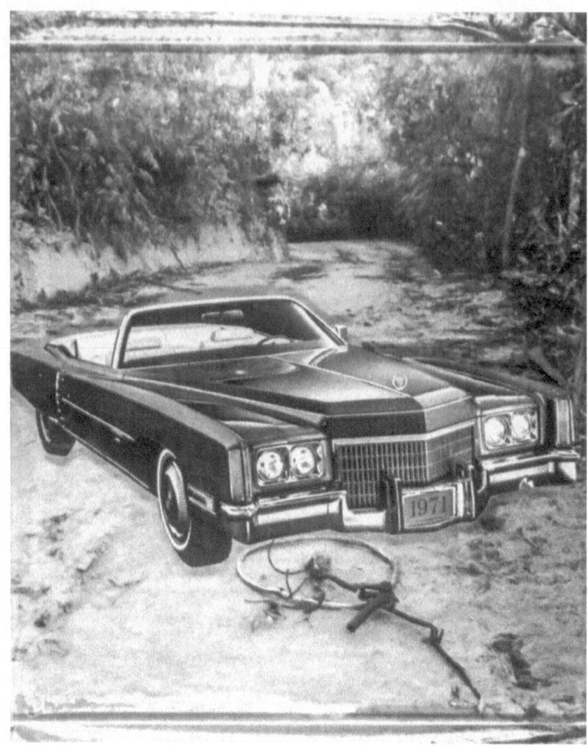

FIGURE 6.5 Martha Rosler, *Booby Trap*, from the series *House Beautiful: Bringing the War Home*. Photomontage. 20 × 24 in. (50.8 × 61 cm.). © Martha Rosler. Courtesy of the artist and Mitchell-Innes & Nash, NY.

ters and spheres of experience is highlighted by a contest of tonalities. Color reproduction, belonging to "lifestyle" sources, opposes black and white, drawn from war reportage or images aligned with it and still considered proper to the seriousness and claims to truth-value of photojournalism. In one of the most widely reproduced images of *Bringing the War Home*, however, that opposition is purposively muted. In *Cleaning the Drapes*, a model-housewife armed with a thoroughly modern vacuum cleaner parts floor-to-ceiling curtains only to reveal battle-weary GIs taking shelter in a rocky outcropping (fig. 6.6). The posture and bodily form of the model and the effect with which she wears and wields the technological apparatus—prosthetic, like the long-range rifles strapped across each soldier's back—that defines her role create not just ideological continuity between the theater of war and the space of mass consumer fantasy, across the symbolic curtain, but also a troubling continuity of practice. Visual rhyming, intensified by the shared register of black-and-white capture, draws the body itself—domestic, female, feminized, conscripted—into the challenge of demonstration: making the traumas of war visible.

That thrust of *Bringing the War Home*, which is not subjective but closely

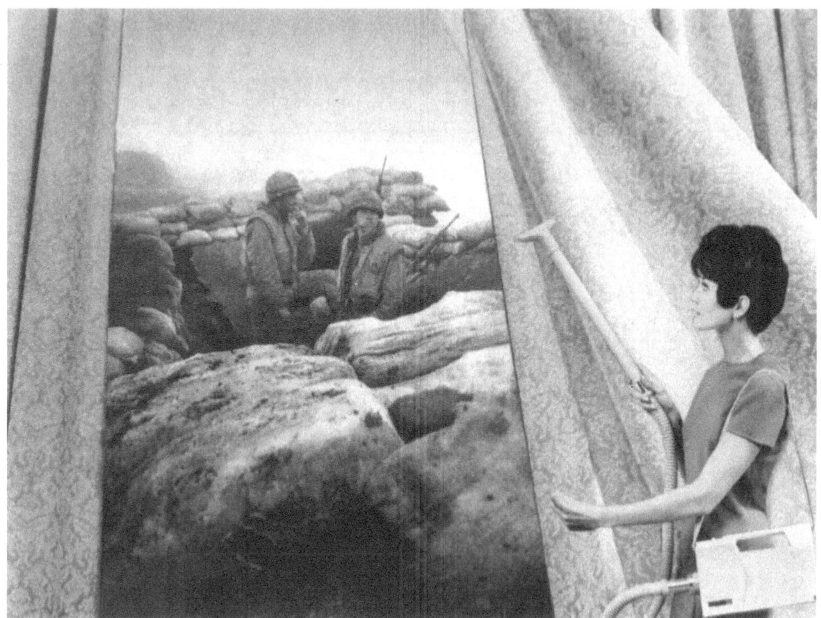

FIGURE 6.6 Martha Rosler, *Cleaning the Drapes*, from the series *House Beautiful: Bringing the War Home*. Photomontage. 20 × 24 in. (50.8 × 61 cm.). © Martha Rosler. Courtesy of the artist and Mitchell-Innes & Nash, NY.

focused on the conditions that produce the experience of the subject, has broader resonance for Rosler's work and its purchase on documentary practice. Notably, she disseminated her project in activist networks—in underground newspapers, like the feminist organ *Goodbye to All That*, produced in San Diego—rather than through conventional art institutions.[66] (That logic governed much of Rosler's work; she declined any gallery representation until 1993, nearly thirty years into her practice.)[67] Part of her aim at this stage of her career, and of the war's, was consciousness-raising among activists themselves about the challenge of visualizing the continuity of endemic imperial warfare and the postwar prosperity program. Whatever it shared with contemporaneous postmodernist theory and practice, Rosler's Vietnam-era photomontage had at its core an attempt to grapple with the question of how systems of representation *work* and with the role that documentational practices might play in more progressive world making.

Consider in this respect the look of Rosler's images. Critics have argued that they have a proto-Photoshop effect, suturing disparate spaces and registers through "precise positioning" of war documentation within domestic frames, in particular mirrors and windows.[68] But the assimilation of these images to the experience of digital production is problematic. If, as art historian Alexander Alberro argues, Rosler aimed to create "the illusion of a coherent new physical space, simplifying and rationalizing the image structure and lowering the emotional temperature," she also rejected the sleek continuity of surface that has become the hallmark of digital manipulation, a fact that has not been widely noted.[69] Alberro for one points to the "clues" left visible in Rosler's broader array of antiwar work—for example, the mark of folds and stapled seams on appropriated magazine illustrations, which tend to become less legible in reproduction in print contexts and on screen. Evidence of the material origin of Rosler's sources, these marks or traces also make visible the act of assemblage, of her own practice and labor.[70] That fact is crucial: it distinguishes Rosler's photomontages from photojournalistic images that can be seamlessly absorbed into the glossy pages of *Life* and *House Beautiful* and unselfconsciously consumed by viewers. It also suggests the possibility of new modes of documentary practice that reflect both on the war as a whole way of life and on the embeddedness of documentary agencies within it.[71]

The Brechtian logic of the trace in *Bringing the War Home* has important resonances in Rosler's evolving practice. More immediately, it marks an important distinction between her work and Avedon's. To their modes of redirecting documentary legacies and documentational practices, very different notions of the artist as producer contribute. With respect to the nature of his portrait practice, Avedon noted in a 1975 interview that "each of my portraits is more a portrait of myself than of someone else—a portrait of what I know, what I feel, what I'm afraid of."[72] The same register of interiority mobilized in "Hard Times" as a resource for making the realities of power visible lends itself after the fact both to challenge the epistemological certitude of traditional documentary, under the sign of objectivity, and to promote the authority of the artist as the aesthetic ideology of modernism conceived and canonized it. In sharp contrast, Rosler has noted that she felt an affinity with the camera, even given its overdetermined claims to truth, neutrality, and transcription, because "photography allowed me to generate an image and not to have it be a representation of my own interiority"; to work with the photograph was to "break the box of interiority, subjectivity, and authenticity."[73] Refusing modes of subjectivism inflected by institutional modernism, Rosler mobilizes documentary practices and conventions to focus instead on their ongoing uses in an emerging age of information and on the subjects—bodies, citizens, mediated social actors—they make and unmake.[74]

During and after her work on *Bringing the War Home*, Rosler extended her practice into the as-yet-uncanonized medium of video. If photography "had no critical history" to limit her conceptual experimentation, she has noted, videos "were like movies made on the cheap out of toilet paper," at this point exempt from the medium-specific standards of still photography and unbeholden to cinematic institutions of distribution.[75] An early video titled *Vital Statistics of a Citizen, Simply Obtained* (first staged as a live performance in 1973, reproduced as a video work in 1977) features Rosler disrobing and then being examined by white-coated figures who record her every possible physical metric, activating her body as a site of ideological struggle and social control. *Semiotics of the Kitchen* (1975), long recognized as a milestone of postwar feminist art, offers Rosler deadpan and aproned before a fixed video camera, robotically demonstrating the uses of kitchen implements from A to Z, transforming that alphabet into a performance of domestic rage.[76]

As these projects attest, Rosler's interest in documentary practices—in particular, the application of "objective" techniques of observation and knowledge-production to the female body—would inform her work of the 1970s across media, from still photography and video to film, installation, and mail art.[77] But photography as a medium and an object of critique had special force in her evolving work, perhaps because it offered such sharp provocation with respect to the question of its cultural authority. If Rosler and her San Diego cohort were focused on the need for socially conscious artists "to develop more complex ways of address," and thereby to engage audiences and fellow citizens outside the institutional spaces of the museum and mass media, "the 'parachuting photographer,' who would go somewhere, take pictures of some crisis, and get the hell out," offered a powerful point of critique and departure.[78] It was against this figure of the documentarian as producer of social knowledge, bulwark against crisis, heroic cultural figure, that Rosler's landmark project, *The Bowery in two inadequate descriptive systems* (1974–75), took aim (figs. 6.7 and 6.8).

Widely exhibited and referenced, Rosler's *Bowery* returns to an iconic site: the last stop for the desperate, inebriate, and down-and-out, a magnet for social reform movements and for documentary observation from the mid-nineteenth century through the end of the twentieth. A major north-south artery of lower Manhattan, the Bowery had long remained the only thoroughfare on the island never to have had a church built on it. It was instead home to bars, saloons, SRO and welfare hotels, soup kitchens, tattoo parlors, and other enterprises serving the indigent, the chronically un-

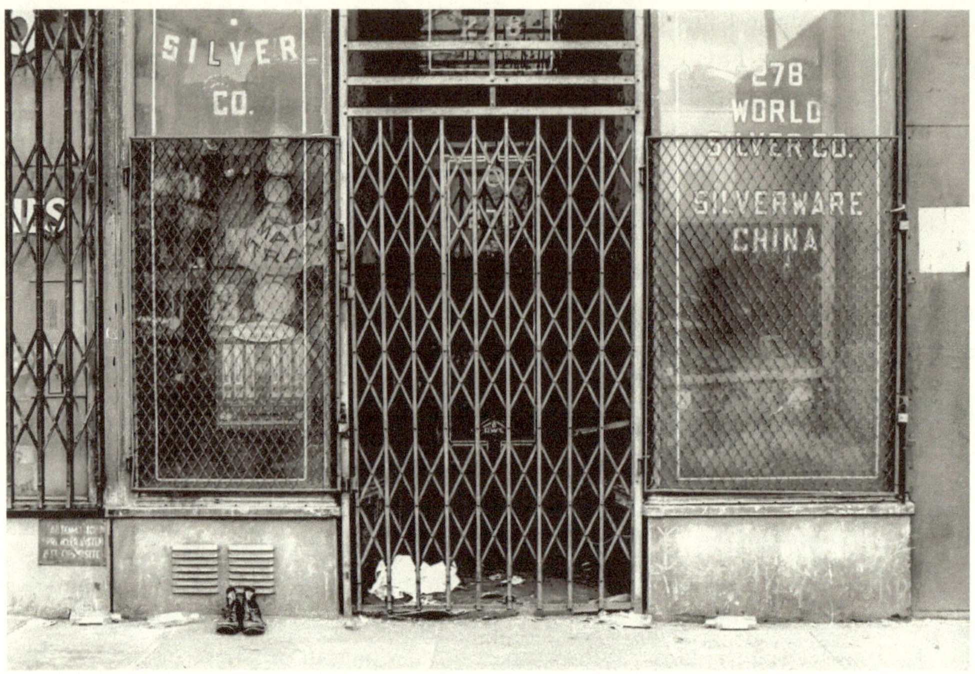

FIGURE 6.7 Detail from Martha Rosler, *The Bowery in two inadequate descriptive systems*. Suite of 45 gelatin silver prints, each framed board: 10 × 22 in. (25.4 × 55.9 cm.). © Martha Rosler. Courtesy of the artist and Mitchell-Innes & Nash, NY.

employed, and otherwise inassimilable classes and had accordingly drawn documentarians to "expose," anatomize, and document the "conditions" of everyday life there from the beginnings of photo-documentary as a project. In choosing the Bowery as her ostensible subject, Rosler meant precisely to revisit these intertwined histories of social marginality and documentary practice in the Vietnam era.

Moving down the Bowery in imitation of the carefully planned surveys of reform photography, she produced a body of familiar images, black and white, mostly frontal, featuring distressed shop fronts, battered facades, and the debris of life on the street. Mimetic of the studied objectivity that was critical to the rhetorical power of documentary in the New Deal era, especially in the work of Walker Evans, Rosler's images call attention to its limits in two striking ways. Most obviously, she leaves the iconic subjects of Bowery documentation—the passed-out, passed-over stalwarts of the doorway and gutter, known as Bowery bums—entirely out of the picture(s). What then is the subject of documentation? Not the exposure of alcoholism, poverty, or dehumanization—which could only reconfirm

soaked	drenched
sodden	flying the ensign
steeped	over the bay
soused	half-seas-over
slóshed	decks awash
saturated	down with the fish

FIGURE 6.8 Detail from Martha Rosler, *The Bowery in two inadequate descriptive systems*. Suite of 45 gelatin silver prints, each framed board: 10 × 22 in. (25.4 × 55.9 cm.). © Martha Rosler. Courtesy of the artist and Mitchell-Innes & Nash, NY.

the status of its subjects as victims or moral failures—but the problematic authority of photo-documentary itself: "What can it tell us," she asks, in the context of documentary's reiterative subjects, "that we don't already know?"[79] Critical to this aim was not just what her work excluded but what it provided as a supplement. Along with images, Rosler produced lists of words describing drunkenness and alcoholism, collected from Bowery denizens, reform agents, and sociological observers. Arranging their language in associative clusters, in the mode of found poems, she typed them onto stock paper and photographed them, pairing them with images for which they serve neither as captions nor as explications. Text and image, metaphor and transcription: however we name the disjunctive systems at work, Rosler insists on their irreducibility to a unified meaning, their inadequacy to meaningful knowledge of a life-world that has been made unknowable in its very saturation by documentary practice.

The twenty-four panels that constitute *The Bowery in two inadequate descriptive systems* have been exhibited with remarkable frequency since their creation, both in museums and in activist and community spaces. The project has been hailed as a landmark of pop, conceptual, and postmodernist art for the questions it raises about the aesthetic and institutional legacies of modernism and its conception of art.[80] But its highest impact may well have been on the conduct of documentary. Revisiting an ur-site, the dead-end Bowery, Rosler argues for received documentary protocols themselves as a dead end. That argument becomes explicit, with devastating force, in a critical essay she wrote to accompany a version of *The Bowery* published in 1981.[81] Her self-titled "afterthoughts" on her work on that site remain "the definitive analysis and demystification" of liberal documentary, theorist and art historian Abigail Solomon-Godeau has noted, and the questions her work raises about social knowledge and power "haunt all documentary photographers to this day."[82] Aligned with projects and generational interests rooted in antiwar activism and focused on institutional critique, Rosler's critical take becomes a documentary to end all documentary.

Yet for all its radical skepticism about the way documentary *works*, particularly in the United States—what it historically has wrought, how it has tended to create glamor and a mantle of heroism for the image maker rather than meaningful social transformation—Rosler's intervention, both critical and productive, theoretical and object-based, expresses an aspiration to remake the practice of documentary. (Of her cohort, she has noted, "We wanted to be documentarians in a way that documentarians haven't been.")[83] Her project has helped make it possible for latter-day theorists to rethink the agency of documentation beyond its institutional contexts, to work in the "post-collapse era of the documentary legacy" toward new understandings of the documentary enterprise.[84] What has come to be known as critical realism—a photographic project founded in social "research," trained on social inequalities and injustices by "an operator who has lived through the situation depicted" and who produces critical views to be "communicated to . . . a community of recipients"—is directly indebted to Rosler's work.[85] So too are current theories of photography that emphasize the extra-institutional life and the radical potential of images to remake social relations between and among viewers, particularly subjects who have been denied visibility, citizenship, and access to civic institutions.[86] Resisting the institutionality and prestige of art, repurposing the stance and modes of objectivity, such critical readings aim to reactivate for the photograph-as-document a transformative agency, a possibility of "inflect[ing]" the experience of spectators "in order to intervene in their way of thinking" about their own relations to key institutions, programs, and powers of corporate life and the state.[87]

If, as Rosler argues in her foundational afterthoughts, practitioners and everyday subjects did "not yet have a real documentary" to inform the era of dissent, she also models the work of finding productive uses for key tensions—between objectivity and subjectivity, the transcriptive and the experiential, the realm of symbolic exchange and that of material circumstance and effect—so as to continue to imagine how "a radical documentary can be brought into existence."[88] Like Avedon's, her shifting affiliations with the legacy and prospects of documentary are part of a provocative, evolving effort to reenvision social agency and to create conditions for meaningful social change—not least in collective practices for inhabiting the image-world and confronting its intensifying power.

NOTES

For their generous support of this work, I am grateful to James Martin and Erin Harris of the Richard Avedon Foundation and to Martha Rosler. Shawn Michelle Smith provided a timely opportunity for testing this argument; Joseph Entin and Franny Nudelman made bracing suggestions for its improvement. Thanks as always to Jonathan Freedman for generous optimism and a clear editorial eye.

1. Livingston, *New York School*, 260, 262.
2. See for a representative account Garner, *Disappearing Witness*, 59–61.
3. Bezner, *Photography and Politics*, provides what is still the most comprehensive account of this problem and of the history of suppression of political aims and context for postwar photography.
4. Foundational accounts of the Photo League include Bezner, *Photography and Politics*, 3–120; Tucker and Cass, *This Was the Photo League*, 9–19; Bethune, "Case of Radical Overkill"; and Klein and Evans, *Radical Camera*.
5. John Szarkowski cited in Bezner, *Photography and Politics*, 14.
6. Bezner, *Photography and Politics*, 37; Szarkowski cited in ibid., 14. See also Guilbaut, *How New York Stole the Idea of Modern Art*.
7. Kroes, *Photographic Memories*, 136.
8. As Bezner, *Photography and Politics*, 2, notes, "Most historians of photography depict the movement toward self-conscious formalism as a natural and positive progression up the evolutionary ladder."
9. John Szarkowsi, introduction to exhibition catalog, cited in Press Release 21, Museum of Modern Art, New Documents, 28 February 1967, available at http://www.moma.org/momaorg/shared/pdfs/docs/press_archives/3860/releases/MOMA_1967_Jan-June_0034_21.pdf, accessed 4 August 2016.
10. Ibid.
11. Allikas, "Looking Back at 'New Documents'"; Gee, *Photography of the Fifties*.
12. Richard Avedon cited in Lawton, "Richard Avedon," citation 38.
13. After being named by the attorney general as a subversive organization in 1947, the Photo League struggled to reclaim its public profile; the exhibition was a key part of its strategy. But during a 1949 trial of alleged Communist Party officials, a league member who had been an FBI informant named the Photo League as a Communist front and singled out its leading teacher, Sid Grossman, as a party recruiter. By 1951, the league had officially disbanded. See Calomiris, *Red Masquerade*, especially 29–30, 73–75.
14. See Avedon and Capote, *Observations*, 68–80.
15. Some of the resulting images can be found in Avedon, *Evidence 1944–1994*, 131–34. The project archive is preserved at the Richard Avedon Foundation, New York.
16. Cited in Livingston, "Art of Richard Avedon," quotation 38.
17. Ibid., 34.
18. Avedon, conversation with Doon Arbus.
19. Roth, "Family Tree," 242–43.

20. Avedon in Madlin, *Legends Online*, cited in Roth "Family Tree," 243; Avedon in Howard Smith, "Scenes," *Village Voice*, 9 November 1969, cited in Roth, "Family Tree," 243.

21. Avedon in Livingston, "Art of Richard Avedon," 36–37.

22. Florynce Kennedy in Avedon and Arbus, *The Sixties*, 66.

23. Richard Avedon, interview by Connie Goldman, 1 July 1970, transcript, Center for Creative Photography, Richard Avedon Foundation, Tucson, Ariz., cited in Roth, "Family Tree," 251.

24. For his intensive reading of this portrait and its context of production, I am indebted to Roth, "Family Tree," 245–46.

25. Ibid., 278, verifies the dating of the Chicago Seven portrait session and notes (245) that in the interval between his periods of attendance at the trial, Avedon participated in demonstrations in New York City around the nationwide Moratorium to End the War in Vietnam.

26. Sekula, "Body and the Archive," citation 6; Gibson, "No Glamorous Poses," cited in Roth, "Family Tree," 247.

27. Roth, "Family Tree," 247.

28. Avedon, interview by Goldman, cited in ibid., 251; see also 248.

29. Livingston, "Art of Richard Avedon," 34.

30. Doon Arbus in Madlin, *Legends Online*.

31. Avedon addresses the version of "Hard Times" published as Avedon and Arbus, *Sixties*, cited in Madlin, *Legends Online*.

32. Abbie Hoffman cited in Avedon and Arbus, *Sixties*, 4–5.

33. E. Nash, "Books in Brief."

34. Vanderbilt, "Courier, Dispatched."

35. For an extended discussion of this context, see Roth, "Family Tree."

36. Larry Hales, letter to Richard Avedon, 20 July 2004, Richard Avedon Foundation, New York; "Richard Avedon: America's War in South Vietnam," March–April 1971, ibid.

37. Stephanie Jay, letter to General Minh, 6 April 1971, ibid.

38. Larry Hales, letter home, 30 March 1971, 29 April 1971, ibid.

39. "Vietnam" files, ibid.

40. Larry Hales, journal, "Richard Avedon," 4 April 1971, ibid.

41. Richard Avedon, letter to Commander Joseph J. Lorfano, Chief of Southeast Asia Division, Office of Assistant Secretary of Defense, 12 March 1981, ibid.

42. Larry Hales, journal, "Richard Avedon," n.d., ibid.

43. A. Scott, "Richard Avedon."

44. Richard Avedon, letter to John Szarkowski, 31 March 1970, Museum of Modern Art, New York, cited in Roth, "Family Tree," 248.

45. Appel, "Avedon," cited in ibid., 249.

46. Roth, "Family Tree," 278n96, notes that Avedon's longtime collaborator Norma Stevens identified Avedon's portrait session with Lt. Joe Hooper as a way for the photographer to "grease the wheels" to secure his session with the Mission Council.

47. Avedon in Livingston, "Art of Richard Avedon" 59.

48. A. Scott, "Richard Avedon."

49. Malcolm, "Men without Props," 119.

50. Roth, "Family Tree," 258–59; Hales, journal, 29 April 1971, Richard Avedon Foundation, New York.

51. Hales, journal, 29 April 1971, Richard Avedon Foundation, New York.

52. O. Edwards, "Pictures of Avedon," 212, cited in Roth, "Family Tree," 259.

53. Emerson, "Avedon Photographs a Harsh Vietnam," cited in Roth, "Family Tree," 259.

54. For groupings, see Avedon and Arbus, *Sixties*, 104–5, 108–12.

55. Gloria Emerson, letter to Richard Avedon [n.d.], Richard Avedon Foundation, New York.

56. Gloria Emerson cited in Avedon and Arbus, *Sixties*, 218–19.

57. Rosler in Michael Rush, "Pure Artist Is Embraced by the Art World." See also Buchloh, "Conversation with Martha Rosler"; "Martha Rosler," in *California Video*; and Bloom, *Jewish Identities in American Feminist Art*, 87–89.

58. In 2004, in the context of the U.S. war on Iraq, Rosler revisited the *House Beautiful: Bringing the War Home* project and began producing a "New Series." See "Martha Rosler: Bringing the War Home," http://www.worcesterart.org/exhibitions/Past/martha_rosler.html, accessed 9 December 2015.

59. Rosler in Buchloh, "Conversation with Martha Rosler," 25.

60. Arlen first introduced the notion in "Living-Room War," citation 200; it became much more widely known with the publication of *Living-Room War*, citation 83, by Viking Press in 1969. Rosler, e-mail to author, 28 March 2017, notes that she came to know Arlen's work only in its book form, after her own had begun.

61. Arlen, *Living-Room War*, 8.

62. Rosler, interview with Laura Cottingham, 23 September 1991, cited in Cottingham, "Inadequacy of Seeing and Believing," citation 157.

63. Cottingham, "War Is Always Home."

64. Luce, "Prospectus for a New Magazine."

65. Mazzucco, "Filming a Revolution."

66. Cottingham, "Inadequacy of Seeing and Believing," 163n2.

67. Rush, "Pure Artist Is Embraced by the Art World."

68. Cottingham, "War Is Always Home," n.p.

69. Alberro, "Dialectics of Everyday Life," citation 80.

70. Ibid., 85.

71. On the matter of materiality and the power of "break with the form," see Rosler and Weinstock, "Interview with Martha Rosler," 82.

72. Lawton, "Richard Avedon," 105.

73. Rosler in Buchloh, "Conversation with Martha Rosler," 39.

74. Ibid., 31.

75. "Martha Rosler," in *California Video*, 200.

76. Rosler, in Buchloh, "Conversation with Martha Rosler," 46; Helmore, "Feminine Mystique"; Martha Rosler video, http://home.earthlink.net/~navva/video/index.html, accessed 25 July 2016.

77. See Alberro, "Dialectics of Everyday Life," 81, 85–86.

78. Rosler, in Buchloh, "Conversation with Martha Rosler," 46.

79. Rosler, "In, around and Afterthoughts," reprinted in *The Contest of Meaning*, citation 322.

80. See, for example, Owens, "Discourse of Others," especially 344; Saper, "Academia's Exquisite Corpse," especially 194; and Batchen, "Looking Askance," especially 231–32.

81. Rosler, "In, around and Afterthoughts," reprinted in *The Contest of Meaning.*

82. Solomon-Godeau, *Photography at The Dock*, 300n4; Batchen, "Looking Askance," 233.

83. Rosler, in Buchloh, "Conversation with Martha Rosler," 33.

84. Van Gelder and Westgeest, *Photography Theory in Historical Perspective*, 9.

85. Van Gelder and Westgeest give a pointed overview of the current concerns of photo theory and critical realism in ibid., 162–63; see also their account of photography's social function and the documentary legacy in relation to "critical authorship," 152–89. Costello and Iversen provide a very useful account from the art historical perspective; see their introduction to *Photography after Conceptual Art*.

86. Ranciere, *Emancipated Spectator*; Azoulay, *Civil Contract of Photography.*

87. Van Gelder and Westgeest, *Photography Theory in Historical Perspective*, 163.

88. Rosler, "In, around and Afterthoughts," reprinted in *The Contest of Meaning*, 306, 307.

Working Photography

Labor Documentary and Documentary Labor in the Neoliberal Age

JOSEPH B. ENTIN

This essay examines work by two documentary labor photographers, Milton Rogovin and Allan Sekula, who for some good reasons are rarely placed side by side. Rogovin was an optometrist-turned-documentarian who came of age in the 1930s, and his photographic series of steel workers, *Working People* (1976–87), follows in the tradition of Lewis Hine and Dorothea Lange. Like Hine, in particular, Rogovin centers his subjects in the frame as they peer forthrightly into the lens, meeting the viewer's gaze. Produced as the neoliberal restructuring of labor through outsourcing and downsizing was beginning and as the Reagan administration was injecting a newly virulent anti-unionism into national discourse, Rogovin's elegant images embody a classic humanist-realist conceit: that photographs can endow workers and other socially disenfranchised figures with cultural legitimacy and spark political reflection and transformation. This idea was fundamental to Progressive- and Depression-era documentarians and has continued to inspire many well-known labor photographers working in the postwar United States, including Ken Light, Earl Dotter, David Bacon, and others.

By contrast, Sekula was a postwar-born, university-trained artist whose approach to photography was shaped by—and helped shape—the postmodern, antihumanist critique of documentary photography authored in the 1970s and 1980s by artists and writers such as Susan Sontag, John Tagg, and Martha Rosler (Sekula's art school classmate). His photographic projects, such as the sprawling photo-textual exploration of economic globalization's maritime dimensions, *Fish Story* (1995), are rigorously theorized, intellectually dense, acutely self-reflexive, and discursive works of art that in many respects have more in common with the work of postconceptual photographers like Jeff Wall and Victor Burgin than they do with traditional labor photographers like Hine and Lange.[1]

Yet despite these differences in generation, training, and approach, Rogovin and Sekula share some crucial tendencies. Significantly, for both, labor photography constitutes an experimental approach to documentary that is motivated by an expressly Marxist commitment to portraying the materiality of labor and the dialectics of working-class collectivity under late capitalism. Notably, despite Sekula's stress on the highly mediated nature of all visual representation, he—like Rogovin—admires Hine, includes portraits of workers in his oeuvre, and is dedicated to a realist project that foregrounds the overlooked role of laboring people in the contemporary world economic system. In turn, while Rogovin may have been insulated from the semiotic theories that were vital to Sekula, his photographic diptychs of workers generate subtle elements of dissonance, discontinuity, and self-reflexiveness that complicate a facile reading of his work as straight social realism. In short, both Rogovin and Sekula blend a materialist focus on the centrality of physical labor to contemporary social reproduction with a self-consciousness about documentary itself as a form of labor—an active, creative, and ultimately unfinished process of remaking rather than merely recording social experience.[2]

My claim, however, is not only that bringing these two photographers together allows us to identify overlooked commonalities between them; reading them side by side also allows us to grasp more fully the crucial differences between them, particularly as they respond to distinct moments in the development of neoliberalism. As a set of policies and practices, including deregulation, the dismantling of the New Deal welfare state, and the implementation of trade agreements designed to facilitate the accelerated mobility of capital across national borders in search of low-cost labor, neoliberalism inaugurated an era of dramatically expanded social and economic precarity for U.S. workers.[3] Rogovin's documentary career began in the early postwar decades, when American industrial production was at its height, but his *Working People* series was undertaken at the cusp of deindustrialization, when the midcentury arrangements that had established a relatively stable environment for organized labor were about to be dramatically undone. Sekula's work on *Fish Story*, conducted in the decade after *Working People* was completed, takes this undoing and the contingency of labor under globalization as central subjects.

Appropriate to the different, if consecutive, historical moments in which they were working, Rogovin and Sekula adopt contrasting conceptual and formal modes to organize their documentary projects. Specifically, Rogovin's images of working people are structured by the logic of the *series*, while

Sekula's are structured by the logic of the *sequence*, or what he calls "sequential montage."[4] A series is a regular, structured ordering of objects, but in Rogovin's work, which is anchored in the use of photographic diptychs—paired portraits of workers at home and on the job—the series becomes a flexible, expandable form that conveys both continuity and difference, that both evokes and questions the potential of the archive to construct secure meanings and render "truth." Depicting industrial laborers who are male and female, black, white, and brown, in an era when neoliberalism's constitutive antiworker ideology was gaining public traction, Rogovin's *Working People* series suggests both the durability of class as a category and the infinite variability of working people as human beings who continually outstrip categorical definitions.

Sekula was a trenchant critic of the curatorial and bureaucratic archive, and for him, the sequence is an experimental, speculative mode of ordering that can challenge the regularity and potential uniformity of the series.[5] For Sekula, the sequence becomes a montage or ensemble form, capable of assimilating heterogeneous materials, including both visual images and verbal text, creating intervals of varying duration, and gesturing to multiple geographic and economic scales. In *Fish Story*, what Sekula describes as the "openness of the sequential ensemble"—its capacity to create cognitive units that defy closure and unitary meaning—allows him to register the unsettling contingency of maritime labor under late capitalist automation, outsourcing, and deskilling.[6] Working out of a shared tradition of labor photography but responding to different, if consecutive and interconnected, moments in labor history, Rogovin and Sekula develop quite distinct documentary modes to convey the shifting conditions of work and working-class collectivity under global capitalism and the fact that, as a form of creative labor, documentary practice itself is an unfinished and open-ended act of social transformation.

Milton Rogovin was born into a Jewish family in New York City in 1909; he attended Columbia and trained as an optometrist, graduating in the midst of the Great Depression. Concerned about the plight of the unemployed, he began taking classes at the Communist Party–sponsored Workers School and became convinced, as he explained later, that "socialism was the path we should take to create a more equitable society."[7] In 1938 he moved to Buffalo and opened an optometric practice; in 1942 he purchased a camera and began experimenting with photography. Rogovin served in the U.S. Army in World War II and then returned to Buffalo, where he continued to be active on the Left. In 1957 he was called before a House Un-American Activities Committee and labeled by the *Buffalo Evening News* as the city's "Number One Red." The same year, he was invited by William Tallmadge, a friend and professor at Buffalo State College, to take pictures in local store-front African American churches where Tallmadge was making sound recordings for a Folkways album of gospel music. Tallmadge finished his work in a few months, but Rogovin continued to work in the churches for three years, eventually completing a series that was published in *Aperture* magazine, with an introduction by W. E. B. DuBois. The store-front church series convinced Rogovin that he wanted to devote himself to social documentary photography, and over the next several decades he undertook a range of projects to document people he referred to as "the forgotten ones": workers, the poor, indigenous peoples, people of color. He photographed miners in Appalachia, Scotland, China, Zimbabwe, France, Germany, Spain, Mexico, and Czechoslovakia; peasants and workers in Mexico and Chile; Native Americans and Yemeni families from the Buffalo area; and residents of Buffalo's historically impoverished Lower West Side. In 1978 he closed his optometric office in order to fully carry out a photographic series in Buffalo-area steel plants, titled *Working People*, which was completed between 1976 and 1987. Inspired by Bertolt Brecht's poem "A Worker Reads History," Rogovin "wanted to show who did the toughest work in industry. I wanted to show them because nobody does. I wanted to show people who are slugging it out at the bottom, especially the women, because women were just coming into the steel mills."[8] Many of the portraits in his *Working People* series are diptychs: pairings of one photograph of an individual on the job and one at home.

Rogovin completed the *Working People* series during a period of seismic loss and decline for industrial labor in the United States, especially in traditional manufacturing cities like Detroit, Pittsburgh, and Buffalo. During these years, the postwar settlement between organized labor and corporate capitalism, which had lifted working-class living standards to unprecedented levels, was shattered by deindustrialization, the rise of neoliberal policies, and the deregulation of several major industries.[9] The beginning of a shift from Fordist modes of production, founded on standardization and labor market stability, to regimes of flexible accumulation, marked by sharply increased capital mobility, outsourcing, and the movement of manufacturing to the Global South and "right-to-work" states, sparked what Mike Davis describes as "ruthless downward spirals of wage cutting and deunionization."[10] Moreover, the political and economic assault on organized labor was accompanied by a cynical attack on the public image of working people—from the media depiction of the so-called hard-hat riots in 1971, which historian Joshua Freeman observes "seemed to confirm a common, middle-class view of manual laborers that held them to be one-dimensional, inarticulate, and intolerant," to Ronald Reagan's highly successful efforts to paint labor unions (starting with the air traffic controllers, whom Reagan unilaterally fired during a strike in 1981) as obstacles to economic efficiency, market freedom, and the American way of life.[11]

Rogovin's *Working People* series represented a forceful challenge to the antiworker ideology of the emerging neoliberal regime. If this regime aimed to demean and degrade the public perception of workers, portraying them as resentful, unintelligent, and irrational figures who stood in the way of economic growth and flexibility, Rogovin's images depict them, by contrast, as a diverse group of competent, thoughtful, complex persons. Rather than a monolithic mass of brawny, white working stiffs, Rogovin's working people are black, brown, and white; men and women; married and single; mothers, fathers, and grandparents. They all work in Buffalo's and Lackawanna's industrial plants, but their home pictures indicate a remarkable variety of interests, living contexts, and relationships. In the most basic sense, then, by showcasing the heterogeneity of ages, races, and family arrangements within the steel-working community, Rogovin's portraits explode the reductive images of working people circulating in much of the period's mass culture.

But in addition to expanding the public view of workers, Rogovin's diptych series constitutes an innovative contribution to documentary practice. First, his photographs are grounded in and make manifest forms of reciprocity and collaboration that challenge the one-sided dynamics of traditional liberal-reformist documentary image-work, which tended to reaffirm the privilege of well-to-do viewers by presenting pity-inducing depictions of socially subordinate subjects.[12] By contrast, and in tune with a growing acknowledgment of the relational nature of documentary practice in the postwar period, Rogovin invites his subjects to pose and present themselves, to claim and assert their agency in the documentary relation. Marked, as critic Melanie Herzog notes, by their "confident poses and direct gazes," the people in Rogovin's photographs are cognizant of his presence; they have paused their labors and turned to the camera to address him, looking directly into the lens.[13] "I never directed them or told them where to stand," he explained, or "how to hold their hands or what to wear. The only thing I asked is that they look into the camera. . . . When you look at these pictures, you know there was no monkey business, and that I was not sneaking around trying to steal pictures of people."[14] In foregrounding his working-class subjects' active participation in the documentary process, Rogovin not only draws on the work of predecessors like Hine but also echoes the oral history practice of Studs Terkel, whose *Working* was published in 1974, and emergent shifts in social science fields like anthropology, which moved away from the putatively objective, structuralist approaches that had dominated the field in the 1950s and 1960s to more fluid, subjective forms of ethnographic work that acknowledged that the observer was also a participant in the field of study rather than a neutral outsider.[15]

The collaborative quality of Rogovin's diptych portraits, as well as the at-times uncanny discrepancies and discontinuities between work and domestic photographs, produces a palpable measure of instability. In granting his subjects autonomy to pose themselves, Rogovin diminishes his own control and opens up what might otherwise be a much more overdetermined, even unilateral, process, dominated by the photographer, to multiple, perhaps even conflicting, impulses and intentions. "As a rule," he explained, "I have no preconceived ideas as to what kind of a face or pose I'm looking for. . . . In the few times that I tried to 'make' a picture by posing the individual . . . the results were so bad that the photograph usually ended up in the waste basket."[16] The domestic images, in particular, in which subjects pose themselves before a widely varied, and sometimes baffling, array of objects and artifacts (family photographs, posters of Elvis, a gilt rococo mirror, a mantle full of porcelain figurines), are often strikingly indeterminate, even disorienting. The fact that Rogovin does not include descriptive captions further amplifies the lack of semiotic closure.

As well, the often startling contrasts between the two images in a diptych, in which it is sometimes difficult to recognize the subject from one photograph to the other, stress the priority of context over essence and the fact that even as these images are carefully composed, they are also products of improvisatory, unpredictable encounters. The divergences in the way workers' appearances, facial expressions, and modes of self-presentation shift between paired photographs remind us that any image is merely one among myriad others and is shaped by circumstance. Each individual image in the series acquires meaning in the context of the others and yet also reminds us that an infinite number of other photographs could have been taken in between or beyond the shots we actually see. The diptychs make us aware of the interstitial moments, the intervals *between* individual shots, and thus the unavoidable flux, fluidity, and indeterminacy that structure even the most seemingly direct forms of documentary representation.

And indeed, several diptychs offer striking discontinuities between work and home photographs. In the work shot in one pairing, a middle-aged blond woman offers up a jaunty pose and sly smile, a huge gear thrown casually over her shoulder, suggesting a confidence, even a playfulness, on the job; in her home shot, where she is the only adult, she has placed herself to the side and smiles more neutrally, giving her children center stage, with a poster of a lion on the wall in the upper right-hand corner, perhaps to signal her protective stance and prowess.

Similarly, in the work photograph in one of the most striking diptychs, a black woman steel cutter is cast as a commanding figure (fig. 7.1). She is shot slightly from below, which elevates her figure, and her authority is enhanced by the thick protective clothes she wears and the long steel-cutting device that she holds quite casually (the iconography of the photograph recalls, and thus recasts and to an extent ironizes, the heroic portraits of white male proletarians from the 1930s). Her home photograph, by contrast, is marked by the broad smiles she and her sons display and the ease and comfort they exude with one another and, it seems, with the photographer (fig. 7.2). This (apparently) single black mother—a figure so often vilified in Reagan-era "family values" discourse—appears in Rogovin's diptych as both a responsible, loving parent and an accomplished, powerful worker.[17]

Yet to highlight the cooperative and open-ended nature of Rogovin's documentary practice is not to say that his work completely rejects photography's power to record and classify. Although each portrait underscores unique, distinctive features of an individual's life and labor, the repetition of the diptych format places each individual image (and each pair, as well) in the context of a larger series, a class.[18] And there is a taxonomic dimension to Rogovin's enterprise: he is, after all, constructing an archive.[19] Yet this archive suggests the rich variety, rather than the typological status, of persons who share a social and economic position as industrial workers. These people are members of a class, but Rogovin's images suggest that their lives, bodies, personalities, and personal relationships cannot be reduced to or wholly contained within class as an abstract category. Oscillating between repetition and variety, commonality and particularity, *Working People* thus invokes and critiques the archive as model of photographic practice and class as a category of social thought and identity. Rogovin's subjects, his images suggest, both are and are not identifiable by and with

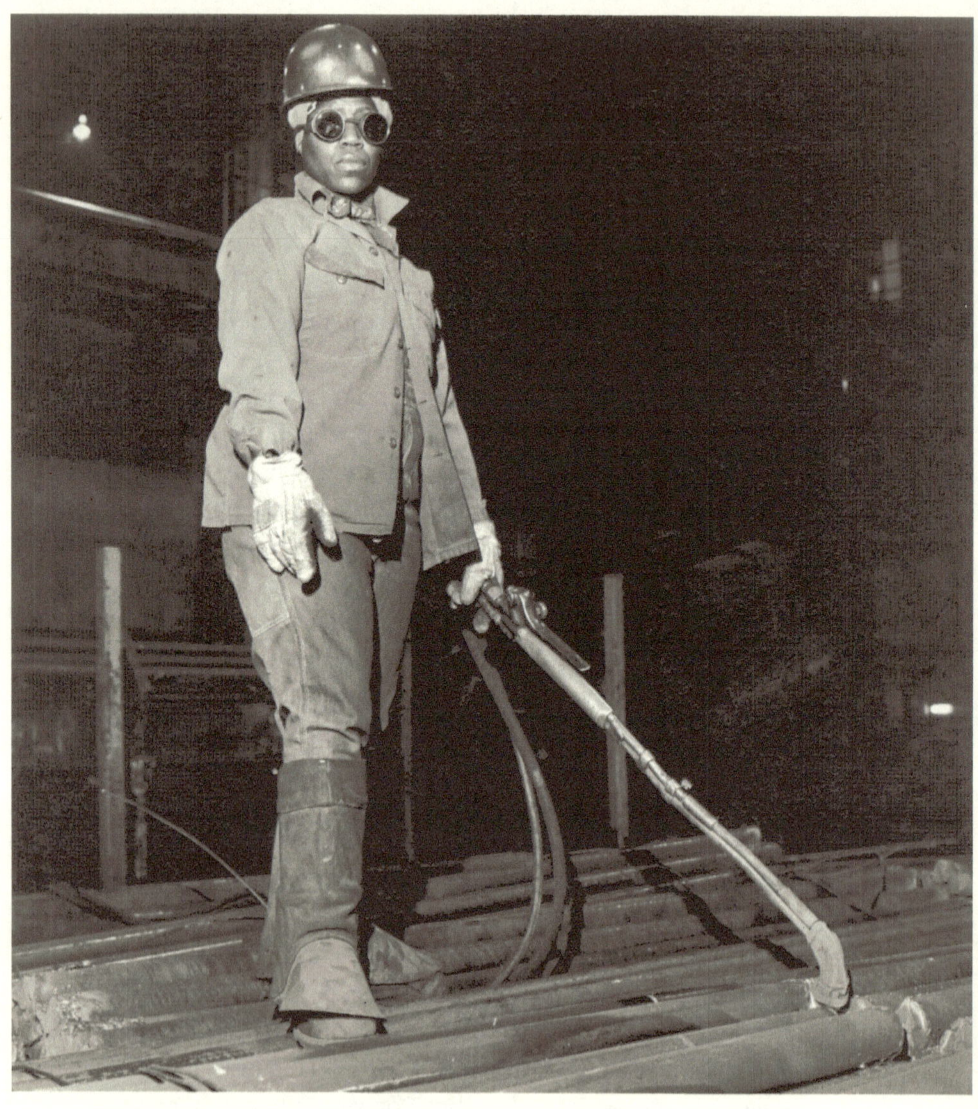

FIGURE 7.1 Milton Rogovin, *Untitled*, in *Working People* series, 1976–1987. Photograph © Milton Rogovin. Courtesy of the Center for Creative Photography, University of Arizona Foundation.

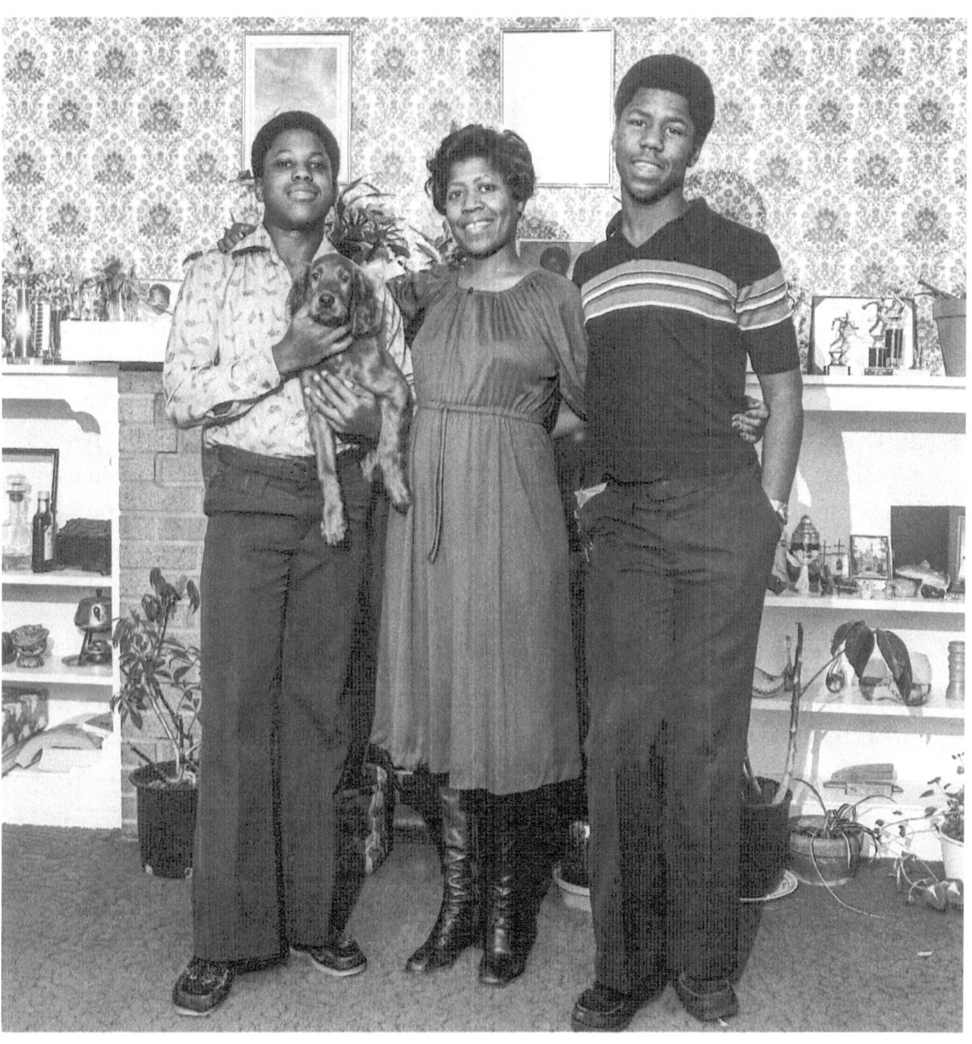

FIGURE 7.2 Milton Rogovin, *Untitled*, in *Working People* series, 1976–1987. Photograph © Milton Rogovin. Courtesy of the Center for Creative Photography, University of Arizona Foundation.

their work; they both inhabit and exceed the series that aspires—and invariably fails—to signify "industrial worker." *Working People* is thus a series but one marked by irregularity as well as regularity. While the work is anchored in the repetition of scenes, locations, and photographic style, it foregrounds not only continuity, consistency, and connection but also discrepancies and inconsistencies that destabilize the serial logic at the heart of the project.

Even more, the striking disparities between work and domestic scenes that mark several of the diptychs silently suggest the impossibility of documenting the full reality of these working people's lives and personalities, thereby subtly exposing the contingency of documentary photographic representation itself. Rogovin's portraits are consistent in their aesthetic clarity and formality, but they neither heroize workers nor condescend to them. They stress the determinations of context, the way that workers may look dramatically different, even unrecognizable, from one milieu to another. If Rogovin's images offer "truths" about the workers, they are multiplicitous, contingent truths. Rather than an essence, we see evidence of change and flux, organized by the intervals, the transformations from one moment, one location, to another.

If Rogovin's *Working People* series represents, as I have argued, a social documentary project that, as it foregrounds the materiality of industrial work, hints at the contingencies of its own form and allows viewers to sense the collaborative and ultimately indeterminate social relations behind its photographs, Allan Sekula's *Fish Story* constitutes a highly self-reflexive text that makes viewers aware of its own constructedness, even as it insists on the agency of documentary to record the transformations of material production in the late capitalist global economy. Rogovin's work gestures, perhaps inadvertently, to the instability of documentary image-making and class as a category; extending and complicating these dynamics significantly, Sekula's project on the world maritime economy takes documentary uncertainty as its conceptual starting point, offering viewers a deeply theorized visual-verbal meditation on the possibilities and problems of representing global labor and the contemporary structures transforming it.

Sekula grew up in the working-class port city of San Pedro, California, and in the late 1960s entered the University of California, San Diego, where he encountered the Marxist critique of modern art and the administered society via the teachings of faculty members Fredric Jameson and Herbert Marcuse (the latter of whom Sekula took a class with) and the antiwar, anti-institutional activism of the period's student social movements. Sekula had planned to major in marine biology but switched to visual art, where he joined with two young faculty members, Phil Lonidier and Phil (later Phel) Steinmetz, and fellow students Martha Rosler and Fred Buck to challenge the medium's role in the maintenance and extension of prevailing state and social power relations. Sekula's perspective was articulated in several now-canonical essays written during the 1970s and 1980s—including "Dismantling Modernism, Reinventing Documentary" (1978), "The Traffic in Photographs" (1981), "Photography between Labor and Capital" (1983), and "The Body and the Archive" (1986)—that offer a searing critique of both photographic realism's faith in scientific truth and canonical modernism's formalist belief in photography's social autonomy.

Collectively, Sekula's essays demonstrate his commitment both to semiotic theory's postrealist stress on the indeterminacy of the verbal and photographic sign *and* to a realist emphasis on photography's capacity to record reality and render the material structures that shape everyday life and meaning. If Rogovin's *Working People* series unconsciously establishes tensions between particularity and abstraction, individual image and serial context, Sekula makes these tensions, and the problematic possibilities of documentary representation more broadly, a presiding subject of his photo-textual practice. Sekula absorbed structuralism and poststructuralism's critique of the sign but rejected what he called "the fortress wall of epistemological skepticism" that inspired many critics to hammer "another nail in the coffin of social documentary."[20] Although he was deeply critical of photography's historic complicity in structures of power, such as prevailing economic relations, the police archive, and the bourgeois division between public and private life, Sekula (like his colleague and sometime collaborator Rosler) was dedicated to reconstructing documentary as a viable enterprise in a world in which the assumptions of realist transparency that had organized so much documentary work in the early part of the twentieth century had been called into question.[21]

Sekula's interest in labor as a documentary, theoretical, and political subject, and in serial montage as a mode for rendering labor's contingency, is an enduring aspect of his career, dating back to *Untitled Slide Sequence* (1972), a twenty-five-photograph series of workers leaving the Convair aerospace factory in San Diego that draws on Edward Muybridge's stop-motion studies; *Aerospace Folktales* (1974), which documents the home life of an unemployed engineer and his family, echoing the black-and-white photographic sequences of Walker Evans's *American Photographs*; and *This*

Ain't China (1974), a "photonovel" about Southern California fast-food workers (including Sekula himself) who threaten to strike, which combines staged photographs and a metanarrative commentary in the spirit of Brecht and Jean-Luc Godard.[22] All three works use experimental, sequential forms to document labor and its negation (*leaving* the factory, *un*employment, and the *withholding* of work via a strike). *Fish Story* extends the focus in these pieces on work, the absence of work, and montage aesthetics through an examination of the sea as a "forgotten space" of global labor and labor struggle.[23]

Fish Story is a hybrid documentary photo-textual book that takes as its central subjects the radical economic and spatial restructuring of the global maritime economy since the 1960s and 1970s, when containerization was introduced, and the European-American literary and artistic traditions in which the sea has historically been depicted. Addressing what Sekula describes as "the imaginary and material geographies of the advanced capitalist world," *Fish Story* is divided into seven "chapters" intercut with a two-part critical essay, "Dismal Science," that examines the history of maritime representations in Western culture, tracing a transition from the classical view of the sea in a panoramic frame to the modern view of the sea, which Sekula argues typically foregrounds fragment and detail.[24] Inspired by modernist montage (the best analogue may be *Battleship Potemkin*, Sergei Eisenstein's 1925 film about naval insurrection during the Russian Revolution that Sekula discusses in one section of "Dismal Science"), *Fish Story* is a complex, composite documentary that brings together radical reportage, experimental photo-textual poetics, and cultural and intellectual history.

In adapting and interweaving these different and at times conflicting literary and photographic modes, Sekula seeks to produce a revisionary, critical—and self-critical—social documentary realism that addresses the material dimensions of labor and transnational economic production while also assimilating the epistemological skepticism and semantic indeterminacy that mark poststructuralist theory. For Sekula, the photographic sign resides, as Benjamin Buchloh has suggested, between discourse and document, between a contextual conception of photography as "a discursively and institutionally determined fiction" and a referential conception of photography "as an actual record of complex material conditions."[25] *Fish Story*'s montage realism emerges between images and accompanying text within a given sequence, between the totalizing narrative of global economics and the accumulation of small details—tensions embodied in one of the more striking, and well-known, photographic diptychs in the book:

one photograph, a close-up of the slightly curved band of red mercury in an inclinometer, gauging a ship's tilt in the mid-Atlantic, and a corresponding mid-Atlantic photograph of a vast expanse of sea, shot over the prow of a ship covered by a jigsaw of multicolored container boxes. While Rogovin's images, which depict workers in individual or small-group portraits at work or at home, occupy the same plane and unfold in a fairly consistent pattern, one worker after another, Sekula's images, by contrast, take up much more capacious contexts and radically different scales. As a result, the gaps between images, as well as the range of perspectives, materials, and geographic locations, are much more varied and uneven in *Fish Story* than in *Working People*.

While Sekula is skeptical of traditional notions of photographic realism, he also holds no truck with high modernism's renunciation of social or political reference. His aim is to contest what he describes as "the old myth that photographs tell the truth" *and* "the new myth that photographs lie."[26] The result is a highly self-reflexive critical realism, allegorized in the book's opening photograph of pay-to-use binoculars on the Staten Island Ferry and, in the distance, a freighter, hazy through a window on which the reflection of the binoculars is faintly visible.[27] The image of the binoculars suggests that the contemporary maritime economy, embodied by the distant ship, is accessible for documentation only through mediating technologies of vision, underscored by the overlapping array of lenses and frames (binoculars, camera, window) in the shot.

Despite the stress on semiotic instability, Sekula's realism seeks to pierce both the abstractions of global capitalism, which reifies concrete social relations through the equivalence of exchange value, and the abstraction of modernist art, which disavows the social world in favor of a myth of aesthetic self-sufficiency—but without ever falling back on a positivist realism, grounded in the illusion of unmediated truth. As such, *Fish Story* might be considered a postmodern version of what I have elsewhere called modernist documentary—in this case, a realism indebted to social documentarians such as Hine and Lange yet produced through the interruptive and experimental techniques advanced by political modernists such as Brecht, Eisenstein, Godard, and Walter Benjamin. *Fish Story* urges us to pursue what Sekula has described as "a new materialist turn, a step backward in the direction of Hine and Marx and forward, with Brecht, in the direction of semiotics and the broader theory of the image."[28] As this volume of essays suggests, the method that Sekula explains, which involves interrogating and assimilating the history of documentary in order to develop innovative practices adequate to the exigencies of present social conditions—in this case, the volatile processes of global commodity production, distribution, and circulation—represents a key feature of much post-1945 documentary practice.

The dialectical quality of Sekula's montage method is visible in *Fish Story*'s depiction of work and workers under contemporary globalization, which is at the heart of the book. Sekula's text documents both the displacement of labor in an increasingly automated system of maritime transit and the persistence of physical labor in a supposedly knowledge-based, high-tech global economy. *Fish Story* is thus on one hand a tale about labor's abstraction in the so-called postindustrial, transnational era, especially through containerization, a process pioneered in the 1950s in an effort to rationalize the global transportation of commodities by undercutting dock and ship labor, which had been militantly organized in the decades before World War II (*FS* 49). And accordingly, *Fish Story* charts a narrative of loss, about the passing of the harbor as haven, about the end of the dock as a human-centered space, and the book contains several photographs of ships, waterfronts, and/or cranes devoid of human figures (*FS* 18, 21, 29, 57, 71, 75, 83, 170, 172, 175, 180, 181).

Yet on the other hand, even as *Fish Story* charts the displacement and disappearance of human labor, it also underscores the concrete, stubbornly material dimensions of maritime work—its grit, grime, and grease, the wear and tear, the individual and collective acts of human effort and expertise that keep ships afloat and moving. Sekula's photographs stress the human presence—whether active or remaindered—in maritime commercial circuits. Challenging the view that "computerization and telecommunications" are the primary engines of the new economy, Sekula insists that "large-scale material flows [and the physical labor necessary to drive those flows] remain intractable" (*FS* 50). Accordingly, the book is punctuated by photographs of workers on docks and in factories and shipyards, as well as unemployed workers who have been displaced by the automation of dockside and shipboard labor under the current global production system.

The contradiction in *Fish Story* between labor as material force and as displaced abstraction is often rendered in photographic diptychs, or pairings.[29] While Rogovin's diptychs feature workers looking directly, even penetratingly, into the lens, Sekula's are much more varied: some pairs contain two different workers (*FS* 24–25), others the same worker but frequently midtask, not looking at the photographer (*FS* 4–5, 58–9); other pairs depict a worker and then a corresponding scene notable for the lack of a human figure. The text's first chapter, for instance, contains the following couplet: on one page, an image of a woman in shorts and a baseball cap worn backwards, seated on the ground before a large wooden box, wearing work gloves and holding a wrench. The caption describes her as "Pancake, a former shipyard sandblaster, scavenging copper from a waterfront scrapyard" (*FS* 30). The image on the facing page depicts the postmodern infrastructure of the mechanized dock labor that has displaced workers like Pancake: a robot-truck transporting a container in Rotterdam beneath a looming array of skeletal cranes. Perhaps an ironic allusion to the "industrial sublime" of Charles Sheeler's photographs of Ford's River Rouge plant, the image of the automated truck is artfully divided between sky and ground, container and cranes, yet off balance, careening to the right, as dark tire marks in the truck's wake pose a potentially disquieting sign of erasure. Together, the two images in the pairing suggest both the supplanting of human labor by mechanization and the persistence of human agency, even if only in the form of a scavenger, scouring the site of organized labor's dislocation.

In *Fish Story*, then, labor appears as both presence and absence, a tension crystallized provocatively in a diptych in chapter 3. The first photograph (fig. 7.3) in the pair is dominated by dark forms created by towering stacks of shipping containers shot from below, which leave a thin, vertical slice of light, in which a remote, tiny human figure crawls upwards below a container that juts ominously above. In the foreground, slimy black and yellow cables snake across the wet deck. The photograph on the facing page (see fig. 7.4) depicts a worker's abandoned coveralls lying on the floor of a ship next to a hose that extends through an open doorway. In the first image, human labor appears amid the apparatus of corporate containerization, but it is fragile, barely visible, under threat; in the second photograph, labor is presented as a trace, an outline, at once embodied and evacuated. Metaphorically, this image suggests that labor is a ghost, a material factor overlooked or suppressed, hidden "below decks," yet still shaping the maritime commercial order via its (grimy, grease-marked) presence.

Refusing conventions of the workers as static, passive victims *or* as monumentalized, heroic figures, Sekula's photographs are frequently askew or off-kilter, less the kind of formal, carefully posed or polished work associated with "art photography" or with the dramatic, eye-catching images of institutionalized photojournalism than with the amateur snapshot.[30] Sekula's is often a purposefully de-professionalized aesthetic of instability, blur, and partiality that reminds viewers of the photographer's own place-

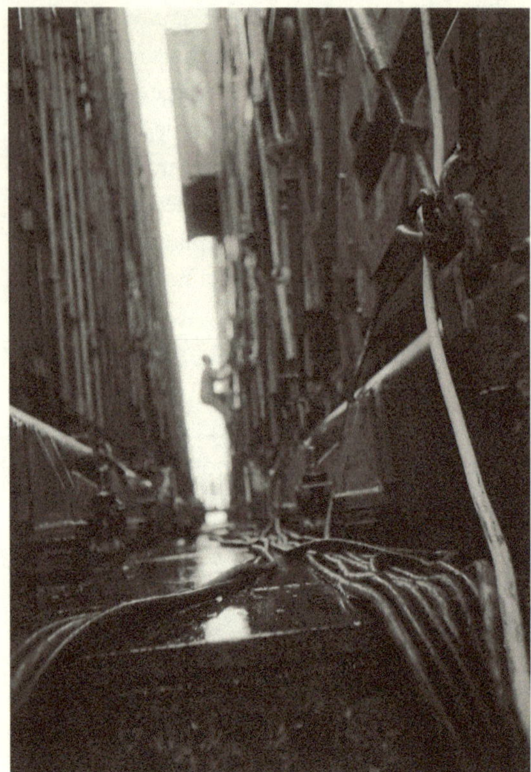

FIGURE 7.3 Allan Sekula, *Chief mate checking temperatures of refrigerated containers. Mid-Atlantic.* From *Fish Story*, 1989–95. © Allan Sekula, with permission of the Allan Sekula Studio LLC. Original photograph in color.

ment and perspective, his material presence in the scene, the knowingly subjective nature of the book's photographic realism. Sekula's photographs of pipe fitters, welders, and steel cutters capture workers in the midst of their labors, rarely facing the camera with the composure or frontal gaze that defines Rogovin's images. Rather, Sekula's maritime workers are often obscured, tangled in pipes or wires, covered by a mask, turning away from our view as they work. His image of an "assistant engineer working on the engine while underway" (image *FS* 61, caption *FS* 76) conveys the paradox: the worker is at the center of the image but concealed behind a thorny snarl of pipes. The photograph reveals, but only partially, reminding us that all documents are incomplete, leaving elements outside the frame or beyond view.

Fish Story is thus an open, unfinished documentary, an assemblage of verbal and visual fragments that defies closure. Blending the material and discursive, fact and fiction, record and representation, the book stands not only as an attempt to trace the tangible and ideological contradictions of the contemporary global economic system but also as an allegory of

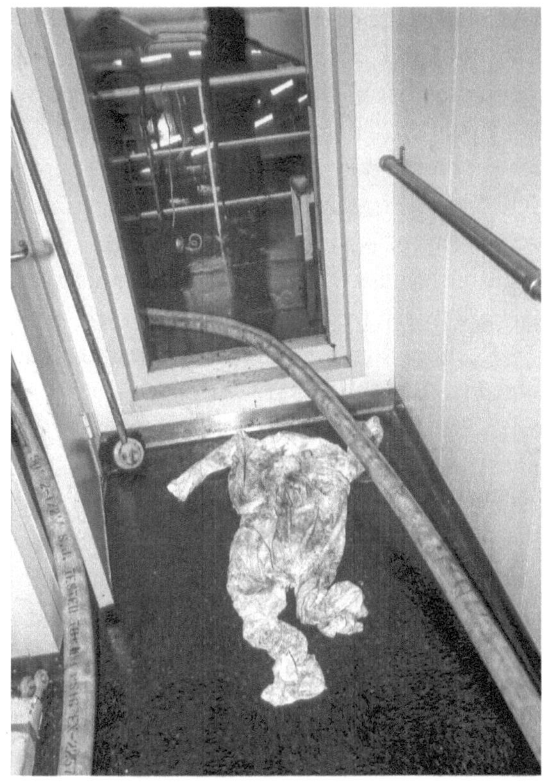

FIGURE 7.4 Allan Sekula, *Filling lifeboat with water equivalent to weight of crew to test the movement of the boat falls before departure. Port Elizabeth, New Jersey.* From *Fish Story*, 1989–95. © Allan Sekula, with permission of the Allan Sekula Studio LLC. Original photograph in color.

working-class formation and collectivity, which is, like the "real" itself, at once material and discursive, institutional and intersubjective, determined and imagined. Class is a matter of abstraction: to imagine the world working class requires thinking beyond and across local contexts and occupations to represent what labor holds in common.[31] Yet class is also a matter of concrete material conditions, always a living, breathing relation that takes meaning in specific contexts, a process of struggle, of becoming rather than being.

Moving between far-flung sites—Rotterdam, Veracruz, Seoul, Los Angeles—Sekula's highly self-conscious mode of denaturalized documentary suggests that knowledge about labor, class, and economics cannot simply be recorded but needs to be made. It is, in one sense, a *work-in-progress* that reminds us that documentary itself is in fact *work*—an ongoing construction, an act of creative transformation rather than a passive recording. Moreover, *Fish Story* suggests that representations of work and working-class collectivity must never lose sight of their own provisionality. As Sekula explained in an interview, "Both socialist realism and liberal capitalist social documentary share in offering us images of labor in its *positivity*. They are necessarily ignorant of any notion of labor's *contingency*. That is to say, labor is always shadowed by the absence of labor, by labor in the negative, by the nightmare of unemployment on one side, and by the utopian dream of genuine freedom from work on the other."[32] Set in dialogue with, yet against, socialist realism, liberal documentary, and modernist experimentalism, Sekula's work calls for forms of labor documentary art that are in keeping with this insight: rigorously dialectical modes that allow us to see the always-unresolved tensions between the abstract and the concrete, the totality and the fragment, the common and the contradiction, the nightmare and the utopian dream of freedom.

Both Rogovin and Sekula were inspired by the documentary work of early twentieth-century practitioners such as Hine and Lange, even as they rework documentary to (in Rogovin's case) delicately question and (in Sekula's case) assertively undercut a putatively unmediated or objective realist approach. In the work of both, key formal features—the use of diptychs, the emphasis on a series or sequence as context for the single image, the stress on the uncanny detail—underscore the gaps, interruptions, and incompleteness of photography's truths. Both use photographic pairings to engender tensions between labor and leisure, presence and absence, individuality and collectivity. As labor photographers, both Rogovin and Sekula are interested not only in human figures but also in the ways that individuals are molded by and respond to the institutional spaces they inhabit, from factories, ships, and docks to their own homes. Both photographers stress documentary as an open-ended form, in which the unfinished nature of representation and of working-class formation is, to varying degrees, palpable. For Rogovin, the openness is a product of his collaborative process, which gives autonomy to his subjects to arrange and pose themselves as they wish, and the serial, diptych form he used, which subtly exposes photography's incapacity to capture the "full picture" of proletarian life. For Sekula, the openness stems both from his never-fully-dialectical diptychs and from his sequential montage method, which brings together multiple literary, theoretical, and photographic registers in a complex, multilayered, and resolutely incomplete text. And for both, I have argued, the open-endedness of the photographic act and documentary text echoes working-class composition, a continuous process always enacted through the slippery channels of representation.

While this essay has identified key commonalities between Rogovin and Sekula, I do not mean to diminish the crucial differences between them.

They work out of different, if adjacent, historical moments (Rogovin, the late 1970s and early 1980s, and Sekula, the 1990s) and different, if interconnected, political traditions (Rogovin out of the 1930s Left, Sekula out of the 1960s Left). I want to suggest that when we read them through one another—chiasmatically, one might say—we can see them each, and the points of convergence and divergence among and between them, anew. When we read Rogovin back through Sekula, we become more attuned to the semantic instability of the earlier photographer's work—the subtle but still tangible ways his images question the foundations of documentary truth that his work is so often thought to exemplify. In turn, reading Sekula through Rogovin allows us to see with greater clarity Sekula's commitment to documentary portraiture, the way his work looks back to early twentieth-century labor photography, as well as forward to conceptual art and poststructuralist theory. But reading them through one another's eyes also enhances our understanding of the radical differences in style, format, method, and intellectual approach that shape their projects. If Rogovin's work gestures quietly, even unintentionally, to photography's semiotic uncertainty, Sekula's highly textual work, while also resolutely materialist and Marxian, is devoted to an expansive, rigorous exploration of photography's discursive dimensions, and his dismantling and reconstruction of documentary image practice is among the most ambitious and innovative of the late twentieth-century period.

Just as Rogovin and Sekula make use of the diptych as a core unit in their serial projects, this essay has posed the two of them as a kind of critical diptych. Reading in pairs points to both continuities and discrepancies and demands that we look, as Sekula puts it in a comment quoted above, backward and forward at once. Such critical reading also draws our attention to the intervals—the spaces between discrete units—and opens the possibility that what seem to be gaps or absences may in fact represent occluded histories not yet seen. A "fish story," in historical vernacular, is always a story of the one that got away, a tale of unfinished business.[33] Perhaps the history of labor photography itself, and the way it is reinvented by post-1945 documentarians working to address the global restructuring of labor, is itself a fish story—temporarily displaced and in need of recovery, not so much lost as waiting to be reimagined and reanimated.

NOTES

For permission to reprint the images in this essay, I am grateful to Mark Rogovin, of the Rogovin Collection, and Sally Stein, of the Allan Sekula Studio. For sustaining support and encouragement, I thank Sophie Bell and Miriam and Rachel Entin-Bell. For invaluable feedback, and for editorial solidarity, I extend my deepest gratitude to Sara Blair and Franny Nudelman.

1. For more on Sekula's relation to conceptual and postconceptual photography, see S. Edwards, "Photography Out of Conceptual Art."

2. On human labor as an active, social creative force that exceeds capitalist forms of abstract, "productive" labor, see Bruno Gulli: "When labor is considered in its ontological sense, as the human activity that goes with life itself, considered in its broadest meaning, and that is, all labor, *all labors*, productive and unproductive, material and immaterial, intellectual and manual, artistic and affective, and so on, then it can be grasped as the power that moves and shapes the entire spectrum of the social: the form of unrest of social movements and struggles is the unrest of living labor." Gulli, *Labor of Fire*, 6.

3. On neoliberalism, see, among many other works, Harvey, *Brief History of Neoliberalism*; Duggan, *Twilight of Equality?*; and Brown, *Undoing the Demos*.

4. Sekula, "On 'Fish Story,'" 49.

5. For a meditation on "speculative documentary," see Daniel Worden's essay on Rachel Carson in this volume.

6. Sekula, "On 'Fish Story,'" 57.

7. Rogovin quoted in Herzog, *Milton Rogovin*, 28.

8. Brutvan, "Interview with Milton Rogovin," 14.

9. For an overview of this period in U.S. labor history, see Freeman, "Labor during the American Century."

10. Davis, *Prisoners of the American Dream*, 137. On "flexible accumulation," see Harvey, *Condition of Postmodernity*. In 1968, Bethlehem Steel employed nearly twenty thousand people in the city; in 1971, half of the workforce of Bethlehem was permanently laid off; by December 1982, the company announced it would be phasing out almost all of its steel making within six months; that same year, Atlas Steel Casting and Republic Steel had likewise closed their Buffalo plants. See Herzog, *Milton Rogovin*, 113. See also Goldman, *City on the Edge*.

11. Freeman, "Hardhats," 741.

12. For a stinging critique of liberal humanist documentary photography, see Rosler, "In, around and Afterthoughts," in *The Contest of Meaning*.

13. Quoted in Herzog, *Milton Rogovin*, 110.

14. Ibid., 92.

15. I am indebted to Sarah Chinn for helping me think through these connections.

16. Quoted in Herzog, *Milton Rogovin*, 109.

17. The space Rogovin creates for his subjects' self-expression flows in part from his use of a Rolleiflex camera, which has a topside viewfinder. Rogovin notes: "I liked the twin-lens Rolleiflex with its waist-level format because it allowed me to look down into the camera. This was a much better way of making photographs as I was sort of bowing in front of my subjects, and this creates a different kind of interaction than aiming the camera directly at them." Quoted in Herzog, *Milton Rogovin*, 92.

18. On class as a form of seriality, see Sartre, *Critique of Dialectical Reason*; and Rose, "Class Formation and the Quintessential Worker."

19. Critics have noted Rogovin's debts to August Sander's encyclopedic survey of 1920s Germany. For instance, James Wood, the president of the Getty Trust, asserted that Rogovin has "created images that allowed us to see our fellow man with an intensity equal to that of Walker Evans or August Sander." Wood quoted in Kennedy, "Showcase." It is worth noting that Sekula, too, looks back to Sander as a model.

20. Sekula, "On 'Fish Story,'" 49.

21. The most crucial historical predecessors to whom he turned for inspiration included radical modernists such as Sergei Eisenstein, Bertolt Brecht, and Walter Benjamin, in whom Sekula found models for fusing aesthetic self-consciousness with a political, realist art. While we tend to associate Benjamin with montage, Sekula notes that Benjamin "built his modernism from an empiricist model, from a mode of careful, idiosyncratic observation of detail. This model could argue both for the photographer as *monteur*, and for the photographer as a revolutionary spy or detective, or more 'respectably,' as critical journalist of the working class." Following Benjamin, Sekula was at once *monteur* and revolutionary spy, critical theorist and documentarian, experimentalist and empiricist. Sekula, "Body and the Archive," 60.

22. See "Found Paintings, Disassembled Movies, World Images."

23. *The Forgotten Space* is the title of the documentary film about maritime labor and globalization that Sekula produced with Noel Burch in 2010 as a follow-up to *Fish Story*. Sekula argues that the sea is the forgotten, "slow" space of material transit and economic exchange that makes modernity possible but that is willfully occluded by modern society's fetish of speed and virtuality.

24. Sekula, *Fish Story*, 202. Further citations appear parenthetically in the body of my text with the abbreviation *FS*.

25. Buchloh, "Allan Sekula," 199.

26. Sekula quoted in Roberts, "Production in View."

27. The photo is paired with an adjacent photograph of a young boy, holding the binoculars, but looking back, away from the ocean and across the photographic plane, toward, the caption asserts, his mother, who is not visible in the image itself.

28. Sekula, "On 'Fish Story,'" 50. Despite Sekula's skepticism about the aspirations to scientific objectivity often embedded in traditional documentary realisms, his commitment to deploying documentary to address the place of labor in the global maritime economy resonates with Hine's desire "to show the meaning of the worker's task, its effect upon him, and the character of his relation to the industry in which he earns a living" (Hine quoted in Trachtenberg, *Reading American Photographs*, 134).

29. For a fabulous reading of Sekula's diptychs, and his images of workers more generally, see Young, "Arresting Figures."

30. Buchloh, "Allan Sekula," 194.

31. On the abstraction necessary to imagine the working class, see Denning, "Representing Global Labor."

32. Sekula, "Conversation between Allan Sekula and Benjamin Buchloh," 48.

33. I am grateful to Sara Blair for suggesting the link between the fish story and the larger arc of this essay and documentary history.

Counterdocuments

Undocumented Youth Activists, Documentary Media, and the Politics of Visibility

REBECCA M. SCHREIBER

In the 2010s, undocumented youth activists have forged a politics premised on reconfiguring self-representation and visibility.[1] During a time in which they began to lead their own organizations and focus on mobilizing other undocumented youth, these activists also used documentary forms to represent themselves in ways that defied the machinations of the U.S. state. They have employed strategies of *countervisibility*, which protects undocumented migrants against state violence, and produced what I term *counterdocuments*. Counterdocumentation is a deliberately oppositional image practice that references the truth claims of traditional documentary film and video in order to provide evidence that challenges official forms of documentation and the state's ability to determine the parameters of political inclusion.[2]

This essay focuses on videos produced by activists involved in the National Immigration Youth Association (NIYA), created before they performed acts of civil disobedience in which they risked being arrested, detained, and deported, as well as during the infiltration of an immigration detention center in 2011. These videos served as a means for undocumented youth activists to frame their depictions and to present public political claims. In order to make these ephemeral actions public, activists distributed their videos through various online media platforms, including activist websites, YouTube, and blogs. These activists' distribution and circulation of documentary realist forms through digital and social media was linked to their emphasis on political mobilization.[3] Yates McKee and Meg McLagan contend that "political acts are encoded in medial forms . . . by which the political becomes manifest in the world," and thus "modes of circulation and making public are forms of political action."[4] In analyzing videos produced by undocumented youth activists before and during their political actions, I study how they have circulated through digital and social media as counterdocuments and were a key part of these activists' political project: reaching other undocumented young people who can be engaged by these politics and further mobilized.

I understand documentation both as an aesthetic practice based in the visual conventions of social realism and as an administrative practice for producing and policing boundaries of inclusion and exclusion within the nation-state. Referring to these activists' videos as counterdocuments is a means to suggest a deliberate connection to other modes of documentary practice, and I argue that the video excerpts that circulated in social media contexts have analogous functions to elements of traditional documentary film, such as testimony or *vérité*-style sequences.

Undocumented youth activists used documentary media to contest the limitations of prosecutorial discretion announced by the Obama administration in August 2011 as "guidelines" that were not legally binding, as well as to expose state agents' disregard of eligibility criteria.[5] While this administration held up prosecutorial discretion as positive, as something that would be given to those who were "deserving" of it, discretion can reinscribe the authority of the state to evaluate undocumented migrants involved in removal proceedings on a case-by-case basis. Seen in this light, discretion is an administrative technology of individuated subjection, which is also based on the exclusion of those who are deemed to be "undeserving."[6] Thus, the politics of visibility for these activists is at once similar to the traditional reformist ethos of documentary "making public" and put in the service of more far-reaching agendas that challenge the meaning of political inclusion.

Since 2010, undocumented youth activists have produced and circulated documentary media as part of a strategy to publicize their political actions. The videos that undocumented youth activists produced before and during these actions developed out of a more confrontational approach to organizing that they took up in response to the limits of the Development, Relief, and Education for Alien Minors Act (DREAM) Act.[7] Their tactics were a reaction to the ways in which U.S. government agencies, including Immigration and Customs Enforcement (ICE), an arm of the Department of Homeland Security (DHS), have deported or threatened to deport undocumented migrants from the United States. These activists' use of documentary media was thus specific to the context of state and federal immigration policies that could render visibility a form of surveillance linked to detention and deportation. Their strategies emerged in response to the Obama administration's policies toward undocumented migrants, which, in contrast to the Bush administration's emphasis on producing spectacles of migrant apprehension, aimed to conceal or minimize publicity around its policing of undocumented migrants. Undocumented youth activists made themselves and their actions public and visible to counter this concealment and mobilized through the circulation of counterdocuments that radiated outward to audiences via digital and social media. Undocumented youth activists publicized their political actions in order to draw attention to the effects of these laws on undocumented migrants and to mobilize supporters. At the same time, they inverted the visual terms of surveillance to shield themselves from possible detention and deportation.[8]

I consider two examples of the ways in which undocumented youth activists have used counterdocuments as part of their broader political strategies. Both are drawn from the work of NIYA, which was formed in 2011 by undocumented youth activists interested in deploying confrontational tactics.[9] Activists in NIYA produced documentary videos, including personal narratives, previous to their actions in part because by protesting and taking part in acts of civil disobedience they risked not only arrest but also detention and deportation, and their videos could be used as part of campaigns to take them out of deportation proceedings. The first set of videos examined here consists of undocumented youth activists videotaping themselves previous to their arrests for participation in a civil disobedience action in North Carolina. While these activists produced the videos as a means of protection in case they were put into deportation proceedings, they also contested the limits of discretion. The second video was recorded by an undocumented youth activist as he was being arrested by Border Patrol agents in Alabama as part of his attempt to infiltrate an immigration detention center. It functioned as a form of evidence that documented how state agents were not using discretion when they encountered undocumented migrants. These videos, which were uploaded onto activist websites, in addition to YouTube and various blogs, have been used to publicize the actions and arrests of undocumented youth and to mobilize others in support of specific political issues and campaigns to release these activists. In both examples, activists used documentary media as a form of protection to counter policing and the state's surveillance of undocumented migrants.

The activists' videos draw upon elements of traditional documentary film and involve performances on the part of the activists who produced them. In creating videos before and during direct actions, undocumented youth activists represent themselves in ways that are deliberately oppositional. Their performances are thus quite distinct from the migrant melodramas that Ana Elena Puga argues are a growing subgenre within a variety of media, including documentary film. She argues that these migrant melodramas, "while sympathetic to migrants, stage suffering so as to create the illusion that the undocumented must naturally, inevitably, necessarily endure physical and psychological pain."[10] Countering this approach, Martin, an undocumented youth activist who took part in an action in North Carolina, was quoted in a press release as saying that he chose "not to present another emotional testimony" or to "ask for sympathy"; instead, he asserted, "We ask for justice. Mere justice!"[11] In this context, Martin's statement functions as a form of disruption in that he refuses to take part in what Puga refers to as "the political economy of suffering," which involves an "exchange of affect—migrant suffering for spectator empathy."[12] As counterdocuments, the videos were created primarily to organize and mobilize other undocumented migrants, and they circulate on the Internet as a means of encouraging the mobilization of other undocumented youth. Counterdocuments, in this sense, strategically protect, confront, and mobilize.

COUNTERDOCUMENTS AS CHALLENGES TO THE LIMITS OF DISCRETION

In September 2011, to prepare for a protest of the discriminatory policies toward undocumented students at Central Piedmont Community College, NIYA activists Marco and Mohammad traveled to Charlotte, North Carolina, to coordinate the action with Viridiana, the cofounder of the North Carolina DREAM Team. The event took place in Charlotte because the Democratic National Convention would meet there in 2012, and the protest was directed toward the Obama administration and the Democratic leadership in Congress. Since Charlotte was located in a 287(g) county, undocumented youth risked arrest, detention, and deportation.[13] Assuming that they would be arrested, undocumented activists in North Carolina made video recordings of themselves before the civil disobedience action, which took place on 6 September 2011.[14] They had learned that by declaring their immigration status and publicizing their actions, they could evade detention and deportation. Mohammad, an activist affiliated with DreamActivist.org, explained, "The more public we are with our stories, the safer we are."[15] These activists believed that declaring their undocumented status could serve as a form of protection for those who wanted to participate in direct actions.

During the protest, a group of activists declared that they were undocumented; they spoke about discriminatory policies toward undocumented students at Central Piedmont Community College; and they explained the effects of the federal government's programs—such as Secure Communities (S-Comm) and 287(g)—on undocumented migrants in North Carolina.[16] Following the rally, activists staged a civil disobedience action at an intersection near the college. Ten activists were arrested.[17] While these activists were in jail, ICE put holds on them, thus initiating their transfer to an immigration detention center in Georgia. In the end, however, not one of the undocumented youth was detained. The activists attributed this decision to the "bad publicity" their detention would have generated for the Obama administration.[18]

This action by undocumented youth activists tested the Obama administration's announcement on 18 August 2011 that ICE was eliminating "low priority" cases in order to focus on deporting undocumented migrants convicted of serious crimes.[19] Young undocumented migrants, many of who came to the United States as children, appeared to be among those who would benefit from this change. Some politicians and migrant rights activists applauded this announcement, but these were not the changes that many undocumented youth and migrant activists had been advocating for—such as stopping any action against undocumented migrants, including those *not* currently facing deportation. Nor did Obama's announcement have any effect on federal policies and programs, such as 287(g) or S-Comm, through which ICE agents continued to arrest, detain, and deport undocumented migrants. Instead of changing immigration laws, the Obama administration attempted to make the current laws less harsh through prosecutorial discretion, which would delay the deportations of young undocumented migrants but would not grant them permanent residency status.[20] The administration was trying to deflect criticism by attempting to make immigration laws more palatable.

NIYA activists wrote a press release in advance of their action in North Carolina in which they critiqued the limits of discretion, arguing that the Obama administration was using it to pacify undocumented youth.[21] In their press release, NIYA activists criticized how discretion involves working within the constraints of the current political context to restrict or partially undo current immigration laws. However, this approach does not account for the shifting ground of immigration policies, which would also change again with a new administration. These activists also questioned the force of discretion within the broader context of punitive U.S. immigration policies.

The significance of the press release emerged in a context in which undocumented youth whom ICE had placed in deportation proceedings were advised by activists involved in the Education Not Deportation (END) campaign to create videos as part of public campaigns to both draw in and mobilize a broader public that could put pressure on ICE to stop their deportation.[22] Because the joint task force overseeing the review of removal cases considered factors such as the pursuit of education, circumstances of arrival, and length of presence in the United States, some elements of an undocumented youth's story were deemed to be very significant in cases of discretion. As a result, the END campaign encouraged undocumented youth to share information such as their names, ages, places of residence, educational histories, community activities, and immigration statuses in their videos. The main targets of these public campaigns included John Morton, director of DHS and ICE, as well as politicians from an individual's state or district.

However, there were limitations to the approaches recommended by activists involved with the END campaign. In order to convince both potential supporters and ICE to use discretion in a certain case, for example, *Education Not Deportation: A Guide for Undocumented Youth in Removal Proceedings* suggested that undocumented youth represent themselves in ways that would make their cases "compelling and worthy of discretion."[23] But this approach had repercussions, as has been noted more recently by activist Tania Unzueta Carrasco.[24] According to Unzueta Carrasco, who helped develop the guide, activists were attempting to "challenge the label of 'criminality' as a qualifier for deportability" by "emphasizing other hegemonic characteristics."[25] Directing undocumented youth to highlight their own "worthiness" implicitly diminished that of others who had not attained this kind of "success," which reaffirmed the prerogative of the state to determine worthiness and supported the presumption that most are less worthy or unworthy of discretion. Producing this kind of public narrative could thus be risky for undocumented migrants.

In addition to advising undocumented youth to create scripts that emphasized elements of their lives fitting the terms of discretion, the *Education Not Deportation* guide also directed them to represent themselves in specific ways. The strategies put forth by the authors of the guide instructed those in removal proceedings to appeal to a broad audience by attempting to mobilize feelings of identification. Undocumented youth were informed that they should speak about elements of their personal lives and include photographs of themselves within the videos, which would encourage viewers to empathize with them.[26] In addition to "making a personal connection," they were to perform the telling of their story.[27] Although the instructions for the video component appear to be simple, including the writing and recording of a public narrative, the guide's authors advise that the stories should appear "natural," and thus individuals should avoid reading these narratives in front of the camera. This approach was intended to produce a "real" aesthetic, although it is important to note that the appearance of "naturalness" involved a carefully rehearsed narrative.

The END campaign's focus on undocumented youth creating videos to prevent their deportation emphasized an appeal for inclusion within the nation, which differed from the counterdocuments produced by activists in North Carolina that drew upon the aesthetic elements of these videos and yet also challenged their approach.[28] Similar to the videos produced as part of the END campaign, these counterdocuments included first-person narratives in which undocumented youth spoke directly to the camera. Each of the videos, which featured a single person, was closely cropped and shot in a simple, straightforward way. Although the aesthetics of these videos are similar, these activists in North Carolina specifically aimed to repurpose these conventional forms to challenge the terms of discretion. Some of the distinctions in the approach to these videos have to do with their different purposes, as well as with the audiences to whom they were addressed. Undocumented youth were already involved in deportation proceedings when they created their videos based on the instructions in the *Education Not Deportation* guide, whereas the activists in North Carolina produced their videos as they were preparing for a direct action, which put them at risk for arrest and possibly deportation. While the guide suggested that videos be directed to Morton and others, those produced by activists in North Carolina were addressed to at least three different audiences, including government agents reviewing cases for discretion, family members, and other undocumented youth.

The distinction between using personal narrative as a case for inclusion in the nation-state and as a means of fundamentally challenging the terms of political inclusion is evident in the videos produced by undocumented youth activists in North Carolina. Although these undocumented youth activists included information about themselves in their videos that was needed to be considered for discretion, they often represented themselves in ways that failed to conform to normative characteristics, such as how the "DREAMer" had been scripted by mainstream immigrant organizations.[29]

The videos made by these activists prior to their arrests served at least two purposes. Some activists recorded these videos as a precaution, in case they were put in deportation proceedings.[30] These videos could then be used as part of antideportation campaigns and included all the information necessary for an individual to be considered for discretion, including the activist's name, age, educational history, and how they came to the United States. These videos were also produced in order to mobilize other undocumented youth to become involved in the struggle against restrictive anti-immigrant laws. As opposed to gaining the support of politicians and leaving the repressive structure of immigration laws in place, these activists directly challenged the laws in their videos by referring to the effects of racism and discrimination against people of color in the United States, which have included racial profiling of Latina/o immigrants, while referencing their own privilege, especially in relation to their parents. The aesthetics of the videos produced by the END campaign and of those produced by activists in North Carolina are similar, conveying direct address and emphasizing a lack of televisual mediation. However, the former is an appeal to the state on its own terms, while the latter challenges these terms as a counterdocument.

In their videos, undocumented youth activists challenged how U.S. immigration law criminalizes undocumented migrants—including their parents—while also critiquing the limits of discretion. The videos produced by the activists in North Carolina included elements of their life stories, including the fact that they were undocumented. They also presented a counternarrative to how the U.S. state deemed their parents—as undocumented migrants—to be deportable. By getting arrested, these activists were testing the Obama administration's policy on discretion, as well as contesting how this policy made some groups eligible for discretion but not others. Unlike the videos featured in the *Education Not Deportation* guide, these activists did not create "compelling" personal narratives to represent themselves as "worthy of discretion." Instead, their videos challenged how politicians and state agents treat undocumented migrants. For example, Angelica stated in her video that she was tired of all the politicians' lies and the ways that local officials treated undocumented migrants as criminals (fig. 8.1).[31] Other activists' videos portrayed how undocumented youth activists contested U.S. immigration policy on behalf of their parents. In Santiago's video, he noted that he was "standing up to power," with the

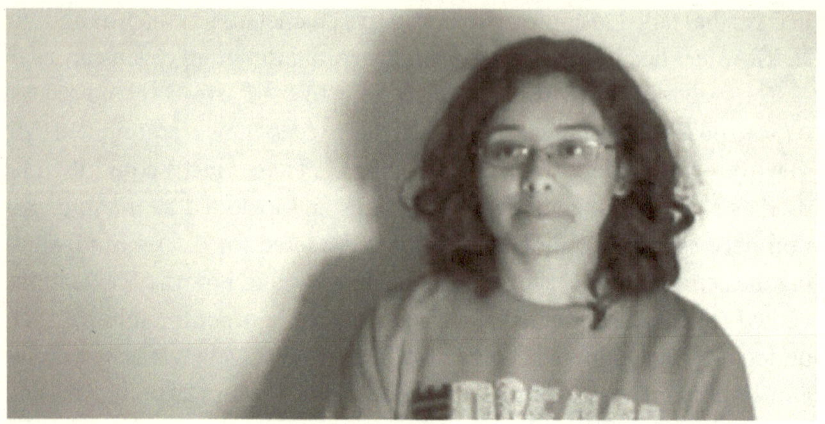

FIGURE 8.1 Screen shot from undocumented youth Angelica's video. Screen capture from digital video.

hope that his parents could also do so someday without the risk of deportation.[32] In their videos, these activists represented their parents in ways that challenged U.S. immigration policies. As opposed to referring to their parents' actions as "illegal" (due to the way in which they crossed the U.S.-Mexico boundary), they instead stated that their parents were brave to travel to the United States to improve families' lives. Instead of participating in the criminalization of their parents, these activists chided politicians for failing to act on behalf of undocumented migrants.[33]

Rather than appealing to the U.S. nation-state for inclusion, the undocumented youth videos were a means to motivate other young migrants to join their cause. In their videos, the activists represented themselves as models whom other undocumented youth could follow to effect real political change.[34] For example, Santiago stated, "[We should not] assimilate to a system that oppresses us and try to belong to that system" and "We need to challenge that system and create a real movement, a movement where we are fighting for human rights for all."[35] Martin also spoke directly to undocumented youth, encouraging them to mobilize on their own behalf: "It's time to step up and do something—we will no longer be placed on hold." Further, he stated, "Doing nothing—waiting to get deported—is a horrible idea. You have to do something about what's going on. No one is going to take care of our issues—we have to take responsibility now to do something about this injustice. So get involved—do something now—there's no time to wait."[36] In creating these counterdocuments, undocumented youth activists challenged the perception that some migrants are not considered to be "deserving" of discretion. They also encouraged undocumented youth to become active in protesting anti-immigrant laws.

Moreover, these videos convey a specific, strategic visibility. After the videos were produced, they were uploaded onto activist websites, as well as onto social networking sites such as Facebook, YouTube, and blogs.[37] McLagan and other scholars argue that digital and social media have shaped how social movements have publicized their campaigns in recent years. Like undocumented youth activists, the human rights activists about whom McLagan writes have also produced "a new kind of media activism" that "not only makes sophisticated and innovative use of techniques of celebrity and publicity through a wide range of forms . . . but that also involves the creation of new organizational structures that provide a kind of scaffolding for the production and distribution of these media."[38] Activists' distribution of these counterdocuments did a certain kind of political work, challenging hierarchies established by the U.S. state and reaffirmed by mainstream immigrant rights groups in efforts to get immigration legislation passed and protecting and mobilizing other undocumented migrants.

In the context of undocumented youth activists' online presence, their websites, such as one developed by the undocumented-led online organization DreamActivist.org, function as "portals into activism."[39] Following the arrest of the undocumented youth activists in North Carolina, Dream Activist.org circulated a petition to President Obama and Janet Napolitano, the secretary of the Department of Homeland Security, to end 287(g) and S-Comm. The authors of this petition noted the contradiction between Obama's August 2011 announcement and the fact that the activists arrested were "put on the fast track to immigration detention."[40] The actions of these undocumented activists highlighted federal laws and policies that continued to place undocumented migrants in detention and deportation proceedings. Their videos also addressed a core constituency of supporters and claimed a digital space for challenging U.S. immigration policy.

In their videos, youth activists in North Carolina represented themselves as disruptive, since they refused to abide by the constraints of discretion. While undocumented youth had focused on lobbying politicians to support the DREAM Act from the early 2000s through 2010, in these videos activists also directed themselves toward other undocumented youth in order to enlist them to act on behalf of all undocumented migrants. Although the END campaign advised activists to represent themselves within the terms of discretion, many refused to abide by these limitations. Through their public actions and their videos, these activists mobilized other undocumented migrants to challenge punitive U.S. immigration laws and policies—such as 287(g) and S-Comm—that have contributed to the increased number of undocumented migrants who have been detained in or deported from the United States.

COUNTERDOCUMENTS AS FORMS OF COUNTERSURVEILLANCE

Soon after the action in North Carolina, NIYA activists escalated their political strategies beyond acts of civil disobedience. The activists arrested in North Carolina were not transferred to an immigrant detention center, yet most undocumented migrants with ICE holds who were in the jail at that time were taken to the Stewart Detention Center in Georgia. By conversing with "low priority" undocumented migrants in the jail, NIYA activists developed a new strategy to infiltrate immigration detention centers to inform undocumented migrants of their rights, as well as to gather information to help release those detained.[41] The production of counterdocuments was central to this strategy. These activists wanted to demonstrate that when the media were not present, "low priority" undocumented migrants were being arrested, put in detention centers, and then funneled into deportation proceedings.

The activists focused on the inconsistencies in the implementation of the guidelines for discretion. This type of action could be performed only by undocumented migrants. As Marco wrote, "We the undocumented . . . have become in effect perfect soldiers to tackle the architects and structures of our detention."[42] While Marco was noting that undocumented migrants could get into detention centers as part of efforts to release those who were detained, Mohammad stated that NIYA members should also use their undocumented status to "flip the power of those who think they are in charge."[43] Government agents believed they had the upper hand, but Mohammad's comment demonstrated that the activists could use their undocumented status to infiltrate detention centers in order to illustrate the inconsistencies between who was being detained and deported and who was not and how this information was being "officially" reported by the Obama administration.[44] These actions relate to what Jonathan Xavier Inda and Julie A. Dowling refer to as "migrant counter-conducts," which are "acts or forms of comportment that contest the criminalization and exclusion of undocumented immigrants."[45] Furthermore, activists' use of everyday technologies such as cell phone cameras and social media—to engage in forms of countersurveillance against state agents—shows how "traditional hierarchies of visibility are being undermined [and] reconfigured," as Kevin Haggerty has described.[46]

The first activists to document the inconsistencies in the enforcement of the guidelines for prosecutorial discretion were Jonathan and Isaac. These two activists were arrested in November 2011 at a Border Patrol office in Mobile, Alabama, and detained at the South Louisiana Correctional Center in Basile. At the time, Jonathan and Isaac were members of the San Gabriel Dream Team, and they traveled from Southern California to Alabama to join activists protesting HB 56, the Beason-Hammon Alabama Taxpayer and Citizen Protection Act. Activists organized rallies and actions in Montgomery to protest the measure, which was based on Arizona Senate Bill 1070 and criminalizes undocumented migrants, prompting many to leave the state. What differentiated the actions in Alabama from those previously organized by undocumented youth activists was that they engaged in civil disobedience along with their parents or with activists of their parents' generation.[47] All the undocumented migrant activists who were involved in civil disobedience in Alabama were arrested. Yet due to the publicity around these actions, everyone—including the adults—was released, avoiding detention centers or deportation proceedings.

The activists' strategy to infiltrate and organize within immigration detention centers was part of a broader campaign to highlight how federal and state agents were not consistently abiding by the terms of prosecutorial discretion, as they continued to arrest, detain, and deport undocumented migrants who were considered "low priority." The jail-to-detention-center pipeline was enabled by ICE's S-Comm program, which connected local police to federal immigration authorities through the use of integrated databases that use biometric technologies—including fingerprinting—to determine the immigration status of arrested individuals.[48] The S-Comm program provided the infrastructure for taking an undocumented migrant who had committed a minor crime—such as a traffic violation—to a detention center or deportation proceedings. As part of the campaign against the S-Comm program, undocumented youth activists held civil disobedience actions at ICE offices nationwide. For example, Jonathan and Isaac participated in a civil disobedience action against ICE in Los Angeles in October 2011, during which young activists blocked a van full of undocumented migrants who were about to get deported.[49] Undocumented youth also took part in and recorded an act of civil disobedience at one of the ICE offices located next to the immigration detention center, which was recorded on the camera of a cell phone and circulated on the Internet.[50] By holding a civil disobedience action in front of a van of undocumented migrants who were about to be deported and in the middle of an ICE office, undocumented youth activists attempted to disrupt the "processing" of undocumented migrants by the ICE "machine." Their actions included recording the activities of government agents, which were largely unseen by the broader public, and exposing the processes by which ICE detained undocumented migrants and then systematically deported them. The activists' use of documentary media functioned as a tactical weapon.

While some undocumented youth activists adopted strategies of countervisibility that protected them from detention and deportation, Jonathan and Isaac also engaged in countersurveillance, as they attempted to infiltrate an immigration detention center. To document what federal agencies were doing behind closed doors—making visible what the state wanted to keep invisible—they performed as "ordinary" undocumented migrants so that their actions did not receive the attention of the news media. Jonathan and Isaac described this infiltration as a "silent action" in which they declared their immigration status before federal immigration agents without the presence of the media.[51] The strategies of these activists—including the "silent action"—developed in response to the Obama administration's predilection for "silent raids" and its more veiled approach to detention and deportation, which stood in contrast to the spectacle associated with ICE workplace raids during the Bush administration.

During their action, Jonathan was the first to enter the office, and he used the video camera on his cell phone to live-stream his interaction with the Border Patrol.[52] He put his cell phone in a jacket pocket with the camera lens directed at the Border Patrol personnel. After entering the office, he speaks to a receptionist, acting as if he is lost. In watching the video, viewers see the Border Patrol staff, but they only hear Jonathan. The camera is shaky, and the aesthetics resemble that of *cinéma vérité*, making the video appear similar to a journalistic exposé. During his interactions with the Border Patrol agents, he questions what they are doing. When the agents explain they are "enforcing immigration law," Jonathan accuses them of deporting people, noting as well that he is "undocumented," a term they do not understand. (Jonathan then translates the term, stating that he is "illegal.") He continues to film the Border Patrol agents as they ask him questions regarding his entry into the United States. Within a short time after his arrival at the Border Patrol office, the agents decide that Jonathan—considered "low priority" by the terms of prosecutorial discretion—will

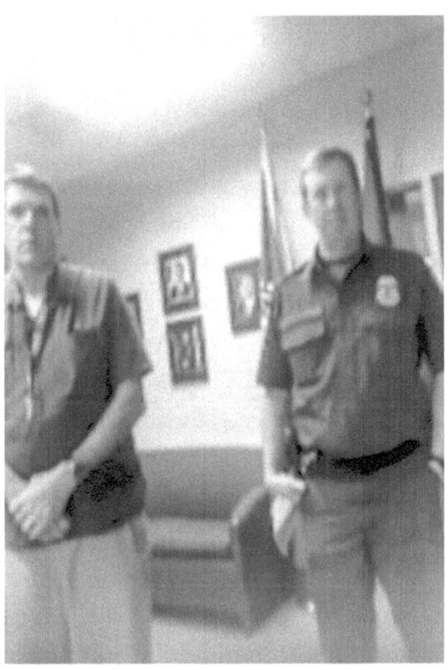

FIGURE 8.2 Screen shot from "Undocumented Youth vs. Border Patrol Round 1—Mobile, Alabama," filmed by Jonathan while he was being questioned in a Border Patrol office in Mobile in November 2011. Screen capture from digital video.

be moved to a detention center. The documentary video exposes how state agents failed to follow the guidelines for discretion.

Jonathan used his cell phone camera as part of a strategy of countersurveillance: "We knew people like us were being deported and we wanted to create a scenario where that could be seen in the public sphere."[53] As such, he documented what happened in the absence of publicity around the case of a "low priority" undocumented migrant. Consequently, Jonathan provided evidence that undocumented migrants—like himself—who met the terms of discretion were being detained. The video highlights the state agents' lack of discretion in their "processing" of undocumented migrants, and it documents this not-so-silent action, as Jonathan's words were heard during the live stream. Jonathan's interaction with Border Patrol agents was posted on YouTube, under the title "Undocumented Youth vs. Border Patrol Round 1—Mobile, Alabama," while he and Isaac were still being held at the detention center in Louisiana (fig. 8.2).[54] Although this action involved countersurveillance, the video also created a counternarrative to the story provided by the Obama administration: that state agents were using discretion.[55] The video served as a counterdocument, circulating Jonathan's interaction with state agents, revealing the limits of the Obama administration's policies around discretion, and demonstrating the ways in which he and Isaac directly challenged the work of the Border Patrol, the DHS, ICE, and the Obama administration.

One of the main strategies of undocumented youth activists in the early 2010s was to publicize their actions through digital and social media in order to bring attention to how U.S. immigration policies was affecting undocumented migrants, which also served as a form of protection against their detention and deportation. These strategies were a response to the Obama administration's minimizing of publicity around its policing of undocumented youth migrants. However, Jonathan's video also reveals the limitations of representing state agents from the perspective of undocumented migrants. After a few minutes of filming the Border Patrol with a cell phone camera, he was arrested by the Border Patrol agents, limiting his ability to document what they were doing after their initial interaction.

The video "Undocumented Youth vs. Border Patrol Round 1" and those produced by activists in North Carolina served as counterdocuments that represented the ways in which undocumented youth activists challenged state and federal immigration laws and policies, mobilized in support of undocumented migrants, and protected those who took part in actions from being detained or deported. The undocumented youth activists involved in these actions contested both state policies and their implementation and configured their self-representations in ways that were oppositional. Further, by disseminating their videos through digital and social media, these activists were able to mobilize other undocumented migrants against anti-immigrant state and federal laws. The videos produced by these activists thus invoked circulation and mobilization as political strategies rather than sought inclusion. As such, they reworked notions of visibility from an *abstract* form of empowerment to a more *specific* strategy, which involved publicizing their political actions that directly challenged immigration laws and policies on the state and federal levels. The activists' decision to record these videos was part of a strategy that they devised in order to communicate their perspectives regarding the effects of programs and policies such as S-Comm and 287(g) on other undocumented migrants. Circulating these videos enabled undocumented youth to provide an example of organizing that served as a model for other undocumented migrants. In their rejection of liberal claims to the inherently transformative capacity of visibility, these activists practiced strategies that also defied conventions of representation and documentation that demand inclusion as a normative imperative.

These activists' counterdocuments speak to both the changing context of documentary practices and the politics of self-representation for undocumented youth. One of the main developments in documentary film and video over the last twenty years has been the dispersion of these forms throughout popular culture, including mainstream cinema, reality television, and digital and social media, including websites like YouTube.[56] The distribution of counterdocuments changes not just the context of documentary but also what the documentary genre of media production is and can do. McLagan argues that "new media refashions previous media forms . . . and this process of 'remediation' upends old ideas about subjects and participants, producers and texts that underpin theories of how media work."[57] Counterdocuments, as forms of digital activism, have the ability to "define the terms of political possibility and create terrain for political acts," as McKee and McLagan suggest.[58] As such, counterdocuments strategically assemble evidence, disrupt, and mobilize.

NOTES

I would like to thank the editors for their feedback on this essay. I am also grateful to Jonathan, Isaac, and Viridiana for sharing their experiences during the "Everyday Forms of Popular Power: Art, Media and Immigration" symposium at the University of New Mexico in November 2012.

1. I describe these individuals as "undocumented youth activists" to distinguish them from either DREAM activists or migrant activists who are not eligible for the DREAM Act or Deferred Action for Childhood Arrivals due to their age. However, I am aware that I am using the term *youth* to describe activists who range from teenagers to young adults. I have intentionally withheld the surnames of activists in this essay.

2. By "official forms of documentation," I am referring to administrative record keeping, monitoring, status adjudication, and so forth.

3. I use the phrase "documentary realist forms" to call attention to the ways in which documentary is an aesthetic practice based in the visual conventions of social realism, with genealogical connections to state record keeping and scientific modes of visual documentation, as in the work of Alphonse Bertillon and Francis Galton, among others. See Sekula's essay "Body and the Archive"; see also Tagg, *Burden of Representation*.

4. McKee and McLagan, introduction to *Sensible Politics*, 17–18.

5. On 18 August 2011, the Obama administration announced that undocumented migrants who fit certain eligibility criteria should *not* be placed into deportation proceedings. A 17 June 2011 memo by John Morton, the director of the Department of Homeland Security, directed agents to use "prosecutorial discretion" with the migrants currently in deportation proceedings. The memo stated that Immigration and Customs Enforcement should focus its work on undocumented migrants convicted of crimes, but this directive was largely ignored by federal immigration officials, who continued to arrest, detain, and deport those who had committed only civil violations. See http://www.ice.gov/doclib/secure-communities/pdf/prosecutorial-discretion-memo.pdf, accessed 18 May 2016.

6. Discretion is clearly a historically fraught concept that is based on interpretation and has allowed for institutional racism. For example, Mexicans crossing the U.S.-Mexico boundary without documentation after 1924 were considered to have entered "illegally" and were thus perceived as criminals and as undeserving of relief. Ngai, *Impossible Subjects*, 89.

7. There were a number of different versions of the DREAM Act proposed in the 2000s.

8. In this sense, the activists I write about have something in common with the queer migrants of color whom Monisha Das Gupta describes and who likewise do not "uncritically embrac[e] visibility as a mode of political empowerment." Das Gupta, *Unruly Immigrants*, 165.

9. For more information, see NIYA's Facebook page.

10. Puga, "Poor Enrique and Poor María," 228.

11. The press release is available on YouTube underneath the activists' videos. See http://www.youtube.com/watch?v=TCRiyhUitok, accessed 19 May 2016.

12. Puga, "Poor Enrique and Poor María," 228.

13. According to ICE, the 287(g) program "allows a state and local law enforcement entity to enter into a partnership with ICE, under a joint Memorandum of Agreement (MOA). The state or local entity receives delegated authority for immigration enforcement within their jurisdictions." See http://www.ice.gov/287g/, accessed 19 May 2016.

14. Most of these videos can be viewed on YouTube under an activist's first name and last initial, location (North Carolina), and "We Will No Longer Remain in the Shadows." The heading for the press release is "Seven Undocumented Youth Speak Out against Federal Inaction and the Lack of Educational Access," posted by DREAMTeamNC, http://www.youtube.com/watch?v=TCRiyhUitok, accessed 18 May 2016.

15. Gomez, "DREAMers Personalize Cases to Stall Deportation."

16. Secure Communities requires local and state enforcement agencies to check both the criminal history and immigration status of individuals whom they have arrested, which they share with ICE.

17. May, "Los Infiltradores."

18. Ibid.

19. See note 5.

20. Prosecutorial discretion is issued by a joint task force—composed of staff members from the DHS and the Department of Justice—that reviews pending removals and can grant deferred action on an individual's deportation. Alexa Alonzo and Mary Kenney, "Practice Advisory," 1 September 2011, www.legalactioncenter.org, accessed 19 May 2016.

21. The press release is available on YouTube, underneath the activists' videos. See http://www.youtube.com/watch?v=TCRiyhUitok, accessed 18 May 2016.

22. According to the website for "United We Dream," the END campaign was initiated in 2010 "to prevent the deportations of young people, thereby allowing immigrant youths to continue their lives in the United States, pursue higher education and achieve their dreams." See http://unitedwedream.org/about/projects/end/, accessed 19 May 2016.

23. *Education Not Deportation: A Guide for Undocumented Youth in Removal Proceed-*

ings was produced by NIYA in collaboration with the Asian Law Caucus, Educators for Fair Consideration, and DreamActivist.org. The sixty-page guide provides legal strategies for undocumented youth in removal proceedings during a period in which the DHS could exercise prosecutorial discretion.

24. Unzueta Carrasco and Seif, "Disrupting the Dream," 288.

25. Ibid., 288.

26. As noted in the guide, "By using pictures you intend to show the public that you are just like them." *Education Not Deportation*, 35.

27. Ibid.

28. I compare the videos produced in North Carolina with the example included in the END guide. See the video made by Herta: "Meet Herta Llusho and Help Stop Her Deportation," YouTube video, posted by DreamActivist, 13 August 2009, https://www.youtube.com/watch?v=kMU_DZofuWQ, accessed 19 May 2016.

29. Walter Nicholls notes that the "DREAMer" was developed by professional associations that were working to get the DREAM Act passed. In creating the "DREAMer," these organizations specified that "these youths were exceptionally good immigrants and particularly deserving of legalization." Nicholls, *DREAMers*, 13.

30. Cristina Beltrán refers to these videos as "cyber-testimonies." Beltrán, "Undocumented, Unafraid, and Unapologetic," 20.

31. See Angelica's video: "Angelica V_ North Carolina: We Will No Longer Remain in the Shadows!," YouTube video, posted by DREAMTeamNC, 6 September 2011, http://www.youtube.com/watch?v=HuqoGX8hP2o, accessed 19 May 2016.

32. See Santiago's video: "SantiagoG__North Carolina: We Will No Longer Remain In The Shadows!," YouTube video, posted by DREAMTeamNC, 6 September 2011, http://www.youtube.com/watch?v=XEvokpyUysY, accessed 19 May 2016.

33. Martin explains that he participated in the action because politicians representing his state—such as Senator Kay Hagan (D-N.C.)—were doing nothing to help undocumented youth. See Martin's video: "MartinR__North Carolina: We Will No Longer Remain In The Shadows!," YouTube video, posted by DREAMTeamNC, 6 September 2011, http://www.youtube.com/watch?v=TCRiyhUitok, accessed 19 May 2016.

34. A few activists did make statements that contained aspects of conventional DREAMer narratives.

35. He also noted that undocumented youth should "embrace the struggles of LGBTQ communities, African American communities, communities of color and immigrant communities of all backgrounds" in order to "create a real movement." See Santiago's video.

36. See Martin's video.

37. These approaches to publicity have been addressed elsewhere, including Choi, "Web of Power."

38. McLagan, "Human Rights, Testimony and Transnational Publicity," 311.

39. Ibid., 312. DreamActivist.org's Facebook page describes the organization as "the largest social media hub for undocumented immigrants to aid organizations, communities and individuals to come together and find new ways to provide help for immigrant communities" (accessed 12 June 2014).

40. The petition blamed President Obama and the Democratic Party, explaining,

"Your recent announcement only acts as a mask to the devastation and injustice that programs like 287(g) and Secure Communities will continue to have in our communities. Your announcements are a symptom of the problem that is the vicious cycle of immigrant criminalization, not a potential cure to the realities of a broken immigration system. We will not tolerate lies designed to court the votes of our community. We will hold you and other Democratic leaders accountable as we demand to be treated with nothing less than dignity and justice." "Support Undocumented Youth Arrested in North Carolina," 8 September 2011, www.dreamactivist.org, accessed 19 May 2016.

41. May, "Los Infiltradores." Marco, an activist arrested in North Carolina, wrote that undocumented migrants began "applying counter-intuitive measures to counter-hegemonic ends" (Pavey and Saavedra, *Shadows Then Light*, n.p.).

42. Quoted in Pavey and Saavedra, *Shadows Then Light*, n.p.

43. Quoted in ibid.

44. Inda and Dowling note that "ICE's law enforcement partners are supposed to target dangerous 'criminal aliens,' but most immigrants who get caught are actually low-level offenders or people who simply crossed paths with local police." Inda and Dowling, "Introduction," 22; Waslin, *Secure Communities Program*.

45. Inda and Dowling, "Introduction," 3. Their concept of "migrant counter-conducts" draws on Michel Foucault's notion of "counter-conduct," which he describes as "the sense of struggle against the processes implemented for conducting others." Foucault, *Security, Territory, Population*, 201.

46. Haggerty, "Tear Down the Walls," 29.

47. Pallares, *Family Activism*, 124–25. See also "People of Alabama vs. HB 56," YouTube video, posted 16 November 2011, http://www.youtube.com/watch?v=wfHQA-zr9-I, accessed 19 May 2016.

48. Inda and Dowling note that "in some locations . . . police officers are engaging in heavy racial profiling of Latinos, making pretextual stops and arrests of people believed to be immigrants so that their information (such as fingerprints) can be checked against the DHS databases." Inda and Dowling, "Introduction," 22; see also Romero, "Keeping Citizenship Rights White."

49. Jonathan and Isaac, presentation at the "Everyday Forms of Popular Power: Art, Media and Immigration" symposium, University of New Mexico, 9 November 2012, https://www.youtube.com/watch?v=4ct6lMyFWfM, accessed 19 May 2016.

50. See, for example, "DREAM Student Protest March at ICE Chief Counsel Office, Los Angeles October 2011," YouTube video, http://www.youtube.com/watch?v=PkxnPixjTts, accessed 19 May 2016.

51. Jonathan and Isaac presentation at "Everyday Forms of Popular Power."

52. Irene Vásquez and Daniel Sonis, "Interview w Jonathan and Isaac 12032011," University of New Mexico, 3 December 2011, YouTube video, posted 3 December 2011, https://www.youtube.com/watch?v=g9yXC_Q68gU; "Going Undercover at the Border Patrol," *Arts of Aztlán*, video, https://vimeo.com/33189634, accessed 19 May 2016.

53. Jonathan and Isaac presentation at "Everyday Forms of Popular Power."

54. "Undocumented Youth vs. Border Patrol Round 1—Mobile, Alabama," YouTube video, posted 20 April 2011, http://www.youtube.com/watch?v=iA54ErBfZ8E, accessed 19 May 2016.

55. Scholars like Mark Andrejevic refer to countersurveillance as "inverse surveillance" that "relies on the ability to offer a convincing counter-narrative to that promulgated by authorities, who may have better access to mainstream media or public relations strategies." Further, he comments that "the success of inverse surveillance depends on the efficacy of such counter-narratives—or, similarly, on the availability to subvert a particular dominant narrative." Andrejevic, "Watching Back, Surveillance as Activism," 180.

56. See Austin and de Jong, introduction to *Rethinking Documentary.*

57. McLagan, "Human Rights, Testimony and Transnational Publicity," 315.

58. McKee and McLagan, introduction to *Sensible Politics*, 9.

At Berkeley

Documenting the University in an Age of Austerity

MICHAEL MARK COHEN AND LEIGH RAIFORD

This essay is an effort to link questions of economic austerity, the crisis in public higher education, and contemporary uses of documentary film and photography. Our subject is a "selfie" of sorts, in that it considers three documentary projects done on and about the university campus upon which we both work, the University of California (UC) at Berkeley. Created between 2009 and 2013, a period of the recent past shaped by steep budget cuts from the state and mass political protests, these projects documented a university facing a confluence of crises. We hope to offer insight into the radical potential of contemporary documentary forms to represent and confront the ongoing crisis of austerity in American public education.

Our argument is that each project represents an explicit confrontation with and representation of this crisis, with each example offering its own political articulation of the crisis of austerity through distinct and conflicting uses of the documentary form. We ask, if documentary is itself a form of producing knowledge, what forms of knowledge are produced in the context of the neoliberal university? The first is a work of documentary as public relations pitch, where the "Thanks to Berkeley . . ." photo wall represented an effort to sell the public university's democratic values to finance an explicit step toward privatization. The second documentary, Frederick Wiseman's film *At Berkeley*, gives us the narrative drama of a university both in crisis and in bloom. Over the course of a sprawling four-hour film, Wiseman offers us an example of university public relations as documentary art film, a branded *cinéma vérité* that also manages to be a defining portrait of the twenty-first-century university. The third is an explicitly pedagogical project, modeled on American studies scholar Matthew Frye Jacobson's Historian's Eye website, in which students undertook research projects and curated archives of their own, documenting the sources and experiences of the 2011–12 Occupy movement in the East Bay. This work also represents a personal effort by two members of the UC Berkeley faculty to translate their on-campus teaching and activism into a work of scholarship, bringing to bear the radical possibilities that remain strong within both multiculturalism and cultural studies to defend public higher education in California. Using these examples, we argue that neoliberal factions within the university used documentary as a means to educate the public as to the economic necessity and personal virtues of privatization, whereas student activists, in explicit dialogue with these administrative efforts, also took up the documentary form to fight the logic of austerity, to confront the reality of an American police state, and to imagine a public university beyond both. Through this conflict of forms and examples, we see how documentary representations become sites of conflict, in which competing visions of the modern university become part of a great debate over the place of public higher education and its future.

"THANKS TO BERKELEY . . ."

In September 2008, on the verge of the nation's financial crisis, UC Berkeley's development office unveiled a photography project called "Thanks to Berkeley . . ." designed to promote the university's most ambitious capital fund drive ever. With a goal of raising $3 billion by 2013, the promotional literature described the "Campaign for Berkeley" as "a wide ranging effort to secure the University's status" and to "strengthen the campus' core mission to serve the public good." Financial contributions to public higher education from the state had been declining in California for decades, forcing universities to raise tuition and cut services. But Berkeley (unlike the California State University system or most of its fellow UC schools) has both the large alumnae and global brand recognition to undertake a major capital drive. To make the pitch, the public face of "Thanks to Berkeley . . ." consisted of thousands of black and white portraits of students, faculty, parents, alumni, and staff, many accompanied by brief handwritten comments by the subjects saying things like "I am going to change the world, Berkeley is going to teach me how," and "It's a place where people provide the experience." According to the promotional literature, the "Thanks to Berkeley . . ." photo project offered "a way for the Berkeley community to meet each other" and to "express its pride and gratitude for all that Cal does."[1]

To facilitate this public expression of gratitude, the university commissioned San Francisco–based advertising photographer Christopher Irion to bring his ongoing "Photobooth Project" to campus. In order to evoke "the mood of an arcade photobooth," the artist used a lightweight portable studio to photograph individuals or small groups, encouraging his sitters to be expressive and playful while behind the curtain. "By creating a private space in a public place," explained Irion, "it allows people to drop that public mask." This privatized public space was then reaggregated into "a vast grid" that revealed what the artist called the "warp and weft of the fabric of the community," which allowed a more intimate view of each person "than you are typically allowed to have when you pass each other on Sproul Plaza," the campus's busy central square. In displaying his work, Irion's primary requirement was that photos be exhibited in an accessible public location so as to "show . . . the community back to itself in a direct and democratic fashion."[2]

Following Irion's documentary directives, the university compiled the images and displayed them on a website, on banners hung along campus walkways, and in promotional literature mailed to solicit alumni and potential donors. Central to all of this, Irion unveiled a seventy-two-foot double-sided wall on a well-trafficked thoroughfare on Berkeley's campus. The wall arranged 426 images into a collective portrait that exuded confidence and pride, a full-throated expression of Cal's official self-image in what then chancellor Robert Birgeneau called a "majestic tapestry."[3] Yet for all its self-confidence and democratic brio, this group portrait represented the marketing pitch for a public university that previously had no need for such branding, thereby marking the photo wall as a direct, material product of the ongoing fiscal crisis.

During his tenure as president of the ten-campus University of California system, Mark Yudof repeatedly asserted that the state government in Sacramento was the source of all of UC's problems. "Due to deep-seated budgetary and governance problems," declared Yudof in 2009, "the state of California has become an unreliable partner for UC."[4] Since 2001, state contributions to higher education have fallen by more than half, and by 2010 state funds made up a mere 12 percent of UC Berkeley's total operating budget.[5] In this climate of state disinvestment in higher education, Berkeley began to turn with new purpose to raising private funds from, as the campaign called them, "the community of people who care deeply about Cal."[6] Tapping into its 420,000-strong alumni pool, the development office saw "huge potential" for this kind of fund-raising in the coming years. Though this manner of fund-raising was once reserved for wealthy private schools like Stanford and those in the Ivy League, as of 2010 private giving has outstripped state contributions to UC Berkeley.

While the "Thanks to Berkeley . . ." campaign was designed and built as a response to state disinvestment, its formal unveiling coincided with the collapse of the American financial system and the start of the Great Recession. In the summer of 2009, the Board of Regents, UC's governing board—which included Governor Arnold Schwarzenegger and real estate developer (and husband of Senator Dianne Feinstein) Richard Blum—declared a fiscal emergency in the UC system and voted to approve a 32 percent tuition increase. This became the first in a series of planned fee increases over the next two years that pushed the cost of a year's in-state tuition at UC to $14,460, marking a doubling of UC student fees between 2006 and 2016. The regents also approved a plan to double the number of non-California residents and international students admitted, selling the Berkeley brand on the global college market to the wealthy for $37,338 per year (plus the cost of room and board).[7] As a result of this dramatic change in public funding for higher education, since 2011 student tuition dollars have now exceeded the state's contribution in the University of California. This marks the fiscal and economic basis for the ongoing identity crisis of what was once regarded as the greatest public university system in the world. Berkeley's low cost—for rich and poor alike—was previously held up as a symbol of its democratic accessibility. But now, the regents viewed this as lost revenue. Berkeley, they argued, must compete in the field of elite higher education, and higher tuition makes Berkeley seem more competitive, more like the Ivy League and less like community college or the schools in the California State University system.[8] But when students pay more than the state, when tuition and student debt grow beyond anything the system's founders could have imagined, how truly public was Berkeley going to remain after the fiscal emergency passed?

But it is not just the university's finances and competitive status that are endangered by the trends toward state austerity; the school's much-celebrated diversity itself has been under serious threat since at least the previous financial crisis in the 1990s. While in the campaign's form, the re-aggregation of a privatized fund-raising public, we see evidence of the immediate crisis, in its content we can read evidence of another, overlapping crisis around racial diversity, particularly the unresolved crisis incurred due to the outlawing of affirmative action and race-based recruiting in California since 1996. In that year, California's Orwellian-sounding California Civil Rights Initiative prohibited the state from using race, sex, or ethnicity to recruit for "public employment, public education, or public contracting."[9]

The effects of this were immediate and continue in a clear trend line. In

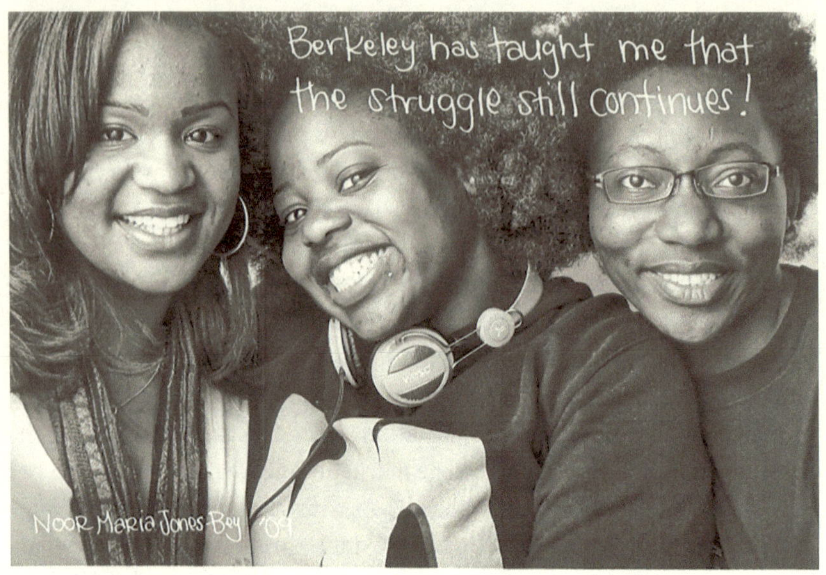

FIGURE 9.1 *Left to right*: Noor Jones-Bey, Tahirah Jones, and LaJuanda Asemota, 2009. "Thanks to Berkeley . . ." photo wall. Photo by authors.

its first year of implementation, enrollment of underrepresented minorities (defined as African American, Native American, and Chicanx/Latinx) dropped from 21.4 percent to 11.2 percent.[10] Figures for 2010 show that African Americans made up only 3.4 percent of the student body, Chicanx/Latinx roughly 10 percent, and Native Americans 0.7 percent. Underrepresented minorities together thus made up 14 percent of the UC Berkeley student body, in a state where these groups constitute 44.8 percent of the total population (while simultaneously representing 77 percent of the prison population).[11] Yet the photo wall included an obviously disproportionate number of black and brown faces. This burden of representation thus fell unequally upon the students of color themselves who walked past their own faces every day going from class to class. Many of the students of color featured on this wall were our students, and many of them when asked by us expressed a feeling of tokenism and exploitation at their representations. They were particularly frustrated by the ways the campaign used these images, their faces, to promote a false diversity in the wake of Proposition 209 and in the context of what many groups have called a "hostile racial climate."[12] One student complained that the campaign, along with continuing harassment from campus police, profiling from campus staff, and courses that belittle racialized subjects, reflected "issues of tokenization [that] can tear away at black students, and are ultimately leaving many people feeling as though they don't belong."[13]

As the university was becoming more unequal and less diverse, the photo wall thus provided a demographically engineered image of a multicultural middle class in the making. But when school spirit becomes an expected burden of representation, we are in the realm of public relations, not public art; brand management, not community building. At work here was the investment theory of education: what was once a public good was now understood as personal value added. Further, the photo booth project and its forms of display adhered to the logics of portraiture in advertising: public images targeting a specific demographic and selling them back to themselves, as transformed by the purchase and consumption of the UC product. What was previously conceived of as opportunity and a right of citizens of the state of California was now framed as returned dividends on one's private investment.

The form of the photo booth itself marked a peculiar individualized and privatized rearticulation of the public face and public space of the public university. By mediating between a possibly intimate encounter with a camera and the potentially anonymous or even contested experience of campus space, the photo booth project created a designed and branded virtual crowd to create a definitive self-representation of the transition from a truly public university to the neoliberal university. Consequently, this combination of utopianism and marketing, community portrait and corporate branding, served to transform this wall from a glossy public relations project of self-gratitude to an object of, and idiom for, student and worker protest.

In the fall of 2009, one academic year after the unveiling of the "Thanks to Berkeley . . ." campaign, the UC Board of Regents declared a financial emergency and raised tuition. In response, the students, faculty, and staff of the UC system mobilized to resist, beginning with a massive wave of public rallies and strikes. In November 2009, as the UC Regents met to vote for the emergency fee increase, they faced a student riot at UC Los Angeles that managed to encircle their meeting hall. Meanwhile, at Berkeley, news of the fee hike's passage led to the overnight takeover of one of the campus's largest classroom buildings, Wheeler Hall, by forty-three students.

The next morning, as news of the occupation spread and activists arrived for the third day of the strike, the first outside supportive action for the occupation began setting up formations in front of the "Thanks to Berkeley . . ." wall display. Campus activists transformed the wall into both

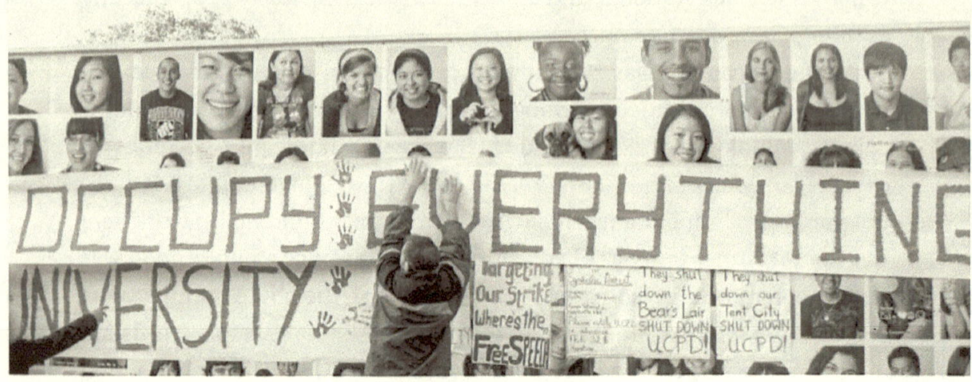

FIGURE 9.2 "Occupy Everything" banner at the University of California, Berkeley, 2009. Photo by authors.

a barricade and object of protest, reminding us that the struggle for public education in the United States is also a struggle over public space. It was here that the Occupy movement found one of its first and most militant expressions.

For the next year, the wall itself became a key site of public struggle. That December, to protest the suppression of free speech on campus during the official celebration of Mario Savio and the Berkeley free speech movement of the early 1960s, students placed orange duct tape over the mouths of the photographs' subjects to illustrate their own silencing. In March 2010, African American students used the wall as a backdrop for their own silent protest against the growing climate of racial hostility after a series of openly racist attacks occurred at UC San Diego and Davis. Other student groups adopted the photo booth idiom to draw attention to rising levels of student debt. With student debt currently surpassing household credit card debt as the single largest source of consumer debt in the United States, students took to photographing each other with signs reading "Thanks to Berkeley I'll be in Debt forever . . ."

The end of this particular story is not a happy one for the photo wall. Against the twin onslaughts of state austerity and popular protest, one act of vandalism seemed to have been the straw that broke the public relation campaign's back, and the wall was taken down two years ahead of schedule. "We struggled with the notion of taking it down," said David Blinder, associate vice chancellor for university relations. "You hate to give in. . . . But given the financial state, you don't want to spend money on what you don't have to spend it on."[14] Yet while the students either were indifferent to or openly hated the photo wall, the capital campaign turned out to be a huge success, raising more than $3 billion in private funds to somehow keep Berkeley "public."

AT BERKELEY

Attracted to UC Berkeley by the activism of 2009, documentarian Frederick Wiseman came to campus in the fall of 2010 to shoot a movie about the American university. Released in 2013, *At Berkeley* offered a four-hour-and-four-minute montage portrait of the public university in a moment of crisis. Widely praised, *New Yorker* film critic David Denby summed up the critical response: "I can't think of another film portrait of higher education that matches this one for comprehensiveness, intellectual depth, and hope."[15] A number of critics said the film made them want to go back to college. To many of us who work at Berkeley, the film feels a lot like a long, if eventful, day on the job, complete with all the excitement, boredom, and politics—both personal and institutional—of a large university. (At this point, in the interests of full disclosure, we need to mention that Wiseman's wide-angle view of Berkeley includes three sequences featuring one of the authors of this essay.)

Wiseman shot *At Berkeley*, his thirty-eighth film, using much the same method he used to make his first, *Titicut Follies*, in 1967. Shot with a three-person crew—director, photographer, and sound recorder—Wiseman's films employ an observational, fly-on-the-wall style, collecting footage as a means of what Wiseman calls "research." He then creates the film in the editing process, organizing the footage into an equally dramatic and pedagogic "report on what I learned." Wiseman quit a job at Boston University Law School to begin making films at the age of thirty, inspired by advances in portable camera and sound equipment that, in his words, "opened up ordinary experience to movies."[16] No interviews, no voice-overs, no titles, nothing staged, just the direct cinematic drama of watching individuals confront social institutions. And Wiseman's films are all about institutions, starting with the State Prison for the Criminally Insane in Bridgewater, Massachusetts, in *Titicut Follies*; Northeast High School in Philadelphia for *High School* (1968); the Ida B. Wells homes in Chicago for *Public Housing* (1997); and the eponymous *Boxing Gym* (2010) in Austin, Texas.

When asked "Why Berkeley?," Wiseman offered a kind of syllogism: "I'm doing a series on institutions, as you know. I wanted to do a university, and I wanted to do a public university. Berkeley is the greatest public university in the world. So I simply wrote a letter to the Chancellor, whom I'd never met, asking if he'd consider the idea."[17] Wiseman got approval and began shooting on campus within weeks, taking his camera into classrooms and labs, student groups, public performances, and protests, and gained special access to top administrative and crisis management meetings. Over the course of twelve weeks of shooting, Wiseman accumulated more than 250 hours of digital video on the Berkeley campus, which he then spent the next fourteen months editing into the finished film.

Wiseman's *At Berkeley* successfully incorporates several older documentary depictions of California higher education. For example, California Newsreel's 1969 short film *SF State on Strike* depicts the public institution in the midst of the months-long battle to establish an ethnic studies program. Challenging the alleged objectivity of direct cinema, the filmmakers understood themselves as the media arm of the era's antiracist, anticolonial movements and sought to make documentaries that in both form and content produced radical progressive visions. The result is a protester's-eye-view of confrontations between truncheon-wielding cops and multicultural student masses, rendering an image of higher education in a state of unending and irresolvable conflict.

Just two years earlier, Ansel Adams and Nancy Newhall's compendium *Fiat Lux* (1967) visualized then UC president Clark Kerr's dream of an expanding public higher education system. Adams turned his prodigious talents at photographing California's mountains toward the midcentury university, and one is immediately struck by the beauty of his images, their technical precision and stability, and the grand scale of his photographic work. Adams gives us the UC as epic vision. Unlike *SF State on Strike*'s noisy encounters, Adams's photographs at once document and perform a futuristic, even utopian vision of UC at the forefront of the Golden State: growing our food, inventing our technologies, designing our weapons, preserving our history, managing and transforming our landscape, solving our social ills, helping the less fortunate, and above all educating the next generation of leaders.[18]

At Berkeley manages to offer both images of overt ideological crisis (in the form of a large anti-austerity protest) and a soothing image of the public university as a pastoral landscape where civic ideals flourish. Above all, Wiseman's film exudes a quiet, listening confidence that convinced many of its hopeful vision of the modern university. Within this setting, the embattled yet enduring values of public education come through in every unscripted and carefully edited moment. For example, we observe a conversation in a windowless classroom between an engineering professor and two students curious about research and their futures. "The principle of this place," the professor explains, "is that this new knowledge has to be publicly disseminated, so one company's narrow economic interest is not going to align very well with that mission." From there we take a montage walk across campus to an administrative meeting in which we watch a pitch for "Operational Excellence," an expensive private consulting plan, in which a man in a suit and tie wielding a laser pointer and PowerPoint slides explains to administrators that the staff are having problems because their "incentives are misaligned" and "there is too much duplication of effort." This language is emblematic of the neoliberal response to the crisis in state funding, a solution in which operational excellence deploys the corporate jargon of managerial efficiency to justify cutbacks and enforce layoffs. In one connected sequence, Wiseman shows us a multifaceted institution affirm its most democratic values before the same institution trades these values away, using the financial crisis as a lever to conform to the logic of a for-profit corporation. This conflict, and this compromise, forms the central drama of the film.

Yet Wiseman's tone in addressing such a topic remains characteristically cool, as he says, "I like to make the film, I don't like to explain it." Rejecting the implication that every documentary has to be some sort of "exposé," Wiseman said that in making *At Berkeley* it was just as important "to show people of good will, intelligence and sensibility."[19] This more optimistic approach taken in *At Berkeley* marks a departure from Wiseman's more confrontational films of the 1960s and 1970s. In films like *Titicut Follies* and *High School*, Wiseman's observational style set the terms for the midcentury documentary exposé, taking his camera into the social margins of the American experience where few visitors wanted to look. As a result, *Titicut Follies* famously faced a legal injunction from the state of Massachusetts and decades of censorship while generating fervent demands for reform. *At Berkeley* provokes neither outrage nor calls for reform. Wiseman told interviewers that he was proud *At Berkeley* could depict "serious, responsible people . . . working hard to maintain the standards, integrity and quality of a great university."[20] In his essay on the film, former Berkeley English professor Stephen Greenblatt wrote, "I confess that I have never before been made to feel so sympathetic to administrators."[21]

The Berkeley administration loved it too. In a series of public appearances with Wiseman at film festivals and at the American Academy of Arts and Sciences, Chancellor Robert Birgeneau and Executive Vice Chancellor and Provost George Breslauer spoke at length about how complicit they were with Wiseman's conceit while praising the film as vindication of their leadership. Though they initially thought it risky to let Wiseman come to campus, especially after the protests of 2009, the film's two leading men said they felt the finished film was an "opportunity to project Cal" and that it was a "great advertisement" for the university.[22]

To gain access to Berkeley through Birgeneau and Breslauer, Wiseman did have to relinquish some measure of control. His camera was not allowed in tenure and promotion meetings. Nor did the administrators let Wiseman film anyone in the university's growing private fund-raising offices, therefore keeping concealed the work of the people who developed the "Thanks to Berkeley . . ." campaign. In a further structural limitation, Wiseman's camera always remained somewhere on the Berkeley campus, meaning that he never filmed UC president Mark Yudof or anyone in the UC's central administration (known as the UC Office of the President and based in Oakland), nor do we see the even more powerful Board of Regents, the largest governing body for the entire UC system.

One of the results of this Berkeley boundary is that it serves to frame the campus protests as a conflict between student activists and the administration. In reality, most of the protests were directed at this higher level of decision making, at the UC president and regents, at the state government, and at the Republican candidate for governor. The result is that we see the administrators calmly managing an immediate crisis created by student disruption, while the protesters speak on a much more totalizing level about structural problems in state governance and the needs for economic justice. Moreover, it is perhaps the greatest limitation of the film itself that student life goes largely unexamined.

While the film takes its time to roam widely across campus, it remains anchored inside California Hall and to the isolated band of administrators who calmly work therein. In meeting after meeting, we hear the chancellor expound on state funds, low-income students, the way to treat protesters, and the meaning of leadership. In all of those meetings, in room after room, it is all the same people listening to the persuasive and self-congratulatory chancellor. Wiseman's observational style is clearly seduced by the campus leadership's deliberative intelligence, yet what we are witnessing in these moments is a portrait of hermetic leadership experiencing a prolonged bout with a bunker mentality. None of the men and women who administer this great public university ever seem to encounter—let alone be forced to listen to—students, faculty, or low-level staff. They lecture department chairs, they explain things to staff representatives, they talk about (but not to) the lone lawn mower, while appearing in the same space with students only when they are singing in an a cappella group wearing matching blue and gold outfits. During the protests, administrators make a principled point of refusing to read student demands, which Birgeneau smugly dismisses as "contradictory" and "all over the place." Though the film depicts the university as a thriving democratic space, an institution in which many voices speak for the university and claim the spirit of Berkeley, the chancellor's open contempt for democracy is startling. In a movie that is visually dominated by images of people listening, the chancellor alone listens to no one.

In its direct cinema form, *At Berkeley* professes to the democratic openness of the public university, offering a vision of the institution with all of its machinery laid bare. But the structural limitations, whether imposed by the filmmaker or by his most powerful subjects, alert us to the insular, closed-door operations that increasingly drove the institution throughout the Great Recession. Unlike the photo wall, which made itself available for a kind of call-and-response of institutional self-representation, *At Berkeley* gives us a singular portrait of institutional hierarchy, albeit one surrounded by a rolling sea of democratic impulses, actions, and desires. While the global critical reception of *At Berkeley* was overwhelmingly positive, in the hallways and cafés of its subject campus, Wiseman's film generated far more critique than praise, due in large part to the fact that in the year between the film's research and its final report, not only had both starring administrators stepped down over their mishandling of student protests, but also many campus activists became engaged in documentary projects of their own designed to articulate and defend their ongoing radical resistance to the politics of austerity.

HISTORIAN'S EYE AND OCCUPY CAL

In the ensuing years, public relations gave way to outright coercion on the Berkeley campus. A year after Wiseman and his crew left campus, in the fall of 2011, police violence rather than slick marketing or direct cinema played the forward role in enforcing student compliance with a predicted future of increased fees and diminished resources. The brutality shown by the campus police against Occupy Cal protesters, widely seen in viral videos of the UC Police Department beating protesters on Sproul Plaza and the even more famous image of campus police pepper-spraying seated protesters at UC Davis, served to make the Regents' push for higher fees politically untenable. A statewide ballot measure to raise taxes on the rich to stabilize the state's education budget passed in November 2012, preempting a proposed 81 percent fee increase. This electoral victory marked a clear, if modest, success for the voices of public education over the pressures of privatization and neoliberalism.

Yet the coverage of these events, and the small successes they claimed, became dominated by mainstream media, the California Democratic Party, and a UC administration that solicited students only as voters while dismissing student-led direct action tactics as the work of "outside agitators." However, as the crisis continued, we noted the increasing presence of students making and circulating their own images of protests, mostly through their cell phones and social media sites like YouTube, Tumblr, Flickr, and Twitter. The students were constantly, reflexively documenting their protests. But, we wondered, was there a documentary archive of this moment? How was one to document this moment from the bottom up? While "Thanks to Berkeley . . ." aimed to reflect the Cal community back to itself for the sake of cultivating donorship and *At Berkeley* sought to reveal the earnest inner workings of the institution to the world, as professors we wondered how might a visual documentary project be made by and for the students themselves—a documentary pedagogy designed to amplify student voices not as potential donors or as a future filmic audience but as historical actors and agents in this place and time. In response, we attempted to enact in the classroom the demand for a different narrative of the crisis announced in the campus's public spaces.

Trained in traditional historical methods, we turned to the Historian's Eye: Our Better History project, scholar Matthew Frye Jacobson's expansive online documentary undertaking, as a model to explore innovative and interdisciplinary ways to document contemporary American history. Our hope was to empower our students to pick up the camera and microphone and record the history going on before their own eyes. Conceived of as a means to document the historic inauguration of the nation's first black president, the Historian's Eye website has grown to collect a wide range of oral histories and black-and-white photographs taken by Jacobson to document the ongoing political and economic crises from various sites around the country. Thinking of the Historian's Eye as an "archive of the present," Jacobson has undertaken an exploration of contemporary history using traditional documentary methods, with the purpose of making this history available to teachers, scholars, and the general public.

Working with a group of student activists, we first took up the challenge of building an online archive of the California Occupy movements while developing methods of bringing the Historian's Eye into the undergraduate classroom, encouraging students to develop their skills in reading images on the website by contributing images of their own and visualizing the social and cultural impact of the Great Recession.[23] Then, in a select seminar on documenting the crisis in California, we began by studying the economic origins of the recession from Wall Street to Washington to Oakland. We interrogated historiographic, cartographic, documentary, and curatorial methodologies of activist documentary and art and then began the process of building a digital archive of present history.

From the beginning, the student documentary projects took us off campus, connecting the crisis in public higher education to communities across the state, tracing the lines between student protests and home foreclosures, gentrification, police brutality, homelessness, plutocracy, and austerity—forces that affected students' own lives and shaped their on-campus choices. If the photo wall project and *At Berkeley* found their formal purpose—and limits—by staying firmly planted on the space of the campus, then the student documentarians sought to place their campus within the larger community, linking the student activism of the present to a world historical crisis of democracy and capitalism. As the Occupy Everything banner first flown on the Berkeley campus in November 2009 became the flag of Occupy Wall Street planted in Zuccotti Park, the movement came full circle, binding the antiauthoritarian struggles in Egypt, Turkey, and Tunisia to the anti-austerity protests in England, Greece, and Oakland. In a crisis of this scope, our students recognized that staying on the Berkeley campus was not an option.

As an experiment from the outset, we gave ourselves license to imagine a utopic classroom: anti-hierarchical, accessible, diverse. As professors raised in analog methods, we wanted the opportunity to learn alongside our students. Thus, we brought in a range of speakers—writers, artists, academics, librarians, technicians—to provide models of engaged scholarship as well as to train us in digital recording methods. We also sought a classroom that was truly diverse, not only along axes of race, ethnicity, class, gender, and sexuality but also of age and experience: our classroom included student parents, formerly incarcerated students, and traditional, transfer, and nontraditional students alike, a kind of diversity that "Thanks to Berkeley . . ." alluded to yet flattened. For us, this is the promise of public education.

The result was a wide range of forms and subjects, ranging from tra-

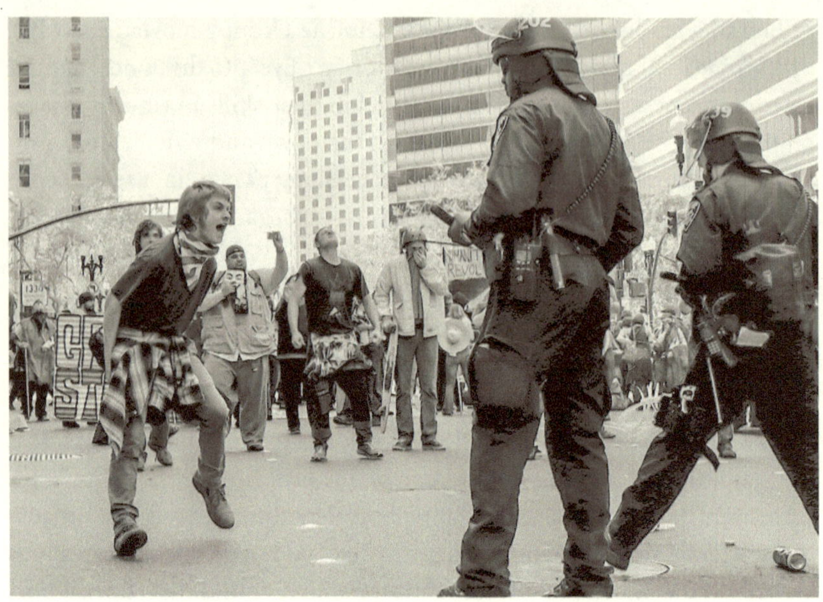

FIGURE 9.3 *Occupy Oakland May Day General Strike*, May 2012. Courtesy of the photographer, Robert Lee. http://historianseye.commons.yale.edu/uc-berkeley-historians-eye-photos-by-photographer/.

ditional oral histories and documentary photography to innovative mapping and visual design projects. Students explored the rapidly gentrifying neighborhoods of Oakland and San Francisco through photography, documented the cartography of Bay Area foreclosures in oil painting, and produced journalistic investigations connecting the drought in the Central Valley to Sacramento politics, oral histories of formerly incarcerated students, and documentary films about Ethiopian immigrant communities and the nonliterary-oriented public services demanded from and provided by the Oakland public libraries.

What we learned from this taught us much about how deeply students sought to create and share knowledge about their own communities and how larger political forces, often imagined only in abstract terms like neoliberalism, privatization, financialization, or gentrification, affected their everyday lives. Far from seeking to close themselves within the walls of the ivory tower, as suggested by "Thanks to Berkeley . . ." and *At Berkeley*, these students used critical documentary methods to map globalized forces, to build bridges between themselves and their communities, and to close the gap between what they learned and what they hoped to change.

Artist Martha Rosler once described documentary photography cynically as "the social conscience of liberal sensibility presented in visual imagery," a medium that relies on moralism and charity in order to compel audiences to reformist rather than revolutionary action.[24] This liberal-reformist definition clearly applies to the first two projects discussed. In the "Thanks to Berkeley . . ." campaign, the compendium of images documenting Berkeley's community, there is nothing radical in the goal of cultivating alumni goodwill and donations. And Wiseman's *At Berkeley* asks very little of its audiences beyond the endurance to watch for four hours, at the end of which one is left with the feeling that Berkeley is in good hands, enduring through the deliberative intelligence of its administrators and professors.

But the Historian's Eye marks a radical departure from the other two endeavors in a way that reflects the argument of scholar Ariella Azoulay, who identifies documentary spectatorship as a "civic duty" that binds documentarian, subject, and audience into new political relations and demands social transformation.[25] Documentary's true potential then lies not necessarily in its form and content but in what documentary's audiences "do" with the knowledge revealed. Emerging from an explicitly pedagogic activist position, the Historian's Eye project sought to imagine this radical transformation in both the process and the final product by encouraging students to develop critical storytelling skills needed to shape and chronicle the events evolving around them. While this last documentary effort might constitute the "most radical" of the three visions of California higher education in crisis, we also recognize that it too has its limitations. If anything, it became clear to us that the public university in the twenty-first century cannot be represented in a single instance or in a single form. Rather, it demands a multiplicity of voices, visions, and approaches reflecting and embracing its diversity. These lessons of art, activism, and documentary remain essential to our current political struggles, because the future remains very much in the balance—not just here in California but across the country and the world.

NOTES

1. *The Promise of Berkeley*, University Relations, UC Berkeley, Fall 2008, http://promise.berkeley.edu/lib/pdf/2008_fall_promise.pdf, 8.

2. All quotes are from *Promise of Berkeley*.

3. Ibid., 8.

4. Mark Yudof, "UC's Road to Recovery Requires Painful Actions," October 2009, http://www.universityofcalifornia.edu/advocacy/youru1009/yudofoct09.html. Based on transcript of remarks of President Mark G. Yudof, UC Board of Regents meeting, UC San Francisco Mission Bay, 16 September 2009.

5. Michael Meranze, "Cells, Classrooms, and State Disinvestment in Higher Ed," 7 May 2014, http://utotherescue.blogspot.com/2014/05/cells-classrooms-and-state.html.

6. *Promise of Berkeley*, 3.

7. See Bill Chappell, "One Year of Public College Can Now Cost $50,000 in California," November 1, 2010, www.npr.org/blogs/thetwo-way/2010/11/01/130978652/one-year-of-public-college-can-now-go-for-50-000; and Lilia Vega, "The History of UC Tuition since 1868," December 22, 2014, http://www.dailycal.org/2014/12/22/history-uc-tuition-since-1868/.

8. University administration's slogan for this policy is called "the high fee / high aid model." What this means is that it raises tuition and then offers generous financial aid packages for lower income students. The administration uses this policy change to argue that Berkeley is currently enrolling more lower income students than ever before. The rich pay more, the working class gets aid, the middle class take out loans, and the share of the university's revenue paid by students goes up. That is the plan, and there are several serious flaws. First, there has to be some limit in order to earn financial aid, so no matter where you set the household income threshold, the middle class gets squeezed. What was once free to everyone in California now becomes a massive financial burden for middle-class Californians. Second, higher fees—regardless of financial aid policies—are known to have a deterrent effect on working-class and first-generation college students who, often unfamiliar with the college application process and complex financial aid forms, experience "sticker shock" and simply do not apply to the UC system. And last, for everyone at every level, this new financial model is driven by debt, student loans, credit cards, second mortgages, and so on, as the high fee / high aid model pumps air into the debt bubble. See Chris Newfield, "Have We Protected Poor Students from Debt?," *Remaking the University* blog, February 9, 2012, http://utotherescue.blogspot.com/2012/02/have-we-protected-poor-students-from.html.

9. From the text of "Proposition 209: Prohibition against Discrimination or Preferential Treatment by State and Other Public Entities," 1996, https://www.calvoter.org/voter/elections/archive/96gen/props/209.html.

10. See UC Berkeley Office of Planning and Analysis, http://opa.berkeley.edu/institutionaldata/archiveenroll.htm.

11. See UC Berkeley Office of Planning and Analysis, http://opa.berkeley.edu/institutionaldata/campusenroll.htm; and United States Census Bureau, http://quickfacts.census.gov/qfd/states/06000.html. Incarceration figures for California (as of July 2013) can be found at Offender Information Reports, California Department of Corrections and Rehabilitation, http://www.cdcr.ca.gov/Reports_Research/Offender_Information_Services_Branch/Offender_Information_Reports.html.

12. See 2014 UC Office of the President Campus Climate Report at Study Results, http://campusclimate.ucop.edu/results/index.html.

13. Asemota, "The Black History Month Façade."

14. Susman, "Wall of Faces Permanently Removed."

15. Denby, "American Gothic."

16. The Seventh Art, "Frederick Wiseman Interview—The Seventh Art," YouTube video, July 18, 2016, https://www.youtube.com/watch?v=I2XWDL3pUHY.

17. Seventh Art Issue 17, section 4, at https://www.youtube.com/watch?v=6HP7wC8EzDg.

18. To this list of documentaries on and about California higher education we should add Mark Kitchell's 1990 film *Berkeley in the Sixties*. This documentary, a high point of baby boomer nostalgia and hagiography, is everything that direct cinema is not, structured by talking head interviews, name tag intertitles, historical stock footage, and explicit moralizing over past events.

19. Seventh Art Issue 17, section 4.

20. See DP/30: The Oral History of Hollywood, "DP/30: Frederick Wiseman @ TIFF '13—At Berkeley," YouTube video, October 7, 2013, https://www.youtube.com/watch?v=A3iyymwTA-g.

21. Greenblatt, "Wonderous, Fragile, Tedious Berkeley."

22. Birgeneau and Breslauer used a series of high-profile public appearances around the film to polish their legacy and defend their own highly unpopular (if entirely local) policies and administrative plans. Breslauer told the Academy of Arts and Sciences that the protesters came off as "vapid" while the administrators were "struggling to deal with really difficult choices." In fact, the pair's publicity for the film was something of a farewell tour, both having faced an Academic Senate condemnation of their handling of Occupy protests on campus (downgraded from a "no-confidence" vote) in November 2011 followed by announcements of their decisions to step down. See Jon Wiener, "Berkeley Faculty: No Confidence in Chancellor Over Campus Police Violence," *The Nation*, November 25, 2011, http://www.thenation.com/blog/164798/berkeley-faculty-no-confidence-chancellor-over-campus-police-violence#.

23. The UC Berkeley Occupy archive can be found at the Historian's Eye: http://hopedespair.yctl.org/uc-berkeley-historians-eye-gallery/.

24. Rosler, "In, around and Afterthoughts," in *Decoys and Disruptions*, 176.

25. Azoulay, *Civil Contract of Photography*.

Afterword

MATTHEW FRYE JACOBSON

In the fall of 2015, a colleague and I were co-teaching Introduction to Documentary Studies at Yale when the campus erupted in protest over a spate of racist incidents, including one college administrator's statement to students in defense of racially insensitive Halloween costumes. The class up to that point had gone pretty much the way college classes do—we had read Errol Morris's obsessive and brilliant meditations on how the mind informs the eye, not the other way around ("believing is seeing"); we had absorbed Paula Rabinowitz's work on documentary genres as a kind of topographical map of progressive thought across the twentieth century; we had wrestled with ethical questions drawing upon Robert Coles and talked through logistical questions with visiting practitioners like Zareena Grewal (*By the Dawn's Early Light*), Rebecca Wexler (*We Break Things*), and Jake Halpern ("Switched at Birth" episode of *This American Life*). We worked to disassemble and dissect the genre—students had watched *Harvest of Shame* without sound and listened to *The Thin Blue Line* without visuals, and they had made several trips to the Yale Art Gallery, where I curated a study wall with images from Lewis Hine, Dorothea Lange, Helen Levitt, Milton Rogovin, and several others. But in retrospect, I now see that students had not learned anything—I mean *really* learned anything—until the day I canceled class.

I come by this honestly, this idea that the classroom is an inconvenient necessity and that the most consequential pedagogy is often to be found outside its walls. My uncle Norman Jacobson was a faculty member at Berkeley during the free speech movement in 1964. In a note posted on the classroom door of Poli Sci 113, he wrote, "As I have tried to absorb the significance of what was taking place before my eyes, it became clear to me that I simply was incapable of violating the palpable air of protest which today surrounds every building on this campus. There will be no class today." He later produced a documentary film titled *Report*, chronicling his experi-

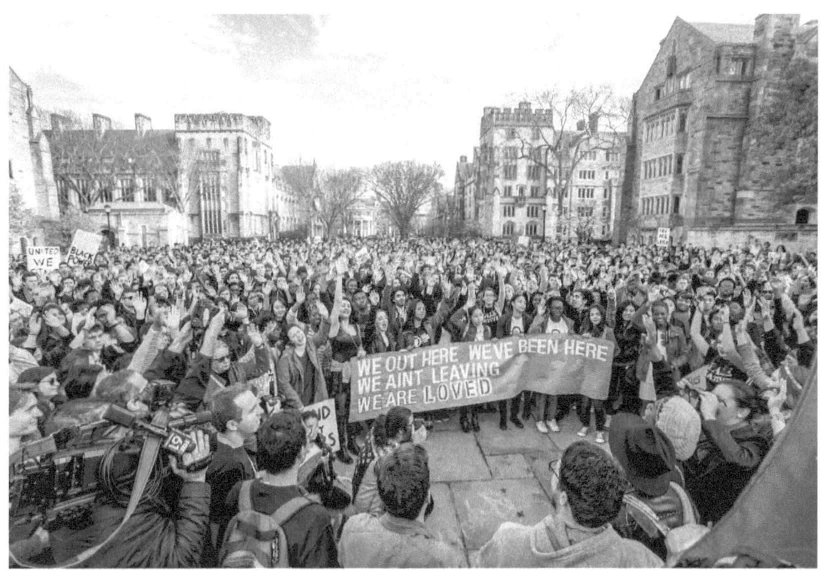

FIGURE A.1 *Yale March of Resilience, 2015*. Courtesy of the photographer, Alexander Zhang.

mental class at Berkeley, Toward the Expression of the Idea of Freedom. My own 1970s undergrad experience was similarly punctuated with teach-ins on U.S. conduct in Central America, among other things; and so to me it was just a matter of course that this 2015 student protest in the streets might require that we abandon the classroom in the name of justice and even, perhaps, in the name of our studies. "I am going to march," I told my students. "I encourage you to join or not as conscience dictates, but I also invite you to take these protests as an occasion to test all those documentary skills and practices you have been discussing so earnestly this semester."

As I marched with the throngs up High Street toward the heart of campus in what has since become known as the March of Resilience, I kept seeing our documentary students along the way: perched atop light poles or fire hydrants, cameras rolling; kneeling in the street amid the onrush of marchers; or shooting from the dais once the marchers had gathered for a series of speeches by student leaders. When you Google "Yale March of Resilience," many of the images that turn up were shot by our students, including the day's definitive images shot from the stage by Alex Zhang. Some truly excellent documentary work came out of that experience—students made very powerful films devoted to race and justice at Yale; they produced photo-essays and compiled interview archives with students, faculty, and administrators. But for our group, the most striking thing that came out of this was the effect that this day's work had on our discussions and on our understanding. As this volume preaches, documentary practice itself is not only a kind of pedagogy but also fully an epistemology—a way of knowing, a method of engaged knowing, an engagement *with* knowing.

After reading *Remaking Reality*, many phrases continue to swirl in my mind, to tantalize and haunt: "participatory documentary" (Hale), "counterdocuments" (Schreiber), "speculative documentary" (Worden), "metaphorical ear" and "cross-talk" (Kahana and Tsika), the documentarian's "deliberate quiet" (Nudelman), "transmedial revision" and the "graphic display of buried knowing" (Wexler), "multiplicitous, contingent truths" and "semantic instability" (Entin), "documentary pedagogy" (Cohen and Raiford), "critical realism" and "transformative agency" (Blair). The phrases stay with me because they so wonderfully capture and convey my own experience—as mentor, as practitioner, as consumer—of documentary work. This is not just any old genre, that is; it is at once a method of teaching and learning, a technique for apprehending the world, a mode of both inquiry and expression, a register of critique, an idiom of protest, a way of mobilizing one's very subjectivity for the struggles at hand and, in the best instance, of mobilizing the subjectivity of others as well. "A camera," Dorothea Lange famously said, "is a tool for learning how to see without a camera."[1] It is the documentarian's hope of hopes that his or her work—both work as "product" and work as "craft"—might likewise teach us to see without documentaries.

Documentary work, then, is at once impossible and necessary. Impossible because the conscientious practitioner is bound to be plagued by a thousand paralyzing questions, not only questions of fidelity—*Did my rendering get it right?*—but ethical and philosophical questions, too: *Was the encounter exploitative? Was the narrative device manipulative? Was the confession coerced?* And yet documentary work is necessary, nonetheless, because in a putative democracy whose participants number in the millions and whose civic exchanges are inevitably mass-mediated, the question is always before us: What is it that we share—that we *can* share—as a foundation for reasonable deliberation and decision-making when it comes to our understanding of prevailing conditions? So on the one hand (to take a case), it may be that John Hersey's approach to realism—as Mary McCarthy charged—flattened the emotive force of his narrative to the extent that Harry Truman's dropping of the atomic bomb evoked no deeper sense of human responsibility than would an earthquake or a typhoon.

And yet on the other hand, as Franny Nudelman argues here, so is it true that Hersey was groping for what he insightfully understood to be the new forms of writing that the advent of atomic warfare required. The documentarian's promise may not always be fulfilled, but it is a promise nonetheless, and these we cannot do without.

Over the past two generations, from *cinéma vérité*'s first hypnotic illusions of unmediated reality, to the video revolution, to our own moment of democratized and ceaseless cell phone witness, a distinctly documentary sensibility—a habit of information gathering and exchange that is at its heart *curatorial*—came over the horizon and steadily took up residence toward the center of our culture. In addition to the proliferation of documentary forms proper, one thinks of a work like poet Claudia Rankine's *Citizen: An American Lyric*, whose own method of exposing and decrying the myriad aggressions and microaggressions of American racism is distinctly archival, curatorial, documentary. One also thinks of the ubiquitous Facebook posts, retweets, Instagram hashtag projects, and Tumblr dashboard feeds that themselves represent widespread, popular exercises in curation. The tendency in the culture has become familiar enough for parody in the faux documentary method of TV's *The Office*, the comic, "archival" flashback cut-ins in the sitcoms *Family Guy* or *Black-ish*, or the real-life documentary interviews punctuating the film *The Big Short*.

Within this cultural context, what decades ago might have been a casual—if interesting—observation on the pedagogies of dissent embodied in documentary work has by now become a possible answer to the nation's very pressing political crisis and to the epistemological crisis that lies beneath it. Perhaps our own epoch began with the chance video footage of Rodney King's brutal beating at the hands of the LAPD. That archive has grown immeasurably, as has the urgency of the social questions at its core. It now includes video from the myriad onlookers on the Bay Area Rapid Transit platform at Fruitvale Station, cell phone cameras poised and rolling, as transit police shot and killed a handcuffed and subdued Oscar Grant. It includes Humberto Navarrete's viral cell phone footage of the Border Patrol at the crossing at San Ysidro, beating and tasing a thirty-two-year-old migrant, Anastasio Hernández-Rojas, until he lay lifeless on the ground. It includes Feidin Santana's video of officer Michael Slager shooting Walter Scott in the back, as Scott fled—unambiguously *away*—across a grassy field in North Charleston, South Carolina. Such instances of brutality have tragically multiplied, as have the guerrilla videos that document them. It is not just our outraged sense of justice that demands perpetual witness of the Rodney King variety, it is our very ability to apprehend the full life of a polity that has outgrown eighteenth-century structures of democratic governance by perhaps a few hundred million people, but—alas—has not outgrown the eighteenth century's legacy of settler colonialism and slavery, nor the Enlightenment's narrow conceptions of proper personhood or full citizenship. Oscar Grant, Anastasio Hernández-Rojas, Walter Scott, Claudia Rankine's nameless citizen—it is on their behalf that the documentarian plies his or her craft.

By "curatorial" I am referring to a distinctive approach to inquiry and presentation that breaks from earlier forms of fact-finding and narration by forging a more continuous relationship between the archive that establishes a certain truth, on the one hand, and the conclusions and passions that that truth arouses, on the other. Evidence itself is never fully autonomous under the curator's hand, no more so than it was (or is) under the hand of the traditional historian, journalist, or lawyer. But in the age of magnetic tape, and later the era of the digital, the archive itself has become multiple, expansive and ever-expanding, accessible, and pliable in ways of vast consequence not only for how we argue but for how we *think*. The distinction can be a subtle one. The historian or the litigator develops an argument based on archival materials and then spins out a line of argumentation using appropriate documents as illustration and evidence. The documentarian, on the other hand, assembles and arranges those materials in such a way that they themselves frame and carry passion, interpretation, and meaning. Here, the evidence *is* the argument.

This is a distinction that first came to me in my photographic work for the Historian's Eye project, some twenty years into my career as an academic historian. Could the camera be an instrument, I wondered, not just for recording history-in-the-making but for advancing an argument about the force of the past in the formation of present? This project—which treated the iconic figure of our first black president, the 2008 crash and its aftermath, the emergence of protest formations like the Tea Party and Occupy, and the hateful obsessions with immigration and Islam that we now know as Trumpism—called for a departure from my writerly, historian's understanding of how meaning is conveyed and consequently from my understanding of the relationship among archive, artifact, insight, interpretation, and argument. For one thing, to build an archive and to mine an existing one are two very different pursuits (though in my experience both might engage a "curatorial" mode of thought). But to my surprise, for another thing, most consequential for me was not the shift from the writer's register of the word to the photographer's register of the image but rather the shift from the analog to the digital. The technologies named by these two terms, I found, cultivate wholly different assumptions and mental worlds. In moving from the work of the gallerist to the work of the data manager (which is how I experienced the learning curve of this work), I came to inhabit modes of thinking defined by an unforeseen scale and bounded by unfamiliar horizons. The archive in this circumstance began to engulf my understanding—not to *in*form but fully to *form*.

My process here is related to what social anthropologist Tim Ingold, in a piece titled "The Art of Inquiry," has called "knowing from the inside"—a thinking *through* observation rather than *after* it. Significantly, Ingold points to artists, craftspeople, architects, and others engaged in "making" as his exemplars: "The way of the craftsman . . . is to allow knowledge to grow from the crucible of our practical and observational engagements with the beings and things around us. . . . In the art of inquiry, the conduct of thought goes along with, and continually answers to, the fluxes and flows of the materials with which we work. These materials think in us, as we think through them." I make no particular claim to artistry for myself here but merely observe that perhaps the documentarian's craft is closer to the experience of working a potter's wheel than it is to traditional academic research and writing, in terms of one's relationship to raw materials, one's hands-on modes of inquiry and reflection, one's "correspondence"—to use another of Ingold's terms—with the world *through* what is otherwise very similar intellectual work. The work of such a practitioner "is not to describe the world, or to represent it," Ingold writes, "but to open up our perception to what is going on there so that we, in turn, can respond to it."[2] It is something very like this quality I have in mind when I describe documentary work itself as a way of knowing, a method of engaged knowing, an engagement *with* knowing.

Nor do such habits of mind necessarily abandon us when we turn our attention to other work. Hip-deep in the Historian's Eye project, soon enough I realized that my lectures in American Studies 191, The Formation of Modern American Culture, had become "curatorial" in this fashion, too. That is, the historical meaning that I was constructing was driven by the multimedia materials gathered, arranged, and projected via PowerPoint, and not the other way around. It is a very different way of thinking and of working: I was no longer "illustrating" my lectures, as I had across two decades of teaching, but—like a museum curator or a documentary photographer—was allowing the archive to fundamentally restructure my understanding and reorient my narrative. The discovery of an image of a southern sheriff arresting and roughly handling a young Martin Luther King Jr., for instance, evolved into an explication of civil rights struggle as "outlawry" that is critical to an understanding of the movement but that popular "Kum ba Yah" renditions of the era do not typically encourage us to reckon with. This is not the historian illustrating his lecture so much as it is the archive speaking *through* the historian. Ingold, I believe, would call it "knowing from the inside."

There are two critical points to make about what I am thinking of here as the curatorial turn that I have experienced myself and that I note in our culture. One is that it has largely been technologically driven. As a broad cultural tendency, its beginnings lie perhaps as far back as the advent of the Kodak Brownie (1900). It then accelerates across several generations marked by similarly democratizing advances in sound and image recording—the Bolex handheld motion picture camera (1924); the magnetic tape recorder (1945); the Instamatic and Polaroid cameras (1963); the affordable video camcorder (1982); digital recording technologies, whose audio and video files are costless and are easily duplicated and transferred (1992); the cell phone camera (2000); and the viral disseminating powers of video-sharing platforms like YouTube (2005). These technologies not only have generated increasingly vast archives of recorded material but also collectively and over time have encouraged a wholly new relationship between media users and consumers on the one hand and the world of the *known* on the other. And so, second, the curatorial turn has also entailed a subtle but consequential epistemological shift in our understanding of those external realities that we fully "know" with some confidence but that we have never actually encountered firsthand. We can "know" many places we have never been—Antarctica, say—in a manner that is wholly different from our grandparents' knowing. It is an obvious point—perhaps so much so that we do not give it the consideration it warrants. When it comes to the documentary impulse and to the conduct of documentary work, these technologically driven shifts in our apprehension of the world have wed fact-finding, understanding, argumentation, and communication in a manner that is a new thing under the sun.

I have used the term *epistemological crisis*, and I do not think this is going too far. One does not know whether to laugh or cry upon hearing the list of things that millions of people accept as truth but that are just not so (Barack Obama's Kenyan birth, for instance). The list of transformative technologies above might have also included innovations in distribution, such as the first basic cable network (1976) or the first dial-up Internet Service Provider (ISP) in the United States (1989). Which is where some new troubles arise. U.S. civic discourse took a bad turn when the coaxial cable remade the world of three networks into a world of many more in the early 1980s—10, 25, 150, and later upwards of 500 cable channels. More bandwidth and more information might have seemed a good thing (did not the preceding paragraphs just imply that they were?), but the discordant, competing, boutiqued realities of narrowcasting turned out to create problems wholly unknown to the "manufactured consent" era of CBS, NBC, and ABC.[3] As a segmented, market-niched populace, we found ourselves hived off from our neighbors and daily exposed not only to divergent opinions or lines of inquiry but also to wildly conflicting data sets on basic facts. (Our civic discourse took a second bad turn when Fox News emerged as one of these many new networks, sowing the chaos of partisanship as objective "news.")[4] This feature of our civic life, so corrosive of commonality, has been ratcheted up even further by the Internet and new media. Opinions and interpretations might be reasonably debated, as might policy prescriptions; but "facts" are more tenacious, no?

This recent history—and the rise of Trumpism, which seems its handiwork—has delivered us to a uniquely exacting historical moment. The documentarian's craft across many media remains one of the most important tools in our kit—the good that is twinned with the bad in this proliferation of information-generating technologies and platforms. This craft includes the documentarian's impulse toward evidence, to be sure, but also that inherently political work, as Grace Hale writes, "based on the tension between the subjective and objective, uninterested in neutrality, and intent on trying to convey its subjects' experience." Facts forged in fire. Which brings me back to my students, marching in the streets and filming, too—protesting, documenting, interviewing, at once giving voice to their dissent and bearing witness, producing proof, and creating a platform for others' voices. As I write, President Trump has taken to decrying reports he dislikes as "fake news," and his White House casually offers what counselor to the president Kellyanne Conway calls "alternative facts." The difference between charges of "media bias" and the blanket dismissal of "fake news" is not a difference of degree but of kind; and if the Republic has been straining under the one, it may well collapse under the weight of the other. In this environment, progressives find themselves rooting for the corporate media they have despised all their lives. But the era has scripted an equally significant role for the documentarian—not only the experienced filmmaker or photographer, whose expensive gear and whose foundation grant bespeak the status of a professional, but also the cell phone legions (let us call them) who, like my own students and like Leigh Raiford and Michael Cohen's before them, came quickly to understand the emergent, twenty-first-century terms of witness, evidence, pedagogy, epistemology, dissent, and voice in their participatory documentary work amid the buffeting waves of history's messy unfolding.

This is not to romanticize a collective state where, as one Shonda Rhimes character snidely puts it, "Every idiot with a cell phone thinks he's Ken Burns." Nor is it to claim that either the curatorial turn or documentary practices in general can resolve the mutual alienation imposed by narrowcast technologies and their hopelessly divided, shrink-wrapped intellectual publics. Rather, it is to recognize that our media environment is part of what got us to where we are and that any set of progressive prescriptions that does not account for or leverage elements of contemporary media practices is bound for failure. Because what passes for "common knowledge" matters. So does the epistemology that underwrites the public conception of what is a "fact." So do the questions of who gets to speak, who gets to be heard, and who bears witness. What is required is a deep understanding of the curatorial, archival force and the pedagogy that documentary work affords, and also an orienting historical grasp of how—for all its flaws, shortcomings, or blind alleys—documentary work across the media, from the democratic spirit of the Farm Security Administration photographers to the participatory documentary of millennials with cell phones, has been part and parcel of progressive history. *Remaking Reality* strikes me as an excellent start.

And remaking reality isn't a bad idea either.

mj
New Haven, March 14, 2017

NOTES

1. Gordon, *Dorothea Lange*, xviii. Quoted somewhat differently but to the same effect in Meltzer, *Dorothea Lange*, vii.

2. Ingold, *Making*, 6, 7, 11. My thanks to Franny Nudelman, Laura Wexler, Carol Chiodo, and Courtney Sato for some clarifying conversations on this subject.

3. Chomsky and Herman, *Manufacturing Consent*.

4. Brock and Rabin-Havt, *Fox Effect*; Skocpol and Williamson, *Tea Party and the Remaking of Republican Conservatism*, 201.

BIBLIOGRAPHY

Archival Collections

Atlanta, Ga.
- The King Center
  - Student Nonviolent Coordinating Committee Papers

Chapel Hill, N.C.
- Southern Folklife Collection, Wilson Library, University of North Carolina
  - Guy and Candie Carawan Collection #20008

College Park, Md.
- National Archives and Records Administration
  - Record Group 111: Records of the Office of the Chief Signal Officer, 1860–1985, 111-M-1241, box 11

New Haven, Conn.
- Yale Collection of American Literature, Beinecke Rare Book and Manuscript Library, Yale University
  - John Hersey Papers

New York, N.Y.
- Museum of Modern Art
- Richard Avedon Foundation

Tucson, Ariz.
- Richard Avedon Foundation
  - Center for Creative Photography

Washington, D.C.
- Library of Congress, American Folklife Center
  - Lomax Family Collections

Films

Barefoot Gen's Hiroshima: The Story of Nakazawa Keiji. Directed by Ishida Yuko. Tokyo: Siglo/Tomo, 2011.

Berkeley in the Sixties. Produced and directed by Mark Kitchell. San Francisco, CA: California News Reel, 1990. DVD.

By the Dawn's Early Light: Chris Jackson's Journey to Islam. Produced and directed by Zareena Grewal. 2004. New York: Cinema Guild, 2004. DVD.

Fires Were Started. Written and directed by Humphrey Jennings. London: Crown Film Unit, 1943.

The Forgotten Space. Written and directed by Allan Sekula and Noël Burch. Brooklyn, NY: Icarus Films, 2010. DVD.

Harvest of Shame. Directed by Fred W. Friendly. Produced and starring Edward R. Murrow. 1960. DVD.

Lessons of Darkness. Directed by Werner Herzog. 1992.Anchor Bay, 2004. DVD.

Psychiatric Procedures in the Combat Area. Directed by Army Pictorial Service, Signal Corps. 1944. Washington, DC: National Archives and Records Administration, 2017. DVD.

The River. Directed by Pare Lorentz. 1938. Naxos, 2007. DVD.

The Sea around Us. Directed by Irwin Allen. 1952. Warner Brothers, 2010. DVD.

The Thin Blue Line. Directed by Errol Morris. 1988. New York: The Criterion Collection, 2015. DVD.

We Break Things. Directed and produced by Rebecca Wexler. 2015.

Books, Articles, and Dissertations

Abbott, Brett. *Engaged Observers: Documentary Photography since the Sixties*. Los Angeles: J. Paul Getty Museum, 2010.

Adams, Jeff. *Documentary Graphic Novels and Social Realism*. Bern, Switzerland: Peter Lang, 2008.

Agee, James. "Films." *Nation*, 15 April 1944, 456.

"The Albany Movement." *Martin Luther King, Jr. and the Global Freedom Struggle*. http://kingencyclopedia.stanford.edu/encyclopedia/encyclopedia/enc_albany_movement/. 28 August 2015.

Alberro, Alexander. "The Dialectics of Everyday Life." In *Martha Rosler: Positions in the Life World*, edited by M. Catherine de Zegher, 73–112. Cambridge, Mass.: MIT Press, 1999.

Allikas, Greg. "Looking Back at 'New Documents.'" *Street Views and News*, 12 July 2012, https://streetshooter45.wordpress.com/2012/07/06/looking-back-at-new-documents/. 4 August 2016.

Allred, Jeff. *American Modernism and Depression Documentary*. New York: Oxford University Press, 2009.

Andrejevic, Mark. "Watching Back, Surveillance as Activism." In *Media and Social Justice*, edited by Sue Curry Jansen, Jefferson Pooley, and Lora Taub-Pervizpour, 177–91. New York: Palgrave Macmillan, 2011.

Appel, Frederick, Jr. "Avedon." *Minnesota Daily*, 2 July 1970.

Arlen, Michael J. "Living-Room War." *New Yorker*, 15 October 1966, 200–202.

———. *Living-Room War*. Syracuse, N.Y.: Syracuse University Press, 1966.

Arsenault, Raymond. *Freedom Riders: 1961 and the Struggle for Racial Justice*. New York: Oxford University Press, 2006.

Asemota, Lajuanda. "The Black History Month Façade." *Daily Californian*, 27 February 2009. http://www.dailycal.org/article/104560/the_black_history_month_facade.

Austin, Thomas, and Wilma de Jong. Introduction to *Rethinking Documentary: New Perspectives, New Practices*, edited by Thomas Austin and Wilma de Jong, 1–10. Maidenhead, England: McGraw Hill / Open University Press, 2008.

Avedon, Richard. Conversation with Doon Arbus. 1999. In Nancy Madlin, ed., *Legends Online: Richard Avedon: Avedon The Sixties*. http://www.pdngallery.com/legends9/. 5 July 2015.

Avedon, Richard, and Doon Arbus. *The Sixties*. New York: Random House, 1999.

Avedon, Richard, and Truman Capote. *Observations*. New York: Simon and Schuster, 1959.

Azoulay, Ariella. *The Civil Contract of Photography*. Translated by Rela Mazali and Ruvik Danieli. New York: Zone Books. Distributed by Cambridge, Mass.: MIT Press, 2008.

Barnett, Erin, and Philomena Mariani, eds. *Hiroshima: Ground Zero 1945*. New York: International Center for Photography, 2011.

Barthes, Roland. *Camera Lucida: Reflections on Photography*. Translated by Richard Howard. New York: Hill and Wang, 1981.

Batchen, Geoffrey. *Burning with Desire: The Conception of Photography*. Cambridge, Mass.: MIT Press, 1997.

———. "Looking Askance." In *Picturing Atrocity: Photography in Crisis*, edited by Geoffrey Batchen, Mick Gidley, Nancy K. Miller, and Jay Prosser, 227–40. London: Reaktion, 2012.

Beltrán, Cristina. "Undocumented, Unafraid, and Unapologetic: DREAM Activists, Cyber-Testimonio, and the Queering of Democracy." In *From Voice to Influence: Understanding Citizenship in a Digital Age*, edited by Danielle Allen and Jennifer Light, 80–104. Chicago: University of Chicago Press, 2015.

Benjamin, Walter. *The Arcades Project*. 4th printing. Cambridge, Mass.: Harvard University Press/Belknap Press, 2003.

Berger, John. *Berger on Drawing*. Edited by Jim Savage. Aghabullogue, Co. Cork, Ireland: Occasional Press, 2005.

———. "Hiroshima." In *The Sense of Sight*, 287–95. New York: Pantheon Books, 1985.

Berger, Martin A. *Seeing through Race: A Reinterpretation of Civil Rights Photography*. Berkeley: University of California Press, 2011.

Bernstein, Robin. "'I'm Very Happy to Be in the Reality-Based Community': Alison Bechdel's *Fun Home*, Digital Photography, and George W. Bush." *American Literature* 89, no. 1 (Winter 2017): 121–54.

Bethune, Beverly M. "A Case of Radical Overkill: The FBI and the New York City Photo League." *Journalism History* 7 (Fall–Winter 1980): 87–91, 108.

Bezner, Lili Corbus. *Photography and Politics in America: From the New Deal into the Cold War*. Baltimore: Johns Hopkins University Press, 1999.

Birmingham, Alabama, 1963—Mass Meeting. Recording. Various artists. Recorded by Candie Carawan and Guy Carawan. FW05487/FD 5487. Smithsonian Center for Folklife and Cultural Heritage. Folkways Records, 1980. Smithsonian Folkways Recordings, 2004.

Bloom, Lisa. *Jewish Identities in American Feminist Art: Ghosts of Ethnicity*. New York: Routledge, 2006.

Bodroghkozy, Aniko. *Equal Time: Television and the Civil Rights Movement*. Urbana: University of Illinois Press, 2012.

Bogre, Michelle. *Photography as Activism: Images for Social Change*. Amsterdam: Focal Press, 2011.

Branch, Taylor. *Parting the Waters: America in the King Years, 1954–63*. New York: Simon and Schuster, 1998.

———. *Pillar of Fire: America in the King Years, 1963–1965*. New York: Simon and Schuster, 1998.

Breines, Wini. *Community and Organization in the New Left, 1962–1968: The Great Refusal*. New Brunswick, N.J.: Rutgers University Press, 1982.

Brock, David, and Ari Rabin-Havt. *The Fox Effect: How Roger Ailes Turned a Network into a Propaganda Machine*. New York: Anchor, 2012.

Brown, Elspeth H., and Thy Phu, eds. *Feeling Photography*. Durham, N.C.: Duke University Press, 2014.

Brown, Wendy. *Undoing the Demos: Neoliberalism's Stealth Revolution*. Brooklyn: Zone Books, 2015.

Brutvan, Cheryl. "Interview with Milton Rogovin." In *The Forgotten Ones*, by Milton Rogovin, 9–23. Seattle: University of Washington Press, 1985.

Bryan-Wilson, Julia. *Art Workers: Radical Practice in the Vietnam War Era*. Berkeley: University of California Press, 2009.

Buchloh, Benjamin. "Allan Sekula: Photography between Discourse and Document." In *Fish Story*, by Allan Sekula, 189–200. Dusseldorf: Richter Verlag, 1995.

———. "A Conversation with Martha Rosler." In *Martha Rosler: Positions in the Life World*, edited by M. Catherine de Zegher, 23–55. Birmingham: Ikon Gallery; Cambridge, Mass.: MIT Press, 1998.

Buell, Lawrence. "Toxic Discourse." *Critical Inquiry* 24, no. 3 (Spring 1998): 639–65.

Butler, Judith. *Frames of War: When Is Life Grievable?* London: Verso, 2009.

Cafaro, Philip. "Rachel Carson's Environmental Ethics." In *Rachel Carson: Legacy and Challenge*, edited by Lisa H. Sideris and Kathleen Dean Moore, 60–78. Albany: State University of New York Press, 2008.

Calomiris, Angela. *Red Masquerade: Undercover for the F.B.I.* New York: Lippincott, 1950.

Canavan, Gerry, and Kim Stanley Robinson, eds. *Green Planets: Ecology and Science Fiction*. Middletown, Conn.: Wesleyan University Press, 2014.

Cantwell, Robert. *When We Were Good: The Folk Revival*. Cambridge, Mass.: Harvard University Press, 1996.

Capote, Truman. *In Cold Blood: A True Account of a Multiple Murder and Its Consequences*. New York: Random House, 1965.

———. Interview with Roy Newquist (1964). In *Truman Capote: Conversations*, edited by M. Thomas Inge, 38–46. Jackson: University Press of Mississippi, 1987.

Carson, Clayborne. *In Struggle: SNCC and the Black Awakening of the 1960s*. Cambridge, Mass.: Harvard University Press, 1995.

Carson, Rachel. *The Sea around Us*. 1951. New York: Oxford University Press, 1991.

———. *Silent Spring*. New York: Houghton Mifflin, 1962.

———. *Under the Sea-Wind*. 1941. New York: Penguin, 2007.

Cha-Jua, Sundiata Keita, and Clarence Lang. "The 'Long Movement' as Vampire: Temporal and Spatial Fallacies in Recent Black Freedom Studies." *Journal of African American History* 92, no. 2 (Spring 2007): 265–88.

Chakrabarty, Dipesh. "The Climate of History: Four Theses." *Critical Inquiry* 35 (Winter 2009): 197–222.

Choi, Jeannie. "A Web of Power: How Online Tools Are Transforming the Way Social Change Happens." *Sojourners Magazine*, July 2011. http://sojo.net/magazine/2011/07/web-power. 19 May 2016.

Chomsky, Noam, and Edward S. Herman. *Manufacturing Consent: The Political Economy of the Mass Media*. New York: Pantheon, 1988.

Chute, Hillary. *Disaster Drawn: Visual Witness, Comics, and Documentary Form*. Cambridge, Mass.: Harvard University Press, 2016.

———. "Joe Sacco: Comics Journalist." *Believer*, June 2011. http://www.believermag.com/issues/201106/?read=interview_sacco.

Collingwood, R. G. *The Idea of History*. Oxford: Oxford University Press, 1946.

Cook, George. "National Guard Confronting Demonstrators." Photograph. In *Road to Freedom: Photographs of the Civil Rights Movement, 1956–1968*, edited by Julian Cox, 86. Seattle: University of Washington Press, 2008.

Cordle, Daniel. *States of Suspense: The Nuclear Age, Postmodernism, and United States Fiction and Prose*. Manchester, UK: Manchester University Press, 2008.

Costello, Diarmuid, and Margaret Iversen. Introduction to *Photography after Conceptual Art*, edited by Diarmuid Costello and Margaret Iversen, 1–12. London: Wiley-Blackwell, 2010.

Cottingham, Laura. "The Inadequacy of Seeing and Believing: The Art of Martha Rosler." In *Inside the Visible: An Elliptical Traverse of 20th Century Art in, of, and from the Feminine*, edited by M. Catherine de Zegher, 157–63. Cambridge, Mass.: MIT Press, 1996.

———. "The War Is Always Home: Martha Rosler." October 1991. martha rosler: reviews & interviews, http://www.martharosler.net/reviews/cottingham.html. 25 July 2016.

Cowie, Elizabeth. *Recording Reality, Desiring the Real*. Minneapolis: University of Minnesota Press, 2011.

Das Gupta, Monisha. *Unruly Immigrants: Rights, Activism, and Transnational South Asian Politics in the United States*. Durham, N.C.: Duke University Press, 2006.

Daston, Lorraine, and Peter Gallison. *Objectivity*. New York: Zone Books, 2007.

Davidson, Steef. *The Penguin Book of Political Comics*. Middlesex, UK: Penguin, 1982.

Davis, Mike. *Prisoners of the American Dream: Politics and Economy in the History of the U.S. Working Class*. New York: Verso, 1985.

Dawes, James. *That the World May Know: Bearing Witness to Atrocity*. Cambridge, Mass.: Harvard University Press, 2007.

Dee, Jonathan. "The Art of Fiction XCII: John Hersey." *Paris Review* 100 (Summer–Fall 1986): 210–49.

Deleuze, Gilles, and Felix Guattari. *A Thousand Plateaus: Capitalism and Schizophrenia*. New York: Continuum, 1992.

Demos, T. J. *The Migrant Image: The Art and Politics of Documentary during Global Crisis*. Durham, N.C.: Duke University Press, 2013.

Denby, David. "American Gothic." *New Yorker*, 18 November 2013. http://www.newyorker.com/magazine/2013/11/18/american-gothic-4.

Denning, Michael. "Representing Global Labor." *Social Text* 25, no. 3 (Fall 2007): 125–45.

Deriu, Davide. "Picturing Ruinscapes." In *The Image and the Witness: Trauma, Memory and Visual Culture*, edited by Frances Guern and Roger Halles, 189–206. London: Wallflower Press, 2007.

De Zegher, M. Catherine, ed. *Inside the Visible: An Elliptical Traverse of 20th Century Art in, of, and from the Feminine*. Cambridge, Mass.: MIT Press, 1996.

"Documents from the Albany & Southwest Georgia Movements." 1961–1964. Civil Rights Movement Veterans. http://www.crmvet.org/docs/albdocs.htm. 28 August 2015.

Duggan, Lisa. *The Twilight of Equality? Neoliberalism, Cultural Politics, and the Attack on Democracy*. Boston: Beacon Press, 2004.

Dunaway, Finis. *Seeing Green: The Use and Abuse of American Environmental Images*. Chicago: University of Chicago Press, 2015.

Edgerton, Gary. "Revisiting the Recordings of Wars Past: Remembering the Documentary Trilogy of John Huston." In *Reflections in a Male Eye: John Huston and the American Experience*, edited by Gaylyn Studlar and David Desser, 33–62. Washington, D.C.: Smithsonian Institution Press, 1993.

Education Not Deportation: A Guide for Undocumented Youth in Removal Proceedings. Produced by Asian Law Caucus, Educators for Fair Consideration, DreamActivist.org, and National Immigrant Youth Alliance, n.d. http://www.e4fc.org/images/E4FC_DeportationGuide.pdf. 19 May 2016.

Edwards, Elizabeth. "Objects of Affect: Photography Beyond the Image." *Annual Review of Anthropology* 41 (October 2012): 221–34.

Edwards, Owen. "Pictures of Avedon." *Playboy*, June 1974, 212.

Edwards, Steve. "Photography Out of Conceptual Art." In *Themes in Contemporary Art*, edited by Gill Perry and Paul Wood, 137–80. New Haven, Conn.: Yale University Press, 2004.

Ellis, John. "Dancing to Different Tunes: Ethical Differences in Approaches to Factual Filmmaking." In *Truth or Dare: Art and Documentary*, edited by Gail Pearce and Cahal McLaughlin, 57–64. Bristol, UK: Intellect Books, 2007.

Emerson, Gloria. "Avedon Photographs a Harsh Vietnam." *New York Times*, 9 May 1971. In Roth, "Family Tree," 259.

Evans, David. "Black Folk Music: Recent Recordings." *Journal of American Folklore* 91, no. 362 (October–December 1972): 983–1001.

Felman, Shoshana, and Dori Laub, *Testimony: Crises of Witnessing in Literature, Psychoanalysis, and History*. New York: Routledge, 1992.

Floyd, Samuel A., Jr. *The Power of Black Music: Interpreting Its History from Africa to the United States*. New York: Oxford University Press, 1995.

Forman, James. Letter to Guy Carawan. November 1962. Box 70, folder 4. Student Nonviolent Coordinating Committee Papers, King Center. Atlanta, Georgia.

———. *The Making of Black Revolutionaries*. Seattle: University of Washington Press, 1972.

Foucault, Michel. *The History of Sexuality: Volume I*. New York: Random House, 1978.

———. *Power/Knowledge: Selected Interviews and Other Writings, 1972–1977*. Edited by Colin Gordon. New York: Random House, 1980.

———. *Security, Territory, Population: Lectures at the Collège de France, 1977–1978*. New York: Palgrave Macmillan, 2007.

"Found Paintings, Disassembled Movies, World Images: Allan Sekula Speaks with Carles Guerra." *Grey Room* 55 (Spring 2014): 130–41.

Formwalt, Lee W. "Albany Movement." 2 December 2003. Revised by NGE Staff, 30 November 2016. *New Georgia Encyclopedia*. http://www.georgia encyclopedia.org/articles/history-archaeology/albany-movement.

———. *Looking Back, Moving Forward: The Southwest Georgia Freedom Struggle, 1814–2014*. Albany, Ga.: Albany Civil Rights Institute, 2014.

———. Sales figures. Vanguard Records file. Reel 10, Student Nonviolent Coordinating Committee Microform Edition. Ann Arbor: UM-I, 1994.

Freeman, Joshua. "Hardhats: Construction Workers, Manliness, and the 1970 Pro-War Demonstrations." *Journal of Social History* 26, no. 4 (Summer 1993): 725–44.

———. "Labor during the American Century: Work, Workers, and Unions Since 1945." In *A Companion to Post-1945 America*, edited by Jean-Christophe Agnew and Roy Rosenzweig, 192–210. Hoboken, N.J.: Wiley-Blackwell, 2006.

Freud, Sigmund. *The Psychopathology of Everyday Life*. Translated by Alan Tyson. New York: W. W. Norton, 1989.

———. *The Psychopathology of Everyday Life*. Translated by Alan Tyson. New York: W. W. Norton, 1960.

Garner, Gretchen. *Disappearing Witness: Change in Twentieth-Century American Photography*. Princeton, N.J.: Princeton University Press, 2003.

Gee, Helen. *Photography of the Fifties: An American Perspective*. Tucson: Center for Creative Photography, 1980.

Gerstle, Dan. "John Hersey and *Hiroshima*." *Dissent* (Spring 2012): 90–94.

Gibson, Richard. "No Glamorous Poses for Photographer Avedon: The Beautiful and Great Become Real and Tragic." *Minneapolis Star*, 1 July 1970.

Gleason, Alan. "Keiji Nakazawa Interview." *Comics Journal* 256 (October 2003). http://www.tcj.com/keiji-nakazawa-interview/.

Goldman, Mark. *City on the Edge: Buffalo, New York, 1900–Present*. New York: Prometheus Books, 2007.

Goldsmith, Peter David. *Making People's Music: Moe Asch and Folkways Records*. Washington, D.C.: Smithsonian Institution Press, 1998.

Gomez, Alan. "DREAMers Personalize Cases to Stall Deportation." *USA Today*, 12 March 2012. http://usatoday30.usatoday.com/news/nation/story/2012-03-12/dream-act-illegal-immigration/53502528/1. 19 May 2016.

Goodman, Paul. "Stoicism and the Holocaust." *New York Review of Books*, 28 March 1968, 15–19.

Gordon, Linda. *Dorothea Lange: A Life beyond Limits*. New York: W. W. Norton, 2010.

Gore, Al. *An Inconvenient Truth: The Planetary Emergency of Global Warming and What We Can Do about It*. New York: Rodale, 2006.

Grausam, Daniel. *On Endings: American Postmodern Fiction and the Cold War*. Charlottesville: University of Virginia Press, 2011.

Greenblatt, Stephen. "Wondrous, Fragile, Tedious Berkeley." *New York Review of Books*, 6 February 2014. http://www.nybooks.com/articles/archives/2014/feb/06/wondrous-fragile-tedious-berkeley/.

Grinker, Roy R., and John P. Spiegel. *Men under Stress*. Philadelphia: Blakiston, 1945.

Guilbaut, Serge. *How New York Stole the Idea of Modern Art: Abstract Expressionism, Freedom, and the Cold War*. Chicago: University of Chicago Press, 1984.

Gulli, Bruno. *Labor of Fire*. Philadelphia: Temple University Press, 2005.

Haggerty, Kevin. "Tear Down the Walls: On Demolishing the Panopticon." In *Theorizing Surveillance*, edited by David Lyon, 23–45. London: Willan, 2006.

Hale, Grace Elizabeth. *Nation of Outsiders: How the White Middle Class Fell in Love with Rebellion in Postwar America*. New York: Oxford University Press, 2011.

Hall, Jacquelyn Dowd. "The Long Civil Rights Movement and the Political Uses of the Past." *Journal of American History* 9, no. 4 (March 2005): 1233–63.

Hariman, Robert, and John Louis Lucaites. *No Caption Needed: Iconic Photographs, Public Culture and Liberal Democracy*. Chicago: University of Chicago Press, 2007.

Harvey, David. *A Brief History of Neoliberalism*. London: Oxford University Press, 2005.

———. *The Condition of Postmodernity*. New York: Blackwell, 1989.

Heise, Ursula K. "Martian Ecologies and the Future of Nature." *Twentieth-Century Literature* 57, no. 3–4 (Fall/Winter 2011): 447–71.

———. *Sense of Place and Sense of Planet: The Environmental Imagination and the Global*. New York: Oxford University Press, 2008.

Helmore, Edward. "Feminine Mystique." *W*, 1 November 2007. http://www.wmagazine.com/story/rosler-jonas. 15 March 2017.

Hersey, John. *Here to Stay*. New York: Paragon House, 1988.

———. *Hiroshima*. 1946. New York: Vintage, 1985.

———. "The Legend on the License." *Yale Review* 70, no. 1 (October 1980): 1–25.

———. "A Short Talk with Erlanger: The Army Is Using a Dramatic Treatment Called Narco-Synthesis to Help Psychiatric Casualties." *Life*, 29 October 1945, 108–22.

Herzog, Melanie. *Milton Rogovin: The Making of a Social Documentary Photographer*. Seattle: University of Washington Press, 2006.

Hogan, Wesley. *Many Minds, One Heart: SNCC's Dream for a New America*. Chapel Hill: University of North Carolina Press, 2007.

Inda, Jonathan Xavier, and Julie A. Dowling. "Introduction: Governing Migrant Illegality." In *Governing Immigration through Crime: A Reader*, edited by Julie A. Dowling and Jonathan Xavier Inda, 1–36. Stanford: Stanford University Press, 2013.

Ingold, Tim. *Making: Anthropology, Archaeology, Art and Architecture*. London: Routledge, 2013.

Jacobs, Lewis. *The Documentary Tradition*. 2nd ed. New York: W. W. Norton, 1979.

Jambet, Christian. "Une interrogation sur les prisons." *Le Monde*, 21 February 1975.

James, David. "Documenting the Vietnam War." In *From Hanoi to Hollywood: The Vietnam War in American Film*, edited by Linda Dittmar and Gene Michaud, 239–54. New Brunswick, N.J.: Rutgers University Press, 1990.

Japanese Broadcasting Corporation (NHK), ed. *Unforgettable Fire: Pictures Drawn by Atomic Bomb Survivors*. New York: Pantheon Books, 1977.

Jay, Stephanie. Letter to General Minh, 6 April 1971. Richard Avedon Foundation, New York.

Johnson, Gaye Theresa. *Spaces of Conflict, Sounds of Solidarity: Music, Race, and Spatial Entitlement in Los Angeles*. Berkeley: University of California Press, 2013.

Jones, Lewis B. "About this Record and Its Documentors." In liner notes of *Freedom in the Air: A Documentary on Albany, Georgia, 1961–1962*. Recording. Student Non-Violent Coordinating Committee, SNCC-627. Produced by Guy Carawan and Alan Lomax. Manufactured by Vanguard Records. Atlanta, Ga. 1962.

Kahana, Jonathan. *Intelligence Work: The Politics of American Documentary*. New York: Columbia University Press, 2008.

Kaplan, Caren. "Dead Reckoning: Aerial Perception and the Social Construction of Targets." *Vectors: Journal of Culture and Technology in a Dynamic Vernacular*, n.d. http://www.vectorsjournal.org/projects/index.php?project=11.

Kelley, Robin. *Race Rebels: Culture, Politics, and the Black Working Class*. New York: Free Press, 2004.

Kennedy, Liam, and Caitlin Patrick, eds. *The Violence of the Image: Photography and International Conflict*. London: I. B. Tauris, 2014.

Kennedy, Randy. "Showcase: Milton Rogovin." *New York Times Lens Blog*, 7 August 2009. http://lens.blogs.nytimes.com/2009/08/07/showcase-milton-rogovin/?_r=0. 6 September 2015.

Kinkela, David. "The Ecological Landscapes of Jane Jacobs and Rachel Carson." *American Quarterly* 61, no. 4 (December 2009): 905–29.

Klein, Mason, and Catherine Evans. *The Radical Camera: New York's Photo League, 1936–1951*. New Haven: Yale University Press, 2011.

Kozol, Wendy. *Distant Wars Visible: The Ambivalence of Witnessing*. Minneapolis: University of Minnesota Press, 2014.

Kroes, Rob. *Photographic Memories: Private Pictures, Public Images, and American History*. Lebanon, N.H.: University Press of New England, 2007.

Kroll, Gary. "Rachel Carson's *The Sea around Us*, Ocean-Centrism, and a Nascent Ocean Ethic." In *Rachel Carson: Legacy and Challenge*, edited by Lisa H. Sideris and Kathleen Dean Moore, 118–35. Albany: State University of New York Press, 2008.

———. "The 'Silent Springs' of Rachel Carson: Mass Media and the Origins of Modern Environmentalism." *Public Understanding of Science* 10 (October 2001): 403–20.

Kun, Josh. *Audiotopia: Music, Race, and America*. Berkeley: University of California Press, 2005.

Lawton, Carol. "Richard Avedon: An Artist Despite His Success?" *New York Times* 7 September 1975, sec. 2, 105.

Leys, Ruth. *Trauma: A Genealogy*. Chicago: University of Chicago Press, 2000.

Liebow, Averill. "Hiroshima Medical Diary, 1945." *Yale Journal of Biology and Medicine* 38 (October 1965): 60–239.

Lifton, Robert Jay. *Death in Life: Survivors of Hiroshima*. New York: Random House, 1968. Reprint, Chapel Hill: University of North Carolina Press, 1991.

———. "Experiments in Advocacy Research." *Newsletter of the American Academy of Psychoanalysis* 16 (February 1972): 1–11.

———. "Home by Ship: Reaction Patterns of American Prisoners of War Repatriated from North Korea." *American Journal of Psychiatry* 110 (April 1954): 732–39.

———. *Thought Reform and the Psychology of Totalism: A Study of "Brainwashing" in China*. 1961. New York: W. W. Norton, 1963.

———. "Victims of Hiroshima." *New York Review of Books*, 25 April 1968.

———. *Witness to an Extreme Century: A Memoir*. New York: Free Press, 2011.

Linfield, Susie. *The Cruel Radiance: Photography and Political Violence*. Chicago: University of Chicago Press, 2010.

Livingston, Jane. "The Art of Richard Avedon." In *Evidence, 1944–1994*, by Richard Avedon, 11–101. New York: Random House, 1994.

———. *The New York School: Photographs 1936–1963*. New York: Stewart Tabori and Change, 1992.

Luce, Henry R. "Prospectus for a New Magazine: Confidential." 1936. *Life* Archive, http://life.tumblr.com/post/17551327132/to-see-life-to-see-the-world-to-eyewitness. 23 July 2016.

Lyon, Danny. *Memories of the Southern Civil Rights Movement*. Chapel Hill: University of North Carolina Press, 1992.

MacDonald, Dwight. "Hersey's 'Hiroshima.'" *politics*, October 1946, 308.

Malcolm, Janet. "Men without Props." *New Yorker*, 22 September 1974, 119.

Marcorelles, Louis, with the collaboration of Nicole Rouzet-Albagli. *Living Cinema: New Directions in Contemporary Filmmaking*. Translated by Isabel Quigly. New York: Praeger, 1973.

Marshall, S. L. A. *Men against Fire*. Washington, D.C.: The Infantry Journal; New York: William Morrow, 1947.
"Martha Rosler." In *California Video: Artists and Histories*, edited by Glenn Phillips, 198–201. Los Angeles: Getty Research Institute/J. Paul Getty Museum, 2008.
"Martha Rosler: Bringing the War Home." martha rosler: reviews & interviews, http://www.worcesterart.org/exhibitions/Past/martha_rosler.html. 9 December 2015.
May, Michael. "Los Infiltradores." *American Prospect*, 21 June 2013. http://prospect.org/authors/michael-may. 18 May 2016.
Mazzucco, Thomas. "Filming a Revolution: The Birth of Graphic Violence in *Bonnie and Clyde*." Reel American History, n.d. http://digital.lib.lehigh.edu/trial/reel_new/films/list/0_63_9. 25 July 2016.
McCarthy, Mary. "The Hiroshima *New Yorker*." *Politics*, November 1946, 367.
McFadden, Frances. "Let There Be Light." *Harper's Bazaar*, May 1946, 116–17, 177.
McGurl, Mark. "The Posthuman Comedy." *Critical Inquiry* 38 (Spring 2012): 533–53.
McKee, Yates, and Meg McLagan. Introduction to *Sensible Politics: The Visual Culture of Nongovernmental Activism*, edited by Yates McKee and Meg McLagan, 9–26. New York: Zone Books, 2013.
McLagan, Meg. "Human Rights, Testimony and Transnational Publicity." In *Nongovernmental Politics*, edited by Michel Feher, Gaëlle Krikorian, and Yates McKee, 304–25. New York: Zone Books, 2007.
Meltzer, Milton. *Dorothea Lange: A Photographer's Life*. New York: Farrar, Straus and Giroux, 1985.
Mickwitz, Nina. *Documentary Comics: Graphic Storytelling in a Skeptical Age*. New York: Palgrave Macmillan, 2016.
"The Midway Movie." *Washington Post*, 20 September 1942, B6.
Miller, Karl Hagstrom. *Segregating Sound: Inventing Folk and Pop Music in the Age of Jim Crow*. Durham, N.C.: Duke University Press, 2010.
Mirzoeff, Nicholas. *The Right to Look: A Counterhistory of Visuality*. Durham, N.C.: Duke University Press, 2011.
Mitchell, W. J. T. *What Do Pictures Want: The Lives and Loves of Images*. Chicago: University of Chicago Press, 2005.
Morton, John. "Exercising Prosecutorial Discretion Consistent with the Civil Immigration Enforcement Priorities of the Agency for the Apprehension, Detention, and Removal of Aliens." Memo, 17 June 2011. http://www.ice.gov/doclib/secure-communities/pdf/prosecutorial-discretion-memo.pdf. 18 May 2016.
Morton, Timothy. *Ecology without Nature: Rethinking Environmental Aesthetics*. Cambridge, Mass.: Harvard University Press, 2007.
Nadel, Alan. *Containment Culture: American Narratives, Postmodernism, and the Atomic Age*. Durham, N.C.: Duke University Press, 1995.
Nakazawa, Keiji. *Barefoot Gen: A Cartoon Story of Hiroshima*. Vol. 1. San Francisco: Last Gasp of San Francisco, 2004.

———. *Barefoot Gen: The Day After.* Vol. 2. San Francisco: Last Gasp of San Francisco, 2004.

———. *Hiroshima: The Autobiography of Barefoot Gen.* Translated and edited by Richard Minear. Lanham, Md.: Rowman and Littlefield, 2010.

Nash, Eric P. "Books in Brief: The Sixties." *New York Times Book Review*, 16 January 2000. Reprinted in *The New York Times Book Reviews 2000*, vol. 1, 96. New York: New York Times, 2000.

Ngai, Mae. *Impossible Subjects: Illegal Aliens and the Making of Modern America.* Princeton, N.J.: Princeton University Press, 2004.

Nicholls, Walter. *The DREAMers: How the Undocumented Youth Movement Transformed the Immigrant Rights Debate.* Stanford, Calif.: Stanford University Press, 2013.

Nichols, Bill. *Introduction to Documentary.* 2nd ed. Bloomington: Indiana University Press, 2010.

———. *Representing Reality: Issues and Concepts in Documentary.* Bloomington: Indiana University Press, 1991.

———. "The Voice of Documentary." *Film Quarterly* 36, no. 3 (Spring 1983): 17–30.

———. "The Voice of Documentary." In *Movies and Methods*, 2:258–72. Berkeley: University of California Press, 1985.

"1963 January–June: Birmingham—the Children's Crusade (April–May)." Civil Rights Movement Veterans. http://www.crmvet.org/tim/timhis63.htm #1963bham. 15 August 2015.

Nixon, Rob. "Rachel Carson's Prescience." *Chronicle of Higher Education*, 3 September 2012. http://chronicle.com/article/Rachel-Carsons-Prescience /134012/.

———. *Slow Violence and the Environmentalism of the Poor.* Cambridge, Mass.: Harvard University Press, 2011.

Norris, Margot. *Writing War in the Twentieth Century.* Charlottesville: University of Virginia Press, 2000.

Olin, Margaret. *Touching Photographs.* Chicago: University of Chicago Press, 2012.

Olmstead, Anthony. *Folkways Records: Moses Asch and His Encyclopedia of Sound.* New York: Routledge, 2003.

Owens, Craig. "The Discourse of Others: Feminists and Postmodernism." In *The Art of Art History: A Critical Anthology*, edited by Donald Preziosi, 335–51. New York: Oxford University Press, 2006.

Pallares, Amalia. *Family Activism: Immigrant Struggles and the Politics of Noncitizenship.* New Brunswick, N.J.: Rutgers University Press, 2015.

Pavey, Steve, and Marco Saavedra. *Shadows Then Light.* Lexington, Ky.: One Horizon Institute, 2012.

Payne, Charles. *I've Got the Light of Freedom: The Organizing Tradition and the Mississippi Freedom Struggle.* Berkeley: University of California Press, 1997.

Payne, Charles Rockwell, and Smith Ely Jelliffe. "War Neuroses and Psychoneuroses." *Journal of Nervous and Mental Disease* 48 (1918): 385–94.

Pells, Richard H. *Radical Visions and American Dreams: Culture and Social Thought in the Depression Years.* New York: Harper and Row, 1973.

Press Release 21, Museum of Modern Art, New Documents, 28 February 1967. http://www.moma.org/momaorg/shared/pdfs/docs/press_archives/3860/releases/MOMA_1967_Jan-June_0034_21.pdf. 4 August 2016.

Puga, Ana Elena. "Poor Enrique and Poor María, or, the Political Economy of Suffering in Two Migrant Melodramas." In *Performance in the Borderlands*, edited by Ramón Rivera-Servera and Harvey Young, 225–247. London: Palgrave Macmillan, 2011.

Rabinowitz, Paula. *They Must Be Represented: The Politics of Documentary*. New York: Verso, 1994.

Raiford, Leigh. *"Imprisoned in a Luminous Glare": Photography and the African American Freedom Struggle*. Chapel Hill: University of North Carolina Press, 2013.

Ranciere, Jacques. *The Emancipated Spectator*. London: Verso, 2009.

Rankine, Claudia. *Citizen: An American Lyric*. Minneapolis: Graywolf Press, 2014.

Reed, T.V. *The Art of Protest: Culture and Activism from the Civil Rights Movement to the Streets of Seattle*. Minneapolis: University of Minnesota Press, 2005.

Renov, Michael. "Imaging the Other: Representations of Vietnam in Sixties Political Documentary." In *From Hanoi to Hollywood: The Vietnam War in American Film*, edited by Linda Dittmar and Gene Michaud, 255–68. New Brunswick, N.J.: Rutgers University Press, 1990.

———. *The Subject of Documentary*. Minneapolis: University of Minnesota Press, 2004.

Reporting Civil Rights: Part One: American Journalism, 1941–1963. New York: Library of America, 2003.

Reporting Civil Rights: Part Two: American Journalism, 1963–1973. New York: Library of America, 2003.

Rifas, Leonard. "Globalizing Comic Books from Below: How Manga Came to America." *International Journal of Comic Art* 6, no. 2 (Fall 2004): 139–71.

Ritchin, Fred. *Bending the Frame: Photojournalism, Documentary, and the Citizen*. London: Aperture, 2013.

Roberts, Bill. "Production in View: Allan Sekula's *Fish Story* and the Thawing of Postmodernism." *Tate Working Papers* 18 (2012). http://www.tate.org.uk/research/publications/tate-papers/production-view-allan-sekulas-fish-story-and-thawing-postmodernism. 4 September 2015.

Romero, Mary. "Keeping Citizenship Rights White: Arizona's Racial Profiling Practices in Immigration Law Enforcement." *Law Journal for Social Justice* 1, no. 1 (2011): 97–113.

Rose, Sonya. "Class Formation and the Quintessential Worker." In *Reworking Class*, edited by John R. Hall, 133–68. Ithaca, N.Y.: Cornell University Press, 1997.

Rosen, Philip. *Change Mummified: Cinema, Historicity, Theory*. Minneapolis: University of Minnesota Press, 2001.

Rosler, Martha. "In, around and Afterthoughts (on Documentary Photography)." Reprinted in *The Contest of Meaning: Critical Histories of Photography*, edited by Richard Bolton, 303–42. Cambridge, Mass.: MIT Press, 1989.

———. "In, around and Afterthoughts (on Documentary Photography)." Reprinted in *Decoys and Disruptions: Selected Writings 1975–2001*, by Martha Rosler, 151–206. Cambridge, Mass.: MIT Press, 2006.
———. "In, around and Afterthoughts (On Documentary Photography)." In *Martha Rosler: 3 Works*, 61–93. Halifax, NS: Press of the Nova Scotia College of Art and Design, 1981.
Rosler, Martha, and Jane Weinstock. "Interview with Martha Rosler." *October* 17 (Summer 1981): 77–98. http://www.jstor.org/stable/778252.
Roth, Paul. "Family Tree: Richard Avedon, Politics, and Power: 1969–1976." In *Richard Avedon: Portraits of Power*, by Richard Avedon, 242–43. Washington, D.C.: Steidl/Corcoran Gallery of Art, 2008.
Rowan, Jamin Creed. "The New York School of Urban Ecology: The *New Yorker*, Rachel Carson, and Jane Jacobs." *American Literature* 82, no. 3 (September 2010): 583–610.
Rush, Michael. "A Pure Artist Is Embraced by the Art World." *New York Times*, 9 July 2000.
Saint-Amour, Paul. "Bombing and the Symptom: Traumatic Earliness and the Nuclear Uncanny." *Diacritics* 30, no. 4 (2000): 59–82.
Saper, Craig. "Academia's Exquisite Corpse: An Ethnography of the Application Process." In *The Exquisite Corpse: Chance and Collaboration in Surrealism's Parlor Game*, edited by Kanta Kochhar-Lindgren, Davis Schneiderman, and Tom Denlinger, 189–204. Lincoln: University of Nebraska Press, 2009.
Sargant, William. *Battle for the Mind: A Physiology of Conversion and Brain-Washing*. London: Pan Books, 1959.
Sartre, Jean-Paul. *Critique of Dialectical Reason, Volume One*. Translated by Alan Sheridan-Smith. New York: Verso, 1991.
Scarry, Elaine. *The Body in Pain: The Making and Unmaking of the World*. Oxford: Oxford University Press, 1985.
Schudson, Michael. *Discovering the News: A Social History of American Newspapers*. New York: Basic, 1978.
Scott, A. O. "Richard Avedon." *Slate*, 17 December 1999. http://www.slate.com/articles/news_and_politics/assessment/1999/12/richard_avedon.html. 9 December 2015.
Scott, Joan. "The Evidence of Experience." *Critical Inquiry* 17, no. 4 (1991): 773–97.
"The Script of *The River*." *The River*, directed by Pare Lorentz, 1938. http://xroads.virginia.edu/~1930s/film/lorentz/riverscript1.html.
Sekula, Allan. "The Body and the Archive." *October* 39 (Winter 1986): 3–64.
———. "Conversation between Allan Sekula and Benjamin Buchloh." In *Performance under Working Conditions*, 21–52. Vienna: Generali Foundation, 2003.
———. *Fish Story*. Düsseldorf: Richter Verlag, 1995.
———. "The Instrumental Image: Steichen at War." In *Photography against the Grain: Essays and Photoworks, 1973–1983*, 33–52. Halifax: Press of the Nova Scotia College of Art and Design, 1984.

———. "On 'Fish Story': The Coffin Learns to Dance." *Camera Austria International* 59/60 (1997): 49–59.
Shank, Barry. *The Political Force of Musical Beauty*. Durham, N.C.: Duke University Press, 2014.
Shephard, Ben. *A War of Nerves: Soldiers and Psychiatrists in the Twentieth Century*. 2000. Cambridge, Mass.: Harvard University Press, 2001.
Skocpol, Theda, and Vanessa Williamson. *The Tea Party and the Remaking of Republican Conservatism*. New York: Oxford University Press, 2013.
Smith, Howard. "Scenes." *Village Voice*, 9 November 1969.
Solomon-Godeau, Abigail. *Photography at the Dock: Essays on Photographic History, Institutions, and Practices*. Minneapolis: University of Minnesota Press, 1994.
Sontag, Susan. *Regarding the Pain of Others*. New York: Farrar, Straus and Giroux, 2003.
Souder, William. *On a Farther Shore: The Life and Legacy of Rachel Carson*. New York: Broadway, 2012.
Spiegelman, Art. "*Barefoot Gen*: Comics after the Bomb, an Introduction." In *Barefoot Gen: A Cartoon Story of Hiroshima*, vol. 1, by Keiji Nakazawa, n.p. San Francisco: Last Gasp of San Francisco, 2004.
Stimson, Blake. *The Pivot of the World: Photography and Its Nation*. Cambridge, Mass.: MIT Press, 2006.
Stott, William. *Documentary Expression and Thirties America*. Chicago: University of Chicago Press, 1973.
Sullivan, Henry Stack. *The Psychiatric Interview*. New York: W. W. Norton, 1954.
Susman, Mary. "Wall of Faces Permanently Removed." *Daily Californian*, 18 January 2011. http://archive.dailycal.org/article.php?id=111521.
"Switched at Birth." *This American Life*. Reported by Jake Halpern. Produced by Jane Marie and Ira Glass. 25 July 2008. https://www.thisamericanlife.org/radio-archives/episode/360/switched-at-birth.
Tagg, John. *The Burden of Representation: Essays on Photographies and Histories*. Minneapolis: University of Minnesota Press, 1988.
Tanter, Richard. "Voice and Silence in the First Nuclear War: Wilfred Burchett and Hiroshima, 1986." *Asia-Pacific Journal: Japan Focus* 3, no. 8 (3 August 2005): n.p. http://www.japanfocus.org/-Richard-Tanter/2066/article.html.
Thompson, Joey. "Nat 'King' Cole's Civil War: How Pop Music's Intimate Sounds and the U.S. Military's Intimate Spaces Ignited Alabama's Racial Tensions in the 1950s." MA thesis. University of Virginia, October 2014.
Torres, Sasha. *Black, White, and in Color: Television and Black Civil Rights*. Princeton, N.J.: Princeton University Press, 2003.
Trachtenberg, Alan. *Reading American Photographs*. New York: Hill and Wang, 1984.
Treat, John Whittier. *Writing Ground Zero: Japanese Literature and the Atomic Bomb*. Chicago: University of Chicago Press, 1995.
Tsika, Noah. *Traumatic Imprints: Cinema, Military Psychiatry, and the Aftermath of War*. Berkeley: University of California Press, forthcoming.

Tsuzuki, Masao. "Report on the Medical Studies of the Effects of the Atomic Bomb." *Atomic Bomb Casualty Commission, General Report 1947*. Appendix no. 9. Tokyo: Japanese National Research Council, 1947.

Tucker, Anne, and Claire Cass. *This Was the Photo League: Compassion and the Camera from the Depression to the Cold War*. Chicago: Stephen Daiter Gallery, 2001.

Unzueta Carrasco, Tania A., and Hinda Seif. "Disrupting the Dream: Undocumented Youth Reframe Citizenship and Deportability through Anti-deportation Activism." *Latino Studies* 12 (June 2014): 279–99.

Vanderbilt, Tom. "Courier, Dispatched." *Slate*, 20 February 2004. http://www.slate.com/articles/business_and_tech/design/2004/02/courier_dispatched.html. 13 February 2015.

Van Gelder, Hilde, and Helen Westgeest. *Photography Theory in Historical Perspective*. Hoboken, N.J.: Wiley-Blackwell, 2011.

Virilio, Paul. *War and Cinema: The Logistics of Perception*. New York: Verso, 1989.

Waslin, Michelle. *The Secure Communities Program: Unanswered Questions and Continuing Concerns*. Washington, D.C.: Immigration Policy Center, 2010.

Waugh, Thomas. "Beyond *Vérité*: Emile de Antonio and the New Documentary of the Seventies." In *Movies and Methods II*, edited by Bill Nichols, 233–58. Berkeley: University of California Press, 1985.

———. *"Show Us Life": Toward a History and Aesthetics of the Committed Documentary*. Lanham, Md.: Scarecrow Press, 1984.

We Shall Overcome: Songs from the Montgomery and Nashville Freedom Movements. Recording. Scholastic Records SH 5519. Distributed by Folkways, 1961.

Wexler, Rebecca. "Heightened Histories: Aerial Archaeology and British Nationalism in England and Iraq." M.Phil. diss., University of Cambridge, 2006.

Winston, Brian. *Fires Were Started*. London: British Film Institute, 1999.

———. "'Honest, Straightforward Re-enactment': The Staging of Reality." In *Joris Ivens and the Documentary Context*, edited by Kees Bakker, 160–70. Amsterdam: Amsterdam University Press, 1999.

Wolfe, Charles. "Historicizing the 'Voice of God': The Place of Voice-Over Commentary in Classical Documentary." *Film History* 9, no. 2 (1997): 149–67.

Wolfe, Tom, and E. W. Johnson, eds. *The New Journalism*. New York: Harper and Row, 1973.

Yagoda, Ben. *About Town: The "New Yorker" and the World It Made*. Boston: Da Capo Press, 2001.

Young, Benjamin. "Arresting Figures." *Grey Room* 55 (Spring 2014): 78–115.

Zelizer, Barbie, and Keren Tenenboim-Weinblatt, eds. *Journalism and Memory*. New York: Palgrave Macmillan, 2014.

CONTRIBUTORS

SARA BLAIR is Patricia S. Yaeger Collegiate Professor of English and a faculty associate of American Culture and Judaic Studies at the University of Michigan. Her publications include *Harlem Crossroads: Black Writers and the Photograph in the Twentieth Century*, *Trauma and Documentary Photography of the FSA* (coauthored with Eric Rosenberg), and numerous essays on visual culture, photography, and documentation in such venues as *American Literary History*, *Images*, *PMLA*, and *The Oxford Handbook of Global Modernisms*. Her new book, *How the Other Half Looks* (forthcoming), focuses on photographic practices on New York City's Lower East Side and their power in shaping literary and cultural narratives of American modernity.

MICHAEL MARK COHEN is an associate teaching professor of American studies and African American studies at the University of California, Berkeley.

JOSEPH B. ENTIN is an associate professor of English and American studies at Brooklyn College, City University of New York. He is the author of *Sensational Modernism: Experimental Fiction and Photography in Thirties America* and a co-editor, with Robert Rosen and Leonard Vogt, of *Controversies in the Classroom: A Radical Teacher Reader*. In 2015, he cofounded the Brooklyn College Listening Project, a community-based interview and oral history initiative: https://bclisteningproject.org.

GRACE ELIZABETH HALE is the Commonwealth Professor of American Studies and History at the University of Virginia. Hale is the author of *Making Whiteness: The Culture of Segregation in the South, 1890–1940*, *A Nation of Outsiders: How the White Middle Class Fell in Love with Rebellion in Postwar America*, and *Cool Town: Athens, Georgia and the Promise of Alternative Culture in Reagan's America* (forthcoming). She has written for the *New York Times*, the *Washington Post*, CNN, the *American Scholar*, the *American Historical Review*, the *Journal of American History*, the *Journal of Southern History*, *Southern Cultures*, *Southern Exposure*, and *Southern Spaces: A Journal of the South*. She created and is the senior editor of the University of North Carolina Press series Studies in U.S. Culture and is a member of the editorial board of *Southern Spaces*.

MATTHEW FRYE JACOBSON is William Robertson Coe Professor of American Studies and History at Yale University. He is the author of six books on race and U.S. political culture, including *Whiteness of a Different Color: European Immi-*

grants and the Alchemy of Race. His documentary work includes a photographic project called *Historian's Eye* (www.historianseye.org) and a recent film, *A Long Way from Home: The Untold Story of Baseball's Desegregation*.

JONATHAN KAHANA teaches in the Department of Film and Digital Media at the University of California, Santa Cruz. He has also taught documentary film and media at New York University, where he was a codirector of the graduate program in culture and media, and at Bryn Mawr College, where he was the founding director of the film studies program. He is the author of *Intelligence Work: The Politics of American Documentary* and the editor of *The Documentary Film Reader: History, Theory, Criticism*.

FRANNY NUDELMAN is an associate professor of English at Carleton University. She is the author of *John Brown's Body: Slavery, Violence, and the Culture of War* and has recently published essays on Mary McCarthy, Susan Sontag, Joan Didion, and the Vietnam Veterans Against the War. She is currently completing a book on militarism and sleep, *Sleeping Soldiers*.

LEIGH RAIFORD is an associate professor of African American studies at the University of California, Berkeley. She is the author of *Imprisoned in a Luminous Glare: Photography and the African American Freedom Struggle*. She is the coeditor (with Renee Romano) of *The Civil Rights Movement in American Memory* and (with Heike Raphael-Hernandez) of *Migrating the Black Body: The African Diaspora and Visual Culture*.

REBECCA M. SCHREIBER is an associate professor in the Department of American Studies at the University of New Mexico. She is the author of *Cold War Exiles in Mexico: U.S. Dissidents and the Culture of Critical Resistance*.

NOAH TSIKA is an assistant professor of media studies at Queens College, City University of New York. His books include *Nollywood Stars: Media and Migration in West Africa and the Diaspora* and *Pink 2.0: Encoding Queer Cinema on the Internet*. His book on documentary film and military psychiatry is forthcoming.

LAURA WEXLER is a professor of American studies, film and media studies, and women's, gender, and sexuality studies at Yale. She is a cochair of the Public Humanities Program, the principal investigator of the Photogrammar Project (photogramar.yale.edu), and the director of the Photographic Memory Workshop. Her scholarship examines representations of race, gender, class, sexuality, and nation within U.S. visual culture. She has written multiple books and critical essays on photography, including *Tender Violence: Domestic Visions in an Age of U.S. Imperialism*, *Pregnant Pictures*, and recent texts on Frederick Douglass, Roman Vishniac, LaToya Ruby Frazier, Donovan Wylie, and Jim Goldberg.

DANIEL WORDEN teaches interdisciplinary humanities in the School of Individualized Study at the Rochester Institute of Technology. He is the author of *Masculine Style: The American West and Literary Modernism*, the editor of *The Comics of Joe Sacco: Journalism in a Visual World*, and the coeditor of *Oil Culture* and *Postmodern/Postwar—and After: Rethinking American Literature*.

INDEX

Page numbers in italics refer to illustrations.

Abernathy, Ralph, 115
Abrams, Creighton W., 133, *134*
Abreaction, 39, 41
Activism, documentary: overview of, 3–6, 9–10; participatory documentary and, 9, 101–3, 115–16. *See also* Audio documentaries; *Silent Spring*; Videos by undocumented youth activists
Adams, Ansel, 200
Adams, Jeff, 60, 79
Aerospace Folktales (Sekula), 161–62
Affect, politically directed, 8
"After 1945," 6
Agee, James, 33n12
Agency of documentary, 5, 102, 121–22, 146, 160
Aioi Bridge, 56, 73, *73*, 80n21
Alabama Christian movement, 113
Alan's War: The Memories of G.I. Alan Cope (Gilbert), 79
Albany, Ga., civil rights movement, 99–100, 101, 103–4, 109–13, *110*
Albany, Ga., mass meeting, 99–100, 101, 107, 117n1
Albany State College, 101, 104, 112
Alberro, Alexander, 142
American Journal of Psychiatry, 47
American Photographs (Evans), 161–62
American Psychological Association, 21–22, 30
Anderson, Candie, 106–7, 118n19. *See also* Carawan, Candie
Andrejevic, Mark, 191n55
Angelica, 179, *180*
Anstey, Edgar, 18
Anthropology, 156
Aperture, 154
Arbus, Doon, 123, 124–28
Arcades Project, The (Benjamin), 74, 81n43
Archives and understanding, 214–16
Arlen, Michael J., 138, 149n60
Army Air Force movies, 22–25, *24*
Army Signal Corps productions: ear of documentary and, 16–18; interviews and, 21, 33n19. *See also specific films*
Art forms and *hibakusha*, expressive, 55, 79–80n2. *See also* Atom bomb manga
"Art of Inquiry, The" (Ingold), 215
Asch, Moses, 104
Asemota, LaJuanda, *196*
Askew, Laurin B., *135*
Association for the Advancement of Psychotherapy, 28
At Berkeley (Wiseman), 192, 199–203, 204, 205, 206, 207, 209n22
Atom bomb manga: images and, 67–75, *68*, *70–73*, 75–78; overview of, 55–57, 78; respect for, 57–60; transmedial revision and, 56–57, 60–61, 75, 78–79. *See also specific works of*

Atomic Bomb Casualty Commission, 65
Audio documentaries, 101, 104–9, 113. *See also* Record albums, documentary; Sound, documentary
Austerity crisis in public education: *At Berkeley* and, 192, 199–203, 209n22; Historian's Eye and Occupy Cal and, 204–4; overview of, 192–93; "Thanks to Berkeley . . ." campaign and, 192, 193–99, *196*
Authenticity: military talking pictures and, 17, 21, 25, 27, 33n11; photography and, 120, 121, 142
Authority, personal documentary, 56, 64, 65
Autobiography: in manga, 56, 59, 63–64, 66, 76; of Nakazawa, 66, 75, 76
Avedon, Richard: background and overview of, 11, 121–23; *Evidence*, 123, 147n15; *Nothing Personal*, 123; *The Sixties*, 128. *See also* "Hard Times"
Azoulay, Ariella, 207

Baez, Joan, 113
Baker, Ella, 107, 113
Baldwin, James, 123
Barefoot Gen (Nakazawa), 56, 58–60, 64, 66, 70–76, *72–73*, 78, 81n37
Barefoot Gen's Hiroshima: The Story of Nakazawa Keiji (film), 57, 63–64
Barnouw, Erik, 15
Barthes, Roland, 77
Battle of Midway, The (Ford), 17, 24–25, 33n11
Battleship Potemkin (Eisenstein), 162
Beason-Hammon Alabama Taxpayer and Citizen Protection Act, 183
Beauty Rest (Rosler), 139
Becker, Harold, 102
Benjamin, Walter, 74, 81n43, 163, 171n21
Berger, John, 55, 75, 76–77, 78
Berger, Samuel D., *135*
Berkeley in the Sixties (Kitchell), 209n18
Bethlehem Steel, 170n10
Bevel, James, 107
Bezner, Lili Corbus, 147n3, 147n8
Big Short, The (film), 213
Billips, Charles, 113–14
Birgeneau, Robert, 194, 201–3, 209n22
Birmingham, Ala., civil rights movement, 113–16
Birmingham, Alabama, 1963: Mass Meeting, 113–16, *114*
Black-ish (television show), 213
Black Natchez (Pincus), 102
Blair, Sara, 10–11, 212
Blinder, David, 198
Blum, Richard, 195
"Body and the Archive, The" (Sekula), 161, 171n21
Bombing of Hiroshima, 63–65, 66; atomic manga and, 10, 61–62, 67, *68*, *74*. *See also* Survivors, Hiroshima
Bonnie and Clyde (Penn), 139
Booby Trap (Rosler), 139, *140*
Bowery, the, 143–44
Bowery in two inadequate descriptive systems, The (Rosler), 143–46, *144–45*
Boxing Gym (Wiseman), 199
Boys Jump Monthly, 66
Brady, Mathew, 124
Brainwashing, 47, 49
Brecht, Bertolt, 154, 163, 171n21
Breines, Wini, 102
Breslauer, George, 202, 209n22
Bridge of San Luis Rey, The (Wilder), 50
BRIDGES 23 and 24, 72, *74*
Buchloh, Benjamin, 162
Buck, Fred, 161
Buell, Lawrence, 88
Buffalo Evening News, 154
Bunka-sha Agency, 56
Bunker, Ellsworth, *135*
Burch, Noel, 171n23
Bush administration, 173–74

Cafaro, Philip, 86
California Civil Rights Initiative, 195–96
California higher education documentaries, 199–203, 209n18
Calley, William, 128
Camera Lucida (Barthes), 77
Cameras, 123, 170n17, 212, 214, 216
Capa, Robert, 138
Capitalism, 94–96, 153, 154, 163. *See also* Austerity crisis in public education; Global capitalism; Neoliberalism
Capote, Truman, 36, 50, 51, 91
Carawan, Candie: about, 9, 106–7, 113–14, 118n19; as audio documentarian, 101, 103, 108, 109, 114, 116; freedom songs and, 107–8
Carawan, Guy: about, 9, 102, 105, 106–7, 113–14, 118n19; as audio documentarian, 101, 103, 108–9, 114, 116; freedom songs and, 107–8
Carson, Rachel: capitalism and, 94–96; *The Edge of the Sea*, 86, 97n8; overview of work of, 12, 83–89; *The Sea around Us*, 83, 86, 88, 95, 96–97nn7–8; *Under the Sea-Wind*, 86, 89, 94–95, 97n8. See also *Silent Spring*
CBS Reports, 85, 92
Censorship, 37, 55, 58, 60, 64–65, 201
Central Piedmont Community College protest, 175–77
Chakrabarty, Dipesh, 96
Cheney, Dick, 85
Chicago Conspirators, 124–27, *126*, 130, 148n25
Chicago Seven, 125–27, *126*, 130, 148n25
Chief mate checking temperatures of refrigerated containers (Sekula), 165, *166*
Chomsky, Noam, 59
Chute, Hillary, 56, 57, 59, 60, 74, 78–79
Cinéma vérité, 14, 16, 20, 184, 192
Citizen: An American Lyric (Rankine), 213
Citizenfour (Poitras), 32
Civil Affairs Digest, 44
Civil disobedience, 174, 176, 183–84
Civil rights movement, 100–103, 106–9, 111, 113–16, 117n9
Clark, Septima, 107
Class, 112–13, 153, 157, 167
Classification, 153, 157–60
Cleaning the Drapes (Rosler), 140, *141*
Climate change, 6, 83–84, 87–88, 96
Clinical interviews, 36–37, 38–41
Cohen, Michael Mark, 9–10, 212
Colantonio, Ernest J., *134*
Cold War, 4, 47, 120–121
Cold Warriors, 120
Cole, Nat King, 106
Cole, Thomas, 139
Combat Exhaustion (film), 17
Comics: origin of, 60–61. *See also* Atom bomb manga
Comics Code, 58
Comics, Comix and Graphic Novels (Sabin), 59
Confessions, filmed, 14, 31–32, 212
Congress for Racial Equality, 102
Connor, Bull, 113–14
Containerization, 95–96, 162, 164, 165, *166*
Contingent truths, 160
Conway, Kellyanne, 217
Cooke, Sam, 106
Cooper, Charles A., *135*
Corporations, 94
Counter-conduct, 182, 190n45
Counterdocuments: about, 9–10, 172, 187; as forms of countersurveillance, 182–87, 190n41, 190nn44–45. *See also* Videos by undocumented youth activists
Countermedia practices, 101–2
Counternarratives, 66, 179, 185, 191n55
Counterpublics, 6, 9
Countersurveillance, 182–87, 191n55
Countervisibility, 172, 184
Courier font, 128

Critical realism, 146, 163
Criticism of documentary, 2, 4–5, 15–16
Cruikshank, George, 61
Cue Recording Studios, 107
Curatorial documentary, 213, 214–16, 218

Darwell, Jane, 17, 24–25
Davidson, Steef, 61
Davis, Mike, 154
Davis, Rennie, *126*
Day After, The (Nakazawa), 70–74, *73*. See also *Barefoot Gen*
DDT, 83, 84–85, 90–92
De Antonio, Emile, 31
Deardorff cameras, 123, 127
Death, 138
"Death in life," 37, 51
Death in Life (Lifton): approach of, 45–46; dying Japanese and, 77–78, 82n56; interviews and, 46, 48–50; overview of, 35, 36–37
Debt, student, 195, 198, 208n8
Deep time, 86, 91, 92–93, 96
Delayed effects, 2
Deliberate quiet, 43, 53n27
Dellinger, Dave, *126*
Demos, T. J., 5
Denby, David, 199
Department of Homeland Security (DHS), 173, 186, 187n5, 188n20
Deportation, 173–74, 175–80, 183–86, 187n5, 188n20
Detachment, 37, 47–48, 49, 52, 129
Détournement, 61
Development, Relief, and Education for Alien Minors (DREAM) Act, 173, 181, 187n1, 188n7, 189n29
DHS (Department of Homeland Security), 173, 186, 187n5, 188n20
Diagnostic and Statistical Manual of Mental Disorders, 21–22, 27–28, 30
"Dialectics at a standstill," 74, 79
Digital and social media, 172–73, 181, 186–87, 213, 215
Diptychs: in *Fish Story*, 162–63, 164–65, *166–67*, 168, 171n27; Rogovin and Sekula as, 169; in *Working People*, 153, 154, 155–57, 160
Direct cinema form, 199, 200, 203
Disaster Drawn: Visual Witness, Comics, and Documentary Form (Chute), 57, 59
Discovering the News (Schudson), 87
Discretion, prosecutorial: challenges to, 175–82, 188n20, 188–89n23; inconsistencies in, 182–83, 190n44, 190n48; overview of, 173, 174, 187–88nn5–6
"Dismal Science" (Sekula), 162
"Dismantling Modernism, Reinventing Documentary" (Sekula), 161
Dispositif, 15
Diversity, 195–97, 207
Documentary: A History of Nonfiction Film (Barnouw), 15
Documentary as pedagogy, 3, 199, 204, 212, 213–14, 218
Documentary as work, 152, 167
Documentary comics, 56, 78–79. *See also* Atom bomb manga
Documentary film. *See* Film, documentary
Documentary Graphic Novels and Social Realism (Adams), 60
Documentary histories, 10–11
Documentary imaging, 4, 11, 122–23
Documentary imagining, 11–12
Documentary making, 2–3. *See also* Documentary practice
Documentary narrative. *See* Narrative, documentary
Documentary practice: about, 6, 116, 120–21, 212, 215–16, 218; counter-documents and, 173, 186–87; Rogovin and, 155; Rosler and, 142–44; Sekula and, 153. *See also specific forms of*
Documentary realism, 11, 75, 162, 171n28

Documentary realist forms, 172, 187n3
Donaldson, Ivanhoe, 102
"Double system" of photographic portraiture, 125
Dowling, Julia A., 182, 190nn44–45, 190n48
Drawing, 75–78, 79. *See also* Transmedial revision
"Drawn to That Moment" (Berger), 55
DREAM (Development, Relief, and Education for Alien Minors) Act, 173, 181, 187n1, 188n7, 189n29
DreamActivist.org, 181, 189n23, 189–90nn39–40
DREAMers, 179, 189n29
DuBois, W. E. B., 154
Dunaway, Finis, 92

Eaarth: Making Life on a Tough New Planet (McKibben), 93
"Eagle Stirreth Her Nest, The," 104, 112
Ear of documentary, 15–18
Edge of the Sea, The (Carson), 86, 97n8
Edgerton, Gary, 20
Education Not Deportation: A Guide for Undocumented Youth in Removal Proceedings, 177–78, 188–89n23, 189n26
Education Not Deportation (END) campaign, 177–78, 179, 181–82, 188n22
EduComics, 56
Effects of the Atomic Bomb on Hiroshima, Japan, 74
Eisenstein, Sergei, 162, 163, 171n21
Elliot, Jack, 105
Ellis, John, 14
Elton, Arthur, 18
Emerson, Gloria, 133–36
END (Education Not Deportation) campaign, 177–78, 179, 181–82, 188n22
Enemy Interrogation of Prisoners (film), 22
Entin, Joseph B., 11, 96, 212
Environmental activism, 84, 85, 93, 96
Environmental humanities, 88
Environmentalist documentary, 84, 86, 93, 95, 96. *See also* Carson, Rachel
Environmental Protection Agency, 83
Epistemological crisis, 2, 213, 216–17
Epistemological skepticism, 161, 162
Evans, Walker, 123, 144, 161
Evidence (Avedon), 123
Executioner's Song (Mailer), 51–52

Fake news, 217
Family Guy (television show), 213
Farm Security Administration, 86–87, 123, 138, 218
Feminist art, 141, 143
Fiat Lux (Adams and Newhall), 200
Fiction techniques, 36, 43, 44, 45, 46
Field Psychiatry for the General Medical Officer, 33n14
Filling lifeboat with water equivalent to weight of crew to test the movement of the boat falls before departure (Sekula), 165, *167*
Film, documentary: activism and, 210–11; counterdocumentation and, 172, 173, 174–75, 187; ear of, 15–18; environmentalist, 84, 86–87, 93–94; interviews and, 14, 18–21, *19*, 22–23, 32, 33n19; mental illness and, 21–23, 25–31; overview of, 7, 11–12, 14; participatory, 102, 103; reenactment in, 15–20, 25, 26–27, 32–33n7, 33n12, 33n14; speech images and, 23–26, *26*; survivor testimony and, 37, 55, 63, 78; universities and, 192, 199–203, 204, 205, 206, 207, 209n18, 209n22. *See also* Military talking pictures; *specific filmmakers*; *specific films*
Films of *Barefoot Gen*, 57, 63–64, 78
Fires Were Started (Jennings), 32–33n7
First Lady (Pat Nixon) (Rosler), 139
Fish Story (Sekula), 95–96, 151, 152–53, 160, 162–68, *166–67*, 171nn27–28
Folk music, 102, 104–5

Folkways Records, 101, 104–5, *114*, 117–18n11
Fonda, Henry, 17, 24–25
Footnotes in Gaza (Sacco), 79
Ford, John, 17, 25, 33n11
Forgotten Space, The (Sekula and Burch), 171n23
Forman, James, 113
Foucault, Michel, 15, 190n45
Fox Movietone newsreels, 18
Freedom in the Air: A Documentary on Albany, Georgia, 1961–1962 (Carawan), 99–100, 101, 104, 109–13, *110*, 117n1, 117–18n11
Freedom Now!, 101
Freedom Riders, 108, 111
Freedom songs, 107–8, 109–13. *See also specific songs*
Freeman, Joshua, 155
French Situationists, 61
Freud, Sigmund, 18, 23
Freudian psychoanalysis, 21–22
Froines, John, *126*
Frontier Films, 102
Frost, A. B., 60–61
Funding for public higher education, 193, 194, 195, 199, 201, 203–4

Gay, Ben, 99–100, 109, 112
Gen of Hiroshima, 58
Gerstle, Dan, 43
Gilbert, Emmanuel, 79
Gilmore, Gary, 51–52
Global capitalism, 5, 153, 163
"Globalizing Comic Books from Below: How Manga Came to America" (Rifas), 57–58
Goebbels, Joseph, 138
Goodbye to All That (Rosler), 141
Goodman, Paul, 45–46, 49
Gore, Al, 84
Grant, Oscar, 213, 214
Grapes of Wrath, The (Ford) (film), 25
"Graphic display of buried knowing," 57
Great Recession, 195, 203, 205
Greenblatt, Stephen, 201
Gregory, Dick, 113
Grinker, Roy, 38, 39, 41, 52n9
Grossman, Sid, 147n13
Gutheil, Emil, 28–29

Hadashi no Gen (Nakazawa), 56, 58, 64
Haggerty, Kevin, 183
Hale, Grace Elizabeth, 9, 212, 217
Hales, Larry, 128–29, 133
Hamilton, Frank, 105
"Hard Times" (Avedon and Arbus): background of, 123–24; Chicago Conspirators and, 124–28, *126*, 148n25; compared to Rosler, 142; Vietnam War and, 128–37, *131–32*, *134–35*
Harper's Bazaar, 29
Hayden, Tom, 124, *126*
HB 56 of Alabama, 183
Heartfield, John, 61, 137
Heise, Ursula K., 88
Hernández-Rojas, Anastasio, 213, 214
Herron, Matt, 102
Hersey, John: about, 12, 37, 212; *Hiroshima* (see *Hiroshima*); "The Legend on the License," 50; "A Short Talk with Erlanger," 37–38, 39–42, 50
Herzog, Melanie, 155
Herzog, Werner, 93–94
Hibakusha, 55, 57, 61, 64–65, 66–67, 73, 79n1. *See also* Survivors, Hiroshima
High fee / high aid model, 208n8
Highlander Folk School, 102, 105, 106–8
High School (Wiseman), 199, 201
Hine, Lewis, 151, 152, 163, 171n28, 210
Hiroshima (Hersey): Hersey's quietness and, 43, 53n27; images in, 50; interviews for, 42; narrative style of, 43, 44–45, 52; overview of, 35, 36–37, 38
Hiroshima Atomic-bomb Hospital, 66

Hiroshima Peace Memorial Museum, 57, 66, 81n37
Hiroshima: The Autobiography of Barefoot Gen (Nakazawa), 66, 75, 76
Historian's Eye: Our Better History project, 192–93, 204–7, 214
Historicist approach, 2–3, 8
Hoffman, Abbie, 124, *126*, 127
Hoffman, Julius, 124–25
Hoffmeister, 25, *26*
"Home by Ship" (Lifton), 47, 49
"Honest, Straightforward Reenactment" (Winston), 32n7
Hooper, Joe, 130, *131*, 148n46
Horton, Zilphia, 105, 106
Houghton Mifflin, 85
House Beautiful, 139
House Beautiful: Bringing the War Home (Rosler), 137–38, 139–42, *140–41*, 149n58
House Un-American Activities Committee (HUAC), 120, 154
Housing Problems (Elton and Anstey), 18
Huet, Henri, 139
Hurst, Arthur, 17
Huston, John: *San Pietro*, 26; *Tunisian Victory*, 17–18. See also *Let There Be Light*
Huston, Walter, 20, 25

Idea of History, The (Collingwood), 15
Immersion techniques, 36, 49, 51, 52
Immigration and Customs Enforcement (ICE), 173, 176–77, 183–84, 187n5, 188n13, 188n16, 190n44
Immigration detention center infiltration, 174, 182–86, 190n41
Imprisoned in a Luminous Glare (Raiford), 117n9
Inclusion, political, 172, 173, 178, 186
In Cold Blood (Capote), 51, 91
Inconvenient Truth, An (Gore), 84
Inda, Jonathan Xavier, 182, 190nn44–45, 190n48
Indoctrination, 46, 48
Infiltration of immigration detention centers, 174, 182–86, 190n41
Ingold, Tim, 215, 216
Interruptions of speech, 23–24
Interviews: clinical, 36–37, 38–41; new journalism and, 50–51; with portrait subjects, 125–28; as a practice of history, 14, 15–16, 37; speech images and, 18–21, 23–24, 25–27; of survivors, 35–36, 38, 42–45, 46, 48–50, 53n27; Vietnam era and after and, 30–32
Interviews with My Lai Veterans (Strick), 30–31
Introduction to the Army, 33n14
Invention as truth, 50–51
Irion, Christopher, 193–94
Isaac, 183, 184, 185–86
I Saw It: The Atomic Bombing of Hiroshima (Nakazawa), 56, 58, 60, 63–64, *68*, *70–71*, 75–76, 81n40
It's Your War, Too (film), 17
Ivanhoe (Becker), 102

Jacobs, Jane, 89, 97n37
Jacobson, George D., *134*
Jacobson, Matthew Frye, 12, 192–93, 204
Jacobson, Norman, 210–11
Jameson, Fredric, 160–61
Japan, military occupation of, 64, 65–66
Jelliffe, Smith Ely, 22, 33n20
Johnson, Bernice, 101, 111
Johnson, Robert, 106
Joint Commission for the Investigation of the Effects of the Atomic Bomb, 57
Jonathan, 183, 184–86, *185*
Jones, Charles, 111–12, 113
Jones, Lewis W., 113
Jones, Tahirah, *196*
Jones-Bey, Noor, *196*
Journal of Nervous and Mental Disease, 22

Kahana, Jonathan, 11, 13n2, 37, 212
Kaiser, Mel, 107
Kelley, Robin, 106
Kennedy, Cleo, 115
Kennedy, Florynce, 124
Kerr, Clark, 200
King, Martin Luther, Jr., 115
King, Rodney, 213
Kitchell, Mark, 209n18
Kleinsorge, Wilhelm, 44
Knowing from the inside, 215, 216
Komsomol-Leader of Electrification (Shub), 18
KPFA, 101
Kroll, Gary, 84, 86, 96–97nn7–8
Kuroi Ame ni Utarete (Nakazawa), 55, 60
Kyodatsu-jōtai, 49

Labor, 152, 154–55, 165, 168, 170n2, 170n10
Labor, documentary as, 152, 167
Labor photography, 11, 151–52, 169. See also *Fish Story*; *Working People*
Lange, Dorothea, 125–27, 138, 151, 210, 212
Lanzmann, Claude, 31
Leacock, Richard, 14
"Leave My Kitten Alone," 111
"Legend on the License, The" (Hersey), 50
Legislative impact, 83, 85–86, 94, 96, 181
Lessons of Darkness (Herzog), 93–94
Lest We Forget (album), 113–16, *114*
Let There Be Light (Huston): about, 11, 16–17, 20–21, 32; "A Short Talk with Erlanger" and, 37–38; authenticity of, 26–27; distribution restriction of, 20, 28–30; interviews and, 18–20, *19*, 33n14; psychology and psychoanalysis and, 21, 22, 39; reenactment and, 15–16, 20; speech image and, 23, 25–26, *26*
Lewis, John, 107
Leys, Ruth, 27–28, 32n6
Liebow, Averill, 57, 62, 80n4
Life: about, 138–39; atomic bombings and, 60, 67; Avedon and, 123, 147n15; *Let There Be Light* and, 29, 37–38; Rosler and, 138, 139
Lifton, Robert Jay: about, 12, 52; "Home by Ship," 47, 49; prisoner of war repatriation and, 46–48. See also *Death in Life*
Living Cinema (Marcorelles), 14
"Living room" war, 138, 149n60
Livingston, Jane, 125
Lomax, Alan, 104, 105–6, 117n1
Lomax, John, 104
Lonidier, Phil, 161
Look, 129
Lorentz, Pare, 17, 86–87
Lott, Eric, 106
Lt. Joe Hooper, The Most Decorated Soldier in Vietnam (Avedon), 130, *131*
Luce, Henry R., 138
Lyon, Danny, 102, 117n4

MacArthur, Douglas, 44
Macdonald, Dwight, 35, 44, 45–46, 52
Mailer, Norman, 36, 50, 51–52
Manga (Gravett), 59
Manga, Manga (Schodt), 59
March of Resilience, 210–12, *211*
Marco, 175, 182, 190n41
Marcorelles, Louis, 14
Marcuse, Herbert, 137, 160–61
Maritime work, 153, 162, 164
Marshall, S. L. A., 23
Marsushige, Yoshito, 82n53
Martin, 175, 180, 189n33
Mason General Hospital, 16, *19*, 20, 25, 40, 44
Maus (Spiegelman), 58, 78
McCarthy, Mary, 35, 51, 212
McGowan, John E., *134*
McGurl, Mark, 92–93
McKee, Yates, 172, 187

McKibben, Bill, 93
McLagan, Meg, 172, 181, 187
Memphis Belle (film), 33n12
Men Under Stress (Grinker and Spiegel), 38, 39
Migrant counter-conducts, 182, 190n45
Migrant melodramas, 175
Military experimentalism, 43–45. *See also* Psychiatric experiments
Military occupation of Japan, 64, 65–66
Military science and Hiroshima victims, 38, 43–45
Military talking pictures: about, 16; ear of documentary and, 15–18; interviews and, 18–21, *19*; mental illness and, 21–23, 25–31; speech image and, 23–26, *26*. *See also specific films*
Miller, Karl Hagstrom, 106
Mills, Hawthorne Q., *134*
Mission Council, Saigon, South Vietnam, The (Avedon), 130–33, *134–35*
Mission Council, U.S., 130–33, *134–35*, 148n46
Mitchell, W. J. T., 62, 80–81n22
Mizuki, Shigeru, 79
Modernist art, 162, 163
Modernist documentary, 163
Mohammad, 175, 182
Montage realism, 162
Morris, Errol, 32, 210
Morton, John, 177, 187n5
Morton, Timothy, 93
Mossler, John R., *135*
Motion Picture Unit of U.S. Army Air Force, 22–23
Music and racial categorization, 106
Muybridge, Edward, 161
Muyokuganbo, 49
Mydans, Carl, 138

Nakazawa, Keiji: bomb story of, 63–67; images by, 67–75, *68*, *70–73*, *75–78*, 82n54; legacy of, 78; overview of, 10, 55–57; respect for, 57–60; transmedial revision and, 60–62, 75, 78–79. *See also specific works of*
Nakazawa, Misayo, 76, 77
Napalm Victim, Saigon, South Vietnam (Avedon), 130, *132*
Narcoanalysis, 38, 39–41, 52n9
Narrative, documentary: atom bomb manga as (*see* Atom bomb manga); autobiographical comics as, 56, 59, 63–64, 66, 76; immersive reporting and, 11, 35–36, 49–50, 51, 52; narrative journalism and, 12, 35–36, 51; speculative documentary and, 12, 83–89, 92–94, 95–96. *See also Death in Life*; *Edge of the Sea, The*; *Hiroshima*; *Sea around Us, The*; "Short Talk with Erlanger, A"; *Silent Spring*; *Under the Sea-Wind*
Narrative journalism, 12, 35, 36, 51. *See also* Narrative, documentary
Narrative nonfiction, 50–51. *See also* Narrative, documentary
Nashville Sit-In Story, The (Carawan), 107, 108, 118n18
Nashville, Tenn., civil rights movement, 106–7, 108, 111
National Association for the Advancement of Colored People Legal Defense Fund, 100
National Immigration Youth Association (NIYA), 172, 174, 175–76, 182, 188–89n23
National Magazine Award, 138–39
Nature writing, 84, 87, 89–90
Navarrete, Humberto, 213
Neoliberal documentaries, 119n28
Neoliberalism, 10, 152–53, 155, 193, 201, 204
New Deal documentary, 3, 83, 86–87, 120, 144
New Documents exhibition, 121
Newhall, Nancy, 200
New journalism, 50–52, 136
New Left, 101, 105, 116, 123, 127
New Pilgrim Baptist Church, 113

Newport Folk Festival, 103
New Yorker, 42, 89, 91, 199
New York Photo League, 120, 122, 147n13
New York Review of Books, 45–46
New York Times, 127, 133
Nicholls, Walter, 189n29
Nichols, Bill, 4, 7, 14, 30, 37
Nickel, Edward J., *134*
Nixon, Richard, 83, 128
Nixon, Rob, 2, 85, 94
NIYA (National Immigration Youth Association), 172, 174, 175–76, 182, 188–89n23
Nonfiction novels, 36, 51
Nothing Personal (Avedon and Baldwin), 123
Nudelman, Franny, 12, 97n29, 212, 213

Obama administration, 173, 175–76, 182, 184, 185–86, 187n5
Objectivity: journalism and, 87; participatory documentary and, 102; photography and, 62, 74–75, 120, 127, 129; realism and, 3–5, 168, 171n28; Rosler and, 143, 144; tension between subjectivity and, 116, 146, 217
Observations (Avedon and Capote), 122
Occupy Everything banner, *198*, 205
Occupy movement, 192, 197–98, *198*, 203–4, 205–6, *206*, 209n22
Occupy Oakland May Day General Strike (Lee), *206*
Occupy Wall Street, 205
Oceans, 88–89
Office, The (television show), 213
Office of War Information, 23
Old Left, 105
Online documentary, 204–5
Operational excellence, 201
Ophüls, Marcel, 31
Ore wa Mita (Nakazawa), 56, 57, 63, 66, 81n40. See also *I Saw It: The Atomic Bombing of Hiroshima*
Organized labor decline, 154–55
Origins of Comics: From William Hogarth to Winsor McCay (Smolderen), 60–61
Ōta, Yōko, 43, 49
"Over My Head," 111

Page, M. S., 101, 110–13
Palestine (Sacco), 79
Pamphlets, documentary, 102, 103
Parks, Gordon, 138
Participation, 102–3, 116
Participatory documentaries, 9–10, 101–3, 116, 117n9. *See also* Audio documentaries
Payne, Charles Rockwell, 22, 33n20
Pedagogy, documentary as, 3, 199, 204, 212, 213–14, 218
Pelted by Black Rain (Nakazawa), 55, 60
Penguin Book of Political Comics, The (Davidson), 61
Penn, Arthur, 139
People of the Cumberlands (film), 102
Personal narratives, 174, 178–79
Pesticides, 83, 84, 90–92
Petition of DreamActivist.org, 181, 189–90n40
Photobooth form, 193–94, 197
"Photobooth Project," 193–94, *196*, 196–99, *198*
Photo-documentary, 11. *See also* Avedon, Richard; Rosler, Martha
Photographer: Into War-Torn Afghanistan with Doctors without Borders, The (Gilbert), 79
Photography: of Hiroshima bombing, 61–62, 67, *68*, 72–73, *74*; photobooth form and, 193–94, 197; photomontage, 137–38, 139–42, *140–41*; postwar overview of, 120–22, 147n3, 147n8; Rosler on, 206–7; "Thanks to Berkeley . . ." campaign and, 193–94, *196*, 196–97; transmedial revision and, 56–57, 60–61, 69–75, 78–79, 82n55;

trauma and, 77, 82n53. *See also* Photo-documentary; Photo-texts; Portraiture; *specific photographs, photographers, projects*
Photography and Politics (Bezner), 147n3, 147n8
"Photography between Labor and Capital" (Sekula), 161
Photo League, New York, 120, 122, 147n13
Photo-texts: *Fish Story*, 95–96, 151, 152–53, 160, 162–68, *166–67*, 171nn27–28; *Life* and, 138; of New Deal era, 125–27; *Observations*, 122; Rosler and, 138. *See also* "Hard Times"
Photo wall of "Thanks to Berkeley . . ." campaign, 192, 194, *196*, 196–99, *198*, 203, 205
Pika, 65–66
Pincus, Edward, 102
Poitras, Laura, 32
Policy toward information on atomic bombings, U.S., 64–65
Political inclusion, 172, 173, 178, 186
Politically directed affect, 8
Politics of visibility, 172, 173–74, 181, 182–83, 184, 186, 188n8
Portraiture: *At Berkeley* and, 199, 203; Avedon and, 123–25, 127–33, *131–32*, *134–35*, 136, 142; Rogovin and, 152, 153, 154, 155, 156, 157, 160; Rosler and, 139; Sekula and, 169; in "Thanks to Berkeley . . ." campaign, 193, 194, 197
Post-traumatic stress disorder (PTSD). *See* PTSD
Postwar documentary, overview of, 120–22
Power of documentary, 4–5
Prefigurative politics, 102
Prisoner of war repatriation, 46–48
Privatization of education, 10, 192, 193, 204
"Project Gen," 58, 78
Prosecutorial discretion. *See* Discretion, prosecutorial
Psychiatric experiments, 36, 37–41, 47, 52n9
Psychiatric Interview, The (Sullivan), 38–39
Psychiatric Procedures in the Combat Area (film), 16–17, 21, 33nn14–15, 33n19
Psychic numbing, 49, 52
Psychoanalysis, 21–22, 25, 33n20. *See also* Narcoanalysis; Psychiatric experiments
Psychological empiricism, 46
Psychology, professional, 38–39
Psychopathology of Everyday Life, The (Freud), 23
PTSD (post-traumatic stress disorder), 27–28, 30–31. *See also* Trauma and traumatic memory
Public Housing (Wiseman), 199
Puga, Ana Elena, 175

Race-based recruiting, 195–96
Racial categorization and sound, 106
Radiation illness, 65–66
Raiford, Leigh, 10, 117n9, 212
Rankine, Claudia, 213, 214
Reagon, Cordell, 101, 103, 111
Realism: comics and, 60, 75; critical, 146, 163; documentary, 11, 15, 162, 171n28; photography and, 162, 163, 166; social, 60, 152, 173, 187n3; socialist, 167–68
Record albums, documentary: about, 9, 101, 104–9; *Birmingham, Alabama, 1963: Mass Meeting*, 113–16, *114*; *Freedom in the Air*, 99–100, 101, 104, 109–13, *110*, 117n1, 117–18n11
Recording equipment, 104, 216
Recording methods, interview, 40
Reenactments, 15–20, 25, 26–27, 32–33n7, 33n12, 33n14, 107
Renov, Michael, 4
Repatriating POWs, 46–48
Report (Jacobson), 210–11
Resisting Enemy Interrogation (film), 22

Rhimes, Shonda, 218
Ribback, Alan, 102
Riefenstahl, Leni, 17
Rifas, Leonard, 58–59, 76, 78–79, 81n37, 81n40
River, The (Lorentz), 86–87
Rivers, W. H. R., 22
Rogovin, Milton: about, 151, 152, 153–54, 170n17, 171n19; compared to Sekula, 152–53, 168–69; *Working People*, 151, 152–53, 154, 155–60, *158–59*
Rolleiflex cameras, 123, 170n17
Rosler, Martha: about, 11, 121–22, 137, 146–47, 151; *The Bowery in two inadequate descriptive systems*, 143–46, *144–45*; *Bringing the War Home*, 137–38, 139–42, *140–41*, 149n58; compared to Avedon, 142; participatory documentary and, 102; on photography, 8, 206–7; Sekula and, 161; *Semiotics of the Kitchen*, 143; video and, 143
Ross, Harold, 42
Roth, Paul, 125
Rowan, Jamin Creed, 89
Rubin, Jerry, 124, *126*

Sabin, Roger, 59
Sacco, Joe, 59, 78–79, 82n62
Safe Area Goražde (Sacco), 79
Sander, August, 171n19
San Pietro (Huston), 26
Santana, Feidin, 213
Santiago, 179–80, 189n35
Sargant, William, 41, 47
Savio, Mario, 198
Scarry, Elaine, 1–2
Scherman, David, 38
Schodt, Frederik, 59
Schreiber, Rebecca M., 9, 212
Schudson, Michael, 87
Schwarzenegger, Arnold, 195
Science Advisory Committee, 85
Science writing, 83–86, 96–97n7
Scientific investigations, 43–45
SCLC (Southern Christian Leadership Conference), 107, 113, 115
S-Comm (Secure Communities), 176, 181, 183, 188n16, 190n40
Scott, Walter, 213, 214
Screening process, soldier, 38–39
Sea around Us, The (Allen) (film), 86–87
Sea around Us, The (Carson), 83, 86, 88, 95, 96–97nn7–8
Sea as a forgotten space, 162, 171n23
Seale, Bobby, 124–25
Secure Communities (S-Comm), 176, 181, 183, 188n16, 190n40
Seduction of the Innocent (Wertham), 59
Seeger, Pete, 105, 108
Sekula, Allan: about, 8–9, 151–52, 160–61, 171n19, 171n21; compared to Rogovin, 152–53, 168–69; double system of portraiture and, 125; essays of, 161, 162, 171n21; *Fish Story*, 95–96, 151, 152–53, 160, 162–68, *166–67*, 171nn27–28; *This Ain't China*, 161–62; *Untitled Slide Sequence*, 161
Self-consciousness, 10, 11, 101, 171n21
Self-representation, 172, 186, 187
Semiotics of the Kitchen (Rosler), 143
Sense of Place and Sense of Planet (Heise), 88
Sequential montage, 153, 162, 168
Sequential narrative, 60–61, 62, 74
SF State on Strike (film), 200
Shackley, Theodore, 133
Shades of Gray (film), 26–27
Sheeler, Charles, 165
Shell shock. *See* Trauma and traumatic memory
Sherrod, Charles, 101, 103, 111, 112, 113
Shoah (Ophüls and Lanzmann), 31
"Short Talk with Erlanger, A" (Hersey), 37–38, 39–42, 50
Showa (Mizuki), 79
Shub, Esfir, 18

Shuttlesworth, Fred, 108, 113
Silent actions, 184
Silent Spring (Carson): capitalism and, 94, 95–96; nature of, 89–93; overview of, 12, 83–84; as speculative documentary, 84–86, 87–88, 89
"Silent Spring of Rachel Carson, The," 92
Simon, Benjamin, 30
Sitcoms, 213
Sixties, The (Arbus and Avedon), 128
Slager, Michael, 213
Slow violence, 7, 83, 92, 96n1
Smith, W. Eugene, 138
Smithsonian Folkways, 118n11
Smolderen, Thierry, 60–61
SNCC (Student Nonviolent Coordinating Committee), 101–2, 104, 107, 109, *110*, 111, 113, 118n21
Snowden, Edward, 32
Social and digital media, 172–73, 181, 186–87, 213, 215
Social impact as an evaluative, 3–4
Socialist realism, 167–68
Social realism, 60, 152, 173, 187n3
Sodium amytal, 25, 39, 40–41
Solomon-Godeau, Abigail, 146
Songbirds, 90–91
Songs, activist, 103, 106, 107–8, 109–13, 115
Sontag, Susan, 5, 151
Sorrow and the Pity, The (Ophüls and Lanzmann), 31
Sound, documentary: background and overview of, 2, 9, 99–103; folk music and, 102, 104–5; freedom songs and, 107–8, 109–13 (*see also specific songs*); interviews and, 40; record albums as (*see* Record albums, documentary)
Southern Christian Leadership Conference (SCLC), 107, 113, 115
Southern Documentary Project, 102
Southern Reach (VanderMeer), 96
Speculation, 1, 46, 53n37
Speculative documentary, 12, 83–89, 92–94, 95–96. See also *Silent Spring*
Speculative imagining, 83, 84, 86, 96
Speech images: interviews and, 18–21, 33n14; reenactments and, 26–27; self-expression and, 24–25; speech therapies and, 22–23; Vietnam era and after and, 30–32
Speech interruptions, 23–24
Spiegel, John, 38, 39, 41, 52n9
Spiegelman, Art, 58, 59, 61, 78
Staging events, 101
Standard Operating Procedure (Morris), 32
Steinmetz, Phil, 161
Stevens, Norma, 148n46
Stewart, Jimmy, 23–25, *24*
Store-front church series of Milton Rogovin, 154
Strick, Joseph, 30–31
Student debt, 195, 198, 208n8
Student Nonviolent Coordinating Committee (SNCC), 101–2, 104, 107, 109, *110*, 111, 113, 118n21
Stuttering, 24–25
Subjectivity, 4–5, 102–3, 116, 142, 146, 217
Subversive Organizations List, 120, 147n13
Suffering, 5, 175
Sullivan, Henry Stack, 38–39, 40
Surveillance, 173–74
Survivor by proxy, 49
Survivors, Hiroshima: atom bomb manga and, 59, 73; isolation of, 61, 64–65; Nakazawa as, 63–67; obstacles of, 55; psychiatry and, 12, 35, 36–37, 46–47, 48–50, 52; testimony of, 37, 38, 42–43, 46, 52, 57
"Swing Low, Sweet Chariot," 115
Szarkowski, John, 121

Talk therapy, 38–39
Tallmadge, William, 154
Tanimoto, Kiyoshi, 42, 44–45, 50, 52

Tanter, Richard, 64–66
Target: Germany (film), 18
Taylor, Paul, 125–27
Technologies, 216–18
Tennessee Valley Authority, 86–87
Terkel, Studs, 156
"Thanks to Berkeley . . ." campaign, 192, 193–99, *196*, 202, 203, 204, 205, 206, 207
This Ain't China (Sekula), 161–62
This Is the Photo League, 122, 147n13
Thoreau, Henry David, 90
Thousand-mile stare, 49
Tiger Cages at Con Son Island prison, 129–30
Titicut Follies (Wiseman), 29, 199, 201
Tokenization, 196–97
Toxicity, 84–85, 88, 89, 90–92
"Traffic in Photographs, The" (Sekula), 161
Transformative potential of documentary, 36, 139, 146
Transmedial revision, 56–57, 60–61, 75, 78–79
Transparency, 3–4
Trauma: A Genealogy (Leys), 27–28, 32n6
Trauma and traumatic memory: about, 21–22, 27–28, 33n20; drawing and, 77; Hiroshima survivors and, 55, 59, 65; Lifton and, 48–49; manga and, 74, 76, 77, 79; military talking pictures and, 11–12, 15–17, 20; narcoanalysis and, 39–42; photography and, 77, 79; Vietnam era and after and, 30–31, 32n6. *See also* PTSD
Treat, John, 6, 52
Triumph of the Will (Riefenstahl), 17
Truman, Harry, 43, 212
Trump, Donald, 217
Trumpism, 214, 217
Tsika, Noah, 11, 37, 212
Tuition increases, 195, 197, 203–4, 208n8
Tunisian Victory (Huston), 17–18
287(g) program, 175, 176, 181, 188n13, 190n40

UC Berkeley, 192; *At Berkeley* and, 192, 199–203, 204, 205, 206, 207, 209n22; fund-raising for, 193, 194, 199; Historian's Eye and Occupy Cal and, 203–7, 214; "Thanks to Berkeley . . ." campaign and, 192, 193–99, *196*, 202, 203, 204, 205, 206, 207
UC Board of Regents, 195, 197, 202
Underground comix movement, 58–59, 80n2
Under the Sea-Wind (Carson), 86, 89, 94–95, 97n8
Undocumented youth activists: about, 172, 187n1; Central Piedmont Community College protest and, 175–77; videos by (*see* Videos by undocumented youth activists)
"Undocumented Youth *vs.* Border Patrol Round 1—Mobile, Alabama," 184–86, *185*
U.S. Fish and Wildlife Service, 85
U.S. Strategic Bombing Survey (USSBS): Hersey and, 42, 44; images of, 61–62, 72–73, *74*, 80n4; Nakazawa and, 57, 60, 61–62, 70, 77, 82n55
Unforgettable Fire, 62, 66, 80n21
University of California (UC), Berkeley. *See* UC Berkeley
Untitled Slide Sequence (Sekula), 161
Unzueta Carrasco, Tania, 177

Vachon, John, 138
Vanguard Records, 104, 117n1
Vaughs, Clifford, 102
Videos by Rosler, 143
Videos by undocumented youth activists: detention center infiltration and, 184–86, *185*; distribution of, 172, 174, 181, 186–87; END campaign and, 177–78, 181–82; made prior to

Central Piedmont Community College protest, 175–77, 178–81, 188n14, 188n34; overview of, 172–73, 174–75, 186–87
Vietnam War: "Hard Times" and, 128–37, *131–32*, *134–35*; *Life* and, 138–39; Rosler and, 138, 139–42, *140–41*; trauma and, 30–31, 32n6
Viridiana, 175
Visibility, 172, 173–74, 181, 182–83, 184, 186, 188n8
Vital Statistics of a Citizen, Simply Obtained (Rosler), 143
Vogue, 129
Voice of documentary, 14–15, 37
Voice-overs, 20, 23
Voyage to the Bottom of the Sea (Allen), 87

Walden (Thoreau), 90
War Department, 28, 44
Warner Bros., 23
War neuroses. *See* Trauma and traumatic memory
War Neuroses (Hurst), 17
Washington Post, 17, 33n11, 133
Waugh, Thomas, 7, 31
Weaponry, 4, 38
Weather Underground, 128
Weiner, Lee, *126*
Wertham, Frederic, 59
We Shall Overcome: Songs from the Montgomery and Nashville Freedom Movements, 108
Wexler, Laura, 10, 212
Wheeler Hall occupation, 197–98
Who Killed the Electric Car (film), 93
Wilder, Thornton, 50
Willard Electronics, 107
Winning Your Wings (recruiting short), 23–25, *24*
Winston, Brian, 32–33n7
Winter Soldier (Winterfilm Collective), 30–31
Wipes, 20
Wiseman, Frederick, 29, 192, 199–203
"Woke Up This Morning with My Mind Stayed on Freedom," 110–11, 112
Wolfe, Charles, 23
Wolfe, Tom, 50, 51
Wood, James, 171n19
Word balloons, 61
Worden, Daniel, 12, 53n37, 212
Work, documentary as, 152, 167
"Worker Reads History, A" (Brecht), 154
Working (Terkel), 156
Working People (Rogovin), 151, 152–53, 154, 155–60, *158–59*
Working people, depiction of, 155–56
World-making, 1–2, 10
World War II: as a documentary turning point, 6, 11, 16, 21, 57, 120; propaganda and training films of, 18–20; psychiatry and, 20, 22–23, 28, 38, 39, 47

Yale March of Resilience (Zhang), *211*
Yale University March of Resilience, 210–12, *211*
"You Better Leave Segregation Alone," 111
Yudof, Mark, 194, 202

Zhang, Alex, 211

www.ingramcontent.com/pod-product-compliance
Lightning Source LLC
LaVergne TN
LVHW050952080826
845145LV00005B/1481

* 9 7 8 1 4 6 9 6 3 8 6 9 0 *